FROM FORT TO PORT

ELIZABETH BARRETT GOULD

From Fort to Port

An Architectural History of Mobile, Alabama, 1711–1918

Published through the generosity of the Mitchell Foundation, Mobile, Alabama

The University of Alabama Press   Tuscaloosa and London

Frontispiece: Bragg-Mitchell House, ca. 1855, 1906 Spring Hill Avenue.
Tall, slender columns and Italianate detailing add distinction to the
antebellum home of Judge John Bragg.
Mr. and Mrs. S. A. Mitchell purchased and restored the property in 1931.
After their death the house and grounds were maintained by
the Mitchell Foundation.
The building is now part of the Exploreum Museum complex.
(Photograph by Michael Thomason.)

Copyright © 1988 by
The University of Alabama Press
Tuscaloosa, Alabama 35487
All rights reserved
Manufactured in the United States of America

Library of Congress Cataloging-in-Publication Data
Gould, Elizabeth Barrett, 1906–
    From fort to port.

    Bibliography: p.
    Includes index.
    1. Architecture—Alabama—Mobile. 2. Mobile (Ala.)—
Buildings, structures, etc. I. Title.
NA735.M62G68 1988   720°.9761'22   85-20364
ISBN 0-8173-0256-5

Design by Cameron Poulter

To my three children,
EDWARD, LANCE, AND
BETSY,
and to the memory of a great
teacher,
DR. CLARENCE WARD

CONTENTS

PREFACE / IX

1 Inheritance: The Colonial Years, 1711–1813 / 1
2 Americans Begin Building, 1813–1830 / 27
3 The Coming of the Greek Revival, 1830–1840 / 57
4 Architecture in Transition, 1840–1850 / 105
5 The Golden Age, 1850–1860 / 129
6 War and the Changing Order, 1860–1870 / 163
7 The End of an Era, 1870–1880 / 183
8 The High Victorian Period, 1880–1900 / 195
9 The Early Twentieth Century, 1900–1918 / 227

APPENDIXES
1. Text of the 1711 Chevillot Map and the 1734 Devin Map / 253
2. Report in the *Mobile Commercial Register* for May 27, 1822 / 255
3. The Fire of 1839: Report in the *Mercantile Advertiser*, October 9, 1839 / 257
4. Toulmin's *Digest of the Laws of the State of Alabama* / 261
5. Sample Contract for a Frame House / 263
6. Building History of the Mobile County Court Houses / 265

Abbreviations / 268

Notes / 269

Bibliography / 297

Index / 309

Preface

The development of a city can be traced in many ways, including by its architectural history. A building is a form wrapped around an activity that occupies interior space. The space and its flow tell much about the customs of the times. The methods of construction reveal the technological and economic conditions, and the details of the elevations reflect the cultural influences. The addition of building to building creates a streetscape, and a series of streetscapes establishes the character of a city. By tracing architectural changes from 1711 to 1918, we may watch Mobile's transformation from an early French Colonial fort to a modern commercial center. The three-dimensional world of architecture can illuminate 207 years of Mobile's history, from the city's existence as a primitive military outpost to its emergence as a deep-water port.

In preparing this manuscript, I consulted primary source material which would not have been available without the cooperation of city and county officials as well as private individuals. I thank: the Mitchell Foundation, which provided funds to photocopy the many contracts found in the County Miscellaneous Books and also to publish this book, with its many illustrations; the Mobile City Commission, and especially Richard Smith and staff, for the use of the city archival material; P. Jay Higginbotham, city archivist; the Mobile County Commission and the Probate Court for the use of their records and for the assistance given by Grace Hood and Kenneth Stafford; the Mobile City Planning Commission, and especially Bailey du Mont, for access to the research files for *Nineteenth Century Mobile Architecture* (1974); the Mobile Historic Development Commission for access to the files containing information on structures within the historic districts (my special thanks to Michael Leventhal, director, for his encouragement to pursue this research); the Historic Mobile Preservation Society for permission to reproduce photographs in its collection; the Title Insurance Company for access to its land grant records and title transfers; the University of South Alabama Photographic Archives for preparing photographs from the Overbey Collection, jointly owned by the Mobile Public Library; and the Mobile Public Library, Special Collections Division, and its staff, especially Robert Zietz, George Schroeter, and Richard Sumrall.

I am also grateful to various individuals who have helped to make this publication a reality: Mrs. Carter Smith, who gave me access to her private archival collection; C. L. Hutchisson, Jr., architect, whose family architectural records go back to 1798; Thomas F. Karwinski, AIA, whose excellent drawings help illustrate this book; Arch Winter, FAIA, AIP, who read the first portion of the manuscript and made valuable suggestions; and Paul Thompson, whose efforts to arrange publication of the book were tireless. For his excellent photography I extend special thanks to Dr. Michael Thomason.

From Fort to Port

1   Inheritance:
    The Colonial Years,
    1711–1813

During the eighteenth century, three powers in succession left their imprint on the southeastern section of the United States. Maps tell the history of the changing times that influenced the development of the built environment. In the years from 1689 to 1748, the English controlled the eastern seaboard, introducing the Medieval and then the Georgian styles of architecture. The French, who were entrenched west of the Mississippi in Louisiana, adapted their distinctive type of half-timber construction to the needs of the climate. The Spanish occupied Florida and concentrated fort development at St. Augustine (figure 1).

By 1763 the distribution of land had changed (figure 2). France had lost its possessions. The territory was divided by England and Spain. Spain held lands west of the Mississippi as well as a strip along the Gulf Coast, including Florida, while England claimed lands east of the Mississippi. The boundary line between England and Spain that extended along the Gulf Coast remained in dispute until the final settlement in 1795, in which both Spain and the Continental Congress recognized thirty-one degrees latitude as the boundary between the two countries (figures 3 and 4). This action divided the Gulf states nationally and in their economic development. Under the leadership of eastern seaboard planters, the central and northern portions of the areas became largely agricultural. The coast, under Spain, remained military in nature. As the Mississippi Territory was gradually divided into states, the coastal property was annexed until Florida, too, was ceded in 1819. In 1813 Mobile was united with the Alabama lands to the north of the thirty-first-degree parallel and changed from a fort to a port.

None of the Colonial buildings of Mobile has survived. Fire, hurricane, and man have destroyed them all. It is possible, however, to establish their architectural characteristics from information in archives and from some features surviving in later extant examples. When the business and professional emigrants from the Atlantic coast came to Mobile, they brought with them a late Georgian and a Federal architecture, a style better suited to the rigor of a colder climate. The enclosed massing of their houses was not as well adapted to the semitropical weather as was the French galleried cottage,

1. 1689–1748 map of North America during the colonial wars. France, England, and Spain all claimed lands on the North American continent. (Reprinted, by permission, from The Pictorial Atlas of United States History, by J. J. Thorndike, copyright © 1966 by the American Heritage Publishing Company, Inc.)

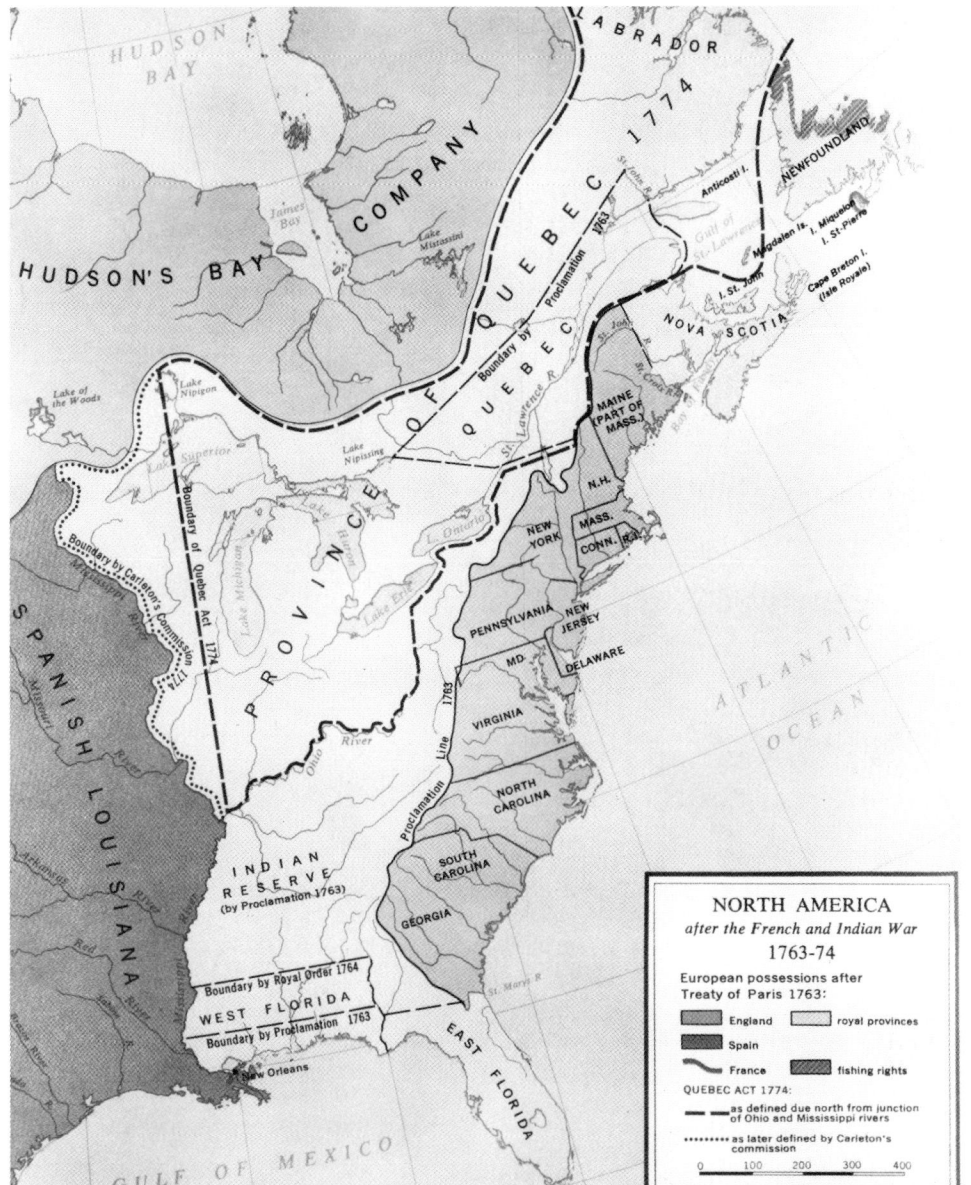

2. 1763–1774 map of North America after the French and Indian War. By the Treaty of Paris, France lost all its lands in the eastern half of the continent. (Reprinted, by permission, from The Pictorial Atlas of United States History, by J. J. Thorndike, copyright © 1966 by the American Heritage Publishing Company, Inc.)

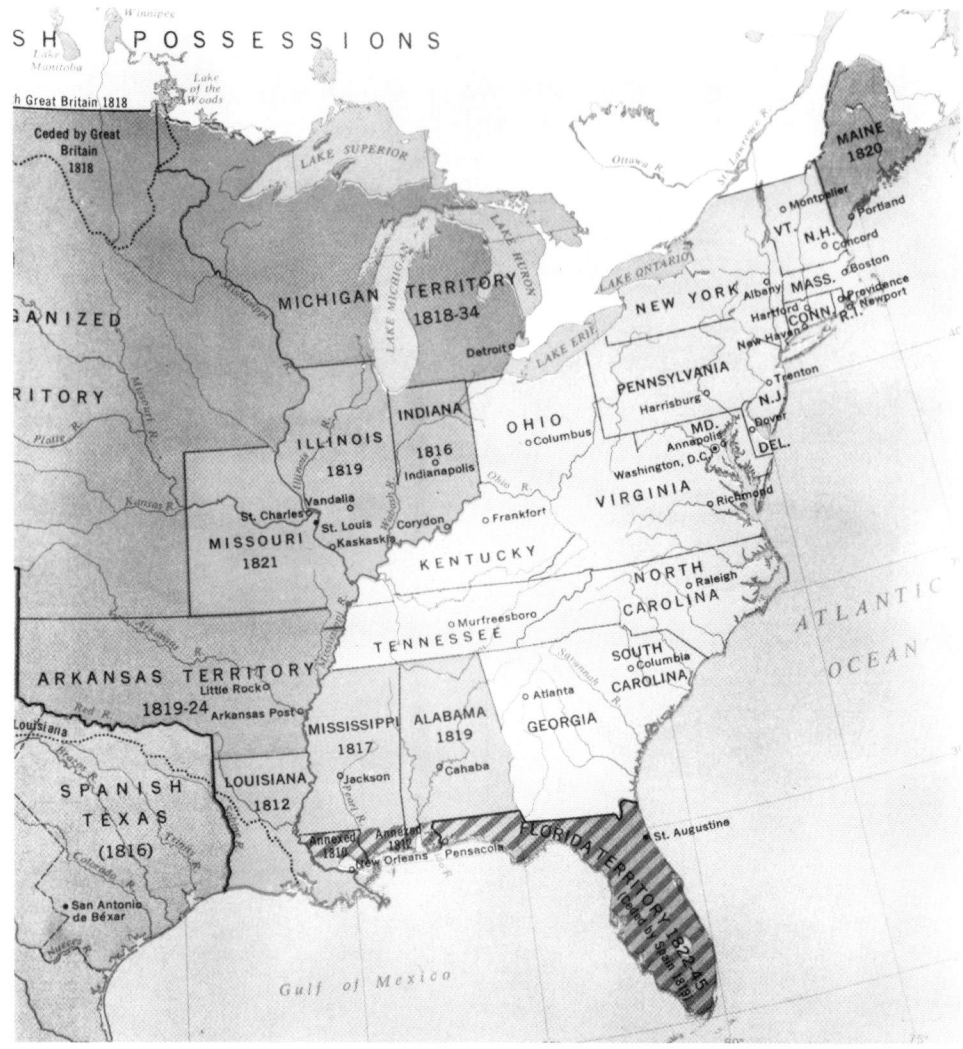

3. 1812–1822 map of the United States, showing Spain in control of Florida and the Gulf Coast. White areas indicate states previously admitted to the Union; light gray areas indicate newly admitted states. U.S. territories appear in dark gray. Spanish Texas is also gray. The Spanish territories, striped in black, were acquired by the United States in 1810 (the Mississippi coast to the Pearl River), 1812 (land between the Pearl River and the Perdido River on the Alabama coast), and 1819 (the rest of east Florida). (Reprinted, by permission, from The Pictorial Atlas of United States History, by J. J. Thorndike, copyright © 1966 by the American Heritage Publishing Company, Inc.)

with its deeply shaded porches and floor-to-ceiling windows that opened up rooms to catch every movement of air (figures 5 and 6). Mobile's buildings may be studied individually and also collectively as they form a city; each successive period of time has brought a change in style and technology as well as in the city's development.

The French Period, 1711–1763

Mobile was founded in 1711 as a result of the removal downstream of an earlier fort constructed in 1702 at Twenty-seven Mile Bluff. The older fort had been located too far from the bay to render adequate military protection and was subject to frequent flooding.[1] A new location at the mouth of the river was selected, and Sieur Chevillot drew plans for a cedar-stockaded fort, with Pailloux laying out the map for the city (figure 7). The streets were set at right angles, following a grid, as in all French fort towns. Because a swamp stretched

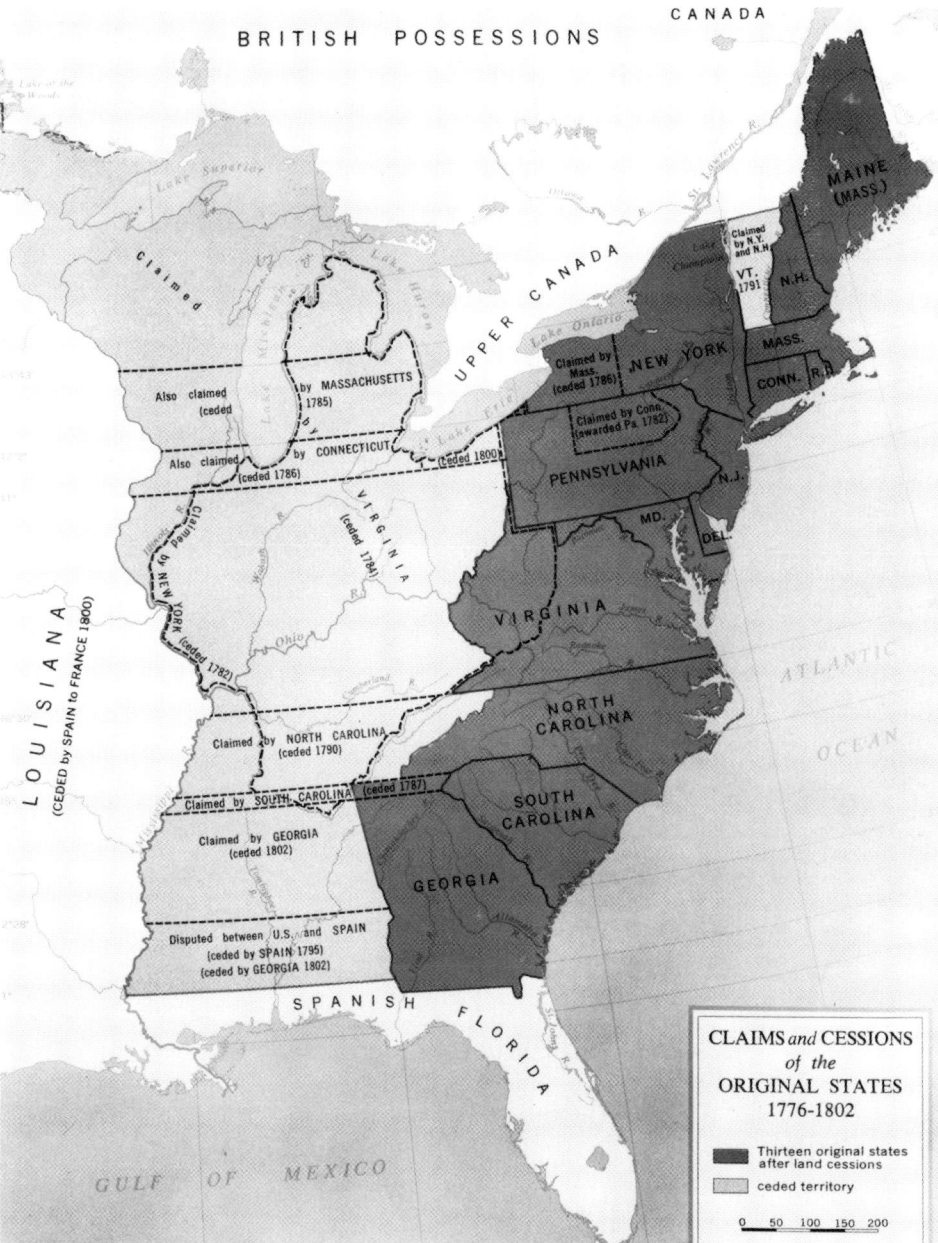

4. *A map of the claims and cessions of the original states, 1776–1822, showing the southern boundary dispute between Spain and the United States. (Reprinted, by permission, from* The Pictorial Atlas of United States History, *by J. J. Thorndike, copyright © 1966 by the American Heritage Publishing Company, Inc.)*

along the river to the south of the fort, the town saw its major development to the north. Both the 1711 Chevillot-Pailloux map and the later Pauger map of 1724 clearly depict the block pattern as it was established during the initial days of the settlement. The legend on the sides of the 1711 map has valuable information, including a description of the layout as well as some details of the buildings: "The officers, soldiers and residents have their abode outside the fort as is indicated, being placed in such a manner that the streets are six toises wide, and all parallel. The blocks are fifty toises square except those opposite the fort, which are sixty toises wide and fifty deep and those nearest the river which are fifty toises wide and sixty deep."[2]

5   *The Colonial Years, 1711–1813*

5. The Wythe House, 1775, Williamsburg, Virginia; Richard Talliaferro, builder. The bold cubic mass, the enclosed space, the window treatment, and the shallow entrance are typical of the eighteenth-century Georgian architecture seen in the homes of Virginia. (Photograph by Paul R. Thompson. Used by permission.)

6. La Couteau, The Lady of the Lake, ca. 1774, located near St. Martinville, Louisiana, and now destroyed. The French colonial plantation house was well adapted to the semitropical climate, with its central mass surrounded by galleries that created an open relationship of form and space. (Photograph by Dr. Eugene Wilson, University of South Alabama. Used by permission.)

7. Plan de la Ville et Fort Lovis de la Lovisiane, 1711—établies par les François en 1711. The map of the Fort was drawn by Chevillot and the grid plan of the town by Pailloux. Following the plan for the Fort, Bienville ordered the construction of a four-bastioned cedar stockade. (Courtesy of the Library of Congress.)

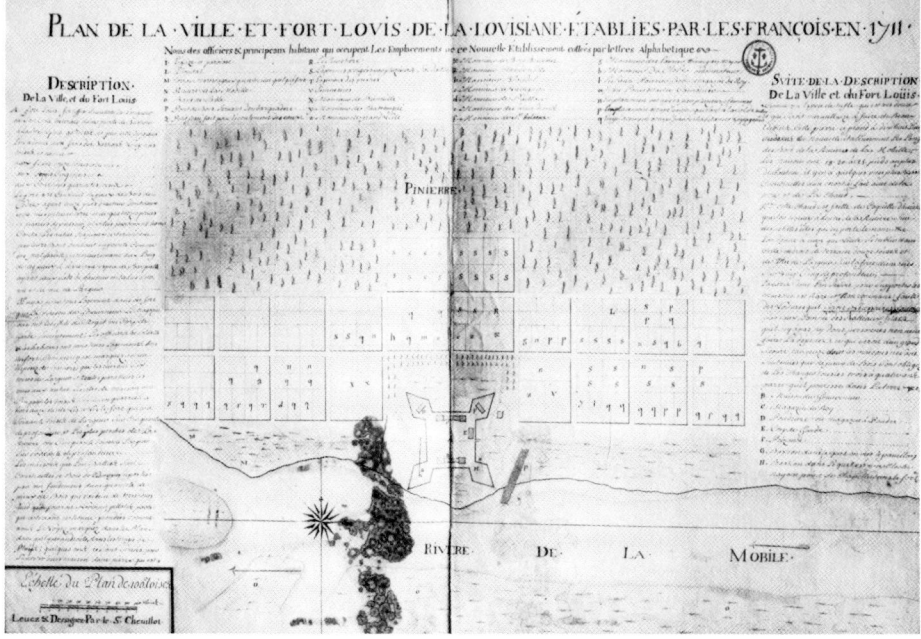

Since the purpose in founding Mobile was to secure the territory for the France of Louis XIV, most of the town was planned for the military. All the blocks west of Fort Condé contained barracks, with more located to both the north and the south of the fortifications. An area was also reserved for the clergy. The northeastern section of the first block north of the Fort was set aside for the seminary priests. The notes at the top of the map include an explanation of the various blocks of the town. One block is marked "Emplacement occupées par plusieurs femmes."

During those early years the building techniques were quite primitive. According to the Chevillot map:

> The houses are constructed of cedar and pine upon a foundation of wooden stakes which project out of the ground one foot and might be called piling, because this soil is inundated in certain localities in times of rain. . . . The houses are 18, 20 to 25 feet high or more, some lower, constructed of a kind of plaster made of earth and lime.[3]

The elevation of the buildings above ground level still did not offer sufficient protection. By 1720 the rotting of the structures had made it necessary to consider replacing the 1711 fort with one made from more permanent materials. A masonry fort was designed by Sieur de Boispinel, with Sieur de Pauger continuing the undertaking after the death of Boispinel in 1723. By late 1723 the work had begun, and the name changed to Fort Condé de la Mobille. A fine series of maps was prepared from 1723 to 1734 by the cartographer and draftsman Sieur Devin, who added details of the buildings at the top of the maps (figures 8, 9, 10). As late as 1743 plans were still progressing, with a proposed enlargement of the Fort by De Batz. Willard B. Robinson has published a definitive explanation of the Fort in the *Journal of the Society of Architectural Historians*.[4]

The Pauger-Devin maps of 1723 to 1734 not only illustrate the placement of buildings throughout the town but also contain information about construction in the elevation and section drawings. The Magazine (figure 10) was of half-timber framing, with posts resting on the sill—*poteaux sur sole*. The cross-bracing, rising the full height of the one-story elevation, was infilled with a form of *bousillée* that was made up of mud, lime, and a fibrous binder. The traditional Mansard roof was used. Unfortunately this type of roof was ill adapted to the weather of the Gulf, with its torrential rains and strong winds. The soft plaster of the walls soon eroded, and the framing rotted. A more streamlined roof was created by adapting the steep pitch of the Norman *pavillon* and extending it out over the porches in an unbroken curve.[5] One of the earliest examples of this form on a military structure is illustrated in the drawing for the Guard House and Prison at the Post of La Balise (figure 11).

The houses of the period were small and rectangular in mass, usually only one room deep and from two to three rooms wide. The ridge of the gable, or hip roof, ran parallel with the long axis of the house. A porch, or *galerie*, was added across the front of the cottage, across both front and rear, or, in the larger examples, around the building in its entirety. All three types appear on the De Batz proposal for the enlargement of the Fort, drawn in 1743 (figures 13a, 13b). In the legend on the Devin map, the governor's lodging is de-

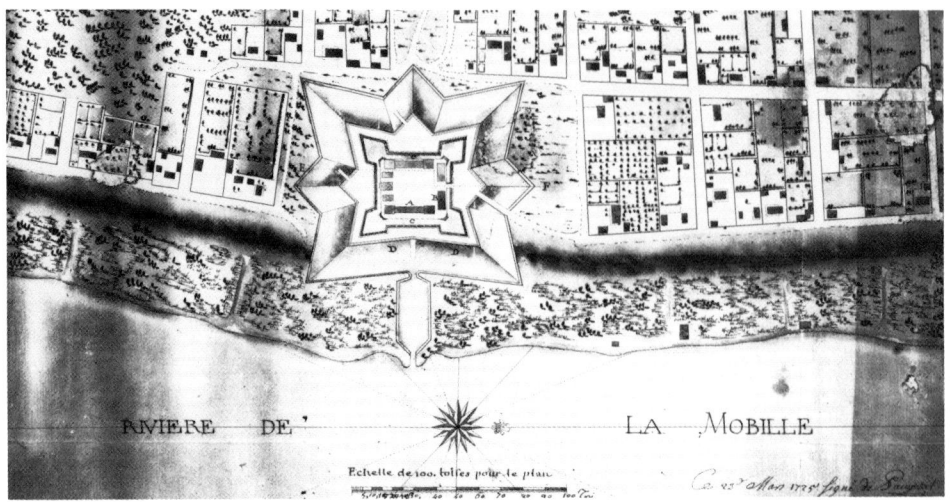

8. Plan of Fort Condé, Mobile. The brick fort was begun in 1723 by Sieur de Boispinel, with the plan drawn by Sieur de Pauger, both engineers-in-second of Louisiana. Upon their deaths, drawings continued to be made by Boispinel's cartographer, Sieur Devin. (Courtesy of the Mobile Public Library, Special Collections Division.)

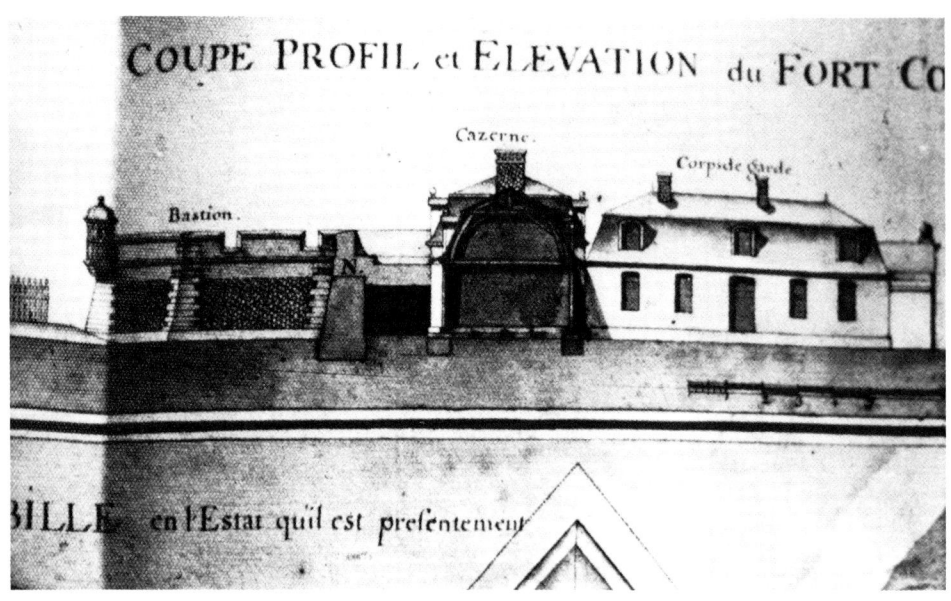

9. Detail of a 1723 drawing by Devin, showing the East Bastion and a cross section of the Barracks and Guard House. The Mansard roof on the Barracks and the Guard House was soon found to be ill suited to the climate. (Courtesy of the Mobile Public Library, Special Collections Division.)

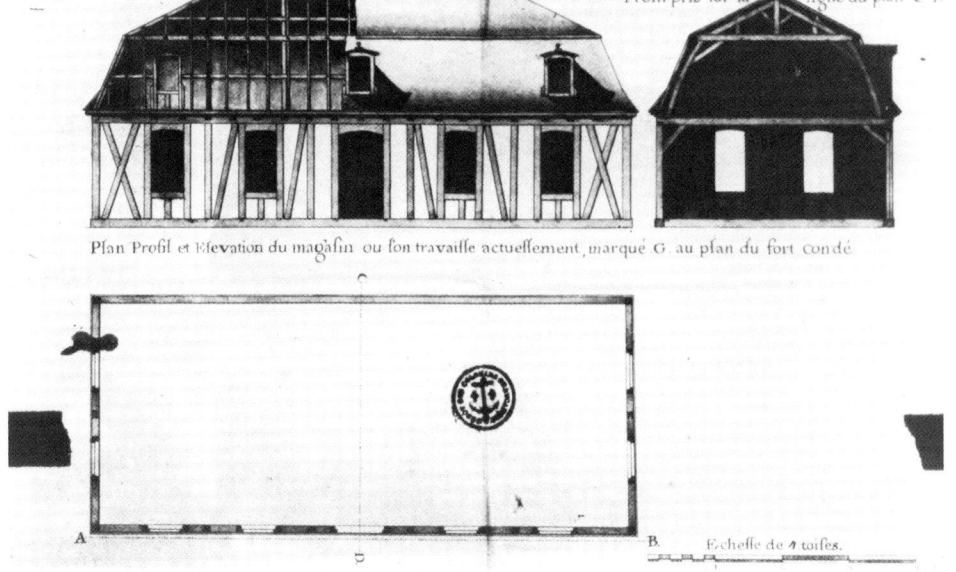

10. Detail of the Magazine, from the 1724 Devin map, showing the half-timber framing, with posts resting on the sill and the trussing needed for a Mansard roof. According to a letter of April 8, 1724, the Magazine had been constructed by Master Carpenter Etienne Fievre. Sieur Devin continued drawings of the Fort into the 1730s, producing an elevation of the Chapel in 1734. (Courtesy of the Mobile Public Library, Special Collections Division.)

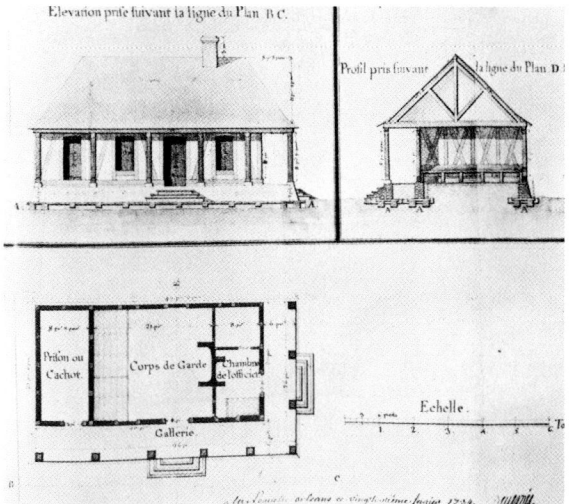

11. Plan, section, and elevation of the Guard House and Prison proposed for the Post of La Balise as drawn by Deverges, 1734. From the ridge of the roof, the unbroken slope extended over the front and side galleries, a design that was well suited to the climate of the Gulf Coast. (Courtesy of the Archives Nationales, Paris.)

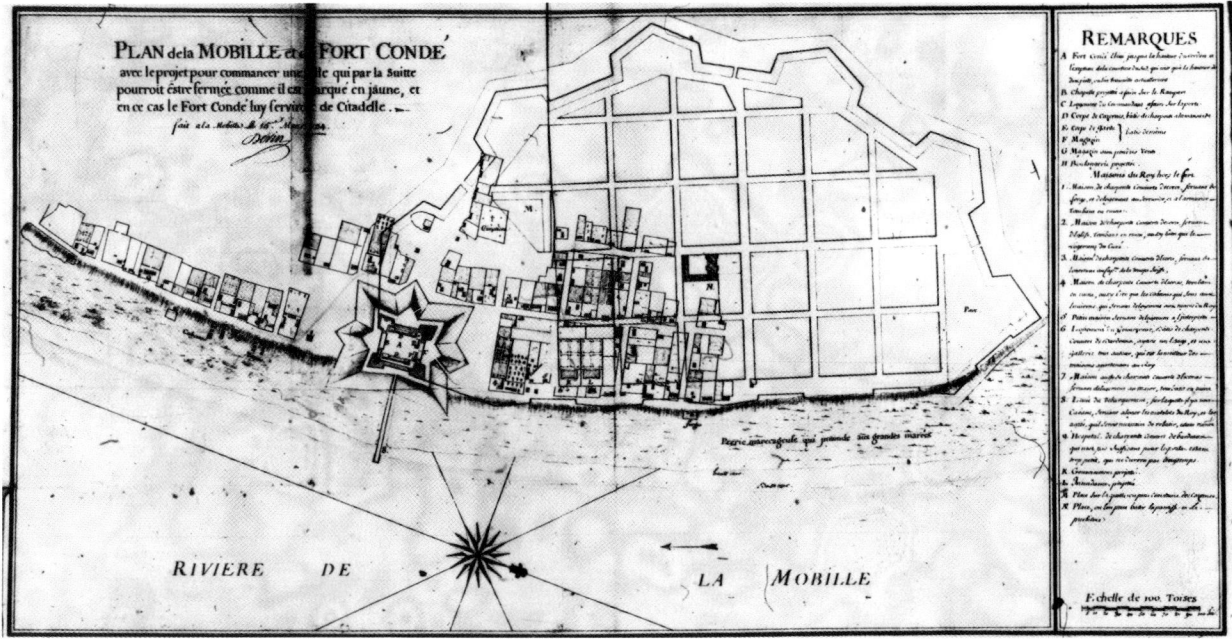

12. Plan of Mobile and of Fort Condé as drawn by Devin, 1734. The Remarques on the right side of the map give important information concerning individual buildings. (Courtesy of the Mobile Public Library, Special Collections Division.)

scribed as "built of wood with roof of shingle, one story and gallery all around" (figure 12). In the drawings, the galleries are indicated by the row of small dots signifying the supporting columns (figure 13b). The roof flared out over the galleries in a smooth curve, forming a protective shelter from the rain and sun. In general the roof material was of bark, but for important structures, such as that of the governor, shingles were employed.

A description of a house of this period has been preserved in an inventory of the property of one Joseph Bock, a sailor drowned while crossing Mobile Bay. It is dated April 4, 1762, the last year that the French retained control of the Gulf Coast:

> We, Jean Baptiste Thibault Guetlin, Officer commanding one half of the Swiss Company garrison at Mobile, having been informed that Joseph Bock, sargeant in said company, was lost at sea while crossing Mobile Bay, went to his house accompanied by Jean Boccard, both sargeants in said company, and found there his wife

The Colonial Years, 1711–1813

13a. Plan du Fort Condé de la Mobille, 1743, probably by De Batz; original in the Archives Nationales, Paris. Proposed enlargement of the Fort, with the existing structures in red and the proposed enlargements in yellow. (Courtesy of the Library of Congress.)

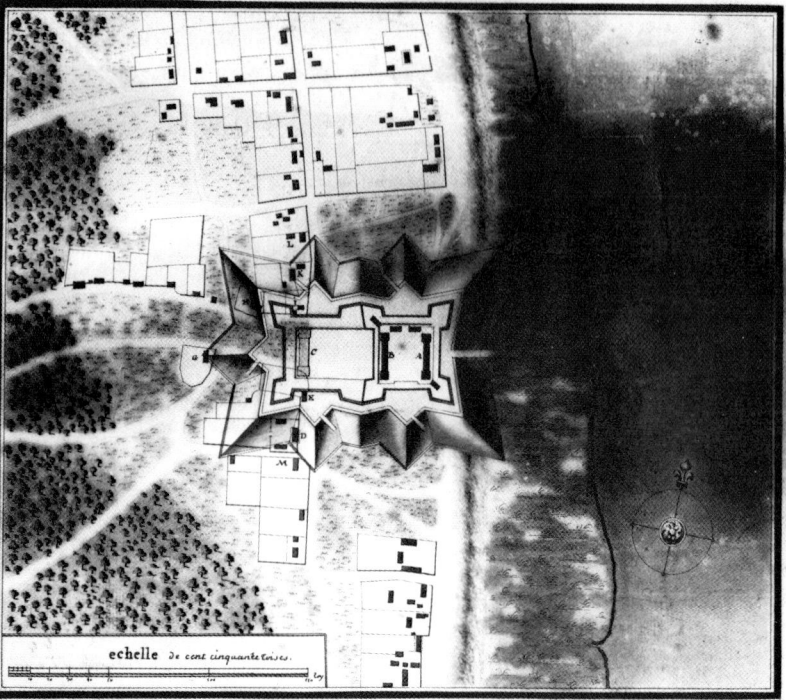

13b. Details of the 1743 map, with proposed enlargements. Cottages are shown with three different gallery arrangements, which are indicated by the dots representing the supporting posts. (Courtesy of the Library of Congress.)

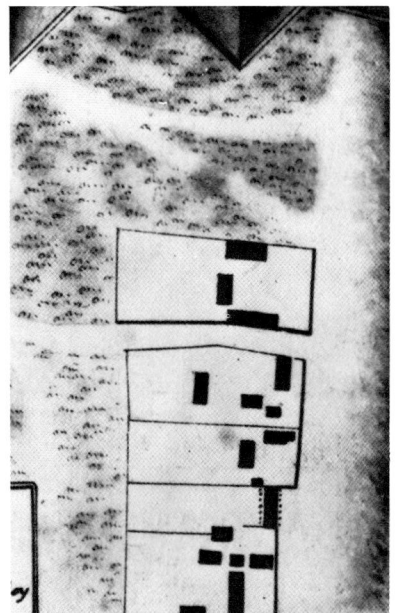
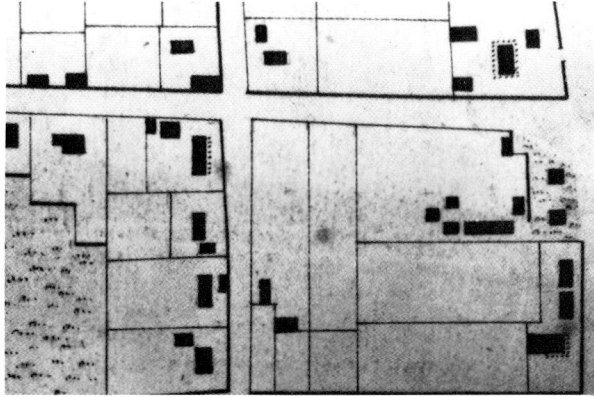

and three children. Widow Bock having been requested to produce all her husbands holdings, so that an inventory could be taken and the seals affixed, stated under oath that nothing had been diverted or secreted and that everything was to be found there. Therefore the following inventory was taken.

A certain piece of ground situated in this city and a house thereon, consisting of a dining room, a bedroom and front and rear galleries, and measuring thirty feet in length by eighteen feet in width. On the same ground also a kitchen, fifteen feet square, with a shed, a yard and a garden. Said ground adjoins on one side of the property of Sieur Lardas and on the other the property of Jacob Lacaze.[6]

14. *Cottage formerly on the corner of Conti and Conception, as drawn by Roderick D. MacKenzie, 1887. The cottage was typical of the early development, with its roof flaring out over the surrounding gallery.*

This type of cottage was based on a plan, shown at right, that was common all along the Gulf Coast in the French settlements. Two rooms were placed side by side, with doors leading to the front and rear galleries. As noted in the inventory, the kitchen was customarily kept in a separate building, so that the heat of cooking stayed away from the main house and so that the fire hazard was also reduced. Sometimes the kitchen was enlarged to contain living quarters for a family slave. According to the Bock inventory: "In the kitchen were found one bed, one mattress and one spread that Widow Bock declared belonged to her negroe, one kitchen table with drawer, three kettles, one brass fish boiler, two iron spits, two copper saucepans,—two choppers, one large saucepan, one pair large andirons with shovel and tongs."[7]

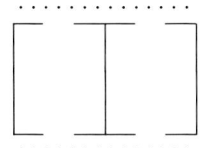

A house similar to that of seaman Bock was described in the French Records of May 1756. Joseph Barbaud de Boisdore bought a cottage constructed of posts with earth infilling in the walls and roofed with bark.[8] The galleried cottage, though modified, continued to be popular into the nineteenth century, as illustrated in the 1887 drawing by Roderick D. MacKenzie (figure 14).

Both Charles Peterson and C. Johnson have published studies of the origins of the French cottage as it evolved from Canadian and Caribbean influences (figure 15). In Canada, the French from Normandy and Brittany had emigrated into Nova Scotia in 1604, and when the English won the war with the French, the French residents refused to swear allegiance to the English king, and so they were expelled and fled south. Many drifted down the Mississippi, settling along the way in Illinois and Missouri. Others continued on down to the bayou country of Louisiana. When they settled new areas, they took their house form with them. In *Building a House in New France* (figure 16), Peter Moogk has authenticated the French Quebec farmhouse: the central rectangular massing with the steeply pitched roof, the plan with a single row of rooms side by side, the one-story elevation constructed of half timber, and the casement windows with exterior shutters.[9]

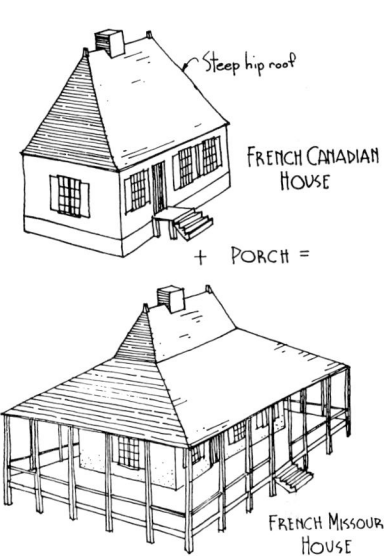

15. *Derivation of the typical Illinois country roof line as drawn by Charles Peterson. The study illustrates the union of the Canadian farmhouse with the galleried dwelling of the Caribbean area. (Reprinted, by permission of the State Historical Society of Missouri, from "The Houses of French St. Louis," by Charles E. Peterson, Missouri Historical Review, January 1941.)*

Meanwhile Colonial French from the Caribbean moved into the Gulf Coast area and the valley of the Mississippi, bringing a less tightly constructed house form that was better suited to the climate of the South. In the house from Livingston (figure 17), a crude form of gallery is covered by the flared roof that provides much-needed shade from the hot sun and protects the walls from the heavy rains.[10] In addition to this structural advantage, the gallery provides outdoor work space when interior rooms would be stifling.

Surviving examples of the early Creole cottages can be found in Sainte Genevieve, Missouri, about sixty-five miles south of St. Louis.

16. *The Paradise House, Charlesbourg, French Canada, as drawn by Carole Richards for Peter N. Moogk,* Building a House in New France. *The rectangular form and the steeply pitched Norman room became the core of the cottages of the Mississippi valley and the Gulf Coast. (Reprinted by permission of the author.)*

17. *A primitive Guatemalan house. This structure continues an early style developed by the colonials of the semitropical regions. (Photograph by Dr. Eugene Wilson, University of South Alabama. Used by permission.)*

Here are more than thirty buildings, most of which bear witness to their French Colonial origin. The most famous of these buildings is the Bolduc House, restored in 1956–1957 (figure 18). An example of the early French construction can be seen at Pascagoula, in the so-called Old Spanish Fort, which was not a fort and was not Spanish (figure 19). The heavy timbers, *poteaux sur sole,* have an infilling of mud, clay, and moss fibers. The walls were originally plastered over, but large areas are now exposed, and the construction is visible. According to the bulletin published by the Old Spanish Fort Museum and the Mississippi Agricultural and Industrial Board, the land was granted to Joseph Simon de La Pointe, who is thought to have built a home there by 1726. The house and most of the outbuildings were destroyed in the 1772 hurricane that is described in Albert J. Pickett's *History of Alabama.* At the time, the property was owned by the daughter of La Pointe and her husband, Hugo E. Krebs. One building is believed to have survived, the old carpenter's shop, which has been called the Old Spanish Fort. It is not known whether it was built by La Pointe or by Krebs, but it is certainly in the French Colonial style.[11]

The same hurricane that destroyed the Krebs property did much damage to Mobile. According to Pickett, "Vessels, boats and logs were driven up into the heart of the town,—salt water overran the gardens—spray rose in the air and fell at the distance of half a mile—houses filled with water several feet deep."[12]

In 1760, toward the end of the French period, Phelypeaux drew a map of Mobile (figure 20). There is a second signature in the lower right corner of the map. After the English territory fell to the Spanish in 1780, Carlos Trudeau, a surveyor, fortunately found the French map and signed his name, adding the line, "Plano que je ha hallado en la tomado de la Mobile, 4 Mayo, 1780." The crown properties are indicated in red on the original. The palisade is outlined in yellow dots, as explained in the title of the map. These two colored areas obviously included most of the town. The main function of the settlement was still to serve the needs of the Fort. The main buildings were labeled: the Commissariat, the Magazine of the king, the Fort, and the Hospital. Barracks occupied the blocks to the north of the Fort as they did on the maps of 1723–1734.

The surface treatment of the buildings has been changed from that of the earlier half-timber construction. Years of experience with the torrential rains had led builders to alter the siding of the buildings. Three years after the Phelypeaux map had been drawn, the "Magazine for the reception of Provisions Constructed in Columbage of Brick [was] surrounded without with Planks, and covered

18. The Bolduc House, Ste. Genevieve, Missouri, ca. 1785, one of the surviving examples of the early French construction that developed in the Mississippi valley. (Photograph by Lee Hoffman, University of South Alabama. Used by permission.)

19. The Old Spanish Fort, Pascagoula, Mississippi, ca. 1726. The building is believed to be the surviving carpenter's shop of the La Pointe–Krebs estate. The construction is French in the roof trussing and has the roof extended over the galleries. The half-timber framing is made of heavy vertical posts infilled with a nogging of oyster shells, mud, and bits of organic material, all covered with a coat of plaster.

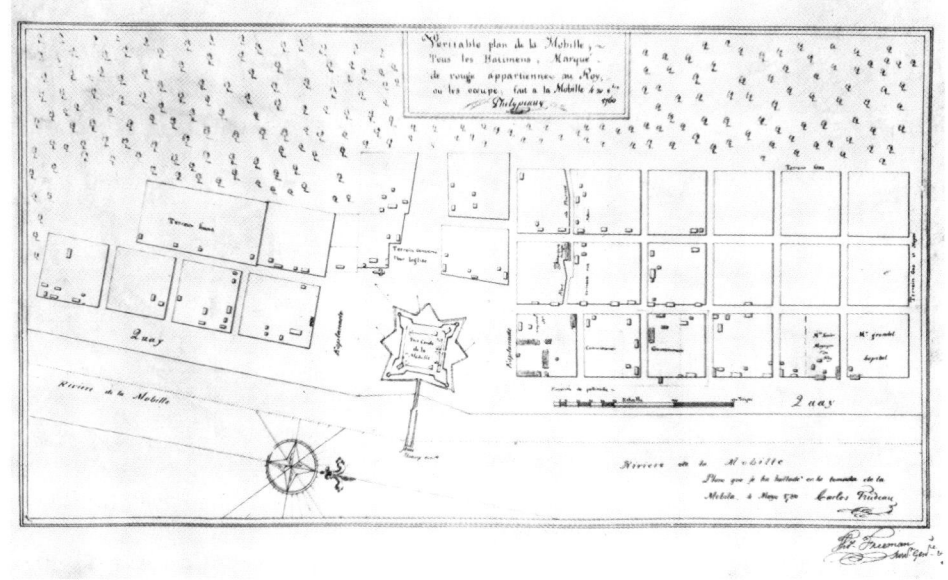

20. Phelypeaux map, "Véritable plan de la Mobille," 1760. The royal properties were indicated in red. (Courtesy of the United States Department of the Interior, Bureau of Land Management.)

with Shingles."[13] The older exterior plaster had been replaced by wood siding and the bark roof by shingles.

The few private dwellings indicated on the map were located either close to the Fort or within the palisaded square to the north, suggesting the continued need for protection in the still untamed wilderness of the mid-eighteenth century. The situation in early Jamestown, Virginia, was similar; the fortified settlement was without the comforts and amenities of the homeland.

The street orientation remained essentially the same as in the early days of the French occupation. While only one street name appears on the 1760 map (figure 20), others must have been adopted, for several of the modern streets have French names: Royal, Dauphin, St. Louis, Conti, and so forth. Where Conti now extends from Water west to Broad, the map shows the Rue de Tournée (not legible in figure 20). It was not uniform in width, like the other

The Colonial Years, 1711–1813

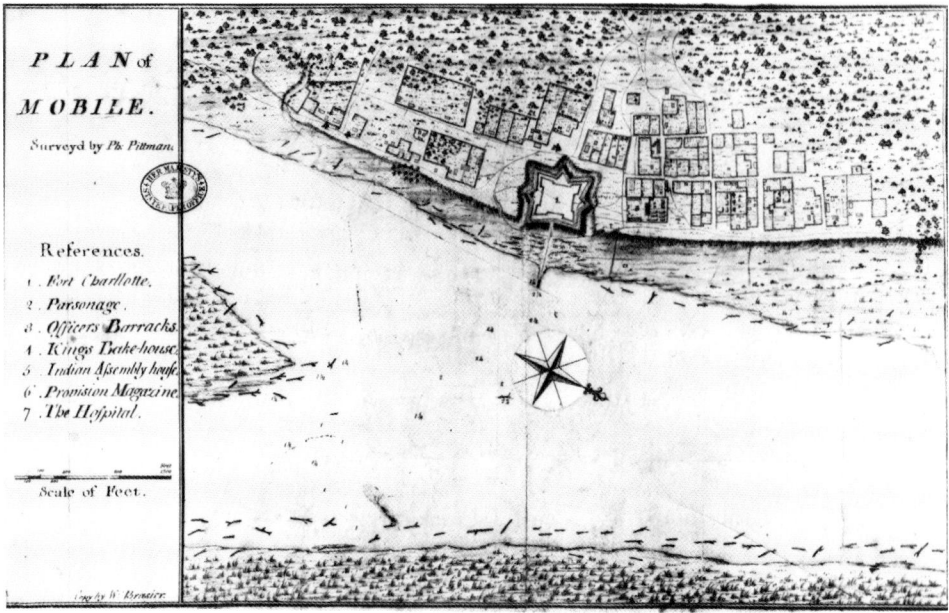

21a. The Pittman map, surveyed by P. Pittman, drawn by W. Brasier, ca. 1768, during the English period. The Indian Assembly building, at number five, was located at the corner of present-day Conti and St. Emanuel streets. (Courtesy of the Library of Congress.)

21b. Detail of the Pittman map, showing the area to the north of the Fort.

French streets. In the western end an open space provides for a building that was marked "haugard, sovager." This was the center for the Indian congresses which were held throughout the French and English periods. The building appeared again on the Pittman map of 1768 (figures 21a, b). The English records give a brief description of the building. It was 100 feet long and 40 feet wide, "divided into two parts, the foundation of wood filled with Earth, surrounded with boards, Covered Shingles, and set around with Guard Beds, several doors and windows wanting."[14]

To the west of the Fort was a religious structure with the designation "Terrein conservé Pour Leglise." A chapel had originally been planned within the Fort, as shown on the Pauger map, but the building was never constructed. Sometime after 1730 and before 1760, the Chapel seems to have been built in the first block west of the Esplanade (figures 21a, b).

On the right side of the map, in land designated as low and swampy ("gos et Moyeé") is located the Hospital under the name of one "Mm Grondel." Later the English records will show that Major Robert Farmer rented the Hospital from Mme Grondel.[15]

Only one wharf is shown on the 1760 map (figure 20), indicating that commerce was limited in nature and that no attempt was made to develop the city as a commercial center. All trade was carried on between the Indians and the representatives of the crown. In 1712, Louis XIV granted rights of trade for fifteen years to Antoine Crozat:

—for these reasons, being desirous to show our favor to him, and to regulate the conditions upon which we mean to grant him the said commerce, after having deliberated this affair in our council, of our certain knowledge, full power and royal authority, we by these present, have appointed and do appoint, the said Crozat, solely to carry on a trade in all lands possessed by us, and bounded by New Mexico and the lands of the English of Carolina—

Signed, Louis XIV
Fontainebleau
September 20, 1712[16]

The Crozat grant was not commercially successful, not surprisingly in view of the fact that at the time there were only "twenty-eight families, twenty negroes, seventy-five Canadians and two companies of infantry of fifty men each, all adding up to 324 souls scattered over the whole territory." Other attempts were made to improve trade, such as the 1717 grant to John Law, but it too had ended in failure by 1721. Even after emigrants had been brought into the territory to increase the population, France never achieved an urban development in which monetary trade could flourish. The French colonial system remained the barter method as it had been founded by Iberville, by which French goods were exchanged for Indian products such as rice, skins, and furs. Since the exchange of goods was carried on by a representative of the crown, only the one wharf at the Fort was needed. Louis XIV never grasped the potential of his Louisiana possessions.[17]

The French agricultural program was no more successful than the growth of trade had been in the central coastal area around Mobile. As a result, no records have yet been discovered that describe the local plantation house. We may reasonably assume that it resembled the eighteenth-century plantation buildings of Louisiana, such as Parlange of 1750. Lisloy was the country home of the Chevalier Montault de Monberaut, located on Fowl River. In his *Mémoire* he listed his manor house with stables, 500 head of cattle, fifty horses, and twenty-six slaves, but he does not describe the house.[18] Plantation grants were made for sites along the Alabama River, but they did not describe buildings. While nothing specific is known about them, it is certain that they bequeathed to subsequent generations a design concept of openness and spatial flow that was well adapted to the climate and that would survive the English and Spanish periods, continuing into the American years.

The end of the French period, sadly, failed to reflect the vision shown by Jean Baptiste Le Moyne de Bienville in 1711. The era's decline was best described by the report of the Fort, written by Peter Hanibal Develle, chevalier of the Royal and Military Order of St. Louis, king's lieutenant and commander of the Fort of Mobile, and by René-Jean Gabriel Fezende, acting as commissary of marine of the same port. The report was addressed to Major Robert Farmer and was written on February 10, 1763, at the time of the surrender:

> The said Port of Mobille situated upon the River of that Name, consisting in different Buildings and works of Fortification, the particulars of which as follows:
>
> The Fort consisting of Four Bastions, Curtains, Rampart and Parapet, with Thirty Eight Embrazures [sic] open, raised in Brick work, the whole being decayed and out of repair. The Cannon, ordinance Stores, and Ammunition taken away.
>
> Twenty three Cazernes Vaulted under the Rampart on the East, North and South Faces, whereof Several doors and Window Shutters are wanting. The rest in very bad repair.
>
> The Powder Magazine in the Interior part of the South East Bastion is of brick work, covered with Shingles, two doors for the said Magazine in tolerable repair.
>
> The Pallisades around the Covered Way, rotten and Several wanting.
>
> A Bake house in the Interior part of the North West Bastion, in

Brick work, and Oven of the same. Entirely Useless at Present.

All the Barracks and Guard-rooms in the Fort, in a ruinous Condition.

The Officers Barracks in the Area, Walls and Roofs good, in all other respects wants a thrô [sic] repair.

The Guard-house and Kitchen in the said Area in good Repair.

The Houses of Offices in bad Repair.[19]

The report written on November 30, 1763, by Major Farmer was even more critical of the condition of the buildings. He wrote of the need to resurface the bastions, the scarp, and the parapets:

—under the Rampart of the Curtains of the Three Fronts are small Casemates Arched with brick, but are very much out of repair and let in Rain, the Rampart having been neglected for some time past were all Covered with Long grass and Shrubs that lodged the Rain, which has very much Destroyed the bricks that cover the tops of the Casemates.

Some of the Platforms, the Sleepers being rotten want entirely to be new Laid and others to be repaired with Planks.

There are Barracks within the Fort for about 216 men, allowing 12 men for each room the whole in very bad repair & wants to be rebuilt, and enlarged by adding another Storry [sic]—There is only one officers room besides the Guard room in the Fort, both in very bad repair.

The Officers Barracks are detached from the Fort about 100 yards, and want a good many Repairs the Floors being mostly rotten, as are many of the windows, they are sash'd [sic] but mostly all the panes broke.[20]

After further listing, there follows a report of all the furnishings and utensils that were handed over to the English. It shows a pitiful lack of materials, illustrating the degree of discomfort experienced by the French garrison at the close of French Colonial control of the Gulf Coast. One era had ended, and another was about to begin.

The English Period, 1763–1780

The war between France and England escalated to include their colonial possessions in the New World, and England was the victor. By the Treaty of Paris, dated February 10, 1763, France lost its lands extending from Canada to the Gulf Coast (figure 2). England also acquired Florida from the Spanish, so that, for seventeen years, England controlled all the lands east of the Mississippi River. The fall of Mobile was recorded in a letter by Major Farmer on January 24, 1764:

My Lord:

I have the Honour to inform your Lordship, that on the 20th of October last, with his Majesty's 22nd and 34th Regiments, I took Possession of the Fort and Town of Mobille; and on the 6th of November detach'd a Subaltern and Thirty men in five Battoes for Tombeckbay who arrived there the 22d and the same day relieved the French troops.—

> Inclosed I have the Honour of Transmitting to your Lordship, Reports of the Condition of the Fort, Number of the French Inhabitants few of whom I believe will remain here, unless the Report of New Orleans being Ceded to the Crown of Spain prove true—.[21]

Major Farmer set up a military government with Mobile as his headquarters and changed the name of the Fort to Fort Charlotte. On October 20, 1763, he issued a manifesto concerning the change from French to English law. He assured the French inhabitants that their rights would be protected if they would "repair to Mobille" to take an oath of allegiance to the English king within three months' time. If they refused to do so, they would have to leave the territory within eighteen months. One hundred and twelve Frenchmen took the oath, their names being listed in the records of October 2, 1764.[22] The roster includes names that still survive in Mobile: Favre, Rochon, Chastang, Dubroca, Durand, and others.

Had the English not been harassed by the events of the years between 1763 and 1780 and by the confrontation between Major Farmer and Governor Johnstone, much might have been accomplished in Mobile. One of the first laws established by Governor Johnstone at his capital at Pensacola was an attempt to encourage settlement:

> One hundred acres of land should be granted to every person, being master or mistress of a family, for himself or herself, and fifty acres for every white or black man, woman or child of which such person's family shall consist—and any further quantity not exceeding 1000 acres over and above what they are entitled to by the number of persons in their family—
>
> for every 50 acres—[he] be obliged within three years to clear and work 3 acres at least—or drain 3 acres of marsh—to put up and keep three neat cattle which he will be obliged to keep on his land until 3 acres of every 50 be fully cleared and improved.—
>
> —further every grantee to erect on some part of his land one good dwelling house to contain at least 20 feet in length by 16 feet in breadth and likewise the 3 neat head of cattle for every 50 acres.[23]

Thus the English attempted to initiate an agricultural development. Land grants were given to military personnel by a proclamation of October 7, 1763, by which 5,000 acres could be acquired by former service field officers, 3,000 acres by captains, 2,000 by staff officers and subalterns, 200 by noncommissioned officers, and 50 by privates. Between 1763 and 1769, 131 grants were platted on a map made by Clinton D. Howard in his book *The British Development of West Florida*. The grants were concentrated around Pensacola, with a scattering along the Mobile River, where 1,000 acres was the average size. Major Farmer claimed two tracts totaling 1,800 acres, one of which was on the Tombigbee River.[24] Bernard Romans, crown surveyor, in 1772 described the Mobile area: "The River also abounds in very Fertile Soil. I cut a Cane on its Banks which Measured Forty-Seven Feet from the third Joint, to its Extremity—nor was this an Extraordinary Case. This River in Process of Time must Indubitably become a fine Settlement not Inferior by itself to any Province now known."[25] Had this agricultural attempt been successful, the Gulf Coast might have developed as did the south Atlantic seaboard territories. The resulting architecture might well have rivaled that found along the James River in Virginia. Such was not to be the case. The English were never able to win the friendship of the local Indians, as the French had done, and no plantation homes survived for long. The Choctaw attacked, as in the case of Dugald Campbell, destroying all his cattle. Three plantations near Dauphin Island had to be abandoned because of attacks by the Creek. Animosity was compounded by the Indians' resentment of the new laws concerning trade and the establishment of the Indian boundaries. In an attempt at reconciliation, the governor appointed le Chevalier Montault de Monberaut (also spelled Montaut Montbereau), a Frenchman, to take charge of Indian affairs. The truce did not last long; when Monberaut had completed the plans for the Creek council, he was dismissed. He left Lisloy, his plantation, to be sold and went to New Orleans. After his departure, tensions between the English and the Indians increased.[26]

While the English were not able to contribute to the development of plantation architecture, they did have some influence on the growth of the city. One year after the English had taken possession, Lord Adam Gordon visited the city and recorded his impression of it:

> The Fort is in an Unwholesome Situation, alth' [sic] it stands rather higher than the Town. It is a Qaurre [sic] of Brick, having a bad dry Ditch, a covered way Stockaded, and a unfinished Glacis. It is casemated and has had Barracks on three Sides, which may contain about three hundred Men. Upon the whole it is Strong enough to resist all Indian Attacks. The Town consists mostly of Straggling houses, built of Wood, or Wood and Brick; the Streets are well laid out, but in the Summer and Autumn, almost everybody is ill of Fevers, Fluxes and Agues; Bark is much Administered and Seldom fails. The water in and near the Town is bad and often brackish, the Natives who remain, fetch what water they drink, at three Miles distance, and in general stand out better than the Garrison, and the New Settlers.[27]

The first major concern of the military was the restoration of the Fort. Its dilapidated condition was reported by the two French officers who handed over the property to Major Farmer, as previously noted. Major Farmer sent home many urgent requests for money and materials for repairs, but the government was slow in responding. In addition to the problems facing the crown, development was shifting away from the Gulf Coast and into the Mississippi valley, especially near Natchez. While legislation was pending on a request by Governor Johnstone for £10,000 to finance public buildings, £21,500 for a naval arsenal and yard for Pensacola, and £33,100 for repairs of the fortification, Major Farmer proceeded cautiously with work that needed to be done. In 1771, Pierre Rochon was appointed to begin mending the Fort.[28] Details of the project were recorded in the financial statements of Major Farmer and included the following.

> The Brick casements were repaired.
> A new platform for the cannon was installed.
> The Barracks within the Fort were put in order.
> The Palisade surrounding the Officers Square was renewed, lathed and spiked.

The Guard Room was floored and white washed.
Six rooms were added to these rooms.
Repairs made to roofs, windows and cupboards.
The late Com't [sic] house had 4 new floors plus doors, hearths and windows put in order.
Chimneys and 5 wells repaired.
The Hospital roof, hearth and walls repaired.
One of the Bake Houses was converted into an Officers' Barracks [where Major Farmer proposed to live].
The second Bake House was put in order.[29]

For all of this work Pierre Rochon received the sum of £2,232, the receipt being dated April 9. The Indian Assembly House was repaired in 1765. The energies and financial resources that were spent on Fort repairs did not alter the basic design of the French military architecture.[30]

The problem of recurrent disease was more difficult to solve than the Fort restorations. The journal of Lord Adam Gordon comments on the epidemic's severity. "In October, 1764, when I was in Mobile, the Garrison which consisted of two Regiments, was so ill, and Weak, as scarce to be able between them to furnish a Subaltern's Guard. Few Guns were mounted, and those that were, were Iron Ship Guns."[31] Another record is that of Governor Johnstone, written to John Pownall:

> A Disorder has been prevalent at Mobile, something in effect like a Plague. The Officers here were summoned to a general Court Martial at Mobile; all who went have been seized with the Disease; three have died and the rest continue ill; I should have imputed it to too many having crowded into the same Apartment in the Heat of Autumn, if every Master of a ship had not been seized with the same disorder.[32]

Dr. John Lorimer, the surgeon general of the military forces of West Florida, noted that Mobile was located in a swamp extending "as far as the eye can see" and that the heat of summer seemed to initiate the onset of the disease. One of the worst epidemics coincided with the arrival of the Second Regiment, which was brought to Mobile from Jamaica.[33]

In an effort to control the disease, it was decided to plan for a series of smaller forts to be built on higher ground for summer occupancy, for example at Red Bluffs (Montrose) and Dauphin Island. The English did not seem to notice that the French who continued to live in the area did not suffer to the same degree. Brigadier General Frederick Haldimand was near the truth when he wrote that "temperate men had nothing to fear in the climate." Pickett in his *History of Alabama* suggested that the English lived too fast, ate too much meat, and drank too much, while the French lived more relaxed lives, drank no liquor during the summer, and always procured pure water from sources outside the city. To help care for the sick, Major Farmer first rented, then purchased the Old French Hospital on the west side of Royal Street, between what would now be St. Louis and St. Anthony streets.[34]

Pensacola was more successful than Mobile in the development of commercial architecture, though two Pensacola companies established centers in Mobile, the William Panton Company and Swanson-McGillivray. William Panton, from South Carolina, brought into the Florida city not only a successful business but also a Georgian influence in his building. The house, which had been erected by 1781, was two and a half stories in height, with semicircular-headed windows and front and rear matching porches supported by square columns.[35]

The Scotchman John McGillivray (also spelled MacGillivary), of the Swanson-McGillivray firm, was an important arbitrator with the Indians, like the rest of his family. Lachlan McGillivray married a half-Creek, Sehoy Marchand. Their son, Alexander, was sent away to be educated and when he returned became one of the most powerful of the Creek chieftains, chief of the tribe of The Wind.[36]

The activity of the early companies affected the growth of Mobile, calling for the construction of residences as well as commercial structures. The Pittman map (figure 21) shows that at the end of the decade there was an increase in the number of buildings located on the blocks to the north and west of the Fort. While as yet no private wharves are shown, the government had passed a bill which encouraged their construction. It was entitled "An Act for Encouraging the Inhabitants of Pensacola and Mobile to Build Wharfs and Establishing the date of Wharfage."[37] During subsequent years the wharves shown on maps indicate the growth of the city.

To plan for the anticipated growth, Elias Durnford platted a map in which lots were set aside for residences and for civic and commercial purposes. Between the years 1763 and 1769, some fifty-four lots were sold. Some deeds referred to older landmarks. There was, for example, the site conveyed to Mme Vedeboncour, "on which the Indian Interpreter's house stands, and a small hut there on." Frances Pousset received one of the king's houses near the Hospital. The Pousset building must have been quite large, for according to the owner, he "had been at considerable expense holding Court at Mobile in his house as no house had been assigned for the Court House." In spite of these grants, living conditions were inadequate. Lord Adam Gordon reported that the sanitary conditions were primitive, "and a roof which did not leak after a heavy downpour was almost a nine day's wonder."[38]

Lots for religious buildings were also requested. One grant went to the trustees of an Anglican parish house. A French chapel was mentioned near a lot granted to one Daniel Clark. While the English were of the Anglican faith, they respected the Catholic beliefs of the French inhabitants and passed laws giving them the freedom to practice their religion and the right to build at their own expense a "Chapel for the decent exercising of their worship; that bells should be allowed for the Chapel, but that public processions in the streets, except for burials, should be prohibited."[39] Included in the requests for military funds were also items concerning the religious and educational welfare of the colony: "1,500 Pounds for a Church at Pensacola and Mobile[;] 100 pounds for the payment of a Minister at Mobile for the time from June 24, 1763 to June 24, 1764 [and] 25 pounds for the payment for a schoolmaster at Mobile for the same period of time."[40] Unfortunately the funds never materialized. The Reverend Sam Mart had to resign, stating that he had grown weary of waiting for the funds to erect the church and that, on the "inconsiderable salary" given, he could no longer support his family.[41]

The advent of the American Revolution checked progress, such as it was, and the project lost its momentum. The town became neglected. All the early attempts to clean up the city, like the 1766 bill that had been passed to cut the "pernicious weeds and the woods around the said town," proved of no help. In 1777 William Bartram wrote:

> The City of Mobile is situated on the easy ascent of a rising bank, extending nearly half a mile back on the level plain above; it has been nearly a mile in length, though now chiefly in ruins, many houses vacant and mouldering to earth; yet there are a few good buildings inhabited by French gentlemen, English, Scotch and Irish and emigrants from the Northern British colonies.[42]

The seventeen years of English domination brought little architectural change from the forms that had been developed by the French. No records have yet been found to indicate that English or south Atlantic coastal tidewater types replaced the galleried French cottage. The military building activity consisted of repairs and restorations, not innovations. Georgian details were seldom mentioned and chiefly in connection with Pensacola, not Mobile. Architecturally, the years from 1763 to 1780 added little to the history of building in Mobile.

The Spanish Period, 1780–1813

From March 9 to March 14, 1780, Don Bernardo de Gálvez laid siege to Mobile. With their successful attack, the Spanish claimed control of the Gulf Coast as far north as thirty-two degrees, twenty-eight minutes of latitude, a line running a little south of Selma. Not until the Treaty of San Lorenzo in 1795 was the boundary dispute finally settled at thirty-one degrees latitude. When the Spanish lost a section of the land they claimed, they had to withdraw from some of their established forts, such as Fort San Esteban de Tombecbé, founded in 1789. The withdrawal also separated them from some agricultural lands that were just beginning to produce cotton.[43]

When Spain began to control the coast, Mobile was in a ruinous state. The English had burned buildings close to the Fort in an effort to improve the visibility for purposes of defense. According to the census recorded by Caughey, only "fort soldiers and personnel, two surgeons, sixty sailors, fifty-four inhabitants and fifty negroes" remained in Mobile at the time of the surrender. By 1787 only 1,230 persons, 62 plantations, 491 horses, and 3,638 cattle were left in the whole area of Mobile, Pascagoula, Bay St. Louis, and the Tensaw and Tombigbee river valleys. Spain lost no time in attempting to enlarge the colony by inviting emigrants from the English Tories of the former American colonies and the French dissidents who preferred Spanish control to the dominion of the newly established United States. Some eighty English and twenty-six French took the oath of fidelity to the Spanish crown. To make this emigration attractive, the Spanish offered free land grants, religious toleration, and commercial privileges free from royal control.[44] With this last step the

22. Plan of Mobile, 1809, Spanish period. Conti Street has been straightened, the Indian Assembly has been removed, and there is a greater concentration of buildings within the city blocks. (Courtesy of the Library of Congress.)

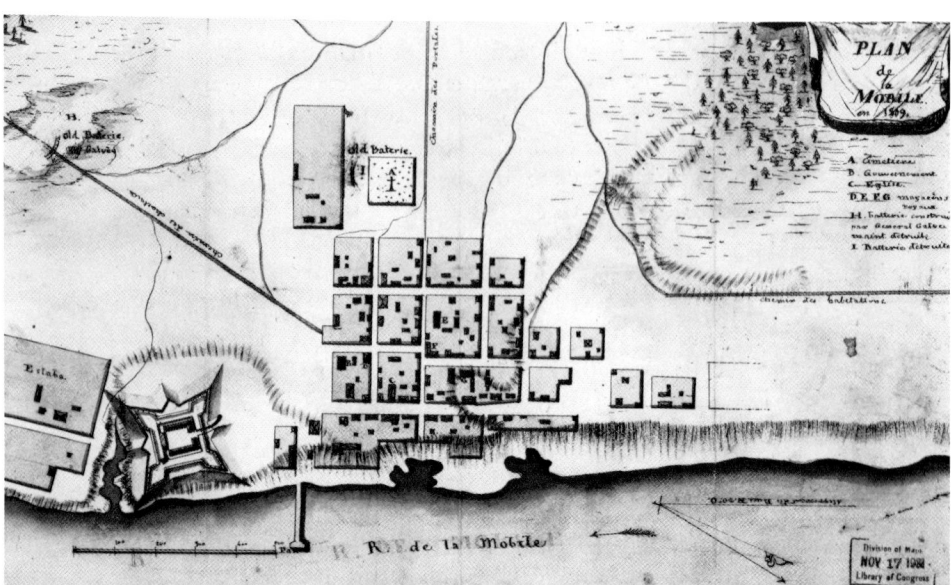

future development of Mobile was established. The city was to bloom during the American period.

The old English company of Panton and Leslie took on new life and with Alexander McGillivray as a silent partner was able to monopolize the Indian trade. A branch of the company was established at Mobile under John Forbes, who by 1802 had built the first wharf for free enterprise in the city. The company also acquired considerable holdings not only within the city but also along the river and the coast. One item of its trade that contributed to architecture was "yellow earth," a coloring that was imported from Pensacola and was mixed in the stucco used to surface exterior walls.[45]

Surprisingly, the increase in trade did not bring a noticeable increase in the area of the city. The Spanish map of 1809 (figure 22) shows a city of much the same size as at the beginning of the Spanish period. The one addition appears along the waterfront, where three partially developed blocks had been reclaimed from the marshy edge of the river. The one wharf on the 1809 map is located at the end of present-day Government Street, and the Old Royal Wharf leading to the fort has been removed. Commerce had progressed far enough to make warehouses necessary, one being erected in 1811, by Lewis Judson.[46] The increased density of occupied commercial sites is evident from the large number of claims made in the courts at the beginning of the American period.

The official naming of the streets also attests to the increased complexity of the city. For street names the Spanish chose the names of saints, and many still appear on signs today. Some names, however, have been changed. Dauphin was called St. John under the Spanish, and Conti was St. Peter, the same street that on the Phelypeaux map of 1760 was marked the Rue de Tournée. The Spanish also straightened St. Peter's Street and removed the old Indian Assembly House (compare the maps in figures 21 and 22). Some of the buildings survived into the nineteenth century to become part of the 1820 street scene. The Spanish Church, located on the west side of Royal, the second building north of St. Peter, was described by a German traveler in 1826. The Old Burying Ground, the Campo Santo, remained until the construction of the Cathedral (not identified in the figure). Unfortunately, few references to Spanish buildings have been preserved, though general descriptions of the city were recorded by early travelers. General Louis Milfort called Mobile "a small earthly paradise where the inhabitants—there were only forty landowners—while not rich, were perfectly happy. Hunting and fishing were abundant, fruits and vegetables as good as in Europe.— Drinking water was brought from a stream a league away." Levi Leland's thesis on Harry Toulmin includes the remark: "To the south stood the small and lethargic Spanish community of Mobile, a Fort carefully surveyed, all commerce plying the river and sea." The *American Gazette* for 1798, published in London, called Mobile "a city of West Florida, formerly of considerable splendor and importance, but now in a state of decline." Early in the Spanish period, Thomas Hutchins wrote:

> Notwithstanding all of these inconveniences in point of navigation, Mobile having been the frontier of the French dominions in Louisiana always was and now is a very considerable place. It has a small regular fort, built with brick, and a neat square of barracks for the officers and soldiers. The town is pretty regular of an oblong figure, on the west bank of the River, where it enters the bay. There is a considerable Indian trade carried on here. Mobile, when in possession of his Britannic Majesty, sent yearly to London, skins and furs amounting from twelve to fifteen thousand sterling; it was then the only stable commodity in this part of the province. The British garrison at Mobile surrendered to the arms of his Catholic Majesty in the year 1780.

Some years later, on May 1, 1804, Ephraim Kirby wrote:

> Nature has designed this position for a great city.—It is at the mouth of one of the finest navigeable waters in the United States, which at some future time, will float down the produce of an extensive and fertile interior country. Surrounding the town stood a few small Spanish settlements of even less note than their American opposites above the 31st parallel.

Finally, Josiah Blakeley in 1812 described Mobile as containing "about ninety houses, all of wood and but one story high."[47] Blakeley's letter suggests that the architecture at the end of the century continued to be dominated by the one-story styles associated with the earlier colonial times. In Pensacola, however, the government buildings show a Spanish influence in an engraving that has survived (figure 23). Here the severely blocked massing, the flat roof, and the cupola reflect Spanish culture. A drawing of the undated Old Spanish Jail (figure 24)[48] shows that the low, galleried cottage had been replaced by a two-story stuccoed wall with a balcony at the second level. The friendly, sociable porch has given way to the private balcony.

A Spanish map has survived that proposed changes in the plan for Mobile (figure 25). While the changes were never executed, the map provided for a shift from a community planned around a fort to one organized into city blocks.[49] Buildings were not located at random in their lots but were arranged so that they faced the corner streets and

23. *View of Spanish Pensacola, 1743. Engraving from the* Universal Magazine, 1 *Hinton, Newgate Street. (Courtesy of Mrs. Carter Smith.)*

privately opened onto large gardens in the rear. This style was to influence the development of the nineteenth-century town house with the rear patio.

The Spanish period saw Mobile start to become a thriving commercial center. Successful businessmen and family dynasties were established, many of whose descendants still live in the city. Men emigrated from northern and southern states: Peter Hobart from Vermont, Lewis Judson and Josiah Blakeley from Connecticut, William and Joshua Kennedy from South Carolina, Thomas Price, the English interpreter for the king of Spain, and Judge Harry Toulmin, who came from Kentucky.[50] These men and others would become leaders during the territorial years and the founders of an American city during early statehood.

24. *The Old Spanish Jail, Pensacola, Florida. The Spanish balcony supported on brackets became an important feature in Gulf Coast architecture. (Drawing by Herbert J. Doherty,* Florida Historical Quarterly *37, no. 3–4, copyright © 1959 by Florida Historical Quarterly. Used by permission.)*

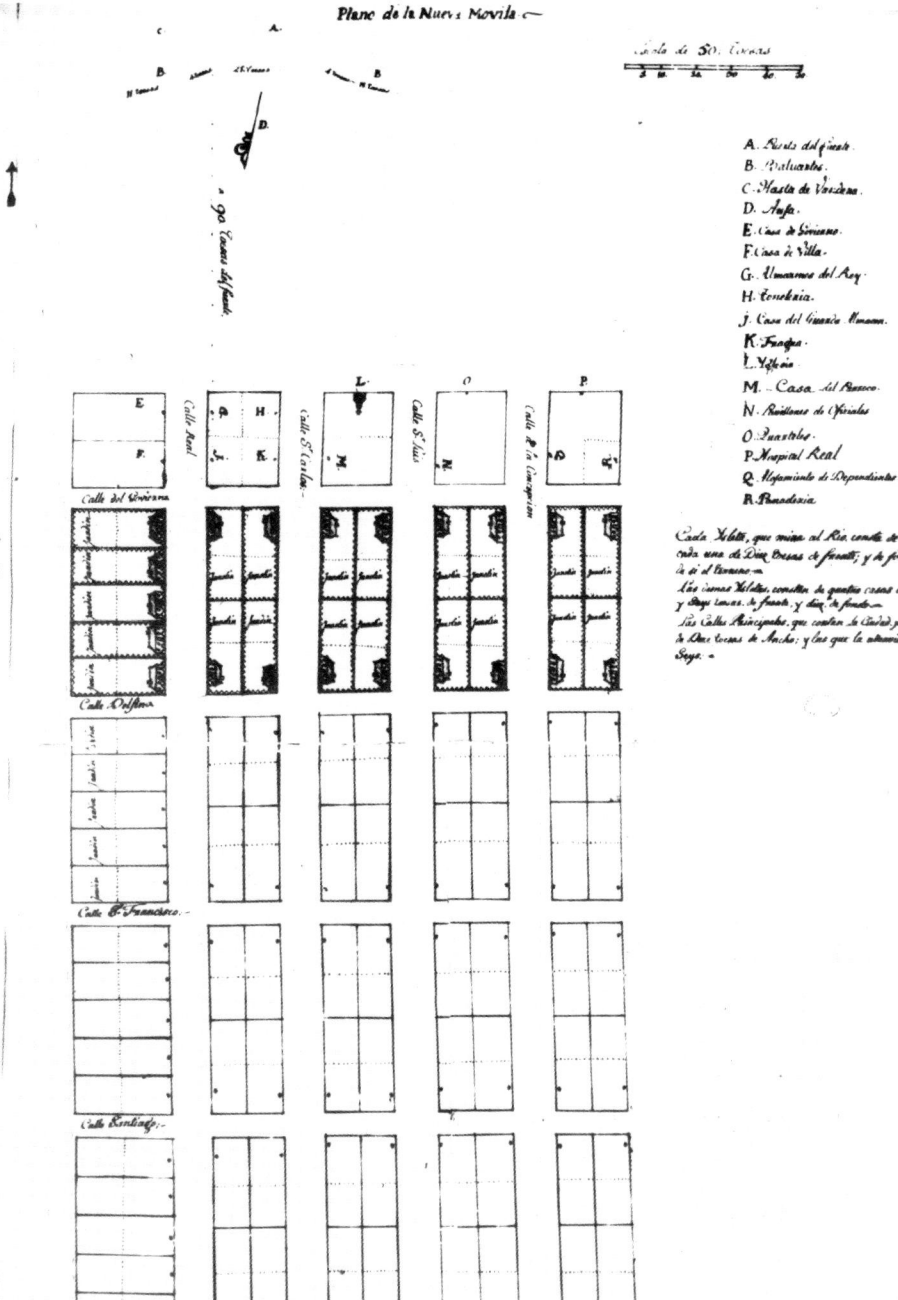

25. "Plano de la Nueva Movila," Spanish period. A proposed plan for Mobile in which every house had space for a garden. (Courtesy of the Mobile Public Library, Special Collections Division.)

The Colonial Years, 1711–1813

26. 1815 map of Mobile. The city blocks perpetuate the colonial configuration shown in the 1809 Spanish map. Street names have been added, and roads to the country have been indicated. A second wharf has been built at a site that will become the foot of Government Street. (From the frontispiece of the 1878 City Atlas, courtesy of the Mobile Public Library, Special Collections Division.)

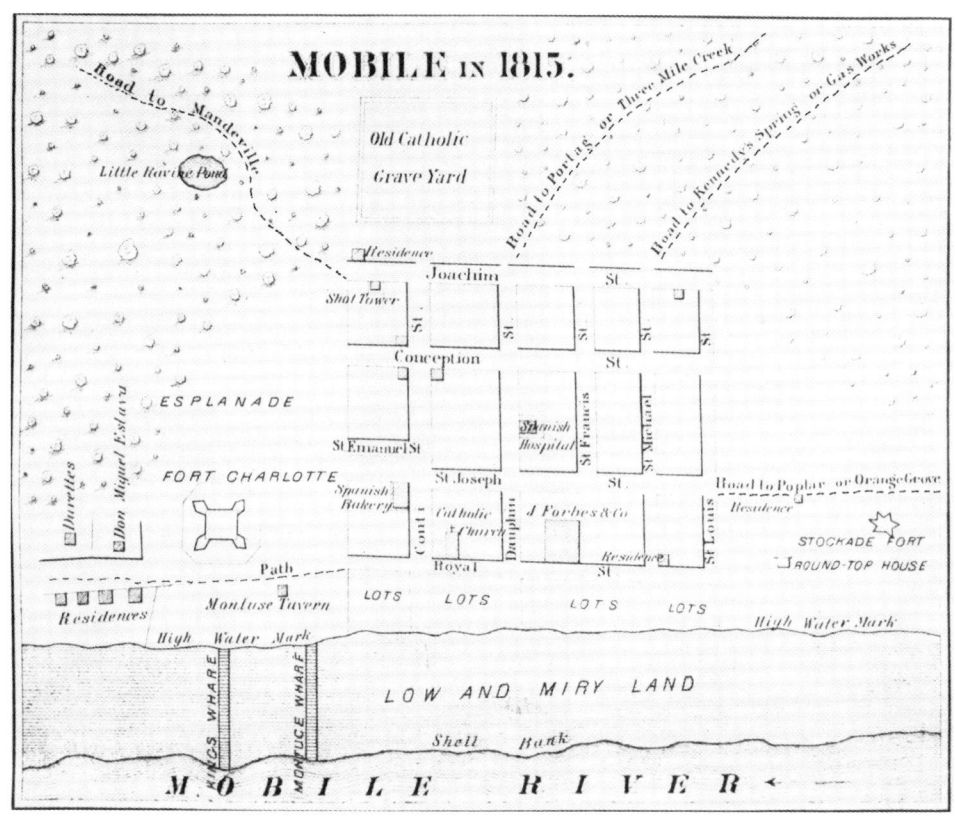

2 Americans Begin Building, 1813–1830

The Territorial Years, 1813–1819

The year 1813 was crucial for Alabama. The Spanish entrenchment along the Gulf Coast was thought to threaten the security of the United States during the War of 1812. President Madison ordered General James Wilkinson to march on Mobile, with the result that the Spanish withdrew from the city on April 15, 1813. The Alabama coast was thus united with the territory to the north of thirty-one degrees latitude. Free trade had been successfully established during the Spanish period, and the rapid development of commerce began during the territorial years. Business and professional men from the Atlantic seaboard eagerly moved into the area. As Alexander Meek wrote, "They came for the purpose of making fortunes and accordingly were business men—industrious, practical, frugal, economically self-reliant and independent."[1]

The schematic map of 1815 (figure 26) suggests rather than records the details of the city and its buildings. The blocks are still largely confined to the old plan, but the city boundaries had been extended on the south to Choctaw Point and on the northwest to Bayou Chotage (Three Mile Creek).[2] A rural residential development is indicated by the four roads, shown on the map by a dotted line, leading to habitations established to the north and west.

Just as the map does not show the new boundaries of the city, it does not show the new buildings that were being erected to meet commercial demands. Instead the buildings indicated are those already familiar to us—the old Fort, the Spanish Church, the Spanish Bakery, the Hospital, the Campo Santo, and the business of Forbes and Company, founded by the Spanish. The main change on the map can be seen along the waterfront. North of the King's Wharf, next to the Montuse Tavern, is a new, small wharf, the first of many that will soon transform the river's edge. In the agricultural center of the Mississippi Territory, cotton was increasingly being cultivated, and Mobile was to become the center for its distribution. In 1818 a modest 7,000 bales passed through the city, but by 1820 the bales had doubled in number.[3] Realizing that the swampy condition of the river's edge hindered navigation, the city commission took action to infill the marshes, creating lots. First the section between Montuse

Tavern and Dauphin was reclaimed, then the work was extended to St. Louis Street. Total reclamation would take another ten years. The increase in the cotton trade brought a corresponding increase in the number of buildings to house and process the product. Cotton presses, warehouses, and wharf facilities were built, together with housing and stores to supply the growing population with commodities.

Steamboats further stimulated the waterfront development. The St. Stephen Steam-boat Company, chartered on February 10, 1818, brought boats into Mobile. On November 28, 1820, the Steam-boat Company of Alabama was established, and in December of the same year, John Fowler was granted the right to run a steam ferry from Mobile to Blakeley. On November 27, 1821, two companies were chartered for Mobile. One was the Mobile Steam-boat Company, under the direction of John B. Hogan, Stephen Chandler, Lewis Judson, Henry Gunnison, William Raser, and Benjamin Vincent. The other was the Navigation Steam-boat Company.[4]

Food supplies for the growing population became a major concern. In 1815 a public market was built at the end of Dauphin Street. Theron Kellogg, the contractor, also built the first County Jail. The market was a "one story building, forty by twenty-five feet, with three rows of five pillars, gables and three foot eaves." Nearby was a private wharf built by Henry Gunnison, who also constructed several stores.[5]

By 1816, frame stores were being erected all along Royal and the newly created Water Street. An interesting contract of 1817 states that Mr. Kellogg of the Mississippi Territory would erect for Mr. Innerarity a "good frame building twenty-two feet in width on the front of Royal Street by forty-five feet in depth" and that it would have a

> brick foundation of at least five layers and two bricks thick: that it shall be two stories in height besides the garret and that the lower and second stories may each be at least eleven feet high, that the whole building shall be thoroughly framed and well braced, that the Sills, Sleepers, Joists, Posts, Braces, Rafters shall be of fully sufficient strength and as stout dimensions as are usual in buildings of this size, and that all the material used shall be of the best quality and the lumber free of sap or defects, that the Building will be covered with shingle Roof, the shingles to be of Juniper or Cypress of Eighteen Inches long by four to six Inches broad, shaved at both ends and perfectly tight, that the walls of the lower story shall be filled in with brick or moss and clay mortar between the posts and shall be ceiled inside with plank & that the whole building shall be weatherboarded with half inch quartered [?] board neatly painted with at least two coats of paint, and completed and finished in a workmanlike manner.—and that the said Theron Kellogg—shall have the building fully completed by eighteen months from and after the date here of the aforesaid business shall be fully completed.[6]

As this contract makes plain, construction methods had not basically changed since Colonial times. The spaces between the supporting members of the frame were still being infilled with nogging. The exterior surfaces of the buildings, however, had been improved by the addition of painted weatherboarding. Other contracts indicate that the interior walls were either ceiled or plastered. No contract called for plaster on lath over studs until the mid-1820s.[7] As rough-surfaced primitive buildings of the early times were supplanted by more finished painted weatherboarding, there were other signs of an increasingly urban setting. Buildings shifted in orientation, with the short sides facing the street and the lengths perpendicular to the street, as indicated by records of the many lots sold at the time. The average lot had 30 feet of frontage and was 120 feet deep, showing that the value of footage on the street had increased.[8] One of the houses built by Kellogg was only 22 feet wide and 45 feet deep. Archival material and the contracts thus demonstrate that, by the end of the territorial years, rows of two-story painted frame buildings had risen in the commercial section of the city, although they do not appear on the 1815 map.

As the town was further organized between 1815 and 1819, civic buildings became a necessity. One of the most essential was a jail. The records of the County Court House contain several receipts for payments for materials and for work on the "gaol." One reads, "The County of Mobile to Clements and Kellogg for building a jail—$419.00." Another, dated April 6, 1816, mentions $219 for completing the building. Other receipts cover the installation of restraining irons and window bars. The first Jail proved inadequate within a very short time, and on November 22, 1818, a territorial law was passed, giving the Mobile commissioners the authority to establish a new jail and a county court house for construction costs not to exceed "fifteen thousand dollars."[9] In spite of the plans, the Court House did not materialize until the next decade.

With the rapid commercial development, a bank became a necessity, and on November 20, 1818, the state passed an act establishing the Bank of Mobile.[10] The building that was to house it appears on the Goodwin and Haire map (figure 27). The majority of the names of the first directors are already familiar to us: Addis Lewis, Henry Gunnison, and Lewis Judson were some of the men who would dominate the development of the city through the territorial period and into the 1820s.

New housing kept pace with the commercial and civic development. Rental properties multiplied, as did private dwellings. Real estate investors prospered. Some citizens built several houses; Samuel Acre, for example, by 1817 had dwellings on St. Michael Street, on Joachim, and on Conception.[11] With much of the land already in the possession of the founding fathers, it became customary for a person who wanted to build a home to erect it on someone else's property. Lots were leased for a stipulated time, and at the termination of the contract the property owner was obligated to pay the builder for the value of the house. Such a contract was made between Diego McBoy and Terry M'Cusker, by which M'Cusker was given the right to build on McBoy's land a "good and substantial house" that he could occupy for a five-year term. At the end of the five years McBoy "covenanted and agreed to pay the said Mc'Cusker for the valuation of the above mentioned house."[12] The descriptions recorded by travelers in the early 1820s indicate that most of the houses were one-story cottages undoubtedly similar to those that had been built earlier. Some were still occupied by the Spanish families who had stayed on, such as the Eslavas and the Espejos.

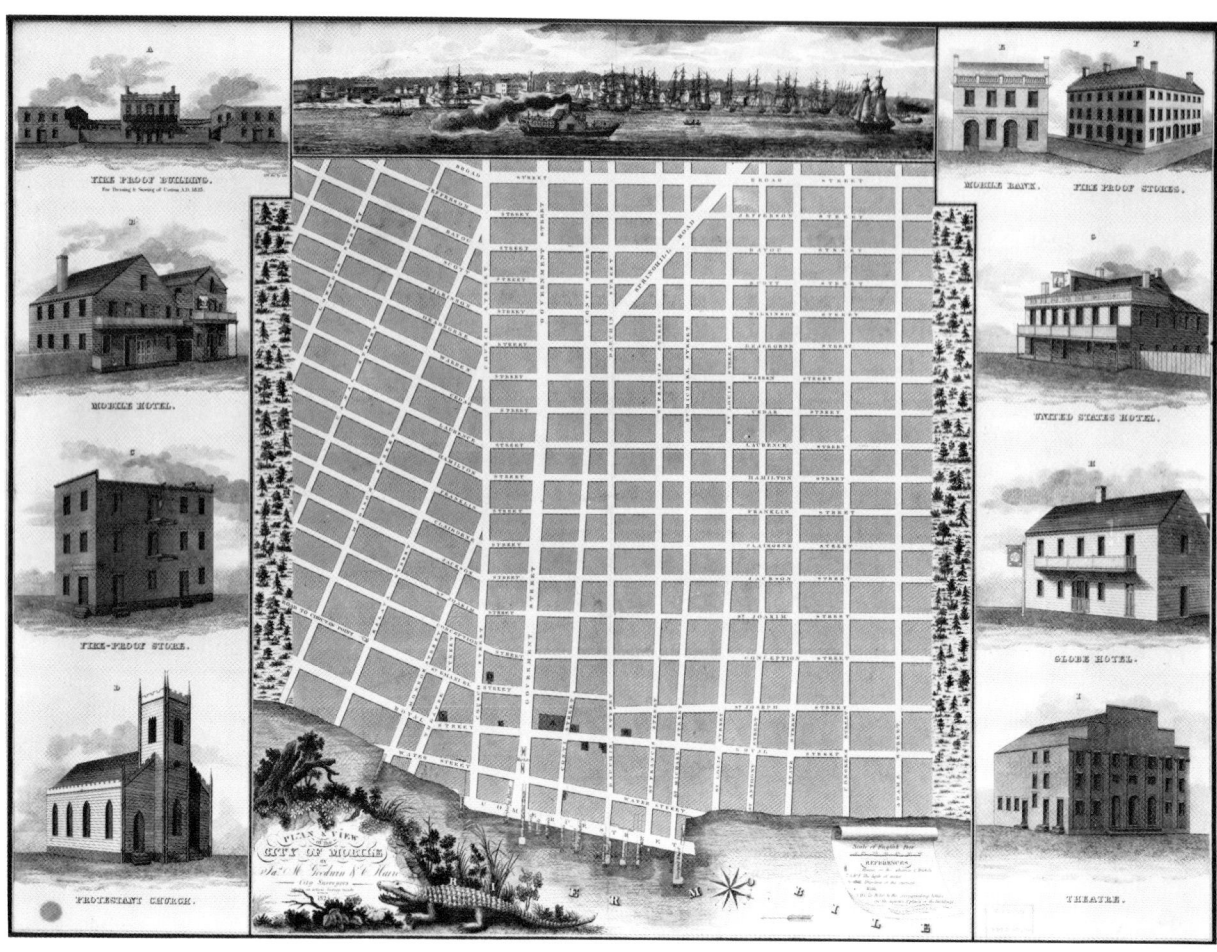

27. The Goodwin and Haire map of Mobile, 1824, with engravings of the important buildings. Increased commercial activity is indicated by the increased number of wharves. (Courtesy of the Library of Congress.)

An important event during the last years of the territorial period affected both the city plan and the city's architecture. On April 20, 1818, the U.S. Congress authorized the sale and removal of Fort Condé-Charlotte. The Fort was not completely destroyed until well into the next decade, but the act of Congress altered the plan of the city, and the main axis moved from Dauphin Street to Government, with developments to the south.

The territorial period closed with the congressional act of December 14, 1819, when Alabama was granted statehood. Three days later, on December 17, the city of Mobile was incorporated and its boundaries established.[13] While no physical evidence remains of the buildings erected during these six years, the records and maps have made it possible to recreate a sense of a place in time, of a city still echoing its past but at the same time entering a new era.

Early Statehood, 1820–1830

Between the years 1820 and 1822, the town took further steps toward becoming a city. Professional and commercial classes moved into the area in increasing numbers, more than tripling the population in ten years' time. In 1820 Mobile had about 800 people, but by 1822 there were "very little, if any, short of 2800, of whom about one third or two fifths are coloured persons and blacks."[14]

The town contained some old one-story, half-timber Colonial buildings interspersed with the painted ones of the territorial years. In about 1820, buildings became larger, and some had two stories. Wood remained the most popular material for construction. A census taken in 1822 illustrates the growth of the city in terms of the buildings:

   240 Dwelling Houses
   110 Stores and Warehouses
   2 Churches (Protestant and Roman Catholic)
   2 limited Seminaries
   2 Printing Offices
   A Post Office and Custom House
   An Incorporated Bank
   A Building used as a Court House
   A County Jail
   3 Commodious Hotels
   With sundry Boarding Houses, and various Mechanical Establishments, including three Bakeries.
   Six well constructed Wharves already built, and two or three more about to be commenced.[15]

Mobile's development is evident not only in the greater number of buildings reflected in the census but also in the numerous street improvements. On December 14, 1820, the city authorized a street survey to be made, with the power to widen, extend, and regulate the streets, providing that the alterations did not infringe upon a dwelling. In the same year $2,591 was expended on street improvements, with an additional sum of $1,528 the following year. New streets were also created, especially along the waterfront. The *Mobile Commercial Register* for February 2, 1822, mentions Water Street and also notes the importance of "Front Street when it is completed," both having been created on originally swampy ground. In addition to the attention paid to the inner-city streets, roads were opened up to neighboring counties, ending Mobile's long isolation. An act of December 3, 1821, authorized a lottery for raising money for a turnpike to Chickasaw Bogue. Fifteen days later Edwin Lewis was given permission to construct an eight-mile-long road to cross Three Mile Creek at his sawmill, and on December 31, 1822, a road from Mobile to the Mississippi line was authorized.[16]

The new street development and the changes in the city plan are all well documented on the Goodwin and Haire map of 1824 (figure 27). On April 16, 1824, it was announced that the survey had been completed; the *Mobile Commercial Register* carried a notice that 150 copies would be made and that the map would include "a correct delineation of streets, squares, etc., a view of the City from Faustina Island and a drawing of some of the principal buildings."

The plan for the city has also been enlarged with a grid to the south, including the site of the old Fort, but it stands at an angle to the original layout.[17] Government Street was made the new central axis of the plan, cutting a thoroughfare 100 feet wide to the western boundary.[18] The new streets and many of the old were still unpaved, so that the rainy season produced quagmires and caused flooding into properties on low-lying areas. By 1825 attempts were being made to correct the situation. Theatre and Royal streets were leveled and graded so as "to cause the water to run into sewers."[19] The Aldermen's Minutes of January 1825 state that the draining of Theatre Street was a necessity "so that the ladies could approach the Theatre without the inconvenience of mud and water." The sewers were described by Mr. Goodacre: as "channels, which may be properly called troughs, about twelve inches wide by six inches deep, formed by squared logs of timber—laid firmly in every street about six or seven inches from the houses and [they] carry off the tremendous wet from the thunder storms, render walking far pleasanter than could be expected."[20] Any port city is built only a few feet above sea level, so that adequate drainage is always a problem.

The need to draw water away from the city was matched by the need to pipe in good water for the residents. Toulmin's *Laws of the State of Alabama* records an act establishing the Aquaduct Company of Mobile on December 20, 1820. The water was transported from Three Mile Creek to six hydrants within the inner city, which were placed for the convenience of the inhabitants and for fire protection. Eight years later, on December 5, 1828, the mayor and aldermen authorized further provisions for water by ordering a "head of water, at the spring below Judge Lipscomb's, and bringing the water from thence to the City on Royal Street, through pine logs of sufficient caliber to afford an ample supply for the use of the city."[21]

The demand for lumber increased as the building programs expanded; the town was built largely of wood and, like any pioneering region, depended upon its natural resources for its building material. The area around Mobile was heavily forested with pine, oak, and cypress. The bogues and streams that emptied into the river made it possible to bring lumber into the city with relative ease. While the English are known to have established lumber as a trade commodity, the industry did not develop until the American period. By 1820 sawmills were well established, as is evident from the numerous newspaper advertisements of the day. One successful establishment was announced for sale:

Steam Saw-Mill for sale
1300 acres, Saw-Mill Creek, 17 miles above Mobile
8 miles from the Mobile River
60 acres cleared
1 two story house, frame, 20 feet by 40 feet with kitchen attached
Negro house, sheds, corn house.
Steam Mill, successful operation
working 5 saws, Work cattle, horses, wheels, carts,
blacksmith shop, together with every necessary thing
for carrying the business on to advantage.
                              signed, Henry Gunnison.[22]

Two years later another mill was offered for sale by Joshua Clemens. It was located to the west of the city on Dog River and was geared for two saws that were guaranteed to cut 5,000 feet of lumber in twenty-four hours. In 1824, William Bayard, Jr., and Company advertised their mill, which operated within the city limits and stocked a "good assortment of lumber always available."[23] The woods encircling Mobile, which had been considered a disadvantage in the eighteenth century, by the nineteenth had been recognized as a basic source of wealth.

Commercial Architecture

Along the sides of the Goodwin and Haire map appear drawings of the important buildings of 1824. One of the most impressive is the Cotton Press, shown in the upper left corner (figure 27). Like lumber, cotton was becoming important in Mobile's economy. The City Directory of 1855–1856 includes the statement that the first Cotton Press was erected in Mobile in 1822. The building contract for the Cotton Press shown on the map is dated September 4, 1822, making it likely that the engraved example is the one that was first established. The building was located on the southwest corner of Royal and Conti, facing on Royal and occupying most of the block. It was built by John Ward for John Lepretre (also spelled Leprete and Leppetre) and Thomas Townsley.[24] Part of the contract reads:

> —to complete all carpenter work required to be done on the brick building about to be erected by John B. Lapretre and Thomas Townsley of the dimensions of Two hundred and twenty six and a half feet on Royal Street, by One hundred thirty feet on Conti Street and to frame the Roof and Prepare same for the masons which Said roof to consist of rafters, and ties of four inches by twelve and be covered with plank of one inch thick well nailed down, the rafters to be placed twenty inches apart in the clear and the roof to project from nine to twelve inches from the piers.[25]

It is interesting to note that even at this early date the builder was fined if he delayed in executing the contract; the contract reads that the builder "shall pay to the said John B. Lepretre and Thomas Townsley the sum of two hundred dollars for every day of delay."

In the City Tax Records for 1829, the company of Lepretre and Townsley was taxed for a brick cotton warehouse and press, located on the southwest corner of Royal and Conti, for the estimated value of $35,000. The building impressed the duke of Saxe-Weimar Eisenach when he visited Mobile in 1825–1826. He wrote:

> A large cotton warehouse, of all the buildings in Mobile, most excited my attention. This consists of a square yard, surrounded on three sides by massive arcades, where the cotton bales coming from the country are brought in and preparatory to their shipment are again pressed.—The Warehouse or Magazine has two such presses. It occupies three sides of the yard, the fourth contains a handsome dwelling house. The whole is built of brick, and has an iron veranda. It belongs to speculators in New Orleans and is known by the name of the "fire proof magazine" although the interior is of wood.[26]

This building complex is the earliest surviving visual evidence of the architectural influence exerted by the Atlantic seaboard. The strong central massing of the residence, with the wings extending to dependencies, is not unlike that of the Georgian plantation homes of the mid–south Atlantic states, and the balustrade at the edge of the eaves is Federal in origin. Also from this influence is the accented second-story central stair window. Such a building was not indigenous to the Gulf Coast. With its enclosing walls and small windows it did not provide the good air circulation needed in the semitropical climate. Surely the early merchants would have been more comfortable in a structure built on a more open plan that allowed the Gulf breezes to help counter the heat of the day.

Fires caused great catastrophes during the first half of the nineteenth century. Several of the buildings on the map are marked fireproof. This was actually a misnomer; although brick was gradually replacing wood on the exterior of buildings, the interiors of the masonry structures were still made of wood, as was all of the roof framing. Very few buildings survived the conflagrations of 1822, 1827, and 1839.[27] The Lepretre and Townsley complex did survive and prospered. The original two partners took on a third, A. F. Stone. They advertised their "General Commission, Factorage and Brokerage Business" in the *Mobile Commercial Register* for December 2, 1823, stating that they had storage facilities for 8,000 bales of cotton, three presses, and "extensive room for Drying and Repacking cotton that may be damaged." They also furnished "Faithful Cartmen and good horses—always in readiness to take Cotton or Goods from any wharf within the limits of the City to their Warehouses."

Another building on the Goodwin and Haire map that was associated with the commercial development was the Mobile Bank. (See figure 27.) With its formal massing and its segmentally arched doorheads, eave edge balustrade, and string course marking the second story, the building would fit comfortably in any eastern street scene in the Federal style. This type of architecture was selected by the bank's founders, men who came from the northern and eastern states. Lewis Judson, for example, was from near Stratford, Connecticut, E. Hall from Philadelphia, H. V. Chamberlain from Massachusetts, and A. W. Gordon from Connecticut.

While there are records that the Bank was founded as early as 1818[28] and that it was in business during the end of the territorial years, an advertisement for a contractor in 1823 indicates that it could not have been constructed before that time:

To Builders
Proposals will be received by the undersigned Committee for erecting a Bank Building intended for Banking House, who will furnish a plan to such persons.
    R. V. Chamberlain, Wm. B. Robertson, Thomas L. Hallett
    Board of Directors, Bank of Mobile[29]

The little Bank was located midway down the block, between Government and Church, on the west side of Royal. In the City Tax Records for 1829, the building was valued at $12,000. It was certainly well regarded by the community. The local newspaper observed, "The Bank of Mobile is a modest, neat little building, the affairs uniformly well managed and it is in a flourishing condition and good credit." Since the building was finished in time to be engraved on the map by Goodwin and Haire, it must have been constructed during 1823. In 1849, the exterior walls were apparently treated with stucco. The change in popular taste is evident in a contemporary comment: "The unsightly face of rough brick is fast disappearing from sight and the building will soon stand perfect in all its parts—a solid piece of masonry and unique in architecture."[30] Thus did the Greek Revival influence and alter the wall texturing of the Federal and Georgian styles.

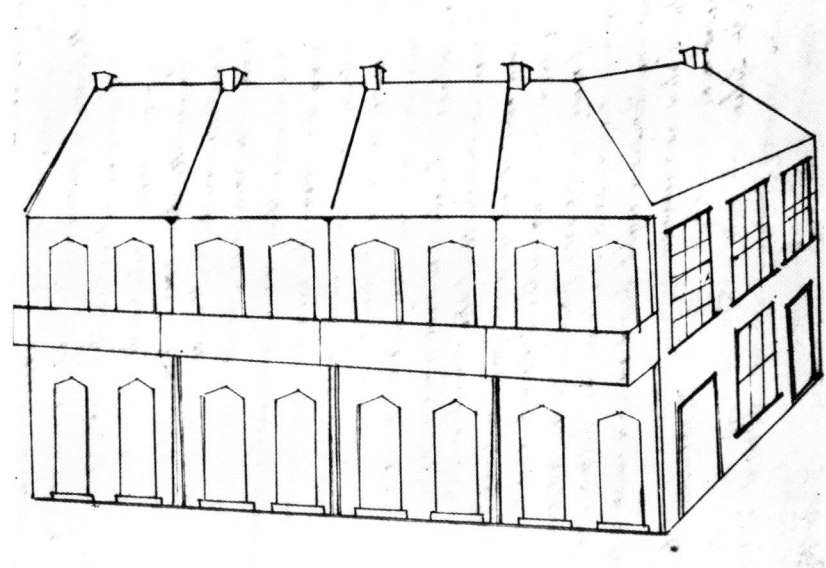

28. *Drawing for a storefront from a contract between Samuel Garrow and Henry Center, builders, and William Robertson and William Barnwall, owners, 1828. (From Miscellaneous Book B, pp. 176–78, dated May 24, 1828.)*

Two other banks were founded during the decade, but nothing is known of the architecture of the Mobile Branch of the State Bank of 1823, and only the value is known of the U.S. Bank. The latter appears in the Tax Records of 1829 with a valuation of $18,000. It was located on the south side of Government Street, between the Court House and the property of Mr. Lewis, and was described as a "splendid and beautiful edifice."[31]

New stores occupied more and more of the commercial section of the city. The two engravings on the Goodwin and Haire map (figure 27, buildings C and F) and the surviving contracts permit accurate description of their appearance and structure. Very few stores at the time were located on individual lots. Most were attached by party walls, so that they formed a continuous frontage, as seen in the elevation drawing in the contract for the row of brick stores built for Robertson and Barnwall and dated May 24, 1828 (figure 28). The stores resembled warehouses more than the "fashionable emporia" so frequently advertised in the newspapers. While a few refinements were occasionally added, an observer would chiefly have remembered a strong rectangular mass with regularly placed rows of windows. The individual units of the row were separated by the extension of the party wall into a low fire wall above the pitch of the roof and sometimes by individual chimneys. Door and window lintels were usually accented by a contrasting texture, though we have no color reproductions that would indicate whether the stucco was whitewashed or whether a white stone was used. Example F on the map shows an entrance with a semicircular head, and both C and F show indications of a projecting rain table at the base of the building. Robertson and Barnwall called for a "Gothic coping" for one structure in their contract with the builder, William L. Little.[32] The commercial buildings' lack of architectural refinements was compensated for in the enthusiasm of a town on the make. Robert Goodacre wrote of Mobile in 1828:

> It is indeed only yet organizing. Civilization is in its boyhood, growing truly with unparallelled rapidity, but like many an over-

35 *Americans Begin Building, 1813–1830*

grown youth without a due symmetry and proportion of limb, bone and muscle. Commerce has usurped nearly the whole attention of man. The minor parts, so to speak, in the drama of residence, are not yet filled up. Extensive wharves, bearing the name of Liverpool Wharf, New York Wharf, Alabama Wharf and vast warehouses all furnish facilities beyond conception in so new a port, for the transacting of business.[33]

The store marked "C" was one of several owned by McLoskey and Hogan. Their property extended along the whole north side of Conti between Royal and Commerce, including a wharf, all of which was valued at $63,000 in the 1829 Tax Records. A contract for one of their three stores on this block has survived. If it was not the same building as that shown on the map, it certainly must have been similar. The contract, dated July 16, 1824, was between the company of McLoskey and Hogan and John W. Ward. At the outset the builder promised, as was usual, to "build, set up and finish" the work "in a good and workman like manner." According to the financial agreement made between the owner and builder, Mr. Ward was to be paid $9,500 in $1,000 installments as the work progressed. The several pages of specifications that follow give us important information regarding building practices of the times:

> The Enclosure to consist of Front Back walls each 107 feet long equal to 214 feet. . . . Two Stores on front Street, each 47 feet front by forty feet depth and two Stories in height with a gate way between them 12 feet wide Two Sheds extending from the back of each Store 100 feet to be 35 feet wide, The walls of each of the above to be 25 feet high independent of gable ends to the two front Stores, to which are to be raised Sufficiently high to give a good pitch to roof; also all the walls as high as the first floor to be 24 Inches thick; and from the first floor to the top to be 14 Inches thick; the whole to be built of Brick laid in the best lime and sand mortar and the Quality of the brick to be equal to the example of 25 bricks placed in the hand of Mr. Sam'l A. Acre—The foundation of the above to consist of good sound pine and cedar timber at least 10 inches square and 6 feet in length Closely laid by the side of each other on and above which transversly a Stretcher or Sill at least thick and sufficiently wide to admit the brick foundation wall of 24 inches above described to commence on the upper side or level of this sill to be 12 inches lower than the upper level of the wood foundation of the Store now building by the said John W. Ward for Col. Judson on Water Street; moreover the foundation walls shall be raised to such height that the first floors of the Two front Stores shall be on a level with the first floor of the Store now occupied by the said Philip McLoskey and further for supporting the Sleeper in the center of the first floor as above, run through each Store. The lower floor of the two Stores consists of sleepers 41 Inches [this seems to be an error in the original contract, for the length is unusually short for a sleeper] by 12 inches and twenty four inches apart to be covered with $1\frac{1}{4}$ inch plank and plained on the upper side and well nailed down the second floor of the two Stores to consist of joists 4 Inches wide by 12 inches deep and eighteen inches apart to be covered by $1\frac{1}{4}$ inch plank plained on both Sides Tongue and groove and well nailed down, across [?] the joists

to be also plained on 3 sides and beed on the two lower corners; The Third floor of the stores to consist of Joists 3 inches wide by 9 Inches deep and twenty four inches apart plained on three sides and beeded on two lower corners to be covered with plank as above plained on one side, Tongue and Groove and well nailed down; for the Support of the floors and roof there shall be a row of light wood pillars running through the center of each Store., In each Store there are to be 2 large doors on the floor and 2 doors on the second floor also two large Windows on the lower Story and four windows on the upper Story—also openings on the second floor of each to admit of Stair ways, To each of the Stores there shall be two Strong flights of Stairs, handsomely plained and with good handrails placed in such situation as said Phillip McLoskey shall point out, also a stair way back and on the outside of each Store to lead to a small gallery or landing place opposite the doors on the second Stories and to be made in the strongest manner with heavy hinges and strong fastenings Window shutters and fastenings to be equally Strong and in good proportion with sashes complete, glazed with the best 10 by 12 inch glass to my [sic] satisfaction of said Philip McLoskey, there shall be two chimneys to each Store with fireplaces and Hearth to each above and below. The whole of the Stores to be handsomely plastered inside after the manner of the Stores occupied by the said Philip McLoskey,—For the sheds there shall be two rows of light wood timbers 12 feet apart running through each, one row being in front and the other in the center for the support of roof, each timber to rest on substantial foundation, also a line of Girders 12 feet apart, resting on the walls and on a sufficient beam or plate in front with an insor anchor or fastening to each through [indecipherable]. The roofs of both Stores and Sheds to be covered with the best Kind of welsh slate: with sufficient pitch or slope to shed water freely and also to be made sufficiently strong to bear without sagging the weight of the Slate the whole to be done in a workmanlike manner Guaranteed by said J. W. Ward from leaks or cracks. The gate between the front Stores to be strong and well fastened after the model of those used at the Cotton Press, to be 14 Inches high and hung on Posts 14 inches square, Sunk in the ground and well secured.[34]

The larger store, pictured at point F on the map, stood on the southeast corner of Royal and Dauphin, the site of the still standing 1891 Pincus Building (figure 196). Structure F was owned by Jonathan Hunt and was valued at $24,000 in the 1829 Tax Records. By 1827 the property was owned by Jesse Tolman, who purchased "one undivided one half" of the corner lot for $8,880.75.[35]

These two buildings are representative of the large number of new brick commercial structures that sprang up along Royal, Dauphin, and lower Conti streets following the 1822 fire, which caused extensive damage. Many references to the growing number of brick buildings can be found in advertisements as well as in building contracts that have been preserved in the City and County Archives. A progress report in the *Mobile Commercial Register* for May 27, 1822, under the heading "Mobile" (see appendix 2) reads:

The walls of no less than Nine Brick Stores have risen up, as if by magic. The spot which but a few weeks since, exhibited a scene of smoky ruins, is now completely covered with five brick tenements, the roofs of which are now going up. . . . In addition to the above, there are ten or twelve new wooden stores and warehouses, of respectable appearance completed and completing.

Local residents were not alone in investing in the growth of the city; businessmen in distant areas were also becoming involved. Charles Brown, of Boston, not only bought property but also sent his own workmen down to erect his building. On December 1, 1827, Brown made a contract with Franklin, Lawyer, and Whitehouse, masons, and with Gidion Horton, carpenter, all of Boston, that they would "danger the sea and sickness" to "build one block of Brick Stores in the City of Mobile." There follows a long contract with specifications for the building dimensions, foundations, construction, and finishing. It differs in several details from those commonly found. The roof was to have the slate "laid in mortar," and the ridgepole was "to be covered with sheet lead." There were frequent references to examples in Boston that the builders were to use as models. The doors, for example, were to be made "the same as those on the Central Wharf at Boston," and the windows and shutters were to copy those of the Boston store. Added protection was provided by covering the doors and their framing with sheet iron or tin. Even a sidewalk of bricks was included that would extend 154 feet along the building and would be 4 feet wide. The contract closes with the usual business determination, but in this case there was the added expense of the travel. Mr. Brown covenanted "to provide the vessel to carry goods to Mobile, plus all the freight for provisions for workmen and passage for all workmen from Boston to Mobile who furnish their own provisions during passage."[36]

The diversity of the mercantile establishments can be appreciated by the advertisements that appeared in the newspapers. The most important events of the day centered around the arrival of the ships bringing the needed supplies:

Schooner *Sophia*, from Philadelphia, Beef, Oats Flour, Whisky, Wine, Cloth.
by the Brig *Fox*, Shoes, Boots, Pumps, Saddles, Bridles, Clothing.
by the schooner *Andea*, Lumber, White Beans, Bricks, Soap, Candles.[37]

Early Mobile had no history of manufacturing or other means of self-support. It had always been a dependent military establishment. The port became the lifeline for the developing city, and the men who were responsible for this growth had contacts with the commercial areas from which they had come. Even the fire of 1827 did not discourage them. The 1828 City Progress Report documents the people's ability to survive:

Since the fire in October last, which swept almost every house between Royal Street and the River and left only a mass of ruins, there have been erected sixty-nine brick stores within those limits besides being between forty and fifty others partly built and the foundations prepared. A great number of small wooden buildings put up immediately after the fire, have already been removed to make room for more permanent improvements, and by the fall,

Commerce Street will present an entire brick front from one end to the other, with the exception of one or two lots.[38]

No description of the commercial development could be complete without mention of the wharves. Many contracts have survived, giving information regarding the methods used in the wharves' construction. Every contract included specifications and an agreement by which the builder would infill his portion of the marshy waterfront. An example is the advertisement that John B. Hogan placed in the newspaper in 1823:

Having leased the east end of Government Street from the Mayor and Aldermen, I am desirous of contracting with some person to fill up the street above the water mark and from Water Street eastwardly 200 feet and to lay a barrier in front of same of good solid logs at least one foot square of pine or cypress, also to run out a table wharf from the center of the Street of 40 feet wide by 250 feet long. The table wharf to be erected on piles of at least 10 inches square and placed ten feet apart, the planks 3 inches thick, to be done by July 1, 1824.[39]

Wharves were of several types. The table wharf was most common, but others had wings projecting at the outer end, and some served as a foundation for a countinghouse or warehouse. The contract for the wharf of James Wilson describes it as "being twenty-five feet wide from end to end and having wings next the stream in addition to the width before mentioned of at least five squares and to construct jutters for weigh offices near the low water mark." Three warehouses were located on the Hallett wharf, and two stores were listed for rent on the Dauphin Street wharf in the newspaper. The Goodwin and Haire map shows only fourteen wharves, but by the end of the decade there were more, making the waterfront resemble that shown on the La Tourrette map of 1838 (figure 40). Wharves necessitated a large investment, as shown in the evaluations in the Tax Records. M. Eslava's wharf was listed at $5,000 in 1829, giving it a value as great as that of many of the brick stores and considerably higher than that of most of the houses. The largest wharf, the Liverpool, owned by Peter Remsen, was valued at $10,000. One of the most interesting of the wharves was owned by Robertson and Barnwall. It was located at the foot of Government Street and served as the live fish market for the city.[40]

Establishments other than stores added to the life of the city. The Theatre was the social delight of Mobilians. It was created by first adapting the Old Hospital and then adding a stage with "new scenery." Thus, in the May 1822 issue of the *Mobile Commercial Register* there appears the welcome announcement that Mr. Judah had "succeeded at considerable expense in fitting up the Hospital as a very neat and commodious Theatre—with the boxes judiciously arranged having a full command of the stage." An acting company was due to arrive from New Orleans, and if the program proved successful, plans would be made for the erection of a new theater. Successful it was, and by December 20, 1822, subscribers for a new theater were being asked to meet at the Mobile Hotel to discuss the matter. By the next Friday a meeting had been held for the purpose of selecting an adequate lot, deemed to be sixty feet by eighty feet, and to authorize the payment of twenty-five dollars for a set of plans for the building, which would have to house an audience of 1,000 persons. The lot selected was on the northwest corner of Royal and Theatre streets. The local archives offer no clue as to the identity of the architect, but Talbot Hamlin in his *Greek Revival Architecture* names Isaiah Rogers, who was in Mobile in 1820–1821. Extracts from Rogers's diary recently published in the *Columbia Library Columns* seem to verify this attribution, but there is a question of dating, since Rogers's diary states he was in Mobile in 1723. The cornerstone for the building was laid April 7, 1823. Though the building was occupied that year, it was not actually finished until January 1824, when stockholders were asked to assemble to help with the last details.[41]

Mr. Vaugh was the new manager. According to one of his advertisements, "the Theatre has been fitted up with Boxes and a Pit (making a proper distinction in the prices of admission) so that families can be accommodated without being liable to annoyance or encroachment upon by the crowd."[42]

A few titles of plays selected at random from the many theater announcements hint at the melodrama popular in the 1820s.

Poor Gentlemen, with Mr. Enberton of Baltimore and Philadelphia
The Honest Thieves, a Laughable Farce
Aboelina; or, The Great Bandit
The Wag of Windsor
The Warlock of the Glen, which has been represented upward of fifty nights in London and is now playing with unbounded applause in the Northern States.[43]

Another, more detailed announcement dated December 14, 1828, read:

Theatre.

The Manager has the pleasure of announcing MR. MATHIS, the celebrated *Parisian Performer*, who stands unrivalled in his performance of *Herculian Feats* and *Olympic Exercises*,—and whose various exhibitions of the power of the human frame, have never yet been attempted by any individual in the United States. He is now engaged for a *few nights*, and will shortly appear.

This Evening, Wednesday Dec. 24.

Will be performed for the first time this season, the beautiful & celebrated Melo Drama of the

LADY OF THE LAKE

Written by Edmund J. Eyre, Esq. and dramatised from W. Scott's Poem of the same name.

The evening's Entertainment to conclude with Garrick's celebrated Farce of the

LYING VALET.

Doors open at Six—Performance to commence at Seven *precisely.*—Box Book open at the Merchants' Exchange, in Water Street, where places can be secured until the end of the first act.—

Performance every night.—No money will be taken at the door under any conditions.—Smoking not allowed in the lobbies.—Checks not transferable.

Tickets for sale at Mr. J. F. Pagles' Store, at the Commercial Hotel, at the Exchange Coffee House in Royal Street, at York House, and at the Meridian Coffee House—next door to the Mayor's Office, Conti Street.[44]

When Bernhard, duke of Saxe-Weimar Eisenach, visited Mobile, he attended the Theatre and described it as having a pit, a row of boxes, and a gallery. The engraving on the 1824 map shows it as a large rectangular mass, the only concession to decorative design being the stepped end gables. A reporter described it in 1828 as a "dull, huge, misshapen pile that would defy the architect to designate to what order it belonged." Another reporter, however, called it "an ornament and credit to the City." The building may not have been an architectural gem, but it certainly provided the community with entertainment. It also inspired some street improvements; lights were installed along Theatre and Royal streets.[45]

This first Theatre was built not by outside investors as a syndicate but through the cooperative effort of the community. Unfortunately, the building was destroyed by fire in November 1838.[46] Drama had by then become an integral part of the social life of the city, however, and a new building soon replaced the old.

Hotels were an important element in the development of the inner city. Unlike the stores, they were constructed of wood in the early decades, as is evident from the Goodwin and Haire map. The three engravings at letters B, G, and H (figure 27) show a similarity to other frontier buildings, such as those found in views of the early West. Of the three buildings shown on the map, the United States Hotel (G, figure 27) was the largest and may have had a brick exterior applied over a wood first story. Its design did make some concessions to refinements, for example the deep cornice parapet with the attic vents, and the full width second-story balcony relieved the austerity of the facade. The date of construction has not yet been determined, but the hotel was part of the Mobile scene as early as 1818, when it served as a meeting place for the organization of the first Fire Company. In 1821 a rental contract was signed between Miguel Eslava, the owner, and James Clarke, in which the hotel and "all shops, cellars, ways, profits, commodities and appurtenances" were "at the disposal of the renter for five years at the monthly stipend of $166.66 and $\frac{2}{3}$ cents."[47]

The Globe, a smaller hotel, while severely geometric in mass had a doorway somewhat influenced by the Federal style, with a wide, arched transom extending over the sidelights. The second-story balcony, extending over the central bays of the building, was a necessity in the days before air conditioning. During the evening hours it afforded a pleasant escape from the heat and stuffiness of interior rooms. The Globe (marked H on figure 27) was located on the east side of Royal Street, between Conti and Dauphin. It was erected in 1820 by Thomas Powell, and on December 1 a five-year lease was signed between the executors of the Powell estate and Seth Stoddard for the new building "commonly known as the Globe Tavern."[48] In 1822 an advertisement signed by William P. Clark announced that the Globe was "prepared for the reception and accommodation of

Boarders and Travelers." He added: "Nothing shall be wanting in his endeavor to give general satisfaction, being determined to set as good a table as the market can afford and to have his Bar supplied with the best Liquors—He is also provided with extensive and convenient Stables, well supplied with Grain and Fodder and attentive Ostlers."[49] The Hotel's charges for meals varied from $0.50 for breakfast to $0.75 for dinner. Board by the day cost $1.25, and board and lodging for the week amounted to $6.25. Horse feed ranged from $0.50 to a week's supply at $5.00.[50]

The Mobile Hotel was the simplest of the three engraved on the map (B, figure 27). It consisted of two unequally sized buildings connected by a rectangular parapet at the eaves' edge and by a carriage passageway at ground level. Each building had its separate gable facing the street, and the two had second-story balconies of differing designs. The Hotel was located on the west side of Royal Street between Dauphin and St. Francis. In June 1825 it was struck by lightning that caused considerable damage which was not repaired until the following November.[51]

While the various advertisements praised the available accommodations, visitors to the city were not as complimentary. Captain and Mrs. Hall arrived in Mobile soon after the 1827 fire. Both described their travels in separate publications. On April 7 Captain Hall wrote: "We reached what remained of Mobile, for the town had been almost entirely burned down not quite ten months before—One of the few buildings which had escaped the fire was a large hotel, and this, as might be supposed, was overcrowded from top to bottom." On being advised to find lodgings elsewhere, the Halls went to the Franklin House, not shown on the 1824 map. They were offered a room with no fireplace, whereupon they sought aid from Mr. Robertson, who graciously offered them his own home while his family was away. They gratefully accepted and, as Mrs. Hall reported, "left the noisy, bustling public table where sixty persons dispatched their unchewed dinner in the course of twenty minutes." Captain Hall described Mr. Robertson's home:

> as neat and trig a little villa, as ever was seen within or without the tropics. This mansion, which in India would be called a Bungalow, was surrounded by white railings, within which lay an ornamental garden intersected by gravel walks, almost too thickly shaded with orange hedge, all in flower. From a light broad veranda we might look out upon the Bay of Mobile, covered with shipping—Many other similar houses nearly as picturesque as our own delightful habitation.—To our eyes all was luxury, attentive servants, sumptuous fare, smooth carpeted floors, soft chairs, voluptuous sofas and hundreds of other comforts.[52]

In spite of the discomfort and the crowding, the hotel business continued to grow. Before the end of the decade, the two-block area between Conti and St. Francis boasted the United States Hotel, the City Hotel, the Globe, the Mobile, and the Franklin House, with the Alabama to be added early in the 1830s. The contract for the City Hotel was the first to call for a brick building. It was located on the east side of Royal, opposite and somewhat farther to the north than the United States Hotel.[53]

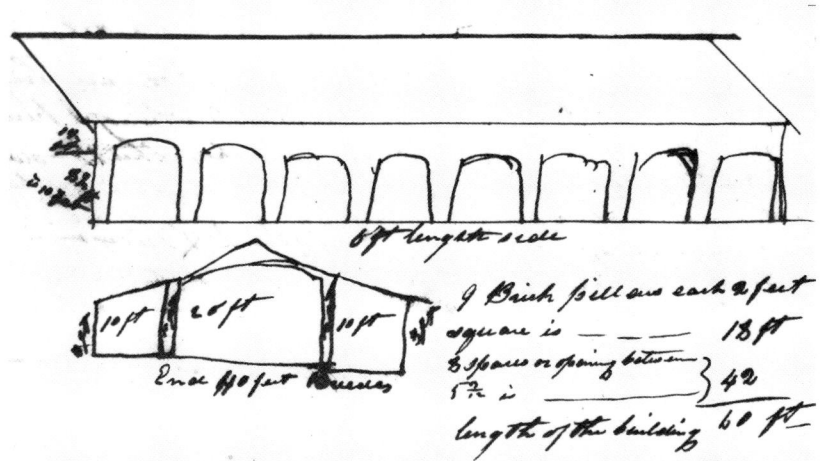

29. *Drawing for the Market, 1823, formerly located at the foot of Government Street; John Ward and Turner Stark, builders. The sixty-foot-long building had open side aisles and a gable roof covered with shingles. (From Miscellaneous Book A, p. 131, dated November 14, 1823.)*

On the lower block of Government Street stood one of the most interesting buildings on the Goodwin and Haire map, the Public Market.[54] It was the center for trade in truck farm produce. Built in 1823, it was constructed by John Ward and Turner Stark, two important builders of the decade. The crude drawing in the contract (figure 29) shows a three-aisled building sixty feet long with the central section twenty feet wide and each open side aisle, or "piazza," as the contract called them, measuring ten feet wide. The central section was supported on brick piers eighteen inches thick which were connected by an arcade. The aisles had wooden columns eight inches thick. The floor was paved with brick, and the gable roof extended to cover the side aisles. The roof was covered with shingles, the contract calling for either pine or cypress. Beneath the roof of the central section, a curved ceiling was installed that was "latticed and plastered," a rather surprising refinement for an outdoor market.

The building was erected at a cost of $1,768. Interestingly, the contract offered the builders' protection in regard to their payment. If the mayor and aldermen failed to meet their financial obligations, they promised to

> appropriate all the money divising from the rent of the stalls of said Market House to the payment of the sum above stipulated—together with such interest as may accruee . . . —and further pledge that all meats, fruits and other articles except fish and oysters usually sold at the Market Houses in towns and cities shall be exposed for sale at said Market House and no where else until the payment be made.[55]

Not everyone was overjoyed by the placing of the Market on Government Street. In the *Mobile Commercial Register* for November 12, 1828, one gentleman wrote that Government Street "had been shorn of more than half of its dignity, by building three market houses, plump in the middle of it—much to the annoyance of one gentleman of the long robe, who lived hard by, and who, in consequence, has disposed of his dwelling for less than half its value."

Americans Begin Building, 1813–1830

Religious Buildings

The last building on the Goodwin and Haire map to be studied is the Gothic Revival Protestant Church engraved in the lower left corner at D. The Gothic Revival was introduced into the United States in 1790 by Benjamin Latrobe in his design for Sedgeley and by Alexander Jackson Davis, architect for Glen Ellen, in 1832. Not until the 1840s did the publications of Andrew Jackson Downing popularize the style in widely scattered areas. Thus it is surprising to find in Mobile the little Protestant Church of Gothic Revival design as early as 1822. The siding is not board and batten, but the lancet windows, the crenellated parapet, and the pinnacled square end tower adapted the Gothic elements incorporated in a wood structure. The architect remains unknown but may have been some local builder who had become familiar with the various builder's guides that were spreading rapidly. The *Mobile Commercial Register* of October 22, 1823, advertised the *Rudiments of Architecture*, first published in 1814. The author, who was not named, must have been Asher Benjamin.

The Church was located on the site of the present Christ Episcopal, on the northwest corner of St. Emanuel and Church streets. It was begun in 1822, for in that year there was reported: "The Protestant Church will, when completed, make a respectable appearance. It is nearly finished. The order somewhat of the Gothic."[56] In May of the same year the newspaper contained an account of the Church:

> We cannot suffer to pass unnoticed the completion of our beautiful little Church. This building is not perhaps surpassed in convenience of plan, tastefulness of execution and neatness of appearance, by any house of public worship, built of wood, of similar dimensions in the Southern States, and although a temple has been erected and dedicated to the "Living God," it is a source of satisfaction to friends of the Society to know that it was destined for a worthier purpose than mere show.[57]

According to Robert Goodacre, the Church was large enough to serve a congregation of 400 people. A bell, cast in Boston, arrived by the ship *Mariner* on April 4, 1823.[58]

There had been a Catholic chapel since Spanish days, but by 1820, the one standing on Royal Street was in very poor condition. The City Progress Report of 1822 described it as "of tolerable size, and though in use, it is in a state of decay." The duke of Saxe-Weimar Eisenach was less kind in his evaluation: "The Catholic Chapel here is a very miserable situation, the Church within resembles a barn, it had a high altar with vessels of tin and a picture of no value, also two little chapels."[59] Goodacre added that it was a wretched old place of Spanish origin.

Plans were made to alter the situation, and in 1826 the trustees of the Church of the Holy Conception resolved to rent to the Right Reverend Bishop Portier the whole of the Old Grave Yard for twenty-one years for a yearly rent of $250. With this contract went the stipulation that the bishop would build thereon a church and would give bond of transfer to his successor. He agreed to "oblige himself to build on the premises hereby devised as soon as possible a Church of sufficient capacity for the use of the congregation and the Trustees." The Miscellaneous Books include a description of the boundaries upon which the new Church was to be built. The actual construction did not begin until the next decade, but after the fire of 1827 had destroyed the old Chapel, a small temporary structure was erected on Conti Street. Archbishop Lipscomb's history of the life of Bishop Portier mentions the hastily constructed little Chapel, twenty feet by thirty feet in dimensions, to which Bishop Portier led his workers for a "Mass of Thanksgiving." It was little more than a shed. Its only furnishings were six small candlesticks and a very unimpressive picture of the Blessed Virgin. The opening of the Chapel can be dated by the announcement in the *Mobile Commercial Register* for December 24, 1828, in which a meeting was called for all Church members to come to the "New Chapel" on Conti Street to elect trustees and select their pews.[60]

Governmental Buildings

By 1822 the attention of the city was being directed to the great need for construction of governmental buildings. The County Court had for years been held in a house rented from Catalina Mottus. From 1820 to 1825 there were repeated references in the press to the need for not only a court house but also a jail, a customs house, a powder magazine, and a poorhouse. In February 1822 the city authorized the Court House, and in March the announcement was made that the legislature had approved not only the Court House but also a "Gaol." Commissioners asked builders to submit proposals by the first of April. The proposal of Peter Hobart and Lewis Judson was chosen from an unknown number. Both Peter Hobart and Lewis Judson were northerners. Peter Hobart, the designer, undoubtedly recalled the Federal and Neoclassical styles that he had seen either at his home or on his journey to the south. His building was the first in the city to have giant two-story columns supporting the portico. Fortunately the contract for the building has survived, so that we can describe it.[61] It was a large building, rectangular in mass, two stories in height above a five-foot basement podium. The first story above the podium contained a large central room forty-two feet long that was flanked by offices, three on one side and two on the other. The sheriff occupied one room, which was connected to the main room as well as to the rear of the building. Situated at the back of the large, central court was a two-run stairway, divided by a platform and leading up to the main court on the upper story. The second-story courtroom was fifty-eight feet long and provided with paneled doors, four-inch pine flooring, and plastered walls.

The exterior of the building must have been quite impressive. A divided stairway led up to the main entrance on the deck of the "piazza," as the contract called the portico. The piazza was twenty feet long and eight feet deep and extended across the central bays of a facade fifty feet wide. The portico roof was supported by columns that rose the full height of the two stories and must have given the structure some of the aspect of a temple. The columns were of plastered brick, but unfortunately no mention was made of the order used. Since there were no directions for the carving of Ionic volutes, it was probably a simple Doric column. The main entrance leading into the large courtroom had an elliptical fan and sidelights, while the two side doors were designated in the contract as being "square headed" with transoms. Richly contrasting colors were provided on the exterior: white marble in the lintels and sills was juxtaposed with the red brick of the walls. The Court House was located on the southwest corner of Royal and Government streets, alongside the newly erected United States Bank.[62]

The old Territorial Jail was completely inadequate for the growing city. A report of February 1822 described the old building as being able "to contain prisoners only in daytime, if well guarded." In December of the same year another reporter found conditions in the Jail appalling, "with no bedding or covering, no fire, a cold damp building. We could scarcely wish our worst enemies such punishment." In 1824 the foundations for the Jail were laid, and the building was finished in 1826. The location of the Jail is established by a newspaper account of 1828:

> The public Jail stands immediately in its [the Theatre's] rear, and but a few steps from it. In the proximity of these two buildings a refined policy is perceptible and I am told that it was benevolently intended to give the votary of pleasure a cautionary lesson in the midst of his mirth, by regaling him with the clanking of chains and to tantalize the prisoner with the sounds of joy that could not be his; thus ingeniously heightening the pleasure of the Theatre and the sorrows of the prisoner, by contrast.[63]

The location of the Jail is further documented by the 1833 Tax Records, which place it on the lot to the north of the Theatre and value it at $4,000.

During the early years of the decade, guard duty was a voluntary effort on the part of the able-bodied men of the town. The Municipal Archives have a memorandum dated November 1, 1821, that lists some 448 men who were liable for duty. Six men were selected for each night, with one of them acting as captain. Many of the names have become familiar to us in connection with business and civic leaders: McLoskey, Hallett, Lewis, Gunnison, and so on. The notes recorded some amusing incidents. On the night of November 27, two guardsmen neglected their duty and were "apprehended at an Oyster House playing cards." They were fined two dollars plus costs, the standard penalty for the misdeed. William Smith, however, was "found about at a late hour" and was placed in jail for the offense of loitering.[64]

One of the important structures of the city was the Powder House. The old one was in disrepair, and a new building was considered essential. On January 6, 1825, a committee was appointed to ascertain the cost of a fireproof brick building that would be thirty feet long by sixteen feet wide and would have walls twelve feet high and one foot thick. The new building was situated on the northwest corner of the lot for the new Hospital, which appears on the La Tourrette map of 1838 (figure 40). The building was begun by Legrand Jennings and was continued by William Quigley. When it was finished on April 18, 1825, the aldermen ordered all the powder removed from the old facility and moved to the new location.[65]

Residential Buildings

The increase in the number of commercial and civic buildings only partially reflects the growth of the city, for the residences make up the major fabric of any community. The houses not only are an indicator of growth but also, and more than the public buildings, embody the cultural patterns of the times, reflecting the collective experience and craftsmanship of the people rather than the outlook of trained architects. During the decade of the 1820s older house forms intermingled with the new. Wood remained the material of choice, and the cottage style was the most popular. Only occasionally did a contract call for brick. In 1828, the duke of Saxe-Weimar Eisenach described a typical Mobile house as having been made of wood covered with shingle and as having piazzas, but he described one brick house with "the two lower stories of red brick and the third of yellow."[66]

Even though the older cottage style persisted, examples differed in construction methods. The old method using half timber with an infilling of clay covered with stucco gave way to framing that called for heavy timbers with studs four inches by four inches on two-foot centers and with four-inch-by-five-inch braces. The exterior was then covered by weatherboarding. The houses were painted white with green shutters, as described by Robert Goodacre. He was impressed by the "handsome porticoes and porches, ornamented with festoons of multiflora rose and other climbing and flowering shrubs." The 1887 drawings by Roderick MacKenzie show the appearance of these homes (figures 14, 30, 31), being typical of those described in surviving contracts. Some of the houses were square, for example that for which William Hale contracted, which measured thirty feet by thirty feet. Others were rectangular, like the cottage for Henry Ellis, which was thirty feet by twenty feet. The plans differed from the older form in the introduction of a central hall, a characteristic

30. *Drawing of a cottage (now destroyed) on St. Anthony Street, two doors east of St. Joseph, by Roderick D. MacKenzie, 1887.*

31. *Drawing by Roderick D. MacKenzie of a typical but unidentified early cottage, now destroyed, with the rear gallery enclosed to create small rooms.*

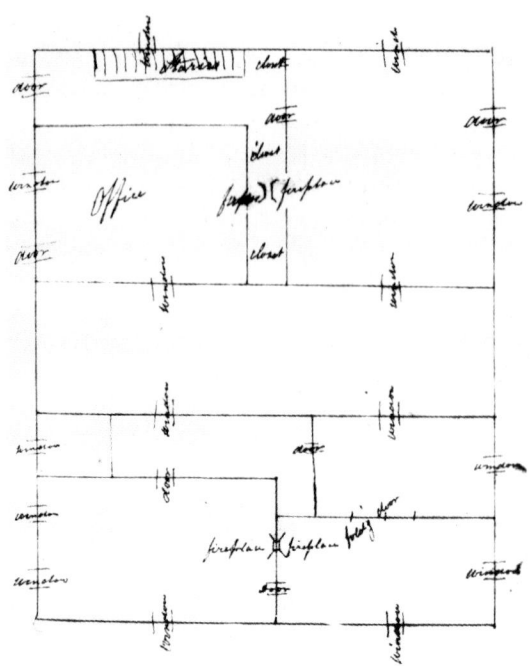

32. *Plan from the contract between George Hilliard, builder, and the trustees of the Catholic Diocese, May 23, 1825. The central-hall plan had the rooms arranged for office as well as residential use. An interior stairway led to garret rooms. (From Miscellaneous Book A, p. 230, dated May 23, 1825.)*

also of some two-story homes and one which was probably introduced by the emigrants from the eastern seaboard. (See figure 32.) As the rough sketch in figure 32 shows, the rooms are now doubled, with two forming the depth of the plan on either side of a hall that runs from front to rear.[67]

The gallery continued to be popular. Some galleries extended along the facade, and others continued around the building. The porches varied in depth from eight to ten feet and were equipped with "handrails and balusters." The supporting columns were usually square in section. In the contract for the house for Charles Batre, six cedar columns were specified. The contract of William Hale called for five columns that were to be five inches on the square. Some of the porch ceilings were of "plained plank"; others were given the refinement of being plastered.[68] The gallery persisted throughout Mobile architectural history, proving its efficiency as a way of protecting walls from the downpour of the tropical rains while also giving pleasure to the residents.

The gable was the most common roof type employed on the wood dwellings, though occasionally a hip was specified.[69] The gable was constructed in two designs. The slope might form a continuous pitch, as in the example on the extreme right of the Roderick D. MacKenzie drawing (figure 30), or the pitch might be broken, either flaring out in a concave curve, as in the older French Colonial profile (figure 30), or forming an angle at the point where the pitch changed (figure 14).

The urban cottage, like its country cousin, was raised on a pier foundation that varied in height from two to six feet, depending on the land elevation (figure 56). As street drainage improved, this ground-level space was used for commercial purposes or for storage. In the country it sometimes also served for household chores.

48   *From Fort to Port*

Walls were covered on the exterior by weatherboarding that averaged a siding cut from seven-inch planks, with an exposure of about five and three-quarters inches. Occasionally the siding was left rough, especially on the side and rear walls, but it was usually planed and painted white.[70]

The interior of the cottages was spacious in spite of the relatively small size. Halls were seven to eight feet wide, ceilings nine to twelve feet high, doors as wide as four feet, and sash windows numerous, all of which added to the free flow of air and the sense of openness. Walls and ceilings were usually lathed and plastered and painted white. While the extant contracts do not specify any color other than white, newspaper advertisements listed a growing number of available paint colors.[71]

All the descriptions of the city written at the time refer to fencing. Cedar was definitely the preferred material, as the Turner Root contract indicates: "The whole to be fenced in a substantial manner with cedar posts and close board fence seven feet high and picketed on top."[72] The street scene created by these white cottages under their protective roofs and with their encircling fences and colorful flowers sounds picturesque today, but we must not forget the dirt thoroughfares deep in mud in the rainy season or the hordes of mosquitoes thriving in the surrounding swamps or the lack of such conveniences as refrigeration.

While the cottage was the preferred form of home, there were also two-story wood dwellings (figure 33). The house tentatively attributed to Samuel H. Garrow certainly did not derive from the early colonial types as they were found on the Gulf Coast. Garrow moved to Mobile from Virginia, and his home bears some relationship to the Georgian houses of his home state.[73] If we compare it with the Charlton House at Williamsburg (figure 34), we see that it has the same general massing, the formal arrangement of windows and end chimneys, the dentil molding at the cornice line, and the small cen-

33. *The early American home of Samuel Garrow, formerly on Government Street. The small windows, the centrally located Neoclassical entrance, the enclosed massing, and the dentil molding at the cornice illustrate architectural features brought from the Atlantic seaboard states. (Courtesy of the Historic Mobile Preservation Society, Wilson Plates.)*

34. *The Charlton House, Williamsburg, Virginia, after 1740. The emigrants to Mobile from the East and Southeast brought with them the architectural style with which they were familiar, though it was not well suited to a semitropical climate. (Colonial Williamsburg Photograph, courtesy of the Colonial Williamsburg Foundation.)*

tral porch, with its classically inspired columns and pediment. The proportions and detailing are probably less refined because the craftsmen living in the pioneering community were less skilled than those in the more established colony of Virginia. The enclosed and inward-oriented space of the Garrow House conceptually differs greatly from the free-flowing openness of the Gulf Coast cottage. It is no wonder that the latter was the more popular form for a dwelling in this semitropical region.

Brick was well established as a material for commercial structures but was rarely used for homes at the time. Only a few of the surviving contracts specify brick construction for homes. The home of Mr. Thomas Daily was a two-story brick dwelling built between Theatre and Church streets. It was quite large, measuring fifty-five feet by twenty-eight feet, with ten-foot-high ceilings and a central hall eight feet wide that extended the full depth of the building. The entrance called for a "Venecian [sic] Door with side lights with a circular head"; the back was to have a neat, six-panel door. There were to be three partition doorways "with double work pannel shutters" and an open newel staircase with enclosed space below for a cupboard. The tongue-and-groove flooring was to be "seven inches wide by one and one-fourth inches thick." The exterior of the brick house described in Winslow Foster's contract was to have a double porch of wood with "full front on the south." The railing and balusters were to be plain. Fifteen-light windows were made of glass, ten by twelve inches, set in simple frames.[74]

With the increased crowding in the inner city, people began to move out to the western hills, forming an early suburbia. The movement was accelerated by the desire to escape from the city during the summer months when the yellow fever was at its worst. As early as 1822, 200 people were living in the Spring Hill area, and in that year not a single case of the fever was reportedly found among them.[75] In February there appeared in the newspaper a report on the disease with the added information: "There is, however, a healthy and not

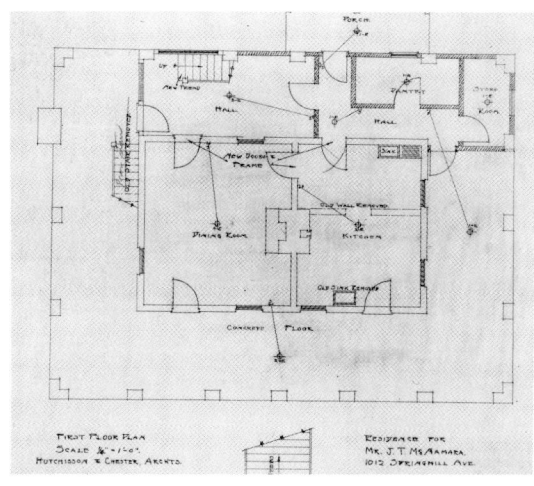

35a. The Vincent House, ca. 1827, with additions made in 1912 and 1927, 1664 Spring Hill Avenue. The house incorporates the Gulf Coast tradition in the elevation of the frame story above a high brick foundation and in the double pitch of the roof that extends over the gallery. (Photograph by Thigpen Photography, courtesy of the Mobile City Planning Commission.)

35b. First-floor plan of the Vincent House, with the 1912 renovation in the enclosure of some gallery space on both the ground level and the upper story. The west side entrance was replaced by one centered on the south facade. Hutchisson and Chester, architects. (Courtesy of Betty Mann Doan.)

35c. Second-floor plan of the Vincent House, 1912 renovation. (Courtesy of Betty Mann Doan.)

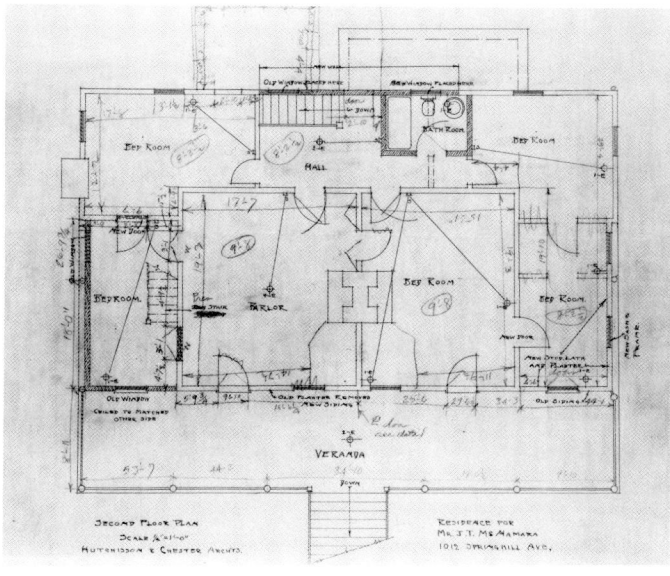

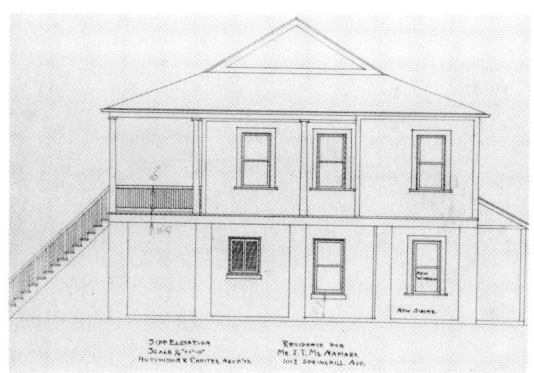

35d. Elevation drawing of the Vincent House, 1912 renovation. Hutchisson and Chester, architects. (Courtesy of Betty Mann Doan.)

unpleasant summer retreat within two or three miles to the westward of the city, to which there is an excellent road and where many respectable families pass the summer, without any interference with their daily attention to business, the ride being short and agreeable."[76] The area meant was probably that known as Summerville, which was located along Spring Hill Avenue in the vicinity of the Convent of Visitation. One of the early homes, located at 1664 Spring Hill Avenue, has survived, though it was altered in the twentieth century. It was built by the pilot Benjamin Vincent in about 1827 and represents the popular two-level house, with the frame story raised on a high brick foundation (figure 35a).[77] In 1912 the firm of Hutchisson and Chester did extensive alterations and prepared drawings of the original walls and the additions being made to them (figures 35b–d). As the plan shows, the original building had three

Americans Begin Building, 1813–1830

rooms on both the ground level and the upper story, with an outside stairway leading up to the deck of the gallery at the northwest corner.[78] A gallery surrounded the building at the second story. The Hutchisson-Chester renovations for J. T. McNamara enclosed the space below the gallery at the rear in order to provide for a hall, an interior stairway, a pantry, and storeroom. The space between the columns of the gallery was enclosed on three sides to provide for sleeping quarters. The old exterior rear northwest stairway was removed, and a monumental front stair was built to give access to the main parlor on the second story. Some alterations were made by Crane, the next owner, and when Alabama Walsh acquired the property in 1927, the firm of Hutchisson, Holmes, and Hutchisson carried out the last major renovations. The main room on the ground floor was enlarged to the west by further infilling of the space below the old gallery, creating the present living room. In the space to the east, a breakfast room or small dining room was added. At that time the tall front stairway was removed and the main entrance established at the ground level. The interior has recently been adapted for use as a bed and breakfast hostel or guesthouse, but the old hand-adzed ceiling summer beam can still be seen in the living room.[79] The house, set far back on its shaded lot, still preserves the atmosphere of the original in spite of the alterations. The two-story massing and the double-pitched roof flaring out over the gallery recall an earlier day.

The Toulmin House is another example of a country home that is still standing, though it has been moved from its original site (figure 36a). It was constructed in 1828 on a 1,930-acre plantation in an area now known as Toulminville. The history of the property goes back to 1733, when the St. Louis tract of 22,500 arpents was granted to M. Diron by Bienville and Salmon. In 1828 Theophilus Toulmin acquired 1,930 acres of the original tract and built his home in time for the birth of his fourth child, Edmund Pendleton.[80] The Toulmin family has been prominent in southern history since 1794, when Harry Toulmin emigrated from England to Kentucky. In 1794 he was made

36a. Toulmin House, ca. 1828, as shown in a photo taken on the original site in Toulminville. Upon removal and restoration, the added Victorian columns were replaced by columns of square section, matching the gallery wall pilasters, and the brick foundation and roof reconstructed. (Photograph by Andrew Dees, University of South Alabama.)

36b. Toulmin House, detail of the heavy brace framing with mortised and pegged joinery, illustrating the early nineteenth-century method of construction.

36c. The frame story of the Toulmin House being moved out to the University of South Alabama.

the president of Transylvania College and was soon involved in compiling the state laws of Kentucky. In 1804 President Thomas Jefferson appointed him judge of the Supreme Court of the Mississippi Territory. When Alabama became a state in 1819, he became the first federal judge of the Tombigbee district. In 1823 Judge Toulmin wrote the *Digest of the Laws* for the new state of Alabama. His son, Theophilus, was born in Kentucky but upon moving to Alabama made his home in Mobile, where he served in the city government as well as in the state legislature. The Toulmin home remained in the family until 1902 and after passing quickly through several hands was purchased by Rebecca Buck, whose family retained ownership until 1975. The growing community of Toulminville had encroached on the old house over the years. In 1975 the house stood in a fast-developing commercial area, crowded between a supermarket parking lot and hamburger stands, gas stations, and other twentieth-century infestations. The building was slated for demolition, so the Mobile Historic Foundation enabled the University of South Alabama to acquire it. It was moved out to the University campus, where it would complete a three-building historic complex. The frame story was removed, the bricks of the foundation were transported to the new site, and in due time the old pegged house (figure 36b) had been remounted on its rebuilt foundation.

The long lines of this 1828 home are typical of the style that had begun with the cottage and had been elaborated by the planters of the Gulf Coast in the early nineteenth century. The use of frame above brick was typical. The supporting piers of the Toulmin House are about seven feet high, furnishing ample room for a shaded passage under the gallery and for rooms where domestic work could be carried on. Sometime during the late nineteenth century, the original square section columns were replaced by Victorian ones, evident in the photograph taken before the building was moved. When the building was restored, columns were made matching the pilasters at the corners of the house to give the shape and the proportions of the original. The plan is the formal central-hall type, with two large rooms of essentially equal size flanking the hall on both sides. In addition there were enclosed end galleries that extended the full depth of the home. The secondary doors off the front gallery led to these end rooms. As was customary, several doors opened onto the interior rooms as well as onto the central hall, thus providing not only easy access but also good ventilation. The framing of the exterior doors and the windows was embellished by channeled surrounds with bull's-eye blocks at the upper corners. All the interior moldings were simple. Only the hall had a ceiling medallion. It was a simple molding of a circular section pressed in plaster.[81]

During the period prior to the Civil War, when plantation architecture was at its height in the central part of the state, there were very few such buildings near the coast. Mobile is fortunate that even one has survived, although not on its original site.

During the decade active expansion occurred about nine miles west of Royal Street. More and more residents took leave of the city during the summer months to live in the hills that became known as Spring Hill. In 1822 a straight road opened to serve this community. So popular did the western adjunct become that a hotel was opened up "some 300 yards from Three Mile Creek." Since much of the acreage was still in the public domain, the city officials wrote a letter to the United States House of Representatives on January 23, 1826, requesting the release of some of the land:

> —I beg leave very respectfully, to the General Assembly to aid the Corporate Authority of the City of Mobile to obtain from the United States four contiguous sections of land at Spring Hill, a quantity equal to four sections—on which to build summer town, or a place of retreat for health.
>
> John Murphy[82]

An 1828 map drawn by William Robertson platted section 13 into five-acre lots (figure 37). On lot 42 are sketched two houses, one belonging to Robert Center and the other to Jack E. Ross. The Center House, an old cottage, is still standing on the same location. According to family records, parts of it date back to the 1828 construction.[83] The Gaillard home, now The Cedars (number 3500), seems to have incorporated the early homestead in its core (figures 38a, b, c). The cottage shows evidence of three building periods. On the right side of the front of the house, now the living room, is a small room covered by a slightly pitched deck. Tradition has it that half of this space was an early trapper's log cabin. On the Robertson map, penned in small letters, are the words "on logs." This cabin seems to have been attached to the core cottage built sometime between 1828 and 1831. The present owner removed some log piers from beneath the house many years ago whose presence bears out the early dating. It is impossible to examine the walls of this room, as the exterior was covered by the same weatherboarding that was used on the cottage core. The main section of the home takes the typical cottage form, with a gable roof flaring out over the surrounding gallery and the roof joining onto that of the front right deck. The present gallery that surrounds the house has some details that suggest a later addition. The house originally faced in the opposite direction from the present orientation, with a porch on this rear side. The columns of this porch have an awkward extension above the capital that resembles a stilt block or a dosseret, suggesting that the present gallery is higher than the original porch. Another unusual detail is the molding, which

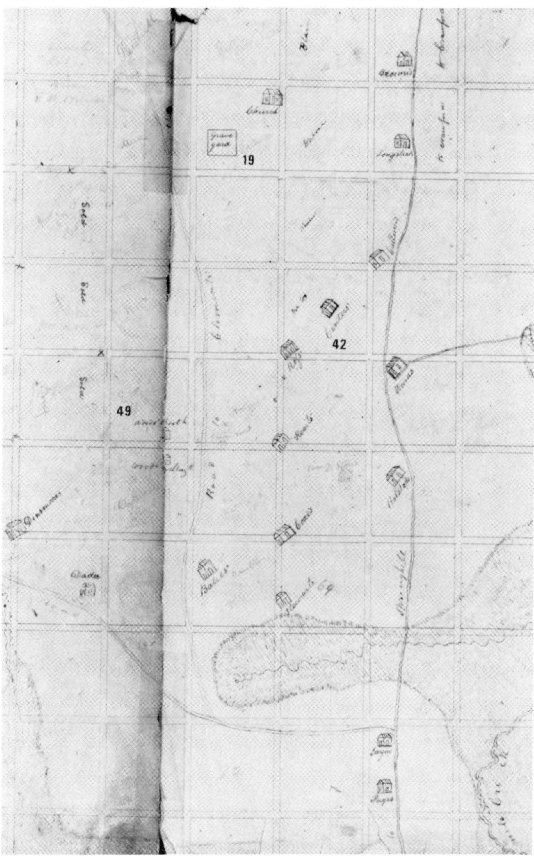

37. *The 1828 Robertson map of the platting of Spring Hill into five-acre parcels. Parcels 19, 42, and 49 still have mid-nineteenth-century houses on their five-acre sites. (From Deed Book 82, n.s., pp. 212–13.)*

38a. *Cottage, before 1830, 3500 The Cedars, standing on parcel 42 of the Robertson map, south and east elevations. Three building periods can be traced, including an old trapper's cabin, a cottage attached on the north, and the later enclosure of the spaces between, with a reorientation of the entrance from the north to the south. (Photograph by Michael Thomason.)*

Americans Begin Building, 1813–1830

38b. 3500 The Cedars. Detail of the old balustrade on the north side, showing the swallowtail cut at the junction of the baluster and the bottom rail. This feature was not found in Mobile after the early 1840s. (Photograph by Michael Thomason.)

38c. The old kitchen house at 3500 The Cedars. The siding is cypress in board-and-batten construction. The original roof was destroyed by Hurricane Frederick in 1979.

drops from the porch entablature like a row of blocks. Parts of the balustrade of the rear porch are still intact, with the rounded top railing and the swallowtail cut at the bottom of the balusters as they join the bottom rail (figure 38b). This balustrade type was also found in the 1830 buildings but seems to have disappeared by mid-1840.

A narrow and very steep interior stairway leads to the garret. Here, where the roof trussing is exposed, the early pegged joinery is evident. The stairway is enclosed and leads from the hall, which instead of being centrally located extends along the west side of the plan. The original entrance to this hall was from the porch facing north toward a road that once led from Mobile to Lewis Hill. The surround of this entrance suggests the Greek Revival, with its horizontal transom and sidelights above simple molded panels. The present main entrance on the south side was created during the twentieth century.

On the lot is an old kitchen house, moved to its present location from a site nearer the house (figure 38c). The small building and its chimney were moved intact. It is a one-story, board-and-batten structure made of cypress, with the same pegged joinery as the cottage and the same drop molding around the entrance that appears on the gallery of the house. The wide cypress boards still retain many of the old nails. While the exact date of the kitchen's construction is not known, it seems to be as old as the cottage and is certainly the oldest surviving structure of its kind in the Mobile area.

The decade of the 1820s set the direction for the city's future development. During this time the street relationships were established, the importance of the waterfront recognized, the concentration of the commercial district initiated, the western expansion begun, and the architectural styles changed from the single building located on a lot to the row-on-row street scene of a city. These ten years were not outstanding in terms of architectural design, but they saw the advent of skilled builders who were ready to carry on the Greek Revival of the next decade, when wealth would support a degree of refinement in architecture that still commands attention today.

3 The Coming of the Greek Revival, 1830–1840

During some periods in history, the energy, optimism, and activities of a people cause an upward swing in their cycle of development. Such times often follow a pioneering phase, a depression, or a catastrophe, bringing release from rigors and dangers. During the halcyon periods the economy makes it possible for men to create and enjoy a life that affords more than mere survival. The history of architecture follows the same pattern. With the decade of the 1830s, Mobile entered a phase of prosperity and growth that permitted men to conceive of the monumental, to evolve structures that were aesthetically pleasing as well as utilitarian. When the 1827 fire (figure 39) destroyed the nine blocks that extended from Government Street to St. Francis and from the waterfront to St. Joseph, the old commercial and civic center of the city was leveled. So vigorous, however, was the economic development that a new city soon replaced the old. The years between 1829 and the fire of 1839 witnessed the erection of impressive civic and religious architecture.

Exploratory moves had been made toward a balanced refinement of the Classical mode in echoes of the Georgian and Federal buildings of the previous decade. Subtle changes in proportions, in orientation, and in the development of the hall plan had been established. Simple chamfered posts had been replaced by columns of circular section, but with the new decade the Greek Revival orders suddenly appeared. Pattern books, such as those of Asher Benjamin, inspired the columns seen in the little Larrouil cottage (figure 58). Architects sought to adjust interior spaces to meet the needs of the times within the confines of the Greek prostyle and distyle-in-antis plans. The drawings and measurements of Stuart and Revett were studied, adapted, and given vernacular alterations that produced the Greek Revival as it found expression in the different parts of the country.[1] The La Tourrette map of 1838 (figures 40a–c) illustrates the impact of the Greek Revival in Mobile; across the top of the map there appear four engravings of buildings erected between 1833 and 1838. These structures contrast vividly with the simplicity and even crudeness of the buildings represented on the edges of the Goodwin and Haire map of 1824 (figure 27). Of the four examples engraved, three are still standing, a Greek Revival legacy that any city would

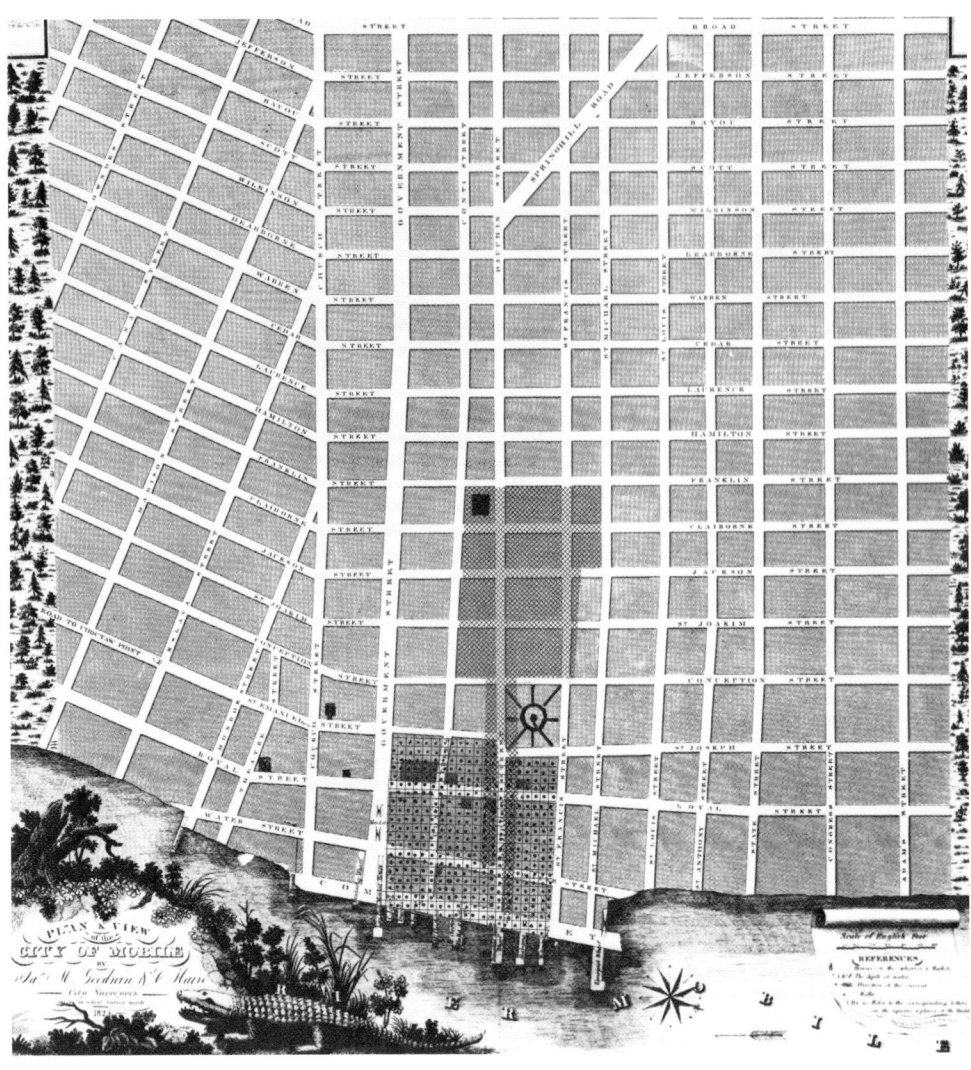

39. *Map of Mobile plotting the fires of 1827 and 1839. Three historic districts are also indicated on the map: Church Street East, de Tonti Square, and the Lower Dauphin Street Commercial District. (Adapted from the Goodwin and Haire map of Mobile, 1824.)*

be proud to claim. The oldest of the four is the City Hospital of 1833–1836 (figures 41a–c).

From the earliest times a hospital of some sort had been located in the city. The French had planned a hospital in the block north of the fort, in the area marked L on the map (figure 7). It would have been located on the east side of what is now Conception Street, between Conti and Dauphin. By the end of the French occupation, the Hospital was located on Royal Street between St. Louis and St. Anthony and was listed under the name of Mme Grondel (figure 20). The English continued to use this building. During the Spanish period, the Hospital was located on the north side of Dauphin between St. Joseph and Conception, about mid-block in present-day Bienville Square. The Old Spanish Hospital located on the map (figure 42) continued to serve the needs of the city until 1824, when it was sold along with the northeast corner of Dauphin and Conception. On October 14, 1824, the city accepted the bid of Mount and Tatum for the construction of a new hospital. On December 28, the building committee was authorized to accept the building if it "were finished agreeable to the contract." Since only two months were allowed for construction and the cost was $1,450 the building was probably a frame structure and quite small. The Minutes of the Mayor and the

From Fort to Port

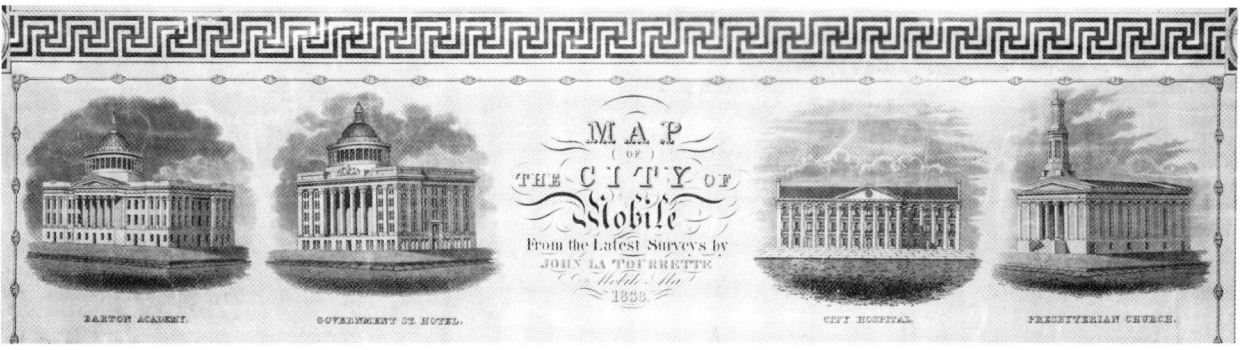

40a. Four engravings of Greek Revival buildings, three of which are still standing, from La Tourrette map of 1838. (Courtesy of the Library of Congress.)

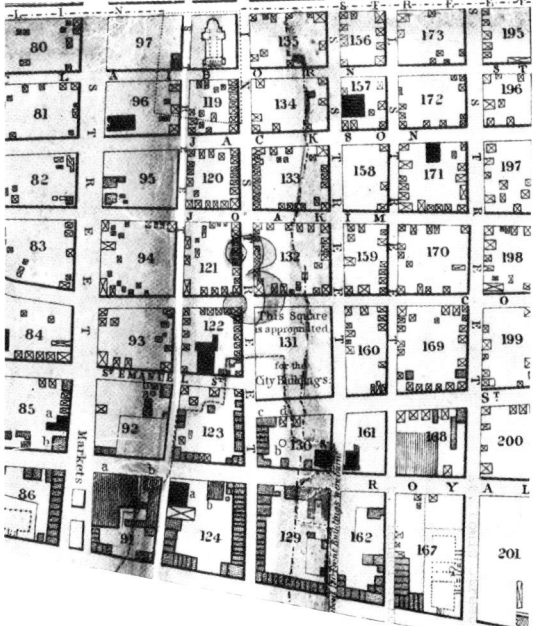

40c. Detail of the legend from the La Tourrette map, including the listing of the wharves. (Courtesy of the Library of Congress.)

40b. Detail of ward 3 of the La Tourrette map, showing the concentration of commercial buildings along the waterfront and up Dauphin Street. (Courtesy of the Library of Congress.)

Board of Aldermen do not mention the location of the Hospital. Information about the 1833 hospital building, however, suggests that the Mount and Tatum building must have been located on the northwest line of the Kennedy tract purchased in 1824 as a site for a new hospital. If so, the structure stood near the present Hospital Street in the Davis Avenue community.[2]

The large Greek Revival Hospital engraved on the La Tourrette map was begun in 1833 (figure 41). On August 23, the mayor and aldermen agreed to accept the plans presented to them by Captain William George. The captain received only seventy-five dollars for the plans of this monumental building, which still stands at 850 St. Anthony Street. The Minutes include detailed records of alterations and amendments made to the plan. Details of construction were recorded, for example the substitution of Welsh slate for shingles to cover the roof and the laying of one and one-half bricks for the thickness of the interior partitions. Especially interesting is the method used to lay the foundation. Because the water table is very high and the land largely sand, it was difficult to supply a foundation for such a large building. As Chicago in the nineteenth century developed the floating slab, Mobile builders erected walls laid on a raft foundation. For the first course, they laid down timber made of "two inch heart pine planks four feet in length placed close together crosswise with the walls." The second course of timber was to be composed of "two inch heart pine planks laid side by side three feet in width and laid transversely with the first course."[3] Upon this foundation the brick structure rested.

41a. The Old City Hospital of 1833–1836, 850 St. Anthony Street; William George, architect, John K. Collins, builder. The Hospital was the first monumental Greek Revival building to be constructed in Mobile. (Erik Overbey/Mobile Public Library Collection, University of South Alabama Photographic Archives.)

The contractor-builder was John K. Collins. All payments to him are recorded in the Treasurer's Day Books covering the years of the construction, from 1833 through 1835. During 1835 alone, his payment was $15,000; the total for the work was $33,420. In 1841 the tax value of the building was $56,000. During the years of construction, two sets of hospital expenses were kept—one set was for the new construction, the other the running expenses of the existing building, presumably the Mount and Tatum structure. The last entry for the old Hospital is dated 1836. It was sold to Mayor J. F. Everett for $150.[4]

In style the City Hospital of 1833 illustrates a free and unacademic interpretation of the Greek Revival. The central bays of the 222-foot-long building form a projecting portico that is 65 feet 10 inches wide, with six stuccoed brick unfluted columns that rise 32 feet 5 inches to the entablature. The proportions of the shafts appear awkward because of the overly enlarged diameter of the lower drums, which goes far beyond the subtle entasis of the classical

Greek refinements. The encircling molding below the capital of the column and the narrow entablature above are more Roman than Greek. The whole design is directed more toward the balance and control of the long horizontal mass than toward refinements of detail. Only the original main entrance had carefully executed embellishments in the fan-shaped transom, which was framed by a torus-scotia molding and had lights divided by a starburst pattern of arrows radiating outward behind an eagle with outstretched wings (figure 41c).[5]

The original building was not as long as the present building, as the engraving (figure 41b) shows; only the colonnade portion belonged to the early period. About 1907 the pilastered end bays were added, increasing the original length of 182 feet 4 inches to the present 222 feet. Behind the impressive colonnade, cast iron galleries 11.5 feet deep create a shadowed space between the sunlit columns and the windowed wall. Because of the building's orientation, the patterns of light and shade constantly change with the movements of the sun. The elevation of the north and east sides of the building is plain, but the west, facing on Broad Street, is divided into bays by

41b. *Engraving of the Old City Hospital, showing the building before the end bays were added. (Reproduced from the Annual Announcement of the Medical College, 1883–1884, courtesy of the Mobile Public Library, Special Collections Division.)*

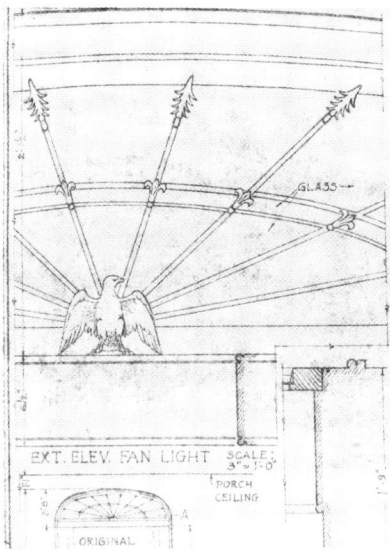

41c. *Detail of the fanlight from the original door of the Old City Hospital. (Drawing by G. Chaudron, courtesy of the Library of Congress, Historic American Building Survey Collection.)*

The Greek Revival, 1830–1840

four pilasters, which rise to an architrave that continues the line of the facade.[6]

The Old City Hospital continued in use until 1965, when it was closed. By 1974 the building had deteriorated. Plaster was peeling on the columns, and there was general damage resulting from neglect and disuse. In 1974 the decision was made to restore the building as offices of the Mobile County Board of Pensions and Securities. A generous grant of $500,000 from the Bedsole Foundation was matched by $600,000 each from the city and the county, making it possible to reclaim the building for the future.

The year after the City Hospital was started, a more sensitive appreciation of the Greek Revival was introduced into Mobile by James Gallier, Sr., and his associate, Charles B. Dakin. They passed through Mobile on their way to New Orleans, where they settled in 1834. Gallier came south after training and experience in the office of Town and Davis. He had also had a year's partnership with Lafever in 1833. Charles B. Dakin joined the staff of Town, Davis, and Dakin when his brother, James, employed him as a draftsman. When James joined the southern migration in 1835, Gallier withdrew from the Gallier-Dakin partnership, and the two brothers formed their own firm. They established two offices. The one in Mobile was known as Charles B. Dakin and Brother, Architects. James headed the New Orleans office. Charles B. Dakin remained in Mobile for about two years, from 1836 to 1838, and had his office on the south side of Government Street, five doors north of Royal.[7]

One of the outstanding examples of the influence of Gallier and Dakin is Barton Academy (figures 43a–d), which appears at the top extreme left of the map (figure 40a). According to Gallier's *Autobiography*, he and Dakin "made plans for a church and for a public school, which were erected there and are still the most important looking buildings on Government Street."[8]

The two buildings planned, Barton Academy and the Government Street Presbyterian Church, exemplify the two major trends of the Greek Revival as it developed in Mobile. One adapted the classical

42. *Section of the 1835 map surveyed by W. Roberts, W. Henshaw, and J. James, deputy surveyors. The last Spanish Hospital is indicated on the northwest corner of Conception and Dauphin, a part of the block now occupied by Bienville Square. (Courtesy of the U.S. Department of the Interior, Bureau of Land Management.)*

62   From Fort to Port

temple elevation; the other applied selected Greek architectural detailing to the monumental domed buildings of a Roman-Renaissance inheritance. Within just a few blocks, Mobile has fine examples of both trends.

It is astonishing that a city with a population of only about 13,000 people should have had the vision and optimism to erect as large a school building as Barton Academy. The moving spirit behind the venture was Judge Henry Hitchcock, who had repeatedly employed Charles Dakin as architect for his own buildings while also urging that he be selected as the builder for public structures. The boundless confidence in the future expressed by the people of Mobile between the years 1833 and the panic of 1837 is demonstrated by the architectural accomplishments of the times. The movement to establish a school system in Mobile County was initiated by Willoughby Barton. In 1826, as a member of the state legislature, he sponsored an act to create a Board of School Commissioners for the Mobile area. In 1830 a suitable site was purchased and plans made to raise the necessary funds for a building. Taxation was to be one source of income, according to the Minutes of the Board of Education, in which appears the phrase, "This being the first effort made in the city to establish a system of instruction upon an extended plan with funds devised from taxation and under the direction of Commissioners elected by the People." A second source of income was to be the proceeds from lotteries, which were made legal by an act of 1836. Later these sources would prove inadequate as Barton finances fell on hard times. By August 1836, the sum of $19,315 in notes and $2,599 in cash had been handed over to the newly selected School Board. At that point the decision was made to proceed with the construction.[9] On December 2, 1835, there appeared in the newspaper a request for bids to erect the school.

The building committee consisted of Henry Hitchcock, Willis Roberts, J. F. Collins, and G. Mordecai. The design or plan selected was that of Gallier and Dakin, as noted in Gallier's *Autobiography*. In view of Henry Hitchcock's confidence in Charles Dakin, it is natural that Dakin was selected to supervise the construction, and his name appears many times in the School Board Minutes. Contractors and builders working under Dakin were Thomas James and John Durden, whose names appear in the Minutes when they received various payments.[10]

Barton Academy is an impressive example of the type of monumental building that was constructed in all parts of the country when state capitols and other civic structures were built. Its dome (figure 43a) is mounted on an octagonal platform and circular drum. The two-story elevation is divided into fenestrated bays by giant pilasters, and the facade is broken by a projecting portico of five bays. End pavilions of three bays project slightly from the plane of the facade, and the space between the pavilions and the portico is also divided into three bays, so that the rhythm across the front is 3, 3, 5, 3, 3. The individual bays are framed by the two-story pilasters that rise from a string course marking the top of the first story. This horizontal string course, or molding, forms a shadow that is an important element in the design, tying the first story to the ground level while at the same time remaining small enough not to interfere with the relationship between the first story and the two above. The horizontal line of the building is further accented by the classical entablature and the parapet above that hides the roof. The only break in this design is the gable roof of the portico that rises at the building's midpoint. The portico becomes an anchor in the design, directing the viewer's attention through the vertical movement of its six giant Ionic columns, which rise from the level of the second story and offer a transition to the small, Ionic columns of the dome above. This subtle relationship is lost in the Dakin drawing for the Government Street Hotel (figure 46), in which the recessed portico seems to lack an adequate support for the weight above and the wide base of the drum isolates the Ionic columns of the drum from those of the portico. In Barton Academy, the interrelationship of the parts is carried on through the cupola, which serves as a point of convergence for the strong vertical lines that begin at the base of the portico columns.[11] Gallier and Dakin again thus skillfully blended the horizontal and the vertical in a well-balanced design that adapts classical features to a large building.

During the years of construction, a frame school building occupied a portion of the site. It was removed and sold on November 9, 1836. The new building, intended to be a free school, was planned for several uses as stated in the Minutes of the Board of Education:

43b. Barton Academy, engraving from Harper's Weekly, July 16, 1887, published in "The Industrial South" with a wharf scene drawn by Charles Graham.

43a. Barton Academy, 1836, 504 Government Street; Gallier and Dakin, architects; Dakin, supervising architect; Thomas James and John Durden, builders. Gallier and Dakin introduced into Mobile specific characteristics of the Greek Revival and the Neoclassical style that permeated vernacular architecture for the next quarter century. (Photograph by Roy C. McAuley.)

The object of the institution being intended to furnish public and popular instruction for the children of the great body of the populace of the city, it becomes the duty of the Commission to arrange the school as to afford the greatest facility for its accomplishment.

For that purpose, the Building is so constructed as to admit of separate schools for the different ages and sexes embracing different grades of instruction from the infant up to and including the Classics.

The first and second stories are each divided into two rooms of sufficient size to accommodate One Hundred Scholars each, the Rooms in the Third Story are subdivided into four rooms which will accommodate Fifty Scholars each, so that the whole building will conveniently accommodate Six Hundred Scholars.[12]

Following this declared purpose, there is a detailed account of the specific use for each room, with the regulations concerning the governing boards.

In 1836 Richard Redwood proposed that an iron fence be erected to enclose the site. According to his plan, a contract of 1837 was signed with Mr. W. Ratcliffe, who agreed to install the brick and granite foundation wall at a cost of $1,700. The order for the fence was given to Mr Magraw for $5,315 (figure 43d).[13]

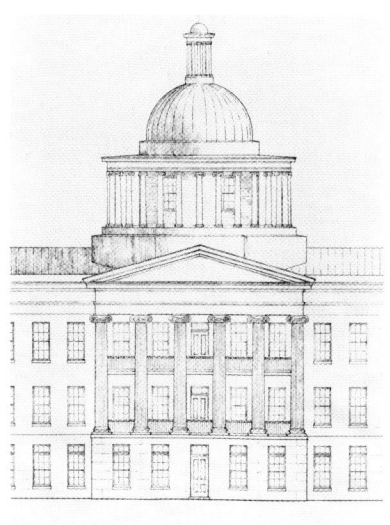

43c. Barton Academy, drawing of the south front elevation. The proportions of the pediment and base of the dome make a subtle transition between the vertical lines of the portico columns and the colonnade of the drum, interrelating the different levels and leading the eye easily from the first story to the top of the lantern. (Drawing by G. Chaudron, courtesy of the Library of Congress, Historic American Building Survey Collection.)

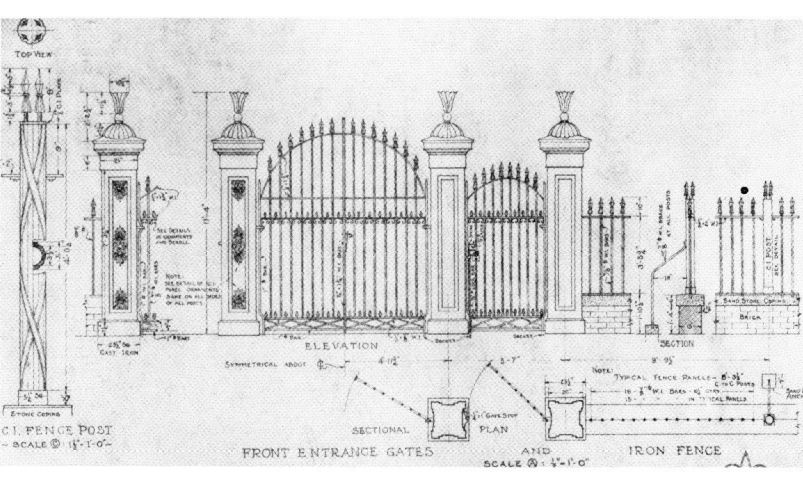

43d. Drawing of Barton Academy fencing and gates. The 1836 plan of Richard Redwood was accepted, and in 1837 Thomas Magraw was paid $5,315 for the completed fence. (Drawing by H. Witherell, courtesy of the Library of Congress, Historic American Building Survey Collection.)

When the building was ready for occupancy, a debt of $12,000 remained, and students who could afford to pay were charged a small fee. Twice during the school's history its financial problems became so severe that plans were made to sell the building, once in August 1838 and again in January 1852. Each time the decision was rescinded. Space was rented when loans were not forthcoming. Rooms on the third floor were rented to civic organizations such as the Franklin Society and the Philomathean. In November 1840 the free school was formally discontinued. In 1845 the whole building was rented on a yearly basis with the stipulation that it must be used for education. During the 1850s, schools were conducted within it by Free Methodist, Bethel, Catholic, and Trinity churches. In 1852 the educational system was reorganized into primary, grammar, and high school divisions, with minimal fees to be charged until the school could afford to be free again. During the Civil War the building was partially occupied as a hospital, but in 1865 it reopened as a girl's school, which it remained until 1875, when it became a public educational facility. As the years went by and the population grew, wings were added at both ends. The additions succeeded, however, in maintaining the equilibrium of the original design. Over the years major repairs were needed. In 1909 the Jett Brothers repaired the roof and reinforced the dome. In 1914 the New Orleans firm of Stevens and Nelson added a wing on the north rear. By 1969 the building could no longer serve its original purpose. The architects Nicholas Holmes and Stuart Dillon March then restored the exterior and renovated the interior for use of the offices of the Board of Education.[14]

Religious Buildings

The third engraving on the La Tourrette map depicts the Government Street Presbyterian Church (figures 44a–e) on the right corner of the upper margin. A drawing for a church facade in the Gallier collection at Tulane University (figure 44b) closely resembles the Government Street Presbyterian Church, with its Ionic distyle-in-antis elevation. This design was made popular through the work of Town and Davis and the Dakins and became part of the vernacular architecture through the pattern books published by men such as Asher Benjamin (figure 44c).[15] Since the Greek temple prototype needed only enough interior space to house a cult figure, the design had to be modified when the derivative style was used for buildings that had greater spatial needs. As in the Roman temples, Greek Revival architects extended the walls to the edge of the foundation and substituted for the free-standing colonnade repetitive pilasters that articulated bays along the side elevations. The wall surfaces in these bays provided for rectangular panels for windows. The skill with which Gallier and Dakin applied the design can be seen in the side elevation of the Government Street Presbyterian Church (figure 44d).

The separate parts are subtly interrelated in the Church's facade. Though each element of wall, column, entablature, and pediment is clearly articulated, they are united in a coordinated whole by their harmonious proportions and the restrained elegance of the detail (figure 44a). The elaboration of the interior design is quite different in spirit, so much so that Arthur Scully, in his chapter on Charles

44a. Government Street Presbyterian Church, 1836, 300 Government Street; Gallier and Dakin, architects; Thomas James and R. J. Barnes, builders. An elegant adaptation of the Greek treasury or small temple using the distyle-in-antis plan. Slender Ionic columns, freestanding between the box pilasters of the end bays, front the recessed porch. (Photograph by Michael Thomason.)

44b. Colored drawing of a church by Gallier that closely resembles the facade of the Government Street Presbyterian Church. (Courtesy of Mrs. Carter Smith.)

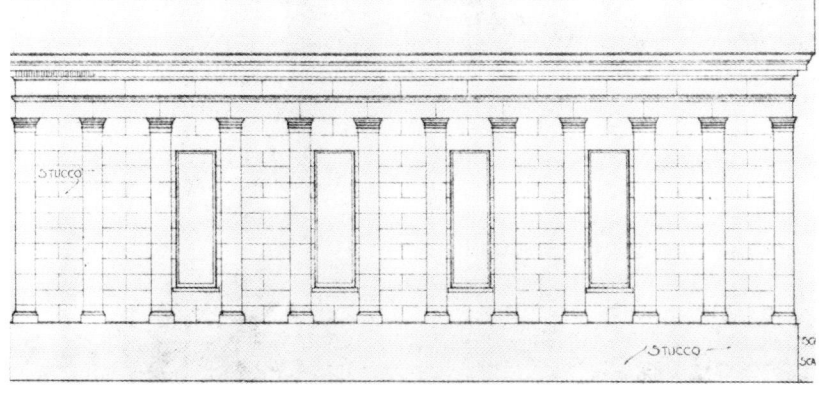
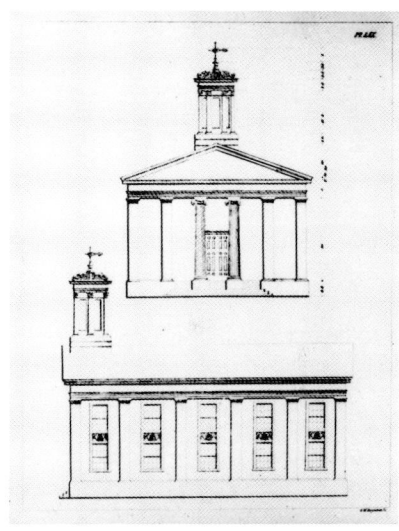

44d. Drawing of the side elevation of the Government Street Presbyterian Church. Similar in design to the side elevation of the Asher Benjamin drawing (figure 44c) but with the windows placed in alternate bays. The brick construction was covered with plaster scored to resemble stone. (Drawing by P. Roberts, courtesy of the Library of Congress, Historic American Building Survey Collection.)

44c. Drawing for a church. In 1837 Charles and James Dakin designed a similar facade using the Doric order for the Methodist Episcopal Church of New Orleans (destroyed in 1851). (From Asher Benjamin, The Builder's Guide [Boston: Perkins and Marvin, 1850].)

Dakin, attributes the exterior design to Gallier and the interior to Dakin. In the main auditorium the balcony is supported by columns of a type used in Athens in the Tower of the Winds, built during the Roman period, 40 B.C. Along the edge of the balcony is a molding with a Greek key, or fret, design. The most striking feature of the interior is the reredos behind the pulpit. Four Corinthian columns support an entablature that is embellished with dentils and an anthemion cresting. The exaggeration of the outward slope of the heavy enframement goes far beyond the classical batter of the Greek key door and suggests an Egyptian heaviness.[16]

The Gallier-Dakin building was not the first Presbyterian church in Mobile. During the tenure of the Reverend John Warren, a frame church on a brick foundation was built for which the contract sur-

44e. *Interior of the Government Street Presbyterian Church. The reredos with its four elaborate Corinthian columns, anthemion cresting, and extreme batter of the enframement suggests that Charles Dakin was the designer of the interior detailing of the Church. (Photograph by Manning, courtesy of the Library of Congress, Historic American Building Survey Collection.)*

vives in the Miscellaneous Books of the county. In it Mr. Moses Wickwire agreed to "frame and adjust the price for the floor of the church on Government Street—to lay the floors of the aisles to run lengthwise with the aisles—to install weatherboards as high up from the floor as the top of the pews, which is thirty-seven inches—and to make eighty pews." The contract goes on to describe the size and shape of the pews. The congregation soon outgrew this building, and under the encouragement of the Reverend William T. Hamilton and Judge Henry Hitchcock, the Greek Revival Church was planned. Bids for construction were advertised in the *Mobile Commercial Register* for December 2, 1835. According to Charles Dakin's receipt book, he paid Thomas James a total of $40,188 for the construction and R. J. Barnes an additional sum.[17] The building was finished in 1837 except that there may have been plans for a steeple. Local tradition has it that a steeple on the building was destroyed during the hurricane of 1852. The Gallier drawing, believed to be a study for the Church, does not have one, though one is present in the engraving on the La Tourrette map. There is no evidence of a foundation for a steeple on the building today. In 1903 the Burgett Memorial Sunday School wing was added on the rear by the architects Lockwood and Seymour, with Seymour as supervising architect. In 1917 C. L. Hutchisson, Sr., added another bay to the rear of the Burgett Memorial and did extensive interior renovations. The exterior of this educational addition continued the same bay division with pilasters that carried on the rhythmic pattern of the Gallier-Dakin Church.

Another fine Greek Revival church was built between 1838 and 1840, too late to be shown on the La Tourrette map. It occupied the same site as the first little Protestant Church shown on the Goodwin and Haire map of 1824 at the northwest corner of Church and St. Emanuel streets. On July 4, 1833, the old Church was partially destroyed when the floor collapsed under the weight of a large crowd. It was decided not to repair the old building, which had been renamed Christ Church in 1828. The congregation then moved to a new building on the southwest corner of St. Francis and Jackson

45a. Christ Episcopal Church, 1838–1840, 114 St. Emanuel Street; Cary Butt, architect; James Barnes, builder. The minutes of the Church also mention Frederick Bunnell as architect with Cary Butt. A Greek Revival distyle-in-antis plan uses the Doric order of columns. The building was erected on the site of the old Gothic Revival Church shown on the Goodwin and Haire map of 1824.

45b. Detail of the facade of Christ Episcopal Church. All the elements of the Greek Doric entablature have been carefully studied to give an academically correct distribution of its parts. (Photograph by Robert Wakeman.)

while plans for rebuilding were being formalized. In November 1835, the building committee reported on two plans that had been submitted, one for a Gothic Revival church and the other for a Greek Revival church. Neither of these plans ever materialized. In 1838 a contract was signed for the building that is now standing. The identity of the architect has been much debated. The contract states that the architect was Cary Butt. On the basis of the relationship between Butt and Dakin, Arthur Scully argues that Dakin was the designer. Still, the Church records for April 20, 1840, note that $150 was paid to Cary W. Butt, architect, and $160 to Frederick Bunnell for plans. Bunnell is the architect who designed the first County Jail and the extant 1842 United States Marine Hospital.[18]

Like the Government Street Presbyterian Church, Christ Episcopal (figures 45a–d) is a distyle-in-antis plan but with columns of the Doric order rather than the Ionic. The impression produced by the two orders is quite different. The Doric creates a feeling of strength and power, while the Ionic is more slender, more graceful, and seemingly more fragile. Each order has its own special characteristic details. The architect of Christ Church carefully designed the facade to include the elements that are traditionally found in the Doric. In the entablature the triglyphs, metopes, guttae, and mutuals are all in their proper sequence (figure 45b). Even the variations in the spacing of the metopes have been observed, so that the triglyphs at the corners form a strong line in place of the weak half metope that would have formed the corner if the triglyph had stood directly above the center of the column. The width of the frieze in relation to that of the architrave reflects the Greek tradition. The only devia-

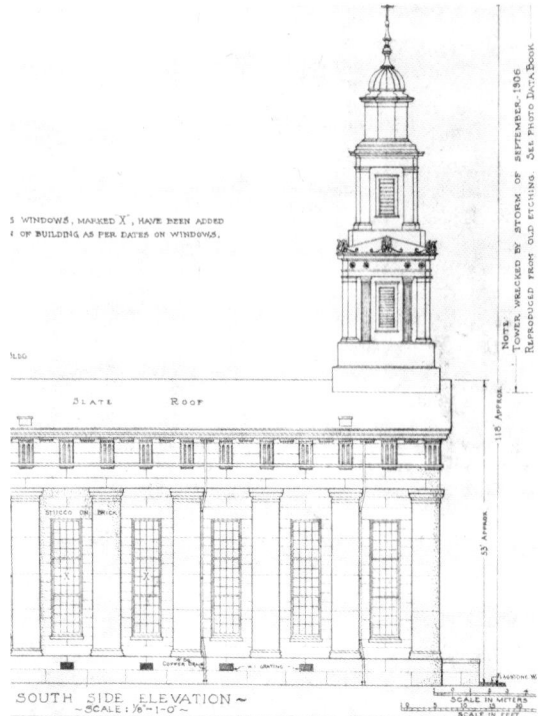

45c. Christ Episcopal Church before the hurricane of 1906, with the steeple still standing. The basic Wren-Gibbs tower form has been adapted with Greek Revival detailing. The first stage of the tower repeats the Doric distyle-in-antis elevation of the main facade but with proportions altered to allow for the central vent. (Courtesy of the Historic Mobile Preservation Society, Wilson Plates.)

45d. Drawing, south side elevation of Christ Episcopal Church. The triglyphs and metopes of the frieze have been placed according to the Greek subtleties, with the end triglyph moved from the axis of the pilaster to the corner. By this realignment, the corner gains in visual strength. (Drawing by H. Witherell, courtesy of the Library of Congress, Historic American Building Survey Collection.)

tion from the Doric style occurs in the vertical line formed by the junction of the flutings of the columns, which here forms a flat fillet instead of the sharp arris found in the Greek prototype. (This detail is not visible in the photograph.) This feature alters the pattern of light and shade along the height of the column.

Unlike the Presbyterian Church, Christ Episcopal bears evidence of a steeple that is no longer present. Engravings exist of the building as it looked before the 1906 hurricane, and the Church's records mention problems with the steeple (figure 45c). The drawing by the Historic American Building Survey carefully defines the details of the spire (figure 45d). Two diminishing cubes have their faces designed to resemble small distyle-in-antis temples or treasuries. The eye is readily attracted to the octagonal lantern and moves up the dome to the crowning pinnacle. This type of steeple design was repeated again and again throughout the eighteenth and nineteenth centuries. The side elevation is formed of fenestrated bays created by pilasters of the same order as the columns. The original windows have been replaced by a fine series of stained glass, with an excellent Cenzo window on the north side next to the chancel. Other windows are Tiffany, and there are some by Franz Mayer of Munich.

The facade and exterior walls stand today as they did at the end of the 1830 decade, when the contractor James Barnes completed his work, except for the exterior stucco, which was not applied until 1852. The building was originally sixty-two feet wide and ninety feet long, but during later years the chancel was elongated. The contract called for a brick building with stone for the door and windowsills and steps. Marble was to be used for the deck of the portico to "match that found in the New Bank on Royal Street."[19] One of the interesting requirements in the contract specified that the foundation walls were to be two feet six inches below the level of the sidewalk and were to splay out for twelve inches on each side "of the base so as to make a firm foundation." The plastered columns were designed to be twenty-nine feet six inches high, including the capitals. The shafts were to taper in diameter from five feet four inches at the base to four feet three inches at the neck, giving a subtle entasis. The roof was to be of tin and "guaranteed not to leak."

The building suffered two major disasters, and the present interior is, therefore, not the original. In 1888 the ceiling plaster collapsed, and a galvanized iron ceiling was installed. Then, in the hurricane of 1906, the steeple fell through the roof, destroying most of the interior except the chancel. Fortunately the contract preserves information about the original interior. It had galleries on the back and on both sides of the sanctuary. The rear gallery was fifteen feet four inches deep; those of the sides measured twelve feet. A balustrade was formed of wood panels with a top molding. The floors were tongue-and-groove yellow pine seven inches wide by one and a fourth inches thick. The walls of the sanctuary called for wainscoting to the height of the windows. The ceiling was coved at the outer edges by an elliptical curve along the sides and end of the sanctuary. The upper line of this curve was accented by fillets of two and a half inches projecting three-fourth inches from the surface. Between the fillets were three flat bands. In the center of the ceiling was a medallion eighteen feet in diameter embellished with acanthus leaf designs. At the corners of the ceiling were rosettes ten inches in diameter. The contract did not describe the pilasters and cornice along the interior walls except to say that they were to be like the "drawing." Unfortunately no drawing has survived. The interior was to be painted white with the "best English white lead," and the hardware and locks were to be silver plated. The contracted price for construction was $21,194.

Commercial Buildings

The last building shown on the La Tourrette map was the Government Street Hotel (figures 46a–b). It was designed by Charles B. Dakin during the time of his residency in Mobile. Unfortunately the fire of 1839 destroyed the building before it was finished. The Hotel was located on the northeast corner of Government and Royal streets (block 91a on the La Tourrette map, figure 40). The land had been acquired by the Mobile Steam Cotton Press and Building Company from Henry Hitchcock, the former owner. Like Barton, the building was a large rectangular building crowned with a dome, but the recessed portico of the Hotel creates a completely different aesthetic effect from the projecting portico of Barton. The Hotel lacks the visual transition from one element of the design to the next, so that the major divisions, the ground level, the portico, and the dome emerge as distinct entities rather than seeming to be progressive steps leading up to the cupola. Because of the shadows produced by

46a. *Study for the Government Street Hotel, called the Lafayette; Charles Dakin, architect; John Collins and R. J. Barnes, builders. The drawing shows the same dome configuration as on the La Tourrette map engraving, with a colonnaded drum forming a transition from the columns of the recessed porch to the dome above. (Dakin Collection, courtesy of the Louisiana Division, New Orleans Public Library.)*

46b. *Second study for the Government Street Hotel; Charles Dakin, architect, 1836. In this elevation the drum of the dome is eliminated and the columns of the recessed porch rise from the ground level rather than from the basement story. (Dakin Collection, courtesy of the Louisiana Division, New Orleans Public Library.)*

the recessed portico, the facade appears less able to support the weight of the large dome, and the sculptured group at the center of the cornice distracts rather than forming a transition with the drum above. The drawing for the United States Hotel by Charles Dakin done in 1836 differs from the engraving on the La Tourrette map. Originally the building was planned as a five-story elevation, but it was modified in 1837, as stated in a contract dated July 14 and signed by Charles B. Dakin and John K. Collins. According to the contract, R. J. Barnes was appointed the carpenter and was employed to construct the Hotel "upon the plan as amended from the original by C. B. Dakin, architect, leaving off the fifth story."[20] The elimination of the fifth story, as shown in the La Tourrette map, weakened the design. Had the building been completed as originally planned, the dome would not have seemed so heavy.

The Hotel was begun in 1836 and promised to be the second largest in the South. When James Silk Buckingham wrote of his visit to Mobile in 1839, he mentioned that the Government Street Hotel was still under construction and added that, when it was finished, it would be "much larger and certainly more handsome than either the Astor House at New York or the Tremont House at Boston." The destruction of the Hotel is recorded in the newspaper and also in the Minutes of the Mayor and Board of Aldermen, which refer to "the City Hotel lately destroyed by fire." On October 12, the Board passed a resolution that "the standing walls of the ruins of the Mansion House and the Government Street Hotel are a nuisance and [must] be required to be pulled down and remove such nuisance within 5 days." Arthur Scully, in his book *James Dakin, Architect*, quoted the *New Orleans Daily Picayune* as saying that "only the walls and lofty arches of the interior" were still standing.[21]

It is easy to imagine the impressive sight that must have greeted a traveler landing at the wharf at the foot of Government Street before the 1839 fire. People who passed the noisy and colorful street market there would have surveyed eleven blocks of an avenue dotted with great examples of Greek Revival buildings towering above rows of two- and three-story red brick and white stuccoed buildings. The bright contrast of exposed red brick with white stuccoed walls symbolized the optimism of the decade. Unfortunately, hard times lay ahead.

The La Tourrette map locates many prominent public buildings that once played an important part in the life of the city but about whose architecture we know little today. For one such building, however, the plans still exist. The St. Michael Street Hotel once stood on the northwest corner of Royal and St. Michael streets, where the parking garage for the Merchant's Bank is now located (figure 40b, block 168). It was designed and built by Charles B. Dakin late in 1836 (figures 47a, b). The St. Michael design was much less ambitious than his grandiose scheme for the unfinished Government Street Hotel. It was a four-story brick building, with a projecting cornice and low parapet, quite in harmony with the rest of the commercial structures that formed the row buildings on Royal and Dauphin. The main entrance was accented by a one-story porch with two Doric columns in antis, supporting the same style of cornice and parapet as that which crowned the whole building. The monotonous repetition of bays and the regularity of fenestration in no way suggest the irregularity of the plan (figure 47b). The enterprise suffered economic decline a few years after construction, seemingly because, as noted in the Minutes of the Mayor and Board of Aldermen for April 23, 1839, "the lot on the northwest corner of Royal and St. Michael Streets known as the St. Michael Hotel, be called a public nuisance." The building survived, however, and was extensively remodeled after a fire in 1845.

47a. Drawing for the St. Michael Street Hotel, 1836; Charles Dakin, architect. The Hotel was formerly located on the northwest corner of St. Michael and Royal streets. The small Greek Revival porch of the first story is not dominant enough to break the monotony of the fenestration. The repetition of the facade elements does not reflect the irregularity of the interior plan. (Dakin Collection, courtesy of the Louisiana Division, New Orleans Public Library.)

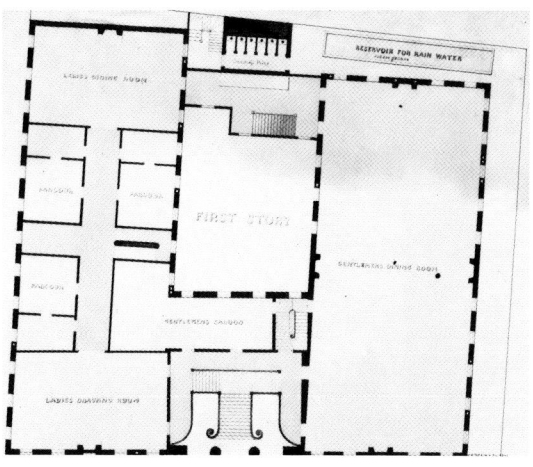

47b. Plan of the first story of the St. Michael Street Hotel; Charles Dakin, architect. The positioning of the stairways and traffic patterns leading to the different levels seems awkward. (Dakin Collection, courtesy of the Louisiana Division, New Orleans Public Library.)

48. *The Planters and Merchants Bank, 1837, as drawn by Charles and James Dakin, architects, formerly on the southeast corner of Royal and Conti and now destroyed. The Mobile Commercial Register of May 10, 1838, praised the "tout ensemble" and the interior finish but was critical of its "awkward and ungainly dome." (Dakin Collection, courtesy of the Louisiana Division, New Orleans Public Library.)*

We do not have descriptions of other hotels, but six are indicated on the La Tourrette map, and at least some were comfortable. When the actor Tyrone Power appeared in the Mobile Theatre, he was favorably impressed with his accommodations and wrote in his *Journal:* "I found here also the best conducted and best appointed hotel in the Southern country, and society congenial and amiable.—The supper was laid out most tastefully upon the galleries surrounding the inner court of the hotel, enclosed for the occasion with canvass, and the pillars wreathed with shrubs and flowers."[22]

The Planters and Merchants Bank (figure 48), another Greek Revival building, was located on the northeast corner of Royal and Conti streets in block 124a of the La Tourrette map (figure 40a). The structure was designed by Charles and James Dakin in 1837. According to the *Mobile Commercial Register* of May 10, 1838, the building was

> a superb one in finish and in architectural arrangement. The massive front Portico and the side view on Conti Street afford as fine and impressive a "tout ensemble" as we have ever seen. The dome which is fortunately for the view not visible on these two sides, is awkward and ungainly, and the observatory on its apex, which of itself is very pretty, is disproportionate to the cumbersome globe which supports it. The banking room and the entrance to it are very beautiful, and the marble pavement, the fluted columns supporting a concave ceiling, the massive pannelling, mahogany counters and fretted ceiling, give it an air of solidarity and substance which is very striking.

The drawing (figure 48) does not reflect some of the details recorded in Dakin's *Account Book*.[23] The 1861 engraving on the certificate from the Fire Department Association that is in the Mobile City Museum was done twenty-two years after the building's destruction in the 1839 fire, so that it cannot be accepted as authoritative where the building's appearance is concerned. Had the two Dakin buildings survived, both the Bank and the Hotel, Mobile's architectural record of the Greek Revival would have been greatly enriched.

The four engravings at the top of the map suggest the richness of the public architecture, but the body of the map tells the story of growth during the 1830 decade. If we judge from the development of the waterfront and the concentration of buildings along the streets of the inner city, Mobile was booming.[24] While the wooden structures would not be eliminated until after the 1839 fire, when an ordinance against them was passed, the streets, lined with rows largely of brick buildings that rose from the sidewalk, were connected by party walls, and were only occasionally individualized by some decorative detail. Surviving examples of such early stores still stand at the southeast corner of Conception and State streets (figure 49). Two stores from an original row of six that extended for 101.3 feet along State were built and advertised for rent in the January 2, 1840, *Mobile Commercial Register.* They are shown on the Troost map of 1840–1846. The facades have been reduced to the simplest terms: the brick walls are pierced by regular rows of identical windows on the second story and, at the sidewalk story, by alternating doors and windows. The gable roofs are not steeply pitched, and parapets above the party walls that form firebreaks mark the limits of the individual units. Originally each of the units had chimneys, but only one is still intact. The only elaboration in the State Street specimen is the narrow string course at the cornice level. At first glance it appears to be dentils, but upon closer inspection it can be identified as bricks set with the corners protruding to make a sawtooth pattern. Beneath this string course are two rows of bricks, one slightly projecting beyond the lower one and forming a slight shadow line along the length of the facade. This elevation characterized the majority of the storefronts of the inner city.

Some of the buildings along the waterfront were larger and more elaborate. None has survived, but extant contracts give a vivid account of them. On June 22, 1831, Charles Barney employed John Collins to construct a large building on the southwest corner of Commerce and St. Francis streets.[25] The building was located on a lot measuring 80 feet by 105.6 feet and faced out on the New York wharf. The structure occupied the whole lot and was attached to property belonging to Henry Hitchcock (figure 50). The three-story structure was brick erected on a timber foundation. It was to have an iron gallery on the facade, though Mr. Collins was not responsible for building the gallery. Mention of an iron gallery in a contract as early as 1831 is noteworthy because tradition has it that such galleries were added only later in the century. The exterior walls of the first

49. *Two remaining units of a row of six stores that once stood on the south side of State Street between Conception and St. Joseph streets, 1839, 161–167 State Street. During the 1830s the streets of Mobile's commercial district were lined with two- and three-story row stores that rose directly from the sidewalk without any galleries or balconies. (Photograph by Thigpen Photography, courtesy of the Mobile City Planning Commission.)*

story were planned to be fourteen feet high and two bricks thick. The party walls were two and a half bricks thick to the height of one foot and were thereafter only one and a half bricks thick. The gable parapets were to rise one foot above the roof. The roof was to be of the "best Welsh slate" with six dormers, three on the front and three on the rear. The specifications stated the sizes and disposition of the various structural members. The total cost of construction was determined to be $14,869, a rather high price for stores at the time.

In almost all the contracts, the first story was reserved for the conduct of public business, with the second story for the "counting rooms" and private offices. The Barney Building had three counting rooms that faced out on Commerce Street, overlooking the waterfront. Each counting room was twenty-five feet deep. The partition walls between them were formed of studs that were lathed and plastered, then painted white. These rooms must have opened on the iron galleries that are mentioned in the contract but are not described, as the builder was not responsible for them.

The building for John Hogan and Philip McLoskey was constructed by Thomas Ellison and William Littell. The building was three stories in height and was constructed of the "best Philadelphia or Baltimore brick." Like the Barney Building it was attached to already existing stores. The first story was more elaborate than the usual storefront of the times, being made of granite blocks:

> strapped to the rear brick wall which with the ballance [sic] of the first story wall are to be built two bricks thick all to commence their base on piles and have a sufficient foundation and have reverse arches of brick work under the doors and windows of the first story over which must be seasoned lintels and blind arches in the first and second stories.[26]

The stone was also planned for use on the caps of the fire walls, on the window and door sills, on the eaves and cornice, on the chimney cap, and on the plinths for the "three turned columns."

The windows of the Hogan-McLoskey Building were unusually large, those on the first story having twenty-five lights, each measuring twelve by eighteen inches in size. The second story had seven windows of eighteen lights, with the lower sash hung with weights and made to slide up into the wall above the upper sash.[27] Four of the windows had jib doors below the sash, so that, when the window was raised and the doors were opened, the space provided a passageway to the galleries. This is the first reference found to jib doors in a commercial building, though homes surviving from the period

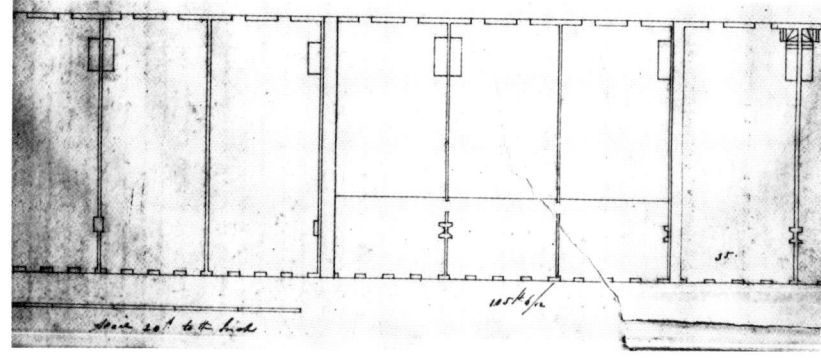

50. Plan for the row stores for Charles Barney, 1831, formerly on the southwest corner of St. Francis and Commerce streets; John Collins, builder; cost, $14,869. The building contract called for an iron gallery across the facade. (From Miscellaneous Book B, pp. 475–76, dated June 22, 1831.)

had them. The roof was covered with slate and had copper gutters. The finished building, based on this design, must have been most impressive and contrasted with simply designed stores such as those illustrated in figure 49.

More than a dozen contracts for commercial buildings have survived, and most repeat the same general design. Only a few have variations that are noteworthy. In a building for Mr. Lopez, the doors were circular headed, and the contract provided for "sash and glass in the circles of each of the two doors in the upper story."[28] The contract for the building also called for a hip roof on the east end, though a gable was specified for the west, where it presumably joined that of its neighbor. This was the first contract to specify an inside privy for a store; most called for an outside "necessary."

The foundation laid for Isaac Spear's store was unusual. It was constructed by James Barnes, the builder of Christ Church. The specifications called for:

> the foundation to be laid 2 feet below the sidewalk, the front and rear Walls to be erected on reverse arches similar to the drawing, $2\frac{1}{2}$ bricks thick, consisting of 7 Piers in front and 4 in the Rear the latter based on a segment arch of Suitable Strength to Support same, the Piers front and rear to rise from the Center of the arches and be continued to the top of the floor joists of the principal Story and $1\frac{1}{2}$ bricks thick to the same in the second Story and 1 brick to the top of the building, the side walls with footings to be carried up 2 bricks thick and to be finished on three sides with fire walls 3 feet high—the principal floor to be laid upon a brick pavement on earth well ramed down to be $1\frac{1}{2}$ inch plank jointed and laid snug together—the roof to be sheathed with 1 inch board tongue and groove—the perlines to run out over the opening far enough to rig a Hoisting Tackle.[29]

In view of the prevalent concern with fire walls and with precautions such as slate for roofs and brick construction, it may seem odd that the 1839 fire could have been so devastating. It must be remembered that timber still played an important part in all the interior framing—in the joists, flooring, roof trussing, and so forth. Water pressure was inadequate, and when a fire started in the closely packed buildings, little could be done to stop it except demolish buildings in its path. To help combat fires, the Creole and Neptune fire companies had been organized in 1819. During the 1830s, six more were created: the Franklin Number Three in 1833; the Merchants Number Four in 1836; the Torrent Number Five in 1838; the Phoenix in 1838; the Mechanics Number Seven in 1839; and the Hook and Ladder Company Number One in 1839.[30]

Richard Redwood, a contractor associated with many public buildings, including Barton, built one of the fire engine houses. The city offered a prize to the first company that reached a fire. The Neptune Fire Company was paid twenty dollars for arriving first at a fire on April 9, 1831. The March 6, 1839, ban on the building of frame structures within the inner city also helped eliminate fires in later decades. In October of the same year, the regulation's jurisdiction was extended to St. Anthony on the north, to Monroe on the south, and to Franklin on the west.[31]

Without an adequate water supply, the fire companies could do little, so in 1830 the city borrowed $35,000 from "Capitalists of Philadelphia" for the purpose of enlarging the supply of water. A new system was established at the old 1828 site at Judge Lipscomb's spring. A large "setting reservoir" was excavated near the spring, from which wood pipes, hollowed out from yellow pine logs and banded with iron, would carry the water to two main reservoirs in town, each reservoir holding 14,000 gallons of water.[32] From these two sources the water was carried to locations convenient for the people and to twelve "cast iron hydrants" for the attachment of fire hoses. This system served the community until Albert Stein took over the equipment and founded the Stein Water Company.

The commercial development of the decade closed with the introduction of steam power. By 1839 sawmills had substituted steam for mule power. The La Tourrette map shows several steam-powered mills. The Deshon Steam Saw Mill was located on block 36 of the map (figure 40a), on Water Street, south of what was then called Massachusetts and is now Charleston. The Brown Steam Saw Mill (figure 40a, block 48) was on Water Street south of Rhode Island, now known as Savannah. The Miscellaneous Books contain contracts for some of the mills outside the city limits.[33]

Government Buildings

The years 1834 and 1835 were ones of great dreams and plans. A block of land in the heart of the city was selected as a site for a municipal building. There the long-anticipated City Hall would be erected. An architectural contest was held for the best design. A plan for the Mobile City Hall signed by Gallier and Dakin and dated 1836 has been preserved (figures 51a, b). There is a record in the Mobile Treasurer's Day Book that James Gallier was paid $250 for first prize, with $150 going to James Longheus for second prize. Except for the stipend, this account agrees with a statement in Gallier's *Autobiography*: "The Corporation of the City of Mobile, having decided upon building a Town Hall, advertised for plans, and we made a design for it which obtained the first prize of three hundred dollars; though but a trifle, it served to place our name before the public; but in consequence of a fire, in which a large portion of Mobile was destroyed, the Hall was never built."[34]

In the lower right corner of the drawing is a small sketch that resembles another drawing (figure 51b), possibly an alternate design. The impressive Greek Revival porticoes with columns were featured in both plans. While Gallier suggested that the fire prevented the construction from proceeding, other factors were involved; the fire did not happen until 1839. On August 28, 1835—five months after the Gallier and Dakin plans had been accepted—an advertisement appeared in the newspaper soliciting bids by November 1 "for erecting City Hall, according to a small plan of Thomas Ellison." The request further stipulated that the construction would have to be finished within eighteen months. While it does not appear on the La Tourrette map, the structure is recorded in the 1839 City Directory as being on the south side of Conti near the corner of St. Emanuel and is listed as number sixty-nine. The Troost map of 1840–1846 shows this corner lot measuring 125 feet on each side as municipal

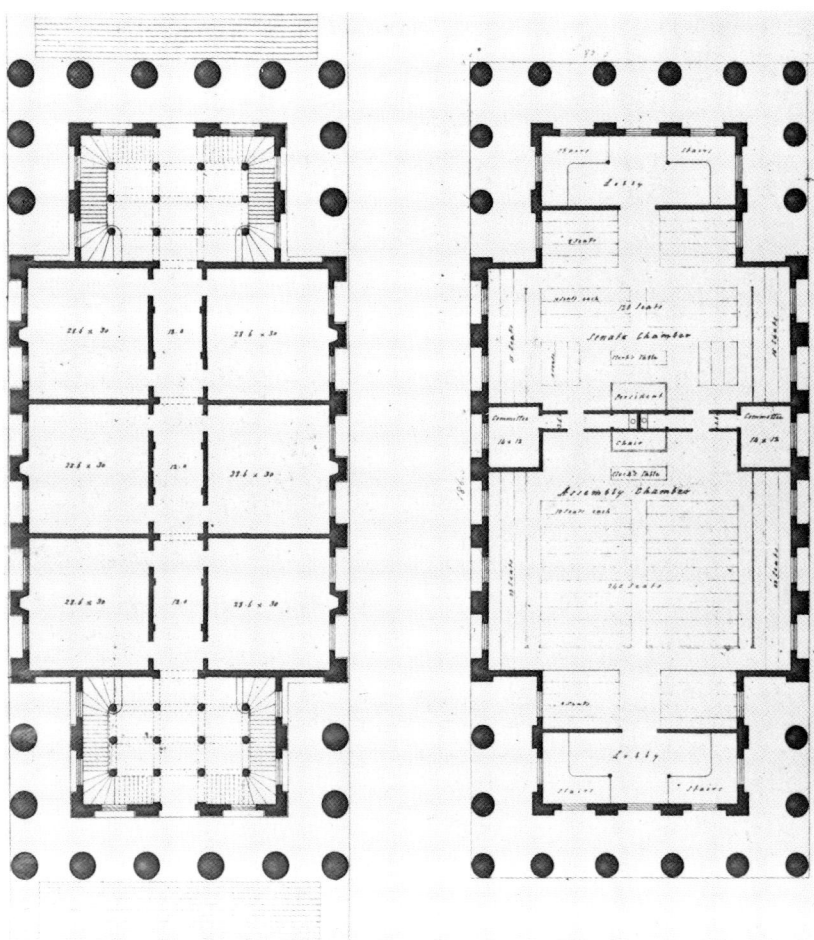

51a. Proposed plan for a city hall, 1836; Gallier and Dakin, architects. The building was planned for construction on the block of the present Bienville Square. Because of adverse economic conditions it was never erected. (Dakin Collection, courtesy of the Louisiana Division, New Orleans Public Library.)

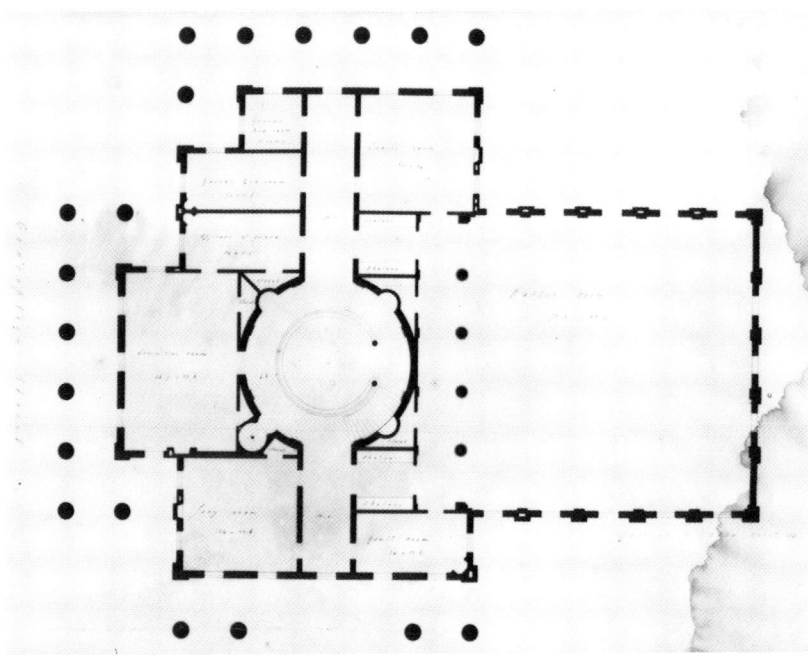

51b. A second proposal for a city hall, believed to be for Mobile; Gallier and Dakin, architects. A small plan at the lower right of the first drawing (figure 51a) not visible in the photograph, seems to be a sketch for the second drawing. According to the Mobile Treasurer's Day Book, March 13, 1835, James Gallier was paid for the plans submitted in the competition. There are drawings for the domed building in both the Dakin Collection of the New Orleans Public Library and the Historic New Orleans Collection of the Kemper and Leila Williams Foundation. (Dakin Collection, courtesy of the Louisiana Division, New Orleans Public Library.)

property. The original site selected for the City Hall was not used and would later become Bienville Square.[35]

To the east of Ellison's City Hall was the 1829 Guard House that had been built by Quigley and Henderson. During the 1830s this building continued to serve but saw improvements during several periods, the most important being the addition of a watch tower twenty feet high and fifteen feet in diameter. On top of the tower was a cupola for the town clock. The general design of this tower would be repeated in the 1842 building that would replace the facility burned down in 1839. The actual plans for the new building had been made in 1839. It was a three-story brick building with a tower that was to have a belfry for the fire bells and an "observatory." The complex was not completed until June 15, 1841, at a cost of $6,397, which was paid to the builder, Mr. Bloodgood (figure 77).[36]

The largest and most impressive of the governmental buildings of the decade was the County Prison. On August 28, 1839, the county selected a block of land behind the City Hospital site that belonged to Mr. Kennedy (figure 52). The contract for the building was signed between Frederick Bunnell, architect, and the Board of Commissioners of Roads and Revenue of the County of Mobile. Frederick Bunnell was mentioned in the Christ Church Minutes as an architect in connection with the building. He also built, during the next decade, the United States Marine Hospital that still stands on St. Anthony Street. The Prison was constructed by the builder John K. Collins, who had built the Mobile City Hospital. At first only the western cells and central block were erected. They were finished within eighteen months. The eastern wing was not added until 1860. The central section was to house the keeper of the Prison and his family. The projected cost of $25,000 seems inadequate for the granite structure, even considering the dollar's purchasing power at the time. The western central cell block was a model for security. It was isolated in an open interior space that rose from floor to roof. The contract (see figure 239) provided for:

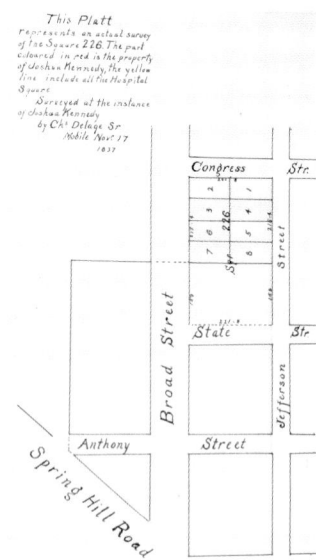

52. Survey of square 226 made by Charles Delage, November 17, 1837. The land was purchased by the County of Mobile for the erection of the new County Jail. (From Deed Book T, p. 302.)

> a block of granite cells thirty two by twenty four feet Square Height of first Story in the Clear, Seven and half feet and the third story seven feet in the clear the second story also seven feet in the clear. The walls to be built of Granite slabs eight inches thick each and reach from bottom to top of a Single Story and to have closed Joists filled in cement. The covering with each range of cells to be heavy stone not less than six inches thick reaching from wall to wall and forming the floor of the cells above. The whole work to be well anchored with strong iron anchors as in the best northern Prisons.
>
> The door hangings and fastenings all to be let into the Granite. Twenty four cells on the first and second Story to measure Eleven feet by four feet and $\frac{6}{8}$ Inches. Cells in the third Story to measure Eleven feet by nine feet and $\frac{3}{8}$ inches as Seen in the drawing.[37]

Every aspect of the Prison was carefully considered—the type of iron doors, fastenings, windows, ventilation grilles, and so forth. An iron balcony was to surround the second and third stories.

Not only was the building well secured, but a wall was built around the lot by John Williams and James Murphy.[38] The foundation was sunk two feet below the surface of the ground and was brick with good cement made of "Choctaw Point sand" with "pillars every nine feet." The top coursing of the fence carried pieces of bottles set in cement. The Prison was still standing during the first quarter of the twentieth century and was demolished in order to make way for a rear wing of the Hospital. The granite blocks were carried out and dumped on a lot in Spring Hill, where they remained until they were used to build a fine house in the western part of the city.

The condition of the Powder Magazine received much attention during the early years of the 1830s. The building had been erected in 1825 and was not architecturally important, but it was a necessity for the town, for it not only housed the powder belonging to the city but also was the repository for all private supplies. The keeper of the magazine was responsible for keeping an inventory and for submitting monthly reports as to amounts withdrawn or deposited, whether public or private. By 1833, the old building had become inadequate, and new provisions had to be made. After considering several locations, the old site west of City Hospital was deemed the best, being far enough from town for safety and yet close enough for convenience. The minutes of December 7, 1833, record the plans that were received and, with slight changes, were approved on December 16. The building was only one story in height, measured thirty feet by fifty feet, and had a twelve-foot-high brick wall enclosing it.[39]

Residential Buildings

City Dwellings of Wood

Wood remained the material of choice for residences and even for the shop-house complex if it lay outside the zone within which brick alone could be used. One such home and business combined stood on the southwest corner of Conti and Franklin. It was built by John Springsteel for Richard St. John.[40] In the two-story building only the center room of the first story was used as a shop, the rest being the residence. The store facade was equipped with two six-foot doors with shutters and two large windows of sixteen lights each. In one of the first-story private rooms was a staircase leading to the upper floor, with another staircase in the rear. The second story was divided into four rooms that were separated by a central hall. A gallery, or "piazer," was mentioned in the contract. The gallery of the St. John House extended across both the Conti and Franklin street facades. It was five feet wide with turned columns, round railing, and square balusters. Since none of the early wood galleries has survived, the descriptions in the contracts are of great value. The ceiling of the galleries was plastered, as were the interior walls.

Throughout the decade the cottage remained the most popular house form. It stayed small, averaging between twenty-four feet long and twenty feet deep to thirty-six feet long and twenty-eight feet deep (figure 54). Cottages were one or one and a half stories in height, raised on a brick foundation ranging from three feet to six feet high. All had galleries (figure 53). One contract specified that the rear gallery should be enclosed at either end by a small room measuring eight feet by ten feet. The galleries ranged in depth from six to eight feet, with either dressed weatherboarding or tongue-and-groove siding on the porch wall. Tongue-and-groove siding was preferred for the ceilings. Of the six examples that I have chosen to illustrate the group, five called for turned columns supporting the gallery and one called for supports of square section. Of the cottages studied, all but one was painted white. The one exception required that the porch columns and railings be painted yellow.[41]

In plan the cottages had no central hall and continued to have two rooms side by side or doubled in depth to make four. Occasionally the rear space was divided into three rooms. A front door opened up into each of the two front rooms, but only one was embellished with a transom, indicating that it would lead into the public parlor (figures 53 and 54). The two rear doors leading from the back rooms to the rear gallery had no transoms. In the contract that specified yellow trim for the porch, the doors were painted to resemble oak. There is no reference to graining, but it seems implied. Windows were double-sash, usually six-over-six lights, with panes of glass measuring ten inches by fourteen inches to ten inches by sixteen inches. Garret windowpanes were six inches by ten inches.

The interiors were quite simple in finish. Doors were usually paneled, but one called for board and batten.[42] Floors were yellow pine six or seven inches wide and one and one-quarter inches thick. Tongue-and-groove floors were reserved for the main rooms, with rough flooring in the garrets. Ceilings were plastered. Kitchens were unattached, and specifications for them are frequently given in the contracts.

The differences in the cottages are apparent in the roof lines and in the type of columns used in the galleries. These changed as the decade progressed. The earliest example of a cottage that I shall discuss is the Ayers House (figures 55a, b). It was once located on the east side of Hamilton, mid-block between Government and Conti streets, near the rear patio of Bernard's Restaurant.[43] There is no hint of the Greek Revival in this cottage. The roof line continues the broken pitch of the early Creole cottage, with the steep central section covering the house proper and then flaring out over the gallery. This structure contrasts with the 1834 Eslava-McMahon House (figure 56), now destroyed, and with the extant cottage standing at 259 North Conception Street (figures 57a,b). In both, the break in the pitch has been eliminated, giving a continuous slope to the gable. In the Conception Street example, a small rear wing cut off part of the rear gallery. This change in plan became more and more popular as city lots became narrower with the increased value placed on frontage.

The change in the shape of the columns reflects a time change also. In the Ayers House (figures 55a–d), the simple square posts lack additional refinement. But by 1837, as shown in the Pascal Larrouil House, the columns have been altered by the influence of the Greek Revival (figure 58). Not only do the columns have a round section, but they are tapered and have a slight entasis.[44] This change in columnar form gives the character of the old cottage a stately quality not seen in the earlier examples. The balustrade style also changed. The early round-top railing became flattened into an oval, and the balusters were no longer always square but were often turned. In the restoration of the Hunter cottage (figure 57), a section of the original balustrade was found embedded in a partition wall that had been added onto the gallery. The balustrade was of the earlier type, with round rail and swallowtail cut at the bottom of the balusters.

The transformation of design by classical detailing is evident

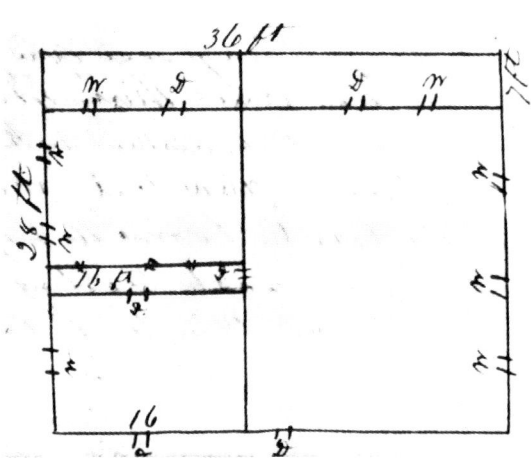

53. The Dade House, 1834, 503 St. Francis Street. A transitional cottage type, retaining the plan and massing of the 1820s but with the roof pitch straightened and dormers added. One of the few examples to have survived the fire of 1839, which destroyed that section of the city. (Photograph by Michael Thomason.)

54. Plan for a cottage, originally located on St. Francis Street; James H. Hutchisson, architect-builder; cost, $1,300. The cottage was raised three and a half feet above ground level. The gallery was seven feet deep and extended the length of the facade. The interior was plastered and painted. (From Miscellaneous Book C, p. 183, dated October 3, 1838.)

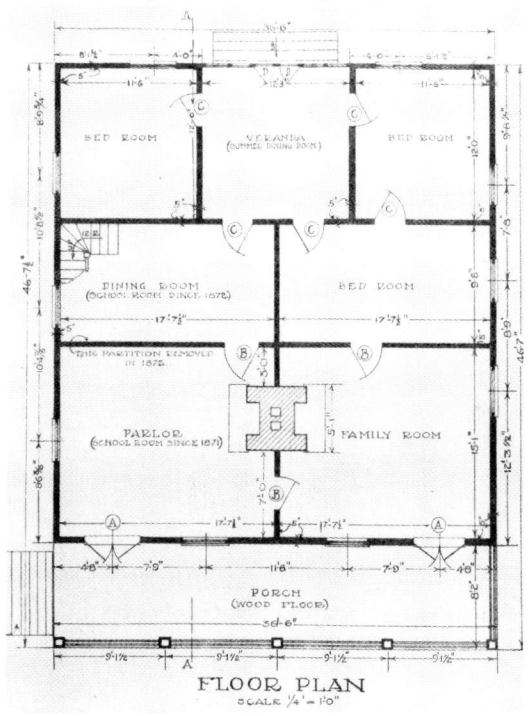

55a. The Ayers cottage, ca. 1832, formerly located on the east side of Hamilton between Government and Conti streets and now destroyed. One of the last cottages built with a roof that still retained the broken pitch. Before its demolition the house was known as Madame Robert's School. (Courtesy of the University of South Alabama Photographic Archives, McNeely Collection.)

55b. Plan of the Ayers cottage. The four rooms with rear gallery enclosed by end rooms form a pattern that is typical of the early cottages. (Drawing by P. V. Chaudron, courtesy of the Library of Congress, Historic American Building Survey Collection.)

The Greek Revival, 1830–1840

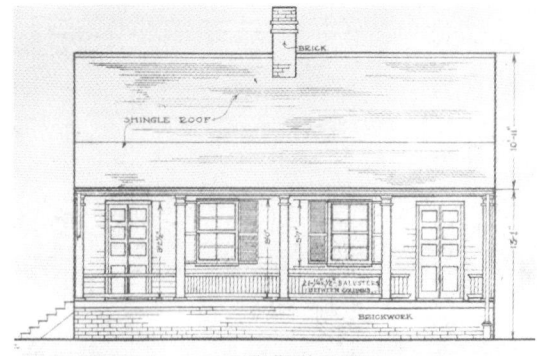
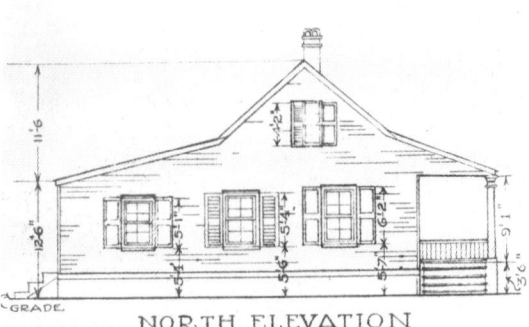

55c. West front elevation of the Ayers House. Each of the front rooms has a separate entrance from the gallery. The stairway is on the side, not the front, built close to the sidewalk. (Courtesy of the Library of Congress, Historic American Building Survey Collection.)

55d. North side elevation of the Ayers cottage. (Drawing by P. V. Chaudron, courtesy of the Library of Congress, Historic American Building Survey Collection.)

56. The Eslava-McMahon cottage, 1834, formerly on the northeast corner of St. Francis and Lawrence streets, now destroyed. The cottage is similar in massing to the Dade home, but the plan has been altered by a central hall and the entrance embellished with sidelights. In 1839 the tax value was $7,000. (Courtesy of the Historic Mobile Preservation Society, Brooks Collection.)

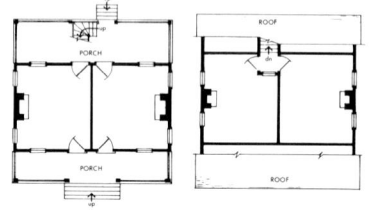

57b. Plan of the original Hunter cottage suggested by an architectural inspection of the building; restoration adviser, Thomas F. Karwinski, AIA. (Drawing by Thomas F. Karwinski, AIA.)

57a. The Hunter cottage, 1836, 259 North Conception Street. One of the houses from the 1830s decade that is still standing in the de Tonti Square Historic District. A recent restoration disclosed a section of the original balustrade with the swallowtail cut of the balusters embedded in a wall of the rear wing.

From Fort to Port

58. *The Pascal Larrouil cottage, before 1837, formerly at 252 South Claiborne, now destroyed. By 1836 the Greek Revival had begun to influence the cottage form, making the columns more classical, smoothing the surface of the gallery wall either by tongue and groove or by plastering, and giving greater emphasis to the central axis. (Courtesy of the Historic Mobile Preservation Society.)*

59. *The Hall House, 1836, 165 St. Emanuel Street. A two-story Greek Revival porch has been added to an older type of building in which the frame story was raised high above a brick ground level. (Photograph by E. W. Russell, courtesy of the Library of Congress, Historic American Building Survey Collection.)*

throughout the decade. It can be seen in the Hall-Ford House of 1836 (figure 59), located at 165 St. Emanuel Street. It is not the typical all-wood, two-story home, nor is it a cottage, since it is two and a half stories high. It somewhat resembles a wide cottage placed high on a brick foundation that has been enlarged as a first story. The upper story is covered by a slight break in the slope of the roof, like that in the earlier form, but the observer's first impression is that it is Greek Revival. The two-story porch of five bays has fluted Doric columns, and fluted pilasters frame the dormer windows. Fortunately the original hardware in the Hall-Ford House is still intact.

All the doors were equipped with Carpenter locks, which appear to have gained popularity about 1835, if we may judge from the contracts of the decade. Carpenter locks were made in England in about 1795 but were not patented until 1823. In 1830 the patent bore the name of Carpenter and Young, and in 1856 the company became known as Carpenter and Tildesley, so that the name on the lock helps to date the hardware. Most of the locks in Mobile belong to the Carpenter-Young period and are marked "Carpenter and Company, patentees," suggesting a date between 1823 and 1830. All have the small circular brass "penny" inserted on the face of the lock box. The innovation in these locks was that the bolt could be drawn back into the lock by means of a knob or a key.[45]

60a. Bishop Portier cottage, ca. 1834, 307 Conti Street. A cottage given highly refined detailing in the treatment of the entrance and the dormer framing. The cottage was the residence of Michael Portier, the first bishop of Mobile.

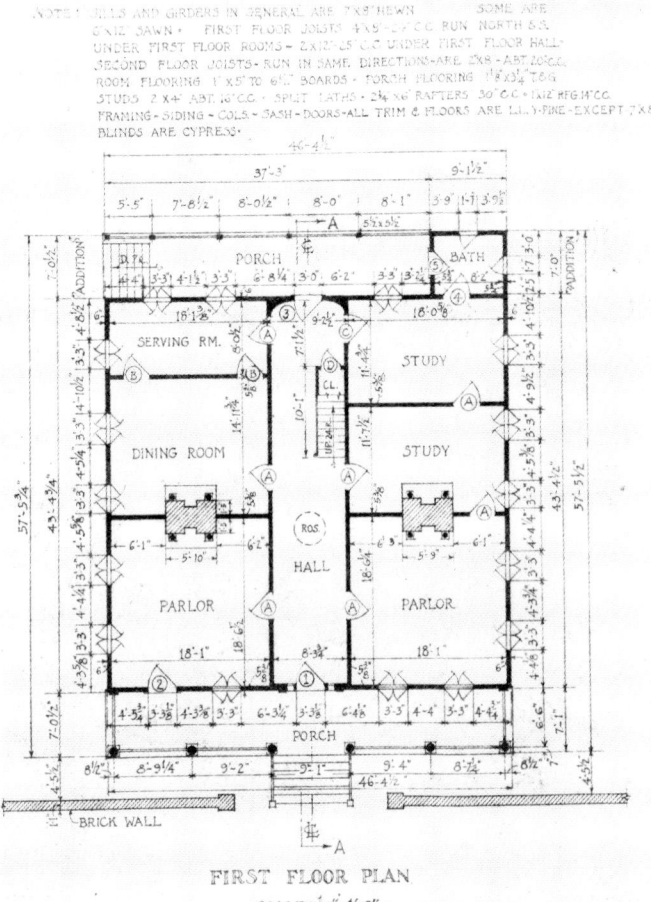

60b. Plan of Bishop Portier's cottage. The central hall is graced by an unusual stairway balustrade in which the balusters are shaped like arrows. The formal plan is broken only by the door on the left, which leads into the room serving as an office. (Drawing by G. Chaudron, courtesy of the Library of Congress, Historic American Building Survey Collection.)

In style, the one-and-a-half-story Bishop Portier cottage of 1834 has lost much of the early Creole influence.[46] Here a sophisticated use of classical motifs suggests that refinements of the Adams brothers and other Federal decor were being incorporated; only the massing continues the early form (figures 60a–e). The treatment of the main entrance is noteworthy. The door is framed by pilasters that rise to an entablature with a very narrow architrave and a frieze that contains closely packed triglyphs and metopes, all crowned by a

60c. East side elevation of the Bishop Portier cottage. (Drawing by G. Chaudron, courtesy of the Library of Congress, Historic American Building Survey Collection.)

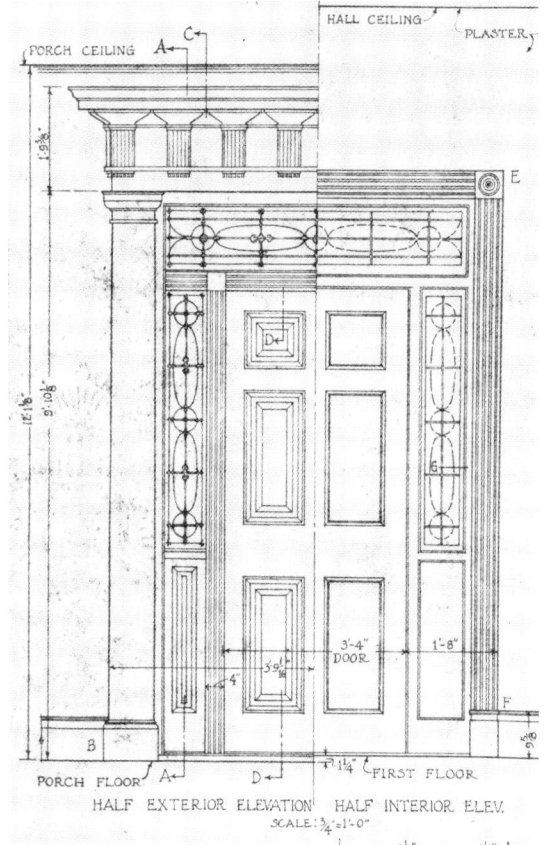

60d. Half exterior and half interior view of details of front door of the Bishop Portier cottage. The delicacy of the detailing and the proportions suggest Federal refinements. (Drawing by G. Chaudron, courtesy of the Library of Congress, Historic American Building Survey Collection.)

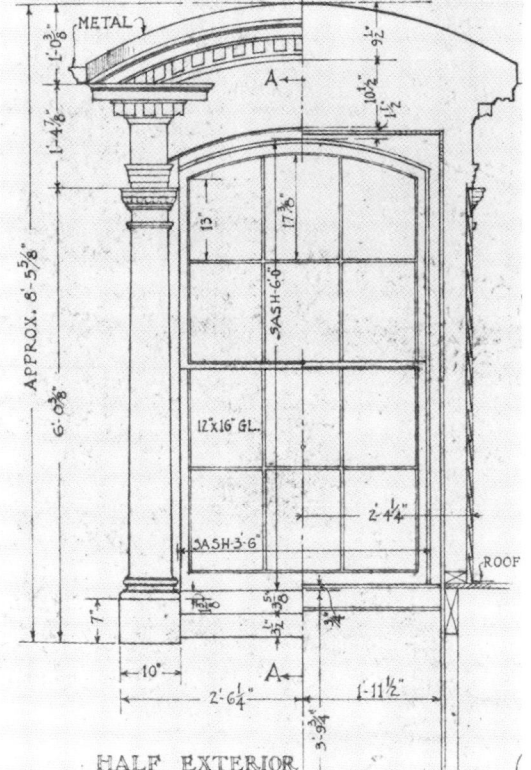

60e. The dormer surround of the Bishop Portier cottage. The segmental architrave is embellished with moldings, and a small dentil course accents the cornice. (Drawing by G. Chaudron, courtesy of the Library of Congress, Historic American Building Survey Collection.)

molding. The transom and sidelights have delicate muntins forming patterns of circles, ovals, and rectangles (figure 60c). The facade windows are casements and are probably a later alteration, for all the rest of the windows are double sash, with six-over-six lights. The upper panes of the three dormer windows have curved heads. Slender colonnettes frame the dormer sashes and rise to a broken pediment that is accented by small dentils (figure 60c). The design of the cottage is attributed to Claude Beroujon, a young seminarian brought from France by Bishop Portier. It is not known whether Beroujon had had any formal architectural training, but he was responsible for several buildings, among them the first Administration Building for Spring Hill College and the body of the Cathedral, though not its facade—buildings that I shall consider later.

The Beal-Hunter House at 205 North Conception Street (1836) completes the transformation of the one-story frame house into a Greek Revival dwelling (figure 61). Here the axis of the old cottage has been reoriented so that the gable end faces the street, creating an elevation that can be called the "temple" facade. Six well-proportioned fluted Doric columns articulate the five bays of the porch, forming a prostyle plan, with the entablature and pediment continuing the typical temple division. On either side of the central entrance are two doors with the upper half glazed and the lower half infilled with molded panels.

None of the original wood fences remains, but the extant contract for one permits an accurate description of their design. Miscellaneous Book C (page 112) carries the description of a fence ordered by the Gordon Land Company for a house to be built on Conception Street. The house was to have been built by Charles Dakin, but it was finished by B. Davenport. The fence was made of wood and stood five feet four inches high, with pickets made of two-and-one-half-inch-by-one-inch boards placed one and one-half inches apart (figure 62). The bottom rail was twelve inches wide by one and one-half inches thick and molded. The top rail was five inches wide by one and one-half inches thick, laid flat upon the top of the posts. The posts were made of cedar with a mushroom-shaped cap. The pickets were sharply pointed.

Some large wood homes were built during the years 1838–1839 in

61. *The Beal-Hunter cottage, ca. 1836, 205 North Conception Street. The earliest surviving example of a cottage in the de Tonti Square Historic District in which the Greek Revival influence reoriented the axis of the structure so that the gable faced the street, thus lending itself to the "temple" elevation.*

spite of the 1837 depression. Two of the most impressive were the Hamilton home on Government Street and the Dorman home on State Street, both of which have now been destroyed but are well documented by their contracts.[17] In the Dorman home a side-hall plan was adopted. This plan became more and more popular for large city houses. Two large parlors, each measuring seventeen feet by eighteen feet, ranged along one side of the hall. The two rooms were connected by folding doors, the framing for which became an important element in the decor. A front piazza (the contracts do not refer to "galleries" in these large houses) was eight feet wide, with four columns connected by a balustrade. The ceilings of the rooms were high, the first story twelve feet in the clear and the second ten feet. The back piazza was enclosed by a closet at one end and a pantry at the other, each measuring seven feet by nine feet. As can be seen in the plan (figure 63), the second story has three fairly large rooms above the two downstairs parlors, with smaller rooms at either end of the upstairs hall. The interior walls were plastered throughout and were painted with "pure lead and oil." Carpenter locks were stipulated for all doors. The unattached two-story kitchen was seventeen feet by twenty-one feet, with a four-foot-wide porch. The first story of this dependency was used as a "cook room and wash room," with a large fireplace and oven in the kitchen. The privy was included in the contract and was described as a "two compartment." A picket fence on a brick foundation was to have the wood elements made of "cedar or cypress." The cost for the whole complex, including the fencing, was listed as $4,100.

The Hamilton home was much more elaborate. The builder was Joseph Vaughan, though the contract named three builders, C. Shaw, B. H. White, and J. S. Vaughan. The entire complex included the house, a two-story brick kitchen, a stable with carriage house, a privy, a special bathhouse, and yards for chickens and for horses, all

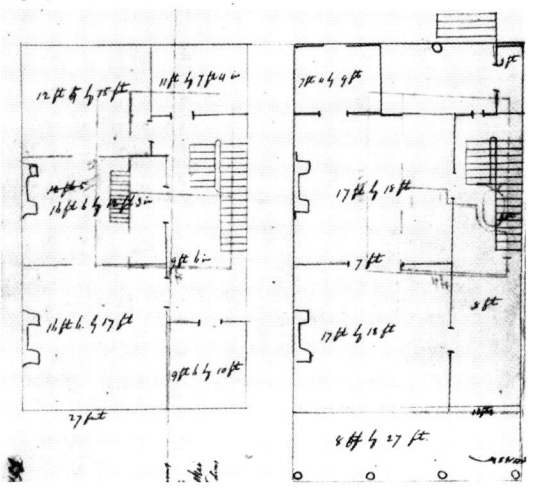

63. Plan for a two-story house from a contract between Benjamin Dorman, owner, and Walker and Nadine, builders, formerly located on St. Louis and Claiborne streets and now destroyed. (From Miscellaneous Book C, pp. 132–33, dated June 9, 1838.)

62. Contract for a picket fence with instructions for shaping the pickets, rails, and posts, dated July 15, 1838. (From Miscellaneous Book C, p. 112; detail only.)

64. *The Gazzam House, formerly near the southeast corner of Government and Ann streets. In 1839 it was taxed at a value of $15,000; it is now destroyed. A fine example of a large Greek Revival home of the 1830s. The refinements of the dormer enframement, the well-proportioned columns, and the wide central-hall entrance with transom and sidelights all reflect the wealth and taste of the time. (Photograph by E. Russell, courtesy of the Library of Congress, Historic American Building Survey Collection.)*

surrounded by 1,600 feet of picket fencing made of cypress. There were six separate entrance gates. Beside the main section of the two-story house, there were two one-story wings, each twenty feet by thirty-two feet, that projected at the back, thus creating a U-shaped plan. A front piazza extended the full width of the facade, and each wing was fronted along its length by a porch. Sixteen "handsomely turned columns" stood on the porches, those on the front being fluted. There were three flights of stairs leading up to the second story, all made of cypress. An unusual feature of the house was a cellar. It measured fifteen feet by eighteen feet, with nine-inch-thick brick walls. (Since the water table in Mobile is very high, cellars were, and are, a rarity.) Another unusual feature was closets. The house had closets not only in each bedroom but also built against the back wall of the rear parlor. With the advent of closets the decline of the armoire had begun.

The finish given the house made it outstanding. The front door and windows were framed by pilasters with "turned corner blocks." The main entrance had both transom and sidelights. The doors had "double faced panelling" and Carpenter locks in all cases. Three coats of plaster covered the interior walls, and even the privy had two coats. Hand-formed plaster moldings and "center pieces" completed the room decor. Mahogany was specified for the main staircase, though cypress was used for all construction. The two-story brick kitchen was covered with slate, an added protection against fire, and attached to the rear of the kitchen house was the special "bath house" fitted to "receive a bathing tub." This was Mobile's first reference to the permanent bathing room.[48]

The one large city house that survived long enough to be photographed was the Gazzam House (figure 64). The documentation by the Historic American Building Survey verifies the refinements that existed in the 1830 homes of the well-to-do and the skill of the builders that produced them. The detailing of the well-proportioned dormers and the delicacy of the sheaf-of-wheat balustrade are ample evidence (figure 64).

City Dwellings of Brick

Brick was used for residences only in the inner city and did not become a common material in country homes for many decades. The ideal combination was a brick home in the city for use during the "winter season" and a wooden house in the country for summer occupancy. None of the brick dwellings of the decade has survived. Of the two structures discussed below, one is only a single unit of what was once a row of twelve built to house "widows of good character."[49]

Photographs of destroyed buildings, as well as contracts, have survived, and so we have some knowledge of brick homes. The general form was a vernacular adaptation of eastern city styles. The buildings were two to four stories in height and were built to rise directly from the sidewalk, without any green strip or fencing in front (figure 65). The narrow axis of the house faced the street, so that the building fit into the narrow but deep city lot. Interior space was achieved by means of a rear wing, which was often as long as the body of the house itself. One such home was built for Frances Ferard by the builders Neville, Silver, Miller, and Sadler early in the year 1840. The dimensions of the house were 37.4 feet across the front by 50 feet deep.[50] In plan the houses had parlors along a side hall. The twin interior end chimneys were connected on the exterior by a solid brick parapet. The main decorative feature of the facade was a small dentil course, marking a very shallow cornice. To this basic form a cast iron balcony might be added or, rarely, as in the James-Ottenstein House (figures 66a–d), a Greek Revival porch.

There were three types of brick structures: the single-family unit (figure 67), the double-family unit (figures 66a–d), and the row buildings. Contracts for the brick houses reveal two important points. The solid walls were commonly formed by setting twenty bricks per cubic foot, and the workmen were paid from fourteen to seventeen dollars per thousand bricks laid. There was no such thing as an hourly wage.[51]

The Staylor House (figure 65) has been destroyed, but it stood long enough to be documented by the Historic American Building Survey. It is an excellent illustration of the development of rental property. The building was located on the corner of St. Francis and Hamilton

65. *Staylor Apartment House, 1834–1836, formerly on the southwest corner of St. Francis and Hamilton streets, now destroyed. The early brick domestic rental property was of the same style as the commercial buildings, with the built-up parapet between the end chimneys and the geometric massing. In the residences the balcony was common. (Erik Overbey/Mobile Public Library Collection, University of South Alabama Photographic Archives.)*

streets, with a seventy-foot front on St. Francis and sixty-five feet on Hamilton. It largely filled the lot, as shown by the photograph made in 1936 by the Historic American Building Survey (figure 65). The site is now an abandoned parking lot, overgrown and neglected. In 1834, Mr. Staylor combined two lots into one. He must have built his complex soon after, because in 1839 he was taxed for property valued at $8,000. The two-and-a-half-story house represents the typical brick town dwelling on an enlarged scale, with the built-up end chimney parapets, the cast iron balcony on brackets along St. Francis Street, and the on-the-sidewalk elevation. On the Hamilton Street side, a one-story brick wall sheltered the courtyard from the main building and the long servants' dependency on the south, providing privacy. A decorative molding with a dentil course marks the level between the first and second stories on the Hamilton Street side.

The James-Ottenstein House (figure 66) stood on the west side of Jackson, near State Street. It was built by Thomas James, who had been associated with the construction of several of Charles Dakin's buildings. James purchased the large corner lot in 1837 and was in the process of building the house during the end of 1838, for the 1839 Tax Records list him as having an "unfinished house, $9,500.00" in value. By 1842, the property had left James's ownership, and by 1863 it was in the possession of the Ottenstein family, for whom it has been named.[52] Behind the imposing two-story Greek Revival porch is the massing of a typical brick building, but because it is a double house, the visual effect of the side-hall plan is lost. The four dormers appear out of place above the roof of the porch balustrade that partially hides them. The eight-light doorways may well have been a later alteration, for they are more typical of Mobile after mid-century than before.

The Louise Cavallero House is still standing at 7 North Jackson, though the first-story facade has been altered to serve various commercial uses. In 1880 the building was used as both a residence and a shop, with the owners living in the second story and running a millinery shop on the first level. The entrance to the original single-family residence was on the right bay, with three windows ranging across

66a. The James-Ottenstein double house, 1838–1839, formerly on the southwest corner of Jackson and State streets and now destroyed. This large brick double house with a classical two-story porch was built and owned by Thomas James, architect-builder. In 1839 he was taxed for an "unfinished house" valued at $9,500. (Photograph by E. W. Russell, courtesy of the Library of Congress, Historic American Building Survey Collection.)

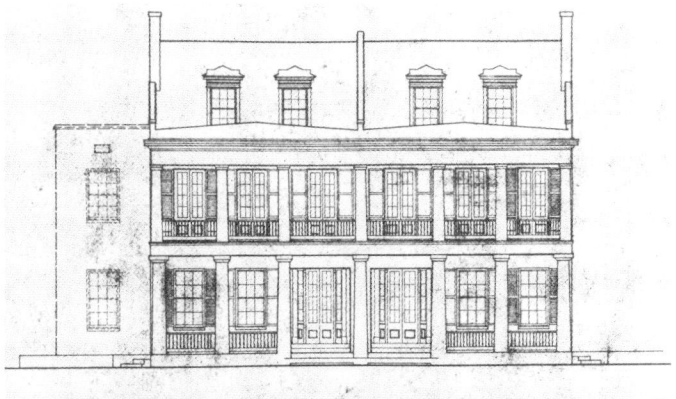

66b. Elevation drawing of the James-Ottenstein House. The double plan of the house is indicated by the doors, the slight pedimentation of the parapet above each half, and the central fire wall that divides the roof. (Drawing by Charles Rubira and D. L. Knapp, courtesy of the Library of Congress, Historic American Building Survey Collection.)

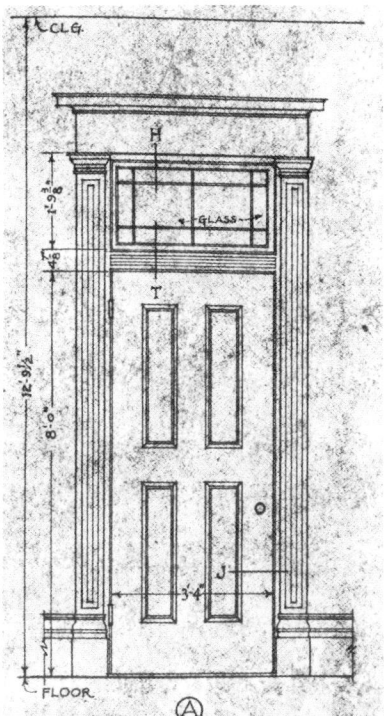

66c. Detail of the interior door surround of the James-Ottenstein House. The paneled jambs and high transom enframe the four-panel door popular in the 1830s. (Drawing by C. Rubira and D. L. Knapp, courtesy of the Library of Congress, Historic American Building Survey Collection.)

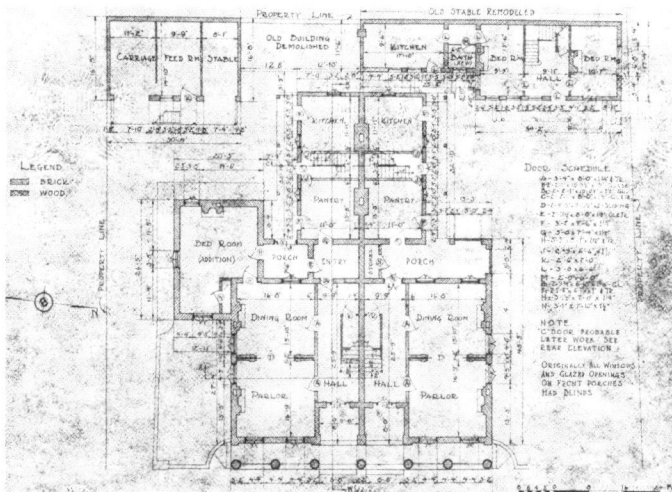

66d. Plan of the James-Ottenstein double house. (Drawing by C. Rubira and D. L. Knapp, courtesy of the Library of Congress, Historic American Building Survey Collection.)

to the left. The central window of the three has now been made into the entrance to the first story, and the original right door leads up a stairway to a separate upper apartment. Two dormers on both the front and rear slopes of the roof have fine detailing, with the upper lights curved in a shallow segmental arch and fluted pilasters that frame the double-sashed windows.[53] The other windows of the facade have had their sashes altered. The small dentil course at the cornice is typical. The Sanborn map of 1885 indicates that there was once a balcony at the second story. The building has recently been purchased for restoration (figure 67).

The Widows' Row unit (figure 68) is the last of the row of twelve that once extended along the whole block on the north side of Eslava, between Warren and Dearborn. The complex was built as a result of the combined philanthropic efforts of Henry Hitchcock and the Female Benevolent Society, which in 1829 perceived a need to assist "impecunious widows." Each unit consisted of a large room about eighteen feet square with a fireplace for cooking. Each had its own entrance, but each two shared a walkway that divided at the low porch. Each had a small garden plot in front and a rear service yard with a well. The Benevolent Society and the churches donated money to support the widows, furnishing them with food, fuel, and other necessities. When the twelve units became too small to serve the growing need, the Benevolent Society purchased the Gazzam House (figure 64) as the widows' residence. Many of the widows were not happy with the move; they lost their semiindependence, and they could no longer cook what they wanted.[54] A few were allowed to remain in the central sections of the original units. In 1897 the complex became the property of the orphanage sponsored by St. John's Episcopal Church, which faced on Monroe Street. The buildings had fallen into disrepair, and soon after the change of ownership, all but two of the units were demolished. This remnant was adapted for use as an infirmary for sick children in the orphanage. A wood addition was made on the rear, and a Victorian porch was added on the front. In 1916 St. John's Church was relocated, and the last section of Widows' Row became slum housing. With the advent of the Community Development Program, the building was purchased for restoration.

Rows of individual brick homes were also built in the 1830s (figure 69). Bloodgood Row once stood in the 300 block of Monroe Street. Its raised three-story units were much sought after by the upper economic class. The surviving photograph illustrates the dilapidated condition into which inner-city homes fell when the wealth moved farther west.

Country Dwellings

A town cannot expand without roads to provide transportation into and away from the commercial centers. The Mobile city and county records of the years 1830–1840 abound with contracts for cutting new roads as well as improving already established streets. Land was opened for settlement south to Choctaw Point and north for the platting of Orange Grove. To the west the area between the city limits and Spring Hill was filling with homes. As in the large wooden city house, the rural complex consisted of a main house and an unattached kitchen that usually had two stories with stables, carriage houses (also often two stories), a necessary, and other rural buildings that were not needed in the city but would be called for on a small farm. Both the cottage and the central-hall plans were popular. An example of the cottage is described in the contract between builder Richard Redwood and M. M. Rowan for a home on Spring Hill near the city limits.[55]

The plan (figure 70) shows the rear gallery enclosed at each end by a small room and the middle section open, with a stairway leading to the second story. The Rowan cottage had the first-story doors paneled, but the doors of the upper level were board and batten. Some of the homes were more decorative, as was the Robert Purvis House, also on Spring Hill. In it the mantelpieces were "finished in imitation marble," establishing that graining by the painters was already popular. Folding doors between major rooms were used instead of sliding doors. Specifications for the 1837 John Elliott House and the 1839 cottage of Edward O'Connor both called for folding

67. Cavallero House, 1835, 7 North Jackson Street. This is the last of the brick townhouses of the 1830s still standing in Mobile. The first story has been altered for commercial purposes. The original entrance door was in the north bay. (Photograph by Michael Thomason.)

68. Widows' Row, early 1830s, 604 Eslava Street. The porch was a Victorian addition. The last two units of a row of twelve brick one-room apartments for "widows of good character." Each widow had a large room, a fireplace for cooking, her own small rear yard with well, and her own private entrance. With the recent restoration the porch has been removed.

69. Bloodgood Row, formerly located on Monroe Street. The last three units (destroyed) were numbered 306–310. During the 1830s these attached four-story houses were considered very elegant. (Courtesy of the University of South Alabama Photographic Archives.)

doors.[56] The small jib doors beneath the front windows were common in country homes, and the more expensive ones had Carpenter locks. The porch wall was treated in several different ways; it might have weatherboarded, tongue-and-groove siding or plaster over lath. The porch ceiling had either plaster or tongue and groove. The roof was made of juniper or cypress shingles but not slate.

Fortunately several country homes have survived through the years. Though some modifications have taken place, enough of the original fabric remains to permit an accurate description of the houses at this time. Four examples have been selected to illustrate the spread from the simplest to the most elaborate. Of these, the simplest is the Collins-Robinson cottage (figure 71a) built in section 14, lot 3 of the Collins property, platted in figure 71b. In 1833 Joshua

The Greek Revival, 1830–1840

Collins purchased the northwest quarter of section 14 from the United States Congress. In 1839 the land was subdivided, and three houses were subsequently built, of which all survive. Of the three, the Collins-Robinson cottage has had the fewest twentieth-century alterations. It was originally a small summer cottage consisting of a hall and two main rooms. There was an unattached kitchen, a dining hall, and several guest cottages for the frequent visitors who came to spend several days after the long buggy ride from town. Letters abound describing these trips and also telling of the movement of furniture, china, and all the supplies needed when the families made their move to the country. After Elizabeth Marston purchased the Collins property in 1870, she decided to enlarge the cottage, and her descendant has the contract of 1889 that describes the addition of two more rooms and the repair of the large chimney.[57] The division between the original two rooms and the addition can be traced in the unusually thick partition wall between the two parts. In 1970 restoration and renovation took place, but the changes were made on the rear, leaving the front body of the cottage intact. A basement was excavated at the back, making room for a garage and a service room. Only the dormers on the front depart from the original facade. The wide front door is framed without transom or sidelights. Doors lead into each of the two front rooms, one on either side of the central hall. While the central-hall plan and the tapered square columns suggest the classical influence, the structure is free of Greek Revival detailing and remains a good example of the 1830 cottage.

A much larger house and one planned originally for year-round living is the Beal-Gaillard residence at 111 Myrtlewood Lane (figures 72a–c). It occupies the center of its early five-acre tract, parcel 49, as platted in the Robertson map of 1828 (figure 37). The house was built in 1836 by Gustavus Beal, who also owned the Greek Revival house on Conception Street (figure 61). If I could discuss only one example of an 1830s country home, I would choose the Beal-Gaillard House. From the heavy pegged framing to the finish of the six-foot-wide paneled cypress door, the house is worthy of special note. Even the site retains a nineteenth-century atmosphere, with its curving driveway, informal plantings, and avenue of native azaleas brought in from the woods (a simpler variety than those imported later). The large central section of the house has been little altered since it was built. Only the rear gallery has been enclosed with windows. Eighteen-foot-square rooms that are sixteen feet high range along the

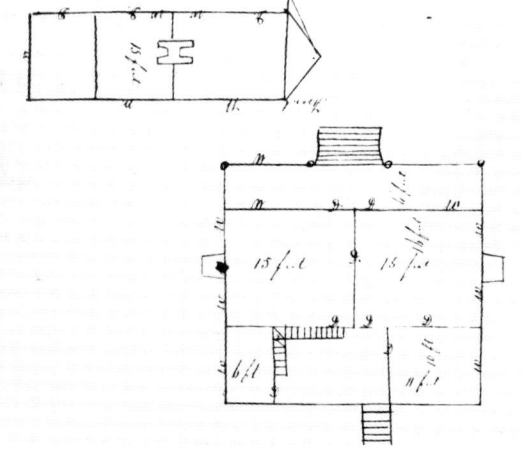

70. *Plan for a country home on Old Spring Hill Road built by Richard Redwood for M. M. Rowan and now destroyed. A typical summer home built in the newly opened Spring Hill area to which people went to escape the yellow fever epidemics during the summer months. (From Miscellaneous Book C, pp. 56–57, dated January 1, 1838.)*

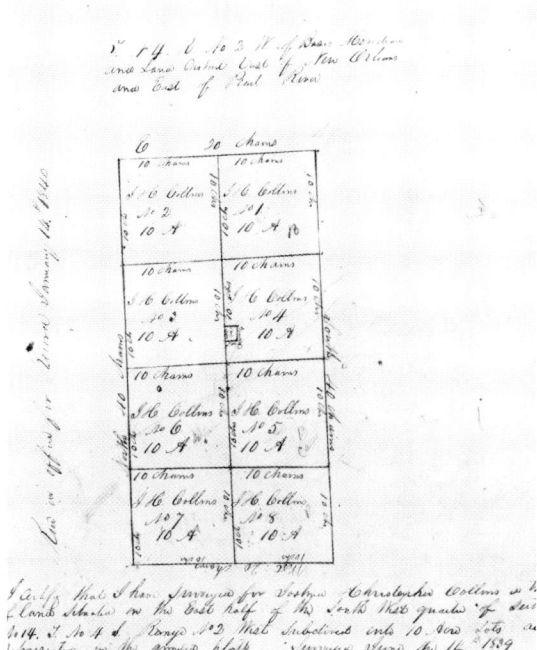

71a. The Collins-Robinson cottage, late 1830s, 56 Oakland Avenue. The small, two-room summer cottage of the 1830s had two rooms added in 1889. Early in the twentieth century the dormers were constructed. The detailing is simple. No sidelights or transom decorates the double-leaf entrance, and the box columns lack Greek Revival refinements.

72a. The Beal-Gaillard home, 1836, 111 Myrtlewood Lane, Spring Hill. The north wing was added during the ownership of Emanuel Jones, 1849–1896. The south wing was added by S. W. Gaillard soon after his purchase in 1903. The main body of the house is the best example in Mobile of the large country house of the 1830s built without Greek Revival influence. Cypress was used in the heavy framing with the pegged joinery.

71b. The 1840 platting of the Collins property in Spring Hill, in which each parcel contained ten acres. The Collins-Robinson House stands on parcel 3. (From Deed Book Z, p. 209, dated January 14, 1840.)

72b. Detail of the porch of the Beal-Gaillard House, showing the tall, slender chamfered columns and the early form of the round-top railing.

72c. The Beal-Gaillard summerhouse still standing on the north side of the property. A matching house originally stood on the south side.

97   *The Greek Revival, 1830–1840*

side of a central hall that is fifteen feet wide and runs through the house from front to rear. The long front gallery extends the full width of the central block. Unusually tall, slender columns are chamfered so sharply that they become polygonal in section. A louvred sun shield extends across the gallery at the height of the column capitals. It is all that remains of the original shutters that once connected the columnar shafts, protecting the porch from the heat of the morning sun.

When Emanuel Jones bought the house in 1849, he added the north wing and in so doing enlarged the dining room, which was in the rear on the north side. He also built two octagonal summerhouses of which the northern one still stands (figure 72c). The south wing was added early in the twentieth century by Samuel Gaillard after he had purchased the property. He also enlarged the north wing by enclosing the old cistern in an open porch (the cistern can still be seen through a trap door in the porch floor). Throughout the house, except in the south wing, cypress was used in the construction. Even the garret flooring is of wide cypress planks, though the main floors are of wide pine. The Carpenter locks are intact, and all the detailing of the house has been carefully maintained by the Gaillard family. Nothing interferes with the flow of the spaces. When the large doors are open, the interior is ideal for a home in a hot climate.

Toward the south of Mobile, near Choctaw Point, lay an area developed by truck farmers. Their homes were built along what was then called the Dog River Road. One of these was a house built by James Miller in 1837 (figure 73). It is located at 1103 South Broad on a site that is so shaded by tall trees that, even before the present wall was erected, the structure was difficult to see. The building has fallen into disrepair, but its fine proportions and dramatically high front steps nevertheless still give it a monumental quality not often seen in a structure of this size. An early photograph of the house in a private collection shows the original front stairway with a landing about a third of the way up the rise.[58] Three families of gardeners owned the property throughout the century—the James Millers, the Thomas Kavanahs, and the John O'Donnells. The last-named family owned the property until just a few years ago. Much of the produce

73. *The Miller Farmhouse, 1837, 1103 Broad Street. When this home was built, it stood in the center of a large area of truck farms that produced vegetables and fruits for the city market. (Photograph by Anne Sieller, courtesy of the Mobile Historic Development Commission.)*

74a. Oakleigh, 1833, 350 Oakleigh Place. James Roper built his fine Greek Revival home on his thirty-three-acre parcel of land during the early years when Mobile was fast becoming a great cotton trading port. The house is now the headquarters of the Historic Mobile Preservation Society and is open to the public. (Photograph by Michael Thomason.)

in the Government Street market came from the farms of these men. It is easy to imagine that the high open space beneath the O'Donnell house was an airy place to sort the vegetables in preparation for the trip to town. The infilling of this ground level by a later renovation altered the original elevation. The simple square columns of the high three-bay porch were connected by an early balustrade with a round-top rail and balusters with the swallowtail lower cut. Many of the balusters are gone, but a few originals remain. In spite of vandalism, the house still has great charm and dignity.

The last of the country homes is the 1833 residence of James Roper, the most photographed house in Mobile (figures 74a–d). It is hard to realize that when it was built it stood on a thirty-three-acre tract. It is now surrounded by the Oakleigh Garden Historic District. Many of the features of the house, taken singly, reflect the local tradition—such as the frame story that stands above a high brick ground level. But many Greek Revival refinements, such as the Greek key door frames and the classical entablatures and columns, give the structure the appearance of a Greek Revival building. The combination of all the elements, the mass, the interplay of spaces, and the symmetry of the wings with their galleries make Oakleigh unique in the city. No other house in Mobile so completely captures an antebellum atmosphere, though other, later buildings may rival it in architectural design. The circular iron staircase leading from the brick terrace to the porch above adds a graceful note to what is predominantly a pattern of interrelated vertical and horizontal lines created by the columns, piers, galleries, entablatures, and cornice. The long front windows of both wings and the central section repeat the rectangular motif with their jib doors. Even the slight batter of the main entrance's jambs and the shallow projection of the window crossettes do not distract from the domination of the rectangular module.

The house formed a wide T, a plan rather unusual for Mobile (figure 74b). In 1852 the property was purchased by A. F. Irwin, who is

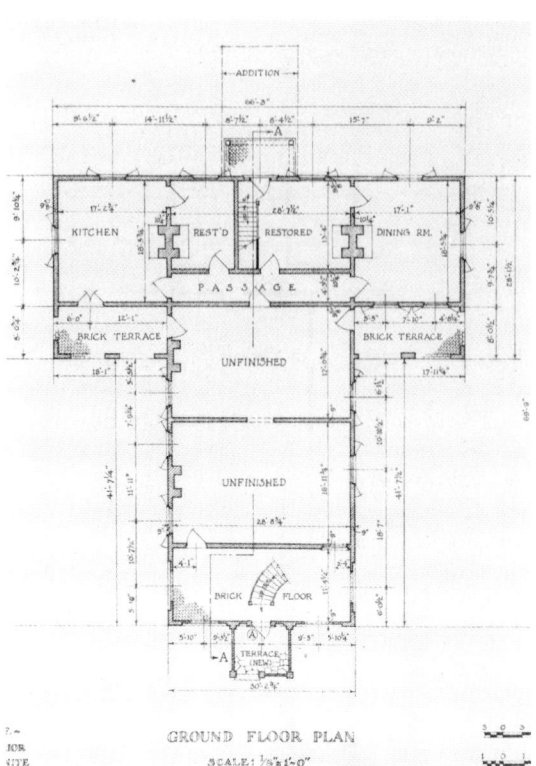

74c. Oakleigh, exterior front stairway. In the large homes of the time, it was customary for the exterior stairway to be located at the center of the facade gallery and to lead from beneath the gallery to the floor above. At Oakleigh the stairs rise in a graceful curve and form an elegant ascent to the main entrance on the second story. (Photograph by Michael Thomason.)

74b. Oakleigh, plan of the ground floor. Early in the twentieth century, the ground level was altered by the Cole and Dennison families. (Drawing by G. Chaudron, courtesy of the Library of Congress, Historic American Building Survey Collection.)

74d. Oakleigh's main entrance, on the second level. The Greek Revival enframement of the entrance, the tongue-and-groove siding of the porch wall, the round-top railing, and the jib doors below the slide-by window are all characteristic of the large homes of antebellum times in the Deep South. (Photograph by Michael Thomason.)

100   From Fort to Port

believed to have added the rear central wing.[59] The drawing made by the Historic American Building Survey (figure 74b) has notations about the interior alterations made by the different owners. All of the owners, however, maintained the basic integrity of the home. From the date when the house was first built, the tax records gave it a high valuation—in 1837 $25,000, three times the amount placed on large brick homes of the day. As the years passed and as the economy suffered various depressions, even this house was neglected. During the Cole family's ownership, from 1916 to 1927, restoration was carried out, together with some renovations. The old earth-packed ground level of the front portion was floored and finished for living quarters. Mrs. Cole worked to restore the gardens. Then, from 1927 to 1945, the Dennison family continued work on the house, replastering the interior walls and building the staircase in the front hall. Since 1955, the building has belonged to the city of Mobile. It is now under lease to the Historic Mobile Preservation Society and is maintained as a historic house open to the public. The best time to visit is at Christmas, when the Historic Mobile Preservation Society holds a festival lasting several days, or in the spring, when all the azaleas are in bloom. At either time the house most vividly recalls its early heritage.

Educational Buildings

The 1830s also witnessed the founding of Spring Hill College and of the Convent of Visitation by the Catholic Diocese, although none of the early buildings has survived. Bishop Portier initiated his dream of a center for higher learning when he procured a quarter section of land on a high point in section 13 in Spring Hill (figure 75). It was a perfect spot for a college. There was plenty of land, trees for timber,

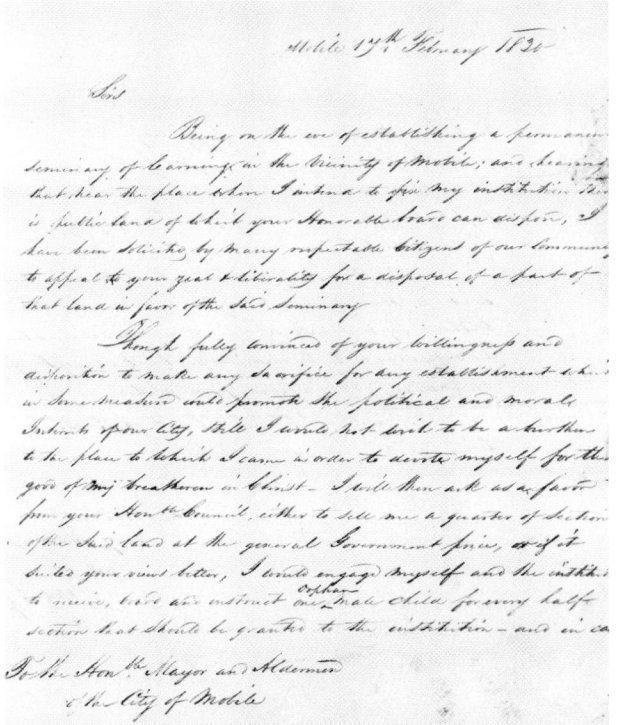
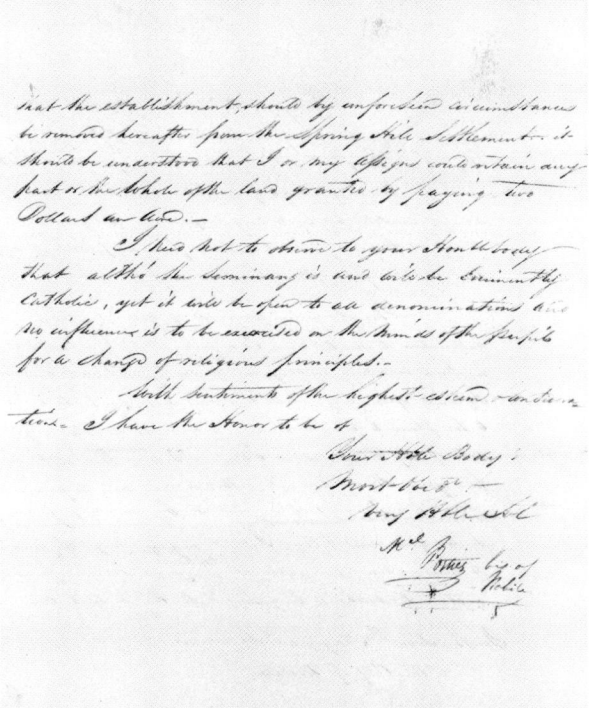

75. Facsimile of the letter written by Bishop Portier to the mayor and Board of Aldermen, requesting land for the location of Spring Hill College. (Courtesy of Spring Hill College.)

The Greek Revival, 1830–1840

76. *The first college building of Spring Hill College, 1831; Claude Beroujon, architect. The wings and fourth story were added in 1859. The structure was destroyed by fire in 1869. (Reproduced, by permission, from* The Torch on the Hill, *1931, courtesy of Spring Hill College.)*

and springs for sufficient water, and nearby was a road from Mobile to Mississippi. In May 1830 the school opened in temporary quarters in the Hotel built by the Baron de Vendel on a hill near the campus site. By July 1830, two two-story wood buildings were ready to receive some fifty boarders and twenty seminarians.[60] Claude Beroujon was given the task of planning the first brick building on the campus. The cornerstone was laid in July 1830, and the structure was finished by May 1831.

An early engraving of the Beroujon building has survived in the College archives (figure 76). The central section in this engraving belongs to the original construction, but the fourth story and the wings were added in 1859. A monumental portico faced to the south, now the rear. Eight columns thirty-six feet tall supported the inner pavilion, and four more formed the classic temple elevation of the portico. Balconies connected the columns at each of the three stories, an idea that was retained when the 1869 building was erected to replace the Beroujon building after it had burned. Had the Beroujon building survived, its fine proportions, facade, and classical detailing would have ranked it with the Government Street buildings of Gallier and Dakin.

The second educational center founded by the Diocese was the Visitation Monastery (now called the Convent of Visitation), located on Spring Hill Avenue in Summerville. An interesting history of the Monastery has been preserved both in the Catholic archives and in a diary in the collection of the Monastery. The earliest building in this complex has not been preserved in any visible form, as was that of the College. The earliest building still standing belongs to the mid-century and will be discussed in chapter 5. Finally, Beroujon in 1833 made the plans for a new cathedral, for which the cornerstone was laid November 19, 1835. Financial problems and other demands made upon the Diocese delayed the construction until the 1840s, and I will therefore discuss the Cathedral in chapter 4.

The Close of the Decade

The start of the decade in 1830 was full of promise and optimism. The closing year of 1839 was one of economic disaster and pessimism. All the forces of nature and man seemed set on destruction. The financial panic of 1837 brought business to a standstill. Notes became worthless, banks suspended payments on specie, and millionaires such as Henry Hitchcock went bankrupt. The bottom dropped out of an economy that was based on trade. In agricultural areas food at least could be home grown, but the port cities were destitute. Then, in the summer of 1839, the yellow fever struck with devastating force. We have many accounts of heroism as inhabitants struggled to care for the sick, to bury the dying, and to provide for the orphans. The added torment of drought lasted from 1839 to 1840, and three great fires broke out on the nights of October 2, 7, and 9, 1839 (figure 39). By the time the last flames had been extinguished, the whole inner city—from Water Street up Dauphin on both sides, over to St. Francis and west to Franklin—lay in ruins. Only occasionally did a building escape, for example the little Dade cottage at 503 St. Francis (figure 53). But buried in all the debris and devastation there was a will to survive, a spirit that would carry the city of Mobile through the lean years of the 1840s into the golden age of the 1850s.

77a. The Old City Prison and Police Station, 1839–1841, formerly on the south side of Conti Street between Royal and St. Emanuel, now destroyed. The complex of several buildings had a watchtower at the center. (Kilburn print from Ballou's Pictorial Drawing Room Companion, *June 1857, courtesy of Mrs. Carter Smith.)*

WATCH AND BELL TOWER, MOBILE, ALABAMA.

4 Architecture in Transition, 1840–1850

During the years 1840–1850, the financial condition of the city government did not allow for construction of more than a few civic buildings. So severe was the financial crisis that, even when the location of the powder magazine was proving to endanger the neighboring hospital, no new facility could be contemplated. Instead, in 1848, all the powder was moved to Fort Morgan and was housed at the United States arsenal, an inconvenience when people wanted their powder. One of the few civic buildings mentioned in the records was the pest house. After the terrible plague in 1839, the health of the community assumed major importance. In November 1841 a plan for an isolation facility was presented by E. B. Shoemaker. It was accepted, and the building had been constructed by January 1842. The brick structure was quite small and resembled a fortress more than a hospital for patients with contagious diseases. The walls were nine inches thick, and the doors and window shutters were covered with sheet iron placed on both the inside and the outside. The roof was covered with slate. The depressing aspect of the building was heightened by its location on a lot near and "convenient to the New Burying Ground." Further isolated by a seven-foot fence of juniper, it certainly was not an encouraging spot in which to be confined during a siege of yellow fever.[1]

The records also mention an armory, though there is no architectural description of it. It stood on St. Emanuel Street on a lot between the mayor's office and the Number Two Engine House. The building cost the city $5,000 and, upon its completion in 1841, was leased to the First Volunteer Regiment under the command of Colonel Thomas A. McCoy, who had supervised the construction.[2]

The third building documented in the Mayor's Minutes was the Jail and Guard House, pictures of which have survived (figures 77a–c). The building has been variously called the Old Guard House, the Old Jail, and the City Prison. It was begun in 1839 and had been completed by June 15, 1841, at a cost of $6,397. Even though the facility was put to immediate use, improvements continued to be made for several years. In 1842, iron doors were added for greater security. The next year a nine-inch brick wall was built along Conti Street, with another running between the old and new building to the west. The last wall was ten feet high, built of boards and capped by large spikes at three-inch intervals along the top.³ The photographs show the massing of the different units, each building having a low gable roof and simple window treatments. Dominating and somewhat unifying the group is the three-stage bell and clock tower, of which the belfry differs in the photograph (figure 77b) from that shown in the engraving (figure 77a). The rear of the complex, seen from St. Emanuel (figure 77c), gives a better idea of the separate buildings' relationship to each other. Before the store was added to the east, as seen in the photograph (figure 77b), the plain stucco wall along Conti Street (see the engraving in figure 77a) hinted at an old Spanish culture, which may account for the inaccurate references to the buildings as the Old Spanish Guard House. With the completion of the Guard House, the corner of Conti and St. Emanuel became the center of the city government, with the mayor's office, Armory, Engine House Number Two, and police headquarters.

77b. The Old City Prison and Police Station facing north on Conti Street, photographed before its demolition in 1895. (Courtesy of the Historic Mobile Preservation Society.)

77c. The view of the Old City Prison and Police Station from St. Emanuel Street, showing the rear elevations and the grouping of the various buildings. (Courtesy of the University of South Alabama Photographic Archives.)

The most important building program of the decade was that for the United States Marine Hospital, which was undertaken by the United States government (figure 78). The site selected was one block east of the City Hospital on St. Anthony, on land purchased from Joshua Kennedy, as shown on the Troost map, vol. 7, page 41. The lot was bounded by 210 feet on St. Anthony and 281 feet on Congress, with a depth of 653.9 feet. Between 1837 and 1839 several plans had been submitted to the United States Treasury, of which those of W. R. Barnes were favored. The construction bid of John Collins was accepted. Before the decision could be implemented, however, a new set of plans was sent to the Treasury by Frederick Bunnell. These seemed better adapted to the purpose and represented a less costly design, so J. B. Hogan, the Mobile collector of customs, was ordered to solicit new bids on the basis of both plans.[4] As a result of this action, the plan of Frederick Bunnell was accepted, and Robert Williamson, as the lowest bidder, was "entitled to the contract and the work to be performed according to Mr. Bunnell's plan for the sum of $17,500.00." The Hospital received its first patient in April 1843. The tax records for that year ascribed a value of $50,000 to the "finished building."

Architecturally the Marine Hospital harmonizes with its neighbor, the City Hospital, but it differs in the use of the classical orders and in other details (compare figure 78 with figure 41a). In the 1842 building the columns, standing upon very high brick pedestals, rise through only the two upper stories of the elevation. Rather than being carried across the face of the portico, the columns are limited to the five bays of the wings, so that the building is divided into three distinct parts. The one-story four-bay porch seems unrelated to the facade even though the columns belong to the same order as those on the wings. The ten years that elapsed between the Old City Hospital and the Marine Hospital show a change in the Greek Revival influence; there is greater freedom in the use of the classical motifs during the 1840s than there had been earlier.

78. *The United States Marine Hospital, 1842, 800 St. Anthony; Frederick Bunnell, architect; Robert Williamson, builder. In this three-story Greek Revival building the full-height colonnade is limited to the wings, leaving only a one-story porch to continue the columnar motif across the central pavilion. (Erik Overbey/Mobile Public Library Collection, University of South Alabama Photographic Archives.)*

Architecture in Transition, 1840–1850

When the building was no longer needed as a marine hospital, it was adapted for use as a tuberculosis sanitarium, and the balconies of the wing bays were infilled with glass. This addition altered the design by reducing the importance of the columns and by disrupting the light-dark patterns that had originally been set up by the deeply shadowed bay spans and the forward-stepping columns. In 1931 the building was further altered by the addition of a rear wing built by the firm of Warren, Knight, and Davis.[5] The structure now serves as offices for the Mobile County Public Health Department.

Some improvements were made during the decade to better the city plan, even though major building programs had to be postponed. Streets were repaired and new ones cut through, gutters were installed, sidewalks were laid, and gas streetlights were set in place. In 1842 the city square was surrounded by a sidewalk, and by 1848 Bienville Square had been formally laid out with paths, trees, and a fence. A good water supply was assured by the agreement made between the city and Albert Stein of Nashville by which the Stein Water Works were established, incorporating the old water system located at Spring Hill.[6] These improvements made the city better prepared for the building boom of the 1850s.

Commercial Buildings

Commercial development, while retarded by the depression, recovered more quickly than did the city government. Brick stores with slate or copper roofs filled in the lots made vacant by the fire. The rapid disappearance of wood buildings brought about an ordinance in 1843 that abolished the old chimney sweep laws as obsolete in a city of brick and tile.[7] Other building codes were passed that affected the design of the street scenes. In 1848, after some thirty-eight requests for permission to build verandas, an ordinance was proposed that would make it lawful to erect a gallery or balcony overhanging a sidewalk if it was fireproof and watertight, if it extended the full width of the building, if it was placed not less than twelve feet above the sidewalk, and if it had iron posts. The proposal was defeated because of a prevailing belief that "verandas would impair if not destroy the beauty and symmetry of the city and greatly injure the comfort and convenience of the public streets.—The committee believe that in as much as it would be inexpedient to grant the permission to erect verandas generally it would be inexpedient to grant it to the petitioners."[8] Thus for several years the stark Federal street scene was preserved, but fortunately the balconies finally won out.

Only a few contracts have survived for a building used only as a store, for during the decade stores were usually combined with residences. An example of the single-purpose store can be seen in the plan for a row of three to be built on Royal Street (figure 79). The one-story buildings were of brick, each unit measuring 16.8 feet by 50 feet.[9] A shed with a single-slope tin roof was added on the rear. Each storefront unit contained a batten door and two stationary windows. Batten shutters protected the rear windows.

Two variations of the store-residence type developed, the more popular being row buildings two or three stories in height, with the

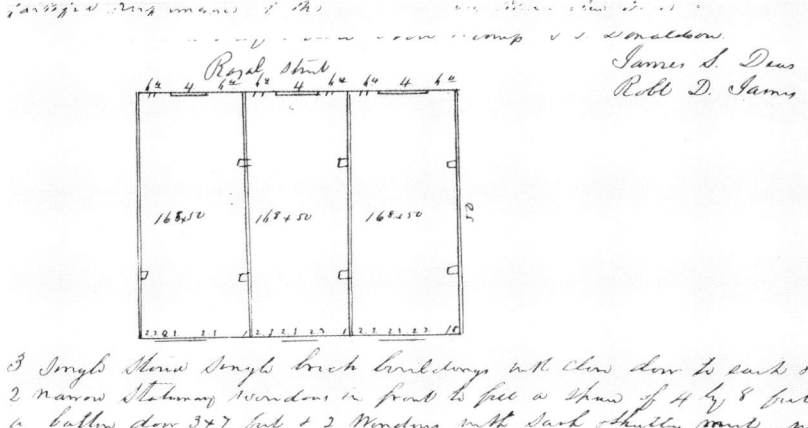

79. *A plan for three stores (now destroyed) to be erected on Royal Street for the Irwin estate; James Deas, builder, 1844; cost, $1,000. (From Miscellaneous Book D, pp. 481–82, dated January 24, 1844.)*

business allocated to the ground level and the living quarters above. The second type was a double building with an alley or corridor dividing the complex. The James F. Hutchisson building erected for Burns and Riley had a nine-foot central corridor, and another Hutchisson building for Eslava and Dumée had an eight-foot separation.[10] Regardless of the type used, there were major similarities in the general treatment. Both types called for additional outbuildings, such as a kitchen, which was usually two story; a carriage house with a stable; a privy; and frequently a fence. One contract included a cistern "large enough to hold 20 hogshead of water, well cemented." Several contracts also called for cellars that were "cemented so that no water could get in."[11]

Without exception, the first story was devoted to the business, and the storefront entrance had stone sills and lintels, usually of granite or Durand stone. The doors had some kind of protection for security, usually sheet iron. Windows had multiple lights, many using twelve-by-sixteen-inch panes of glass, but a few introduced large sheets of glass, such as the store for John Lyons that was built by William Smith, in which the contract called for panes measuring twenty-two and one-half inches by twenty-eight inches.[12]

The facing brick was hard fired (frequently Baltimore brick) and was laid in smooth-struck white mortar joints. Softer brick was used for the other walls and was laid in common bond.[13] A molded brick course with dentils projecting only slightly from the cornice served to accent the roof line. Fire walls extended from one to two feet above the roof pitch and were finished with stone coping. Dormers, while not yet common, were sometimes specified.

Some kind of balcony was usually requested, even though the city code required that balconies be of fireproof construction and even though a variance had to be obtained before they could be installed. To meet the growing need for a local source of iron, the Skate and Spear foundries were built during the decade. As time went on, the balcony became accepted. When the residence was on the second story, the balcony became the front porch for the occupants. Floor-length double-sash windows, the lower sash being a slide-by, and jib doors below, afforded easy passage from interior rooms to the balcony. The rear galleries were more often of wood, usually two stories in height with square columns. One such was lengthened to include a two-story "water closet" with two seats on the first-story level and one on the second.[14]

The interior finish of the buildings varied somewhat, depending on the expense involved. Some called for artificial graining of the doors, some to resemble oak, others mahogany. The height of the interior rooms seems to have been fairly constant, usually twelve feet for the first story, eleven feet for the second, and ten for the third. Mantels were usually painted black. In the residential area the flooring was tongue and groove, but the store might have brick or flagstone. Interior walls were furred, plastered, and painted white. Baseboards were as much as ten inches high. There were no references to crown moldings in the contracts, though one did call for a chair railing.[15] Between the parlor and the dining room was an opening about nine feet wide and ten feet high that could be closed by a pair of folding or sliding doors.

In a conspicuous change from the previous decade, the picket fence was replaced by a brick wall. One example is described in Mr. Bunnell's plan for Mr. Payan. The brick wall was seven feet six inches above ground level, with a cap formed of two courses of brick, the upper course projecting slightly over the lower. The wall was reinforced by brick piers that were set in "good Thomaston lime mortar."[16]

Increased commercial activity was reflected in the new wharves and warehouses that were constructed along the waterfront (figure 80). The plan for the typical warehouse appears in figure 81. A series of storage rooms were separated by high fire walls. These storage rooms could be arranged around a central courtyard (figure 81) or, as in the cotton warehouse built for D. E. Hall (figure 82), in rows of three or more. The entrance end of the yards contained large doors from twelve to sixteen feet in height and fourteen feet in width. Both doors and windows were well secured with iron wire mesh and flat iron bars. Frequently iron shutters were added. Sometimes the yard was roofed with a king post truss supporting the slate roofing. At other times, the yard was partially open, with only four-foot-wide eaves projecting from the walls of the storage rooms. Near the entrance to the warehouse an office was walled off. Outer walls were given additional support by applied pilasters on both the interior and exterior surfaces.[17] In one case tie rods were added for greater strength.

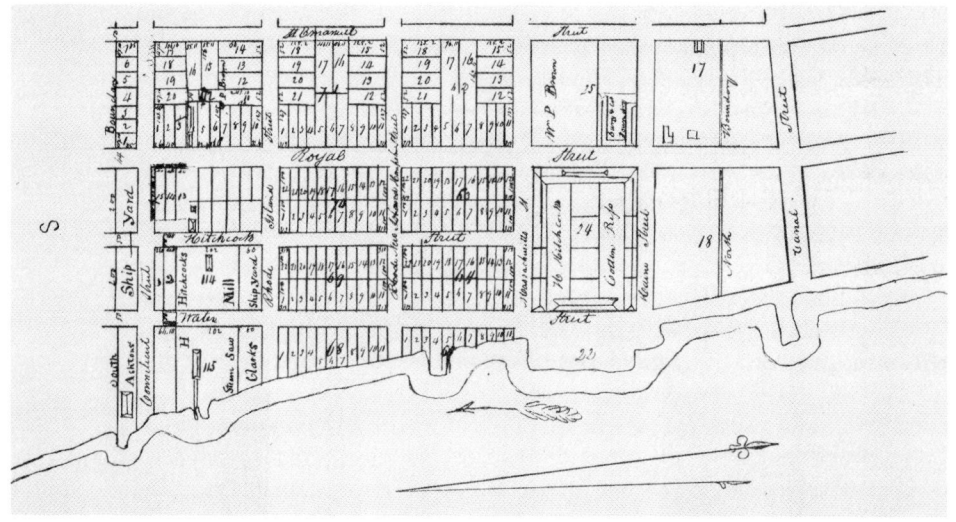

80. *Map of Mobile south of Canal, with Henry Hitchcock's large cotton press and warehouse covering the block between Maine (now Palmetto) and Massachusetts (now Charleston). (From Deed Book Z, p. 205.)*

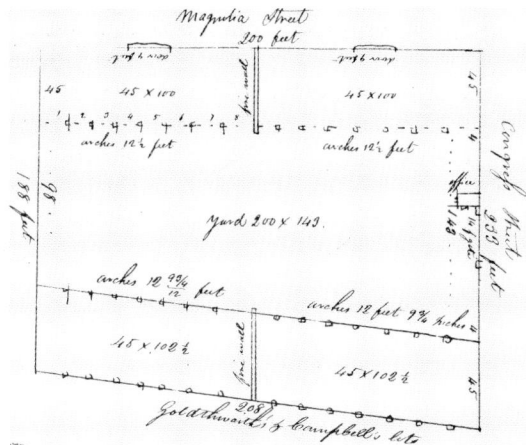

81. *Plan for a cotton warehouse for William Pritchard, originally on Congress and Magnolia and now destroyed; James Deas, builder; cost, $10,093. The plan is typical, with a large open yard flanked by storage stalls. (From Miscellaneous Book D, pp. 304–6, dated February 3, 1842.)*

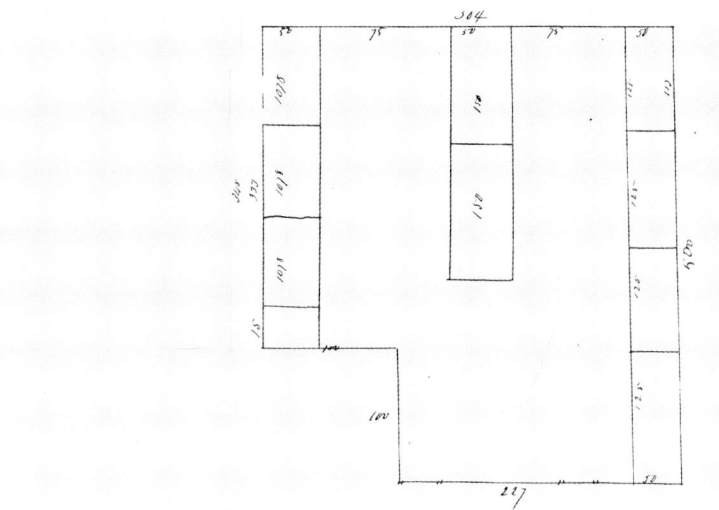

82. *Plan for a double-shed cotton warehouse, formerly on Front Street (now destroyed); D. E. Hall, owner; James Deas, builder; cost, $6,000. (From Miscellaneous Book D, pp. 410–12, dated March 15, 1843.)*

83. *The Magnolia Cotton warehouse, 1866, 62 Lipscomb Street (destroyed in 1981). No photographs of the earlier cotton warehouses are known to exist, but the Magnolia of 1866 illustrates the type. (Courtesy of the Library of Congress, Historic American Building Survey Collection.)*

111   Architecture in Transition, 1840–1850

84. *The Lafayette Hotel, early 1840s, formerly on the southwest corner of Royal and St. Michael streets, now destroyed. The building served as a hotel until 1873, when it was purchased by the Mobile Press Register, which carried out extensive renovations. The older style, with its parapet built up between the end chimneys, stands in striking contrast to the Greek Revival St. Michael Street Hotel across the way. (Courtesy of the Historic Mobile Preservation Society.)*

The interior of the warehouses was divided into different sections either by walls or by arcaded passageways supported by rows of wood columns standing on foundation piers of cypress (figure 81). A cotton warehouse built in 1866 was still standing in 1980 (figure 83), and while it is of a later date, it illustrates the simplicity and the strength of the warehouse facades.[18]

With the coming of the automobile, one of the essential structures of the nineteenth century has been forgotten—the livery stable, the garage of its day. A contract has survived for the construction of one located on the east side of Royal Street, between Government and Conti, next to the Mansion House.[19] The building was two stories in height, with fifty feet of frontage on Royal. The specifications established that the building had refinements not to be expected in a livery stable. The two entrances had "two fold" doors with outside shutters; the twelve-light windows had large panes of glass, twelve inches by twenty inches, with the central window given prominence by sidelights. In the *Register* for October 4, 1849, is a description of this "horse mansion," which was run by Mr. Barney, as a

> building neat and beautiful in exterior, and said to be finely, comfortably and conveniently arranged in its interior—and, withal, well fitted with all the living "critters" that those who are fond of handling the "ribbons" delight to follow. Carriages, tasteful and elegant, may there be had, while the Barber that flourishes in the front part of this neat structure will prepare the exquisite for a showy and pleasant ride.

With the loss of the hotels from the fire of 1839, new facilities were needed to supplement older ones that were being refurbished. During the 1840s, the Lafayette Hotel (figure 84) stood on the southwest corner of Royal and St. Michael streets, opposite from the site of the old St. Michael Hotel. The building was owned by William Hallett, who in 1841 was taxed for it at a value of $16,000. The contrast between the Lafayette and the former St. Michael built by Dakin is startling and illustrates the difference between the two decades in architectural style (figures 84 and 47a). The Greek Revival buildings stood isolated in their monumentality, while the 1840 buildings became part of a street scene. Cast iron replaced Greek columns. Apart from the advertisement, the Lafayette offered few clues that it was a hotel rather than just another commercial building on the block. The three-story brick massing with its dormers and parapet built up between the end chimneys continued the design of the neighboring stores. The Lafayette continued to serve the community for some thirty-five years, though sometimes not to the satisfaction of the conservative members of the city. On January 23, 1846, a petition from "sundry citizens" was submitted to the mayor's council requesting that "the corporate authorities prohibit the House being used for the purpose of Cock Fighting and for Fancy Balls."[20] In 1867 the name of the Hotel was changed to Roper House, and in 1873 it was purchased by the *Mobile Press Register*.

Religious Buildings

New churches played an important part in the building program of the last half of the decade. The most ambitious plans were those of the Cathedral of the Immaculate Conception. The building occupies an entire block, bounded by Dauphin on the north, by Conti on the south, by Franklin on the west, and by Claiborne on the east (figures 85a,b). It was begun in August of 1834, with the cornerstone laid the following November. As previously noted in chapter 3, financial problems delayed the project.[21] By 1843, funding seemed sufficient to permit construction, and a contract signed with Claude Beroujon stipulated that he would furnish all necessary plans, would supervise the construction, would keep all records subject to review by the committee, and would "travel north to select all the Baltimore brick and the granite to be cut for the building."[22] The contract concerned only the main body of the Cathedral and specifically omitted from consideration the altar, the communion rail, the pulpit, the front portico with its four planned columns, and the granite steps front and back. Also omitted were the front corner towers, which were to be raised only "to the height of the columns." The present portico with its eight columns was the work of James H. Hutchisson in 1875–1887 and was finished by his son, James F. Hutchisson, on August 31, 1890. The towers were completed by James F. Hutchisson in 1895 (see chapter 8). Beroujon was to be paid 8 percent of the cost until the sum reached $50,000 and was thereafter to receive no stipend.

While Beroujon was responsible for the building, he may have received advice from other sources. Earlier plans had been sent to the Diocese (to Brother Mathias Loras) in 1830, and in 1833 plans were requested from Bishop Rosati.[23] Further research into archives in

Rome would be necessary to ascertain whether these plans were in any way connected with the plan of Beroujon. The original architectural features of the building can best be seen from the west, the corner of Conti and Franklin streets. From this position, Beroujon's elevations of the sides and rear of the Cathedral can be studied. The forty-foot-high walls are divided into bays by white pilasters that strongly contrast with the red brick. Each bay has a double semicircular arched window with a keystone at the apex of the outer arch. The water table, pilaster bases, abacus blocks, and keystones are all of gray granite. Granite was also used for the windowsills, and for the taenia in the entablature that separates the stuccoed brick architrave and frieze. A granite course was also used in the horizontal cornice. Thus the elevation is a pleasing harmony of red brick, white stucco, and gray granite.

85a. *The Cathedral of the Immaculate Conception, 1834–1849, 4 South Claiborne Street; Claude Beroujon, architect; elevation from the southwest, showing the main body of the Cathedral as it was designed by Beroujon. T. E. Giraud, an architect from New Orleans, was consultant for the roof and vault, but they were built by J. F. Hutchisson. The east facade was a later addition. (Photograph by Michael Thomason.)*

85b. *Face of the Cathedral of the Immaculate Conception, 1875–1890; James H. Hutchisson, architect from 1875 to 1887, James F. Hutchisson, architect from 1887 to 1890. The upper stages of the towers were not finished until 1895 (James F. Hutchisson, architect). (From* Mobile, Alabama, in Photogravure, *by the Zadex Jewelry Company, 1892, courtesy of the Historic Mobile Preservation Society.)*

From Fort to Port

The work progressed between 1844 and 1849. The roof presented some problems, and T. E. Giraud, of New Orleans, was called in as consultant. The contract for construction was signed with James F. Hutchisson, who received a silver pitcher with an engraving expressing appreciation for his services.[24] The dedication of the Cathedral took place on December 5, 1850.

Great care was taken in the erection of the building so that it would be able to withstand many years of use. In 1963 the foundations were examined during an extensive restoration program. The walls at ground level were found to be ten feet thick, and the foundation walls for the interior columns were six feet thick. Reverse arches embedded in the masonry further strengthened the foundation.[25]

An account in the newspaper of August 22, 1849, describes the building as it stood at the time of the dedication:

> The foundation—being of the best masonry and resting on a bed of hard clay, is perfectly solid, and will doubtless sustain the immense superstructure for ages. The side, rear and middle walls are ten feet thick at the ground, while those for the steeples and the front walls for the support of the columns of the portico are eleven feet thick, with reversed arches under each column, inside and outside. The Church stands on a basement five feet above the level of the surrounding plain and is 164 feet in length. It has a front breadth including the two steeples, of 103 feet—the main body 88 feet and the rear 94 feet wide. The windows are arched and semi-circle, $7\frac{1}{2}$ feet wide by 23 feet in height, their sills being granite and all the framework cast iron. There are six on each side, three in the rear and two in front.—In front there are three doorways under the portico, the centre one 8 by 16 feet and the others 6 by 12 feet. All their jams [sic], sills and lentals [sic] are made of finely wrought granite. There is also a door in the rear, 8 by 12 feet, ornamented with a fine portico which is supported by two fluted columns and entablature, likewise of the best grade of granite, the bases of the column and jams [sic] of the door being of polished granite and of the most chaste design and greatly admired by everyone. This portico, like the balance of the church is of the Roman Doric order.
>
> There are to be four columns in front making six in all. These with the pilasters all around the building, are 40 feet in length and the entablature 10 feet which with the basement and parapet wall, make the entire height of the edifice more than 60 feet. The steeples are 20 feet square and when completed will have an altitude of 150 feet.

The newspaper article continued with details of the exterior, then described the interior. Since the present interior does not contain the original fabric, the contemporary account is important.

> The interior when completed, will be grand and imposing. It is divided into three naves, the center one being 42 feet wide and the side aisles 19 feet. They are separated by two rows of columns, six each. The side walls will be ornamented with pilasters of a type to correspond with the columns. The sanctuary will form a semi-circle of about 40 feet in the diameter, with an elevation of two feet. In the rear of the main altar, the circular wall will also be

ornamented with columns. The ceiling of the middle nave will be 60 feet from the floor. There will be but one gallery and that above the entrance.[26]

Besides the activity on the Cathedral of the Immaculate Conception, the Catholic Diocese continued the development of Spring Hill College and the Visitation Monastery and, through the Catholic Female Charitable Society, established an orphanage on the site now occupied by the Cathedral Towers on the south side of Conti Street.[27]

The Protestants too were busy erecting churches during the decade. The Second Presbyterian congregation built on the northeast corner of St. Francis and Conception streets, now the site of the new Colonial Bank. The three pages of specifications in the contract address different topics separately: excavations, foundations, brickwork, plastering, stonework, roofing, carpentry work, cornices, windows, doors, and the interior details of altar, pews, and so forth.[28] In design the Church continued in the classical tradition, reflecting the Roman temple form, with the body of the Church on a high podium. The exterior of the side walls was divided into bays by pilasters. The portico was of the distyle-in-antis plan, formed by two fluted pilasters and brick columns plastered to resemble stone. The columns were 4 feet in diameter at the base and 24.6 feet tall. Kreb's "Bird's Eye View of Mobile" for 1873 contains a drawing of the building (figure 86, detail of map). A curving, divided stairway led up to the portico level. As in the Cathedral, granite was used for the doorsills and for the projection between the pilaster capitals and the brick cornice above. In the interior, twenty cast iron columns in the basement supported the framing of the auditorium above. As in previously reported contracts, oak graining was used for the doors.

The increase in the number of orphanages shows that life at the time was precarious. After the 1839 plague, the women of five Protestant churches cooperated in a mutual effort to provide for children who had lost their parents. A permanent facility was finally found in 1845 in the building that still stands at 911 Dauphin Street (figure 87). It was designed and built under the supervision of Henry Moffat

86. *The Second Presbyterian Church, 1844, formerly on the northeast corner of St. Francis and Conception (now destroyed); I. P. Pond, E. W. Irvin, and B. H. Scattergood, builders. The temple style of the Greek Revival was built on a high podium. (From Ehrgotte Kreb's "Bird's Eye View" map of 1873, courtesy of the Museum of the City of Mobile.)*

87. *Protestant Children's Home, 1845, 911 Dauphin Street; Henry Moffat, architect. The orphanage was built to house children who lost their parents in the yellow fever epidemics. The original building has been enlarged by additions to the rear in 1924 and 1950, and the two-story front gallery was altered.*

of Philadelphia. Two years later the architect succumbed to the plague while he was in Mobile. The central section of the building and the offset east wing belong to the original fabric. Over the years additions have been made as the building was adapted for various uses. The building has the same clearly defined massing as the other 1840s structures, with the usual shallow cornice accented by the small dentil course. The present entrance porch has the characteristics of a later style.

Residential Buildings

City Dwellings of Wood

During the 1840s the Gulf Coast cottage, locally called the Creole, evolved into its final form. It is still popular today (figures 88, 90). In mass it was a little longer than the earlier form, having a five-bay porch instead of the older three or four bays. The long axis still ran parallel to the street, but the roof line had altered. The break in the slope was abandoned; the roof extended over the front porch. The columns were usually of square section, about twelve inches on a side, giving the structure a rather stocky appearance. The column capitals were formed of simple moldings. Square balusters were universally used, and the top railing formed a flattened oval rather than being circular, as in the previous decade. The swallowtail cut at the bottom of the balusters disappeared after about 1843, and in its place was a squared cut where the baluster joined the bottom rail in a right angle, a place where water was certain to collect and cause rot. Cornices were of the box type. Entablatures were either left plain or divided by a single taenia molding. While a few examples continued to use the two-door front entrances, the common plan called for a single central entrance and a central hall. Contracts specified that the doors should have four panels with transom and sidelights, the early sidelights being quite narrow. Windows for cottages still had double sashes and six-over-six lights, but some few called for weights to assist in the raising and lowering of the sashes. All the cottages had front and rear galleries; some had rear galleries partially enclosed, with small end rooms. Interior end chimneys completed the axial balance of the massing. The main variation in the style seems to have been the height to which the cottage was raised, which varied from two to six feet. White remained the interior color for the ten-foot-high rooms. Baseboards, called washboards in the contracts, were eight inches high. The average cost of such a cottage was $500.

A good example of the 1840s cottage is the Carlen House (figure 88), now a museum open to the public. It is located to the north of Murphy High School at 54 Carlen Street. In 1843 it was built by Michael Carlen on his small, twenty-acre farm. The old heavy pegged framing was covered by hand-split lath and was then plastered. The house, facing east, is of a central-hall plan, with a reverse stairway at the rear of the hall. The hall has an entrance on both the front and rear porches. Four rooms, two on each side, form the downstairs plan. There are no front dormers, but when the building was restored by the architect Nicholas Holmes, he found evidence that there had been a single rear dormer. It was rebuilt, and the garret was finished with two rooms.[29]

Over the years the cottages were frequently bastardized by additions such as the winged brackets added to the columns of the I. I. Jones cottage of 1840 (figure 89). The simplicity of the original building, raised on a high foundation, was disrupted by the incongruous Victorian brackets and the balustrade. Israel Jones came to Mobile from London and brought with him some progressive ideas. He operated the first streetcar line in the city and was president of the Mobile Musical Association and benefactor of the Protestant Orphanage. In 1840 he helped form the first Jewish congregation, which was incorporated in 1844. He served as the first president of the congregation and remained in that office for thirty years. Mr. Jones contributed his expertise to the development of Mobile as a member of the city council. The site on which his home once stood

88. *The Carlen cottage, 1843, 54 Carlen Street. The final development of the Gulf Coast cottage is well demonstrated in the five-bay gallery, the central-hall plan, the stocky box columns, and the refinements of the door surround. The house is part of the museum system of the city and is open to the public.*

89. *The I. I. Jones cottage, ca. 1840, formerly at 910 Conti Street and now destroyed. A typical 1840s cottage with Victorian decor added to the box columns and the balustrade. (Courtesy of A. Bailey du Mont.)*

90a. The Clemmons cottage, 1849, still on its original site at 503 Church. The original configuration was covered by aluminum awnings, canopies, and asbestos siding.

90b. The Clemmons cottage, seen in 1981, after it was moved half a block and restored, 551 Church Street.

and in which he lived for forty years is now a vacant overgrown lot.

The small Clemmons cottage that formerly stood a half block east of its present location would hardly have been recognized as an early cottage, so hidden was it behind asbestos siding, aluminum awnings, and added wings. When all the accretions were stripped away during a recent restoration, the 1849 cottage stood exposed in its original state (figures 90a,b). Joseph Clemmons was a man of some means, being a bar pilot captain, and had his home built with some refinements, such as the channeling of the door and dormer framing and the segmental curving of the upper sash of the dormers. The restored cottage now standing at 551 Church Street has been adapted for use as a law office. While it is no longer a residence, it is an important addition to the Church Street East Historic District, being one of the earliest buildings in that area.

Country Dwellings of Wood

The country homes that have survived were larger variations on the city cottage. Since many were built by wealthy cotton factors, more attention was paid to refinements such as columns and moldings than in the less expensive city cottage. Macready's *Reminiscences* of 1844 described the actor-author's delight in a sightseeing drive in the country: "My drive today among some very pretty suburban villas with their many flowers and their richly blossoming pink trees, oranges in bloom, was very lovely. The air was quite delicious. We came frequently to the water side, looking from a low cliff over the extensive bay."[30]

Country homes were erected along three main roads, two of which led from Mobile to the western hills, with the third heading toward the bay to the south. At that time, Spring Hill Road ran northwest, making a branch of St. Stephens path, crossing and recrossing Three Mile Creek at several points, with the major residential development about four miles out of town in Summerville.[31]

91. *The Gates country home, 1842, 1570–1572 Dauphin Street. Originally out in the country, this long, galleried home was given maximum ventilation by French doors that led from the porch into every room.*

92. *Georgia cottage, ca. 1845, 2564 Spring Hill Avenue. The cottage form has here been expanded into a large country dwelling of great charm. The plan and the symmetry of the balancing wings show classical influence. The gable roof has been superseded by the hip. (Photograph by Michael Thomason.)*

Dauphin Road extended west to Spring Hill College, with a scattering of homes along its length. The present Old Shell was originally called Isabel and extended only to the city limits. In the 1850s it was cut through to the west and was called Dauphin Way. In about 1904 it was renamed Spring Hill Old Shell Road, which was finally shortened to Old Shell.

On Dauphin Way, about three miles out, Hezekiah Gates built an 1842 country home (figure 91). The long low lines and the seven-bay gallery perpetuate the older style, with chamfered columns and a swallowtail baluster cut. Doors led into every room from the gallery, but there was a wide central hall, to which a more elaborately framed door gave access. When I first examined the building in 1970, the east rear wing was still intact, though it had badly deteriorated. In one room the fireplace still had the cooking angle irons in place. During restoration the wings had to be destroyed.

More typical of the 1840s is Georgia cottage (figure 92), built in 1845 on Spring Hill Road. The building still stands, well preserved, at 2564 Spring Hill Avenue, the only alterations having been made in the rear, where provisions for utilities had to be provided. A comparison of this home with the Vincent House of 1827 (figure 35) illustrates the changes that had occurred within twenty years. While it is not strictly Greek Revival, the Georgia cottage shows a refine-

93a. Carolina Hall, ca. 1845, at 76 South McGregor Avenue, named for the state from which the builder, William Dawson, had emigrated. The house harmoniously combines several styles of nineteenth-century architecture, with the double-storied portico reminiscent of the late eighteenth-century homes of Charleston. (Photograph by Michael Thomason.)

ment and harmonious balance in its masses that reflect a classical influence. A strong central axis is enhanced by the five-bay porch and the offset matching wings. The converging lines of the hip roof tend to draw the eye toward the entrance, where the cornice leads the eye toward the horizontal. The home's location on a wooded site preserves the sense of space once common in residences and now rare within the confines of the city. The long lane that leads back to the house is bordered by magnificent old oaks and azaleas that recall a time when gracious living was the order of the day and the only early morning sounds were the songs of the mockingbirds and the clomping of horses' hoofs.

Upon approaching the house, the observer is impressed by the harmonious proportions and the purity of the design. No superficial decoration is needed to please the eye. Interior detailing is in the same spirit, with restrained scotia and torus crown moldings and ceiling medallions. Shallow crossettes project from the door architraves, and the batter of the jambs is understated and subtle.

The large two-story mansion built about 1845 by the Charleston-born William Dawson (figures 93a–h) is completely different in style. The main fabric of the house belongs to the 1840 decade, but some interior modifications were made by the F. A. Luling family after 1883 and later in the early twentieth century under the direction of George Rogers, architect. The general massing of the house derived from Charlestonian prototypes that must have been familiar to the builder. As in the Miles Brewton House in Charleston, which is of late Georgian style, the Neoclassical portico is two storied.

93b. *The decorative capitals and the crown moldings of the west parlor, Carolina Hall. Greek Revival motifs embellish the moldings throughout the house. Acanthus and water leaves adorn the capitals. (Photograph by Michael Thomason.)*

93c. *An acanthus swirl surrounded by an egg-and-dart motif form the center medallions of the parlors at Carolina Hall. (Photograph by Michael Thomason.)*

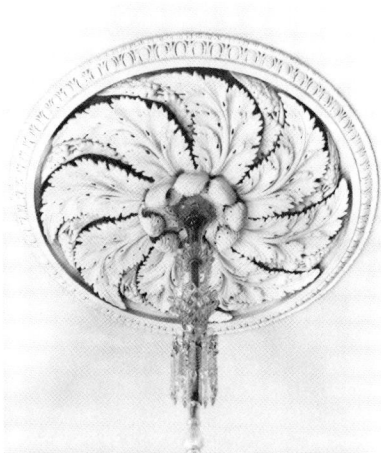

93d. *Carolina Hall dining room ceiling medallion in designs of leaves and flowers. (Photograph by Michael Thomason.)*

There is a matching portico on the rear. While the massing was derived from this source, the detailing was nineteenth century, incorporating Italianate characteristics such as the twin brackets under the raking cornice of the gable roof. The side-hall plan also breaks the axial balance of the classical tradition. Two large parlors range along the west side of the hall, and the dining room is in an offset wing on the east. The interior plaster work is among the finest found in Mobile. Greek Revival motifs abound—egg and dart, leaf and dart, bead and reel, grapevine, acanthus, and so forth (figure 93b). The ceilings of the parlors are embellished by a panel formed by a border molding representing a bundle of slender rods joined by delicate flowers. The three different types of ceiling medallions are designed to be in harmony with the function of the room in which they appear. In the parlors they are formed of acanthus leaves enclosed by a circular border of egg and dart, very formal and in low relief (figure 93c). In the dining room the medallion forms a rectangular shape, the design freer and more deeply carved, with organic motifs of flowers and fruits (figure 93d). In the rear gallery the medallion has a full-blown acanthus design of Baroque movement.

The two parlors are separated by a crossbeam supported at the walls by fluted pilasters and in the opening by two fluted columns. The parlor windows and doors are framed by paneled pilasters (figure 93e), and all capitals have a row of acanthus leaves below a circle of water leaves. The crown moldings are elaborate, being made of several different motifs (figure 93b). Above each of the parlor doors is a rectangular panel embellished with leafy tendrils in a low-relief stucco (figure 93e). Throughout the house the decor has grown from the classical vocabulary except for the staircase in the front hall. Here the cusped silhouette of the balusters reflects the Gothic Revival (figure 93f). The Luling renovation may have been responsible for this staircase, for during the Lulings' ownership the entrance doorway was enhanced by the Bohemian glass in the transom and by sidelights and the etched central panel with their initials.

Still surviving is the little "playhouse" that originally stood on the east side of the house and was moved to the west upon the recent restoration. It is of board-and-batten construction, with a palmetto tree motif carved above the door. During part of its history it was a billiard room (figure 93h).

93e. The decorative panel above the parlor doors of Carolina Hall. (Photograph by Michael Thomason.)

93f. Detail of the front stairway of Carolina Hall. The Gothic Revival balustrade is thought to date to the renovations done by F. A. Luling after his purchase of the property in 1883. (Photograph by Michael Thomason.)

93g. The enclosed rear gallery with stairs curving up to the second story. (Photograph by Michael Thomason.)

93h. The unattached dependency of Carolina Hall, used first as a children's playhouse and later as a billiard room. The palmetto tree motif may have come from the design used on the South Carolina flag. (Photograph by Michael Thomason.)

Architecture in Transition, 1840–1850

94. *The Parmly Houses, 1842 and 1852, 303–305–307 Conception Street. The three units of a row of brick city dwellings are typical of the 1840 developments. The two houses on the left are from 1842 and are earlier in style than the Greek Revival design of the building on the right.*

95a. *The Tarleton House, 1846, formerly at 351–353 St. Louis Street. This fine, large single-family dwelling made of brick once stood on a fashionable residential street in the inner city. Commercial encroachment brought alteration of the first story, and the building was finally destroyed in 1972. (Photograph by Robert Wakeman.)*

95b. *Tarleton House, detail of door. The monumental door is typical of its time, with its exaggerated batter and the straight-capped architrave. (Photograph by Robert Wakeman.)*

City Dwellings of Brick

Wood was the material of choice for the city cottage but not for the two-story residences, for which brick was preferred. Of the fine surviving examples, I have selected three for discussion. All had the same blocky massing and differed only in size (figures 94, 95a,b). The shallow cornices were accented by small dentil moldings as in the stores. The gable end of the roofs was hidden by a solid parapet built up between the end chimneys (figures 95a, 96). The side-hall plan was universally used. Chimneys, located only on the parlor side of the house, created an unequal balance in the massing. One contract for such a home called for a false chimney on the hall side in order to rectify the problem.[32] Garrets were given windows and ventilation either by a dormer, as in the Parmly Houses (figure 94), or by twin windows in the gable end (figures 95a, 96). The brick walls commonly used white mortar for the facades and brown for the rest of the building. The white accent, combined with the stone or stucco of the windowsills and door lintels, made a lively contrast with the red of the brick. Front galleries were not customary, as they were in the cottages. Instead, a small second-story cast iron balcony was placed at the central bay (figure 94, left; the two-story iron gallery on the middle building in the illustration is a later addition). The Sanborn maps show that some brick houses located outside the restricted zone did have wood galleries. One example was the Silver House (figure 96), which had a two-story wood gallery surrounding the building on three sides that was later replaced by the present cast iron gallery on the facade. Doors received any of several treatments. They could be plain, with a small transom of three lights, as in the Parmly Houses (figure 94), or they could have pilasters framing the door, as in the Silver House (figure 96), or they could have a capped architrave and battered jambs, as in the Tarleton House (figure 95).

The cast iron galleries of elaborate design that were added later to the earlier buildings make it difficult to see the original elevations

96. *The Silver House, 1845, 251 St. Francis Street. A two-story frame porch originally surrounded the building on three sides. As with many other brick buildings, the early porches were replaced by cast iron later in the century. (Photograph by Robert Wakeman.)*

clearly. The date of some of the additions can be determined approximately on the basis of the design motifs shown in iron—whether classical, Gothic Revival, or Victorian in origin, whether strongly three dimensional or flat, thin, and brittle geometric configurations dating to the end of the century. A case in point is the iron on the 1844–1845 Chandler House standing at 205 Church Street, in which an elaborate Victorian design was superimposed on an earlier facade (figures 97a,b).[33]

Unique in Mobile is the small building at 110 Claiborne (figure 98). In 1868 Moses Waring added to his Government Street property the little 1840 Nugent building, now known as the Waring Texas. Mr. Waring's purpose was to adapt the building as a *garçonnière* for his boys. The local explanation of the name is that it derived from a phrase "going to Texas," meaning an escape to a distant land. The building recalls the Charleston side entrance plan, in which the house had its windowed short end on the street and the gallery extended along the side, access being gained through a privacy fence. Mr. Nugent built three houses on Claiborne, two of brick and one of wood. Of the three, only the one purchased by Mr. Waring remains. A letter written by the great-granddaughter of Moses Waring mentioned that the little building had been a schoolhouse.[34] In 1966 the Mystic Society bought the building for its headquarters.

97a. The Chandler House, 1844, 205 Church Street. A typical brick home of the 1840s, to which cast iron of a later period has been added.

97b. Chandler House, detail of the cast iron gallery, with typical Victorian design.

126   *From Fort to Port*

98. *The Waring Texas, ca. 1840, 110 South Claiborne. The old Nugent House bought by Moses Waring in 1868 for use as a "garçonnière."*

The decade that opened so inauspiciously closed with renewed vigor. Two far-reaching events brought about the economic prosperity that made possible the architectural boom of the 1850s. In April 1848, a railroad was planned to extend from Mobile to the mouth of the Ohio River. Charters were granted by all states through which the line would pass. Subscriptions for stock were issued May 2, and in early 1849, the Mobile authorities levied a real estate tax to raise $300,000 to cover the local assessment.[35]

In addition to the new connections by land, Mobile was selected as a port for the Royal East Indies Steamship Line, greatly increasing the opportunity for international trade.[36] Thus Mobile was in a position by both land and sea to emerge from its isolation and to develop into an important center of trade extending far beyond the borders of the Gulf. The time was right: cotton was fast becoming the gold of the South.

99. The Richards House, 1860, 256 North Joachim Street. Detail of the cast iron, with figures of the four seasons, framed by arabesques. (Photograph by Michael Thomason.)

100. Row stores, formerly on the west side of Royal, south of Dauphin, now destroyed. Tucker Drug Store was on the corner. The two to the south were owned by A. Carmelich, who was taxed for them in 1850 at a value of $15,000. (Courtesy of the Historic Mobile Preservation Society, Wilson Plates.)

5 The Golden Age, 1850–1860

The decade of the 1830s in Mobile was charged with the strength and youthful vigor of the early Greek Revival, in which excellence of proportions and restraint of detail were architecturally dominant. With the cotton-produced wealth of the 1850s, the more elaborate Italianate took precedence over the simplicity of the early Greek Revival, and Mobile builders adopted more complex designs and rich plaster ornamentation in the moldings and medallions. The decorative patterns were of Renaissance origin—arabesques, leafy rinceau, swags, and occasionally small Arcadian figures (figure 99). Cast iron began a period of importance, with the Skate and Spear foundries producing structural iron. Decorative iron was still largely imported, though within a short time local foundries would begin to fill the demand.

The Robertson maps of 1853 and 1856 (figures 101a–c) do not indicate the growth in the number of buildings. Except for the wharves, which have proliferated along the waterfront, the city in the Robertson map appears much as it did on the La Tourrette map of 1838. Not indicated is the fact that the inner-city streets were solidly lined with rows of two- and three-story brick commercial buildings (figure 100). The legend on the side of the map (figure 101c) lists only the major structures. Travelers of the decade described Mobile as a city "on the make." Charles Olliffe wrote in 1853 that anyone visiting Mobile would find it the most flourishing city in Alabama.

> He would need only to stroll briefly through its main thoroughfares and especially along its wharves in order to observe there the extraordinary business activity evident on all sides. . . . Anyone desiring to take a jaunt to the outskirts of the city will feel overwhelmed by the wealth of choices confronting him. Everywhere so far as one can see, there is nothing but thick green groves, picturesque rolling country, meadows decked with flowers and carpeted with luxuriant grass, a striking contrast to the swamp and mud holes encountered in the country surrounding the "Crescent City" of New Orleans.[1]

101a. Robertson map of Mobile, 1856. The west boundary is indicated on a line between Monterey and Houston streets. (Courtesy of the Library of Congress.)

101b. Robertson map, detail of the wards of the inner city, with the increase in the number of wharves indicated along the waterfront. (Courtesy of the Library of Congress.)

Fredrika Bremer, another visitor, was intrigued by the Indian population still camped in the area. On a walk to the Indians' area, she wrote, "In order to reach their camp I must walk up Government Street, the principal street of the city, a broad straight alley of beautiful villas surrounded by trees and garden plots; the most beautiful young orange trees covered with fruit, shine in the sun."[2] A less romantic record of the city is suggested by the 1855 census reported in the *Mobile Weekly Advertiser* of Wednesday, October 31. The residents were counted during the summer, when many were away on vacation. Undoubtedly the figures would have been higher had the census been taken during the winter. The total number of residents was given as 29,744, which included 8,366 slaves and 1,041 free blacks. The four public schools in the city had a total of 1,079 pupils; ten county schools had 454 pupils. The twenty-three private schools had 721 pupils, and the eight Catholic schools accommodated an additional 1,081. The growth in churches was amazing: four Episcopal, thirteen Methodist (including those in the county), five Presbyterian, five Baptist, six Catholic (including those in the county), and two Jewish.

With such activity we would expect both the city and county governments to initiate some ambitious architectural programs. When Hobart's 1822 County Court House burned early in the 1850s,

101c. Robertson map, detail of the legend, listing the important buildings. (Courtesy of the Library of Congress.)

131   *The Golden Age, 1850–1860*

a contract was signed between the Board of Revenue of the city and county and the builder James Barnes. Barnes was to erect a new County Court House on the same site as the old one, following plans drawn by William S. Alderson. While Barnes signed the contract for the construction, Alderson was retained as the superintendent.[3] The building was to be brick and three stories in elevation, with rough stucco on the exterior in "imitation of stone" and with the classic features of columns, pilasters, and brick molded triglyphs.[4] Two kinds of stone were employed, white granite for the steps on the Royal and Government street entrances, for the doorsills, and for all window trim, and a Tennessee blue marble for the water table and for the square bases and capitals of the columns. Yorkshire flagging was used on the lower story. The directions for the installation of the parapet and the stone cap of the fire walls suggest that the exterior design continued the traditional practices of the times, but the interior plans incorporated several innovations. One was the groined vaults in the courtrooms and vestibules, which supplanted the flat ceilings. The contract issued careful instructions regarding the centering of the vaults so that the brick arches would not be injured when the supporting scaffolding was removed. The surface of the vaults was finished by plaster and paneling.

A second innovation was the installation of a hot air furnace with "cast iron conductors" set in the walls. As the contract explained: "All the walls of the second story, to have an opening of Two Inches left between the outer body of the wall and the inner core of Brick, in all cases to be filled up solid. . . . the two Walls to be bound together . . . as the Superintendent may direct, to build the Cast Iron conduits in such places as shall be pointed out." The furnace was unusual for Mobile in the 1850s. Sheet iron and iron reinforcements in the window framing were also specified. The first-story shutters were made of sheet iron. The windows were different in that they were made in three sashes, with the central section stationary, while pulleys controlled the movement of the upper and lower lights. The architect called for French glass of double thickness in all the windows except those of the third story and the jury room. The double thickness served to strengthen the windows while also acting as insulation. The interior wood trim was without extravagant detailing, the only refinements being cherry in the courtroom and mahogany for the stair railing. Yellow pine and cypress furnished the structural members, and white pine was used for the window sash. Such a well-built structure should have survived until the present, but as in the case of many other buildings in Mobile, within ten years it had burned down.

The city of Mobile was more fortunate in the Market that it erected in 1856, as it still stands on the east side of Royal Street, between Government and Church. The structure was severely damaged by the winds and water sweeping in from the bay during the 1979 hurricane, but it has now been restored. The building reflected two decisions made by the mayor and Board of Aldermen (figures 102a–d). The first plan addressed the need for a new market to replace the old one located on lower Government and shown on the Goodwin and Haire map of 1824. This open air Market had grown until it sprawled over sidewalks and neighboring stores and was finally condemned. Several solutions were suggested. Moses Waring in 1852 offered his cotton shed, which was located on the block bounded by Water,

Church, and Royal streets. He agreed to brick the floor, plaster the ceiling, and install seventy windows with iron bars, for which he would receive the rents of the market in payment.[5] This offer was not accepted. Later, on July 27, 1854, the committee for the new Market recommended that two markets be built, one in the south part of the city and the other in the north. This plan was approved, and on August 12, 1854, $30,000 to $40,000 was appropriated for the land for the southern Market. In December 1854, the land bounded by Royal on the west, Church on the south, Water on the east, and Hitchcock Alley on the north was purchased. The lots acquired had been owned by Moses Waring, Bernard Tim, John Bloodgood, John Weaver, Sidney Smith, and H. Lyons.[6] By February 1, 1855, plans for the building had been approved but were stopped because of a report brought in by the Public Property Committee.[7] The condition of the building being used as the City Hall had deteriorated to such a point that it could not be repaired without great expense. The committee reported that the roof leaked, the timbers and floor were rotten, and there was no longer enough space to contain the offices for the city surveyor, the tax collector, and other officials. Furthermore, the public records were in jeopardy. A recent fire in the mayor's office had made further use of the building impossible. It was proposed that a second story be added to the new Market to house the municipal offices. On February 1, 1855, the new plan was approved, and an additional $6,000 was allocated for the changes. To cover the expense of the whole project, the city issued forty-four bonds valued at $1,000 each.[8] Thomas S. James, the builder, estimated that he could complete the project in about six weeks and was

> agreeable to the original plan at a cost of between thirty three and thirty five hundred dollars and that five offices: the Mayor, the City Clerk, the Treasurer and rooms for two boards can be completed in ten weeks and be ready for occupancy at a cost of between fifteen and eighteen hundred dollars—but that these rooms and offices can be finished with the exception of the plastering for a less sum.[9]

Some public criticism of the expenses involved was expressed in the *Mobile Daily Register* for December 30, 1855, in which John Forsyth, the editor, wrote that "the new market erected after the plan of Mr. Architect James' 'pretty pictures,' although a beautiful structure and quite the pride of Mobilians, has cost a pretty sum of money. How much cannot be precisely learned, for the Market Committee reports that 'the unfortunate fire in the Mayor's office consumed all the records, papers, vouchers, etc.'" James did not finish the building, however, for a second contract, dated September 27, 1856, was signed by Richard Redwood, Benjamin Scattergood, George Gregory, Thomas Riley, and E. S. Dargan, in which they agreed to complete the Market–City Hall complex. The final contract for the iron grilles was signed on September 22, 1856, with William Rouse representing the New York Wire Railing Company, which furnished the iron wire in the arcades.[10]

The final building consisted of the Market on the first-floor level, with open stalls filling the large courtyard east of the building and extending to Water Street. Closed stalls occupied the length of the south wing that faced onto Church Street. The municipal offices ex-

CITY HALL AND NEW MARKET, MOBILE, ALABAMA.

102a. *City Hall, 1856–1857, 111 South Royal Street; first building program, 1855, Thomas James, architect; second building program, 1856, B. F. Scattergood, R. H. Redwood, G. Gregory, T. Riley, and E. S. Dargan, builders. The building housed both the municipal government and the local Market. (Engraving from Ballou,* Pictorial Drawing Room Companion, *June 1857, courtesy of Mrs. Carter Smith.)*

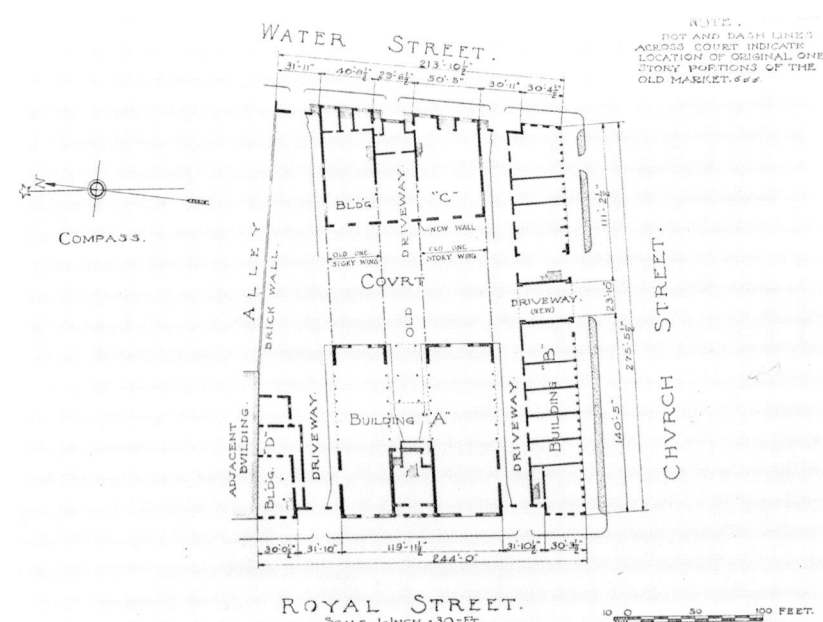

102b. *City Hall, first-floor plan. (Drawing by Kenneth Engwall, courtesy of the Library of Congress, Historic American Building Survey Collection.)*

tended across the complex located in the second story of the two main buildings, with the courtroom forming a bridge over the entrance to the Market (figure 102b). The second story of the south wing was turned over to the Regimental Company as headquarters, drill room, and armory.

Very few exterior alterations have been made over the years. The original stall doorways on the Church Street side of the south wing have been changed to windows (figure 102a and b). The major interior changes have resulted from the gradual elimination of the Market and the adaptation of the space for municipal offices. The once

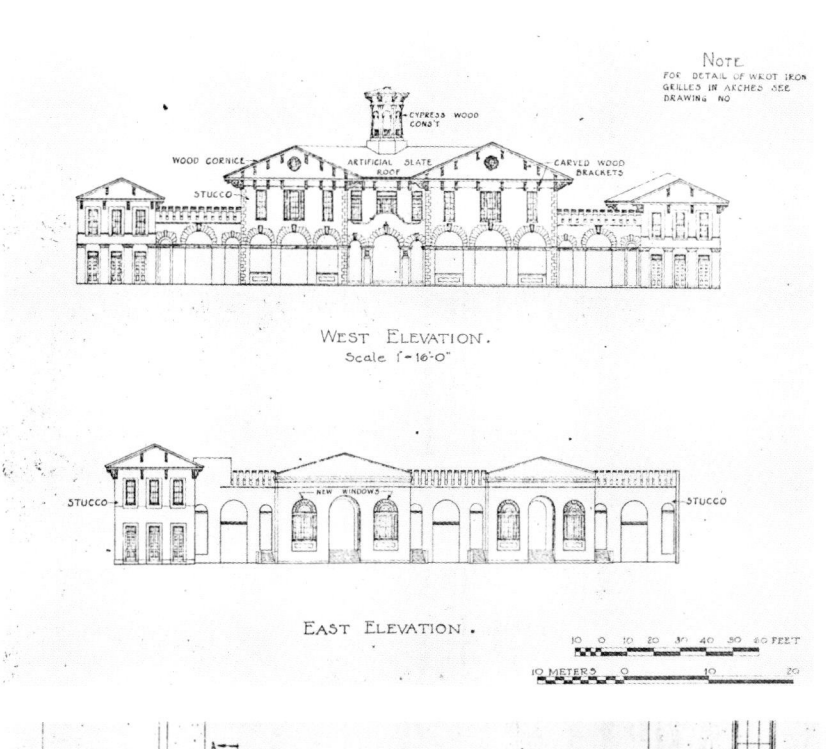

102c. City Hall, elevation drawings. (Drawings by Kenneth Engwall, courtesy of the Library of Congress, Historic American Building Survey Collection.)

102d. City Hall, drawing of the iron gates opening into the city Market. (Drawing by Paul Dowling, courtesy of the Library of Congress, Historic American Building Survey Collection.)

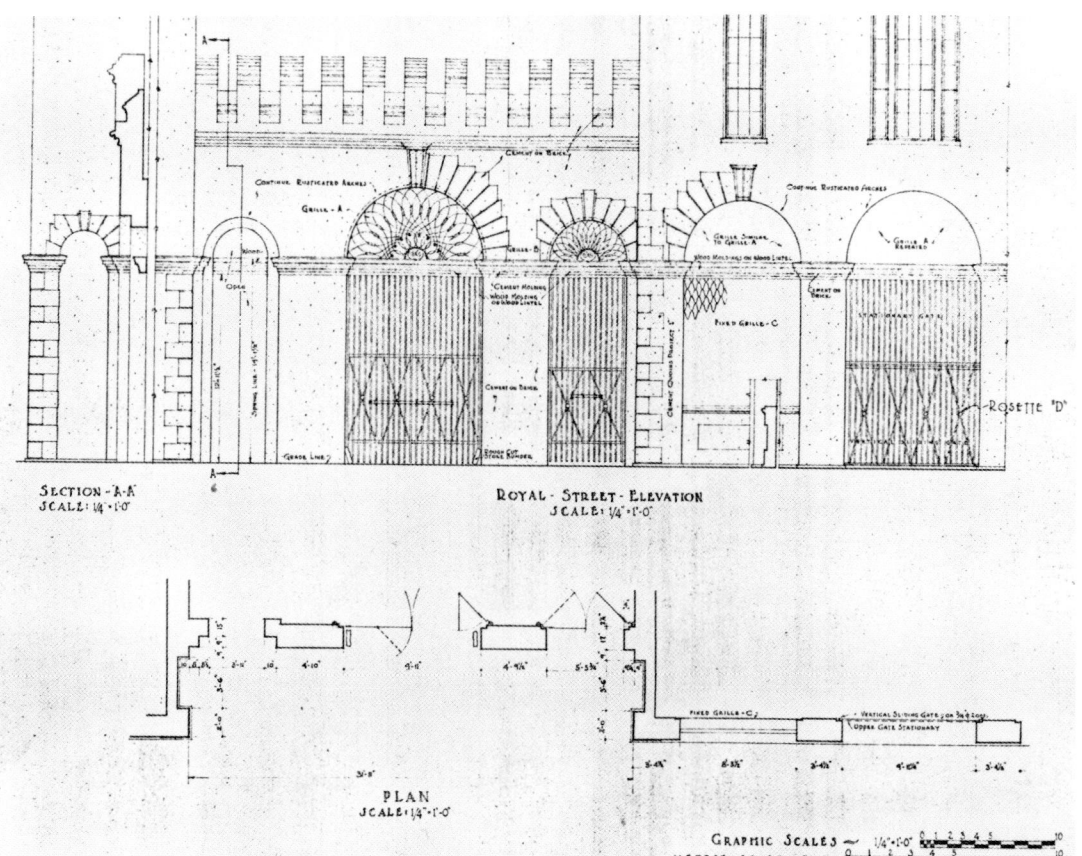

open passageway has been made into a foyer with a monumental stairway to the upper level. In design the building makes an interesting contrast with the Greek Revival public buildings of the 1830s. Here elements of the Renaissance have been selected to embellish

135   *The Golden Age, 1850–1860*

103a. The United States Customs House, 1852–1856, formerly located on the southwest corner of Royal and St. Francis, was authorized in 1850 and was finished in 1856 at a cost of $379,564.93. Ammi Burnham Young was the supervising architect for the United States Treasury, 1852–1862. (Courtesy of the Mobile Public Library.)

the plane of the stuccoed walls, creating a design that contains the spirit of a Latin culture more in harmony with the origins of the city. The semicircular arcades, the deeply overhanging bracketed cornice, the quoining, and the iron grilles belong to a place free from the influences imported by the merchants of the eastern seaboard. The building more truly expresses a particular location than does the monumental Barton Academy of 1836.

In the 1830s the nationally known architects Gallier and Dakin influenced the trend of Mobile architecture toward the Greek Revival. Twenty years later, Ammi B. Young, architect in charge of the Federal buildings in Washington (1852–1862), introduced the Italianate into Mobile. Ammi Young's 1852 plan for the United States Customs House and Post Office was the first major building of the city to incorporate the characteristics of the style to the fullest extent (figures 103a–d). The imposing three-story building stood on the southwest corner of Royal and St. Francis streets, the site of the present First National Bank. As was the case with many of the United States government buildings, the United States Customs House was built of granite, an unusual material for a city accustomed to brick and wood. The building was reported in the 1855 Directory to have cost $360,000. The stone was laid in interlocking joints; therefore the Aalco Company of St. Louis found its demolition in 1964 a difficult task. The contrasting textures on the surfaces of the different stories were also new to Mobile. As in the John Notman Athenaeum in Philadelphia (1845–1847; figure 104), the upper levels received a smooth ashlar surface, while the ground level had slightly beveled stones set in recessed mortar joints. Quoining too made its first appearance in Mobile at this time. In both the Notman and the Young buildings, the stone balcony played an essential part in effecting the visual transition between the first and second stories. Other Italianate features that were to become popular in Mobile buildings were the bracketed cornice and the molded band that marked the level of each story. Both the Renaissance elements in the

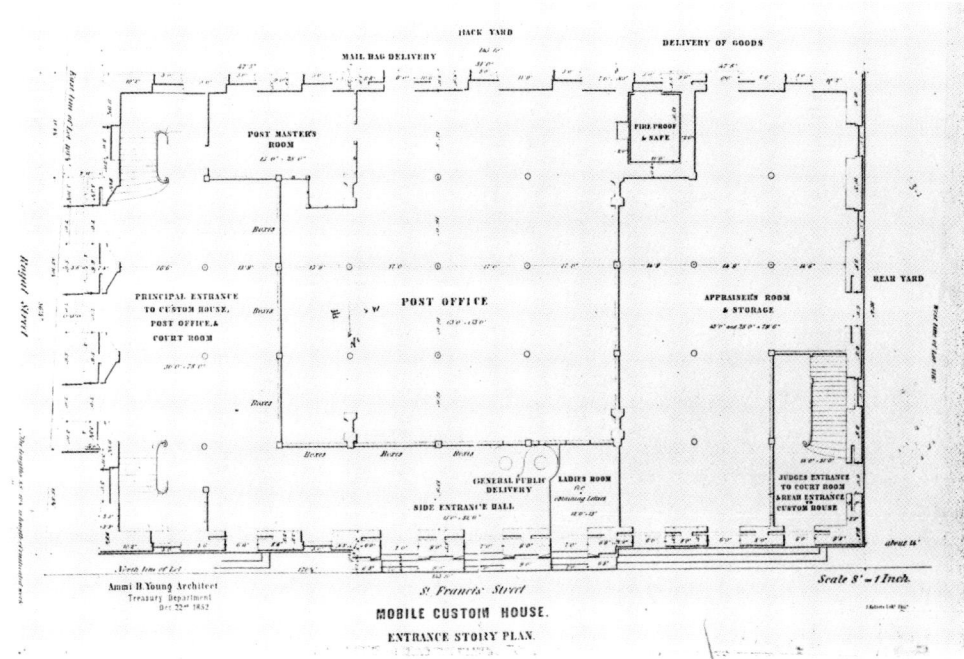

103b. *The United States Customs House, plan of the first story. (Courtesy of the Mobile Public Library, Special Collections Division.)*

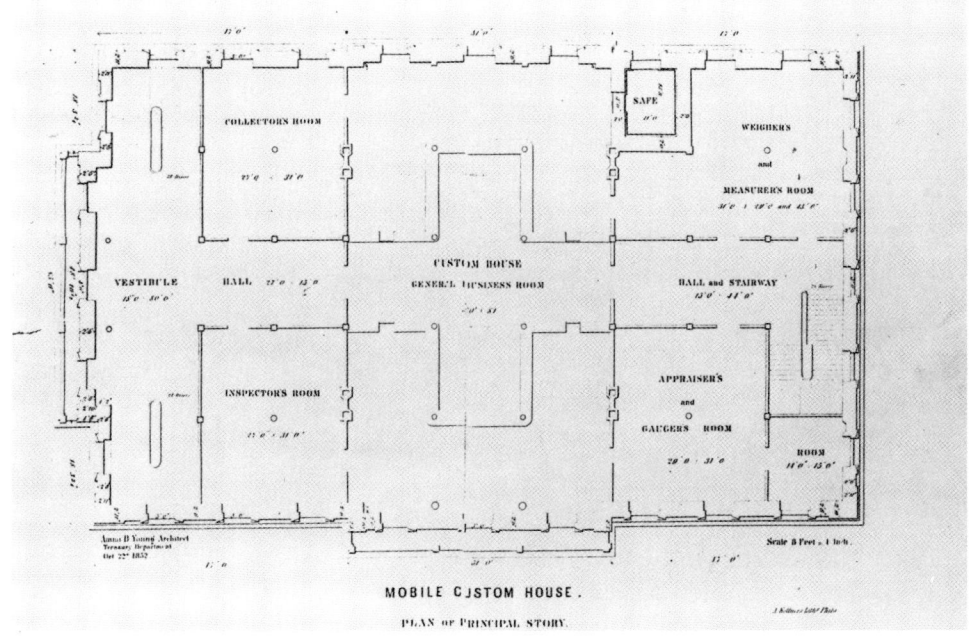

103c. *The United States Customs House, plan of the second story. (Courtesy of the Mobile Public Library, Special Collections Division.)*

window framing and the Greek Revival use of rosettes to elaborate the door surrounds were to appear in later buildings of the decade. Several of the doors in Hitchcock Row (figure 111) used the same decorative treatment for the main entrances.

An interesting structural feature of the Customs House was the foundation. Until this time, it was common practice to set brick walls on an overlapping layer of cypress logs. For a heavy granite building, such a foundation was not adequate. At the time of demolition, the *Mobile Press Register* of February 22, 1964, published an account of the foundation and photographs of its substructures. Some fifteen or twenty feet below the surface of the ground, a foundation bed of twelve-inch-thick heart pine had been placed over

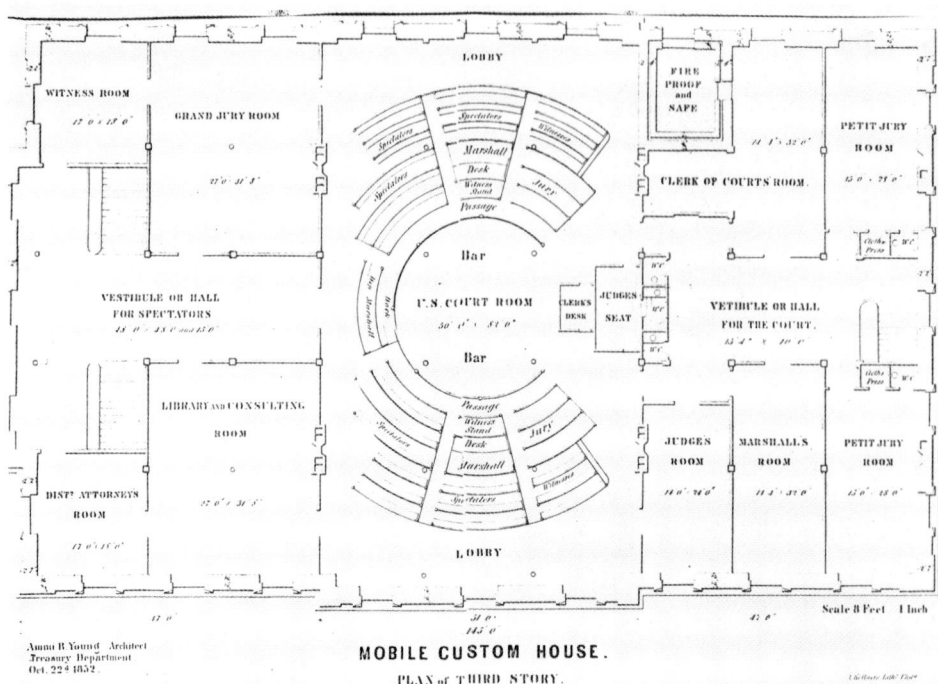

103d. *The United States Customs House, plan of the third story. (Courtesy of the Mobile Public Library, Special Collections Division.)*

hard clay. On this platform five-foot-wide brick foundation walls had been laid, with reverse arches between them acting as buttresses to help support the weight above. These walls were tapered as they rose to the ground surface, where they received the coursing of the exposed walls. Each coping stone weighed five tons. In a coastal area where the water table is high and the sand deposits are deep, foundations are a problem.

The first floor of the Customs House served as the Post Office (figure 103b). It was divided into three main rooms, with vestibules and offices. In the northwest corner leading in from St. Francis Street was a stair hall leading up to the second (main) story, which contained the offices and workrooms connected with the customs department (figure 103c). Stairways at both the front and the rear of the building led up to the top story, which contained the main courtroom and auxiliary chambers (figure 103d). It is unfortunate that such a well-designed building and one of such importance to the history of Mobile architecture was not preserved.

The Italianate became the dominant style during the late 1850s and early 1860s, but during the early years of the decade, the Greek Revival continued in popularity for both civic and domestic construction. One of the surviving examples of the former is the small Fire Station Number Five standing at 7 North Lawrence, which was built in 1851, soon after the Washington Fire Engine Company Number Eight bought its lot. The Annual Report of the chief engineer of the Mobile Fire Department, 1860–1861, listed the cost of the 1851 firehouse at $5,500 (figures 105a,b). The building is important both architecturally and historically. It is an excellent example of a functional building designed in the Greek Revival style. The basic classic divisions of the front elevation, the excellent proportions, the simplicity of the moldings, and the classic rhythms give the old fire station its distinction. The building is simultaneously a historical monument, recalling the time when private companies

104. The Athenaeum, Philadelphia, Pennsylvania, 1845–1847; John Notman, architect. (Photograph by Peter Olson, courtesy of the Athenaeum.)

105a. Number Five Fire Station, 1851, 7 North Lawrence Street. Following the national movement, local builders selected elements of the Greek Revival to adorn the facades of even small buildings. (From Souvenir History of the Mobile Fire and Police Department, 1902, courtesy of the Mobile Public Library, Special Collections Division.)

furnished the fire protection for the city. In 1843 the Washington Company Number Eight was incorporated under state law, and in 1851 it bought the land upon which to construct its building. The company continued to serve the community until 1888, when it and other companies were purchased by the municipal authorities as the city established a fire department. At that time the building was renamed Number Five. While it has been altered in the course of service in various commercial enterprises, the basic fabric remains, and if the commercial store windows were removed and the iron balcony restored, the original design would be intact (figure 105b).

Two developments of the decade affected the growth of the city and indirectly influenced its architecture by improving the means of transportation. On October 20, 1859, the Mobile Omnibus Company petitioned the city for permission to build and operate a horse-drawn street railroad system. Iron tracks were to extend west along Dauphin Street to Ann, with a double track for a turnaround on

105b. Number Five Fire Station. Time and alterations have changed the facade design, but the basic elevation is still intact. (Photograph by Michael Thomason.)

139   The Golden Age, 1850–1860

Broad. The tracks were laid four feet six inches apart. The area between them was filled with shell. When this system had been completed early in the 1860s, it greatly increased the possibilities for a residential expansion to the west, extending the boundaries of the city far beyond the confines of the original colonial limits. As the Robertson map of 1856 (figure 101) shows, the northern boundary was still at Three Mile Creek, but the western line extended just beyond Reed. This expansion was furthered by the opening up of Old Shell Road. By a legislative act of February 13, 1850, Isabella Street was extended into the toll road known then as Spring Hill Shell Road and later called just Old Shell. The Spring Hill neighborhood six miles out thus became more accessible. With the improvement in transportation, more architectural activity was possible.

Religious Buildings

The Gothic Revival took precedence over the Classical style in Mobile churches during the 1850s. Inspired by the idea that a "Christian architecture" might serve as a prototype rather than a "pagan temple," the movement was stimulated by both an emotional drive and the greater flexibility with which the style could be adapted to the wood and brick materials that were easily obtainable in Mobile. Unlike the Gothic Revival of the East in the work of Richard Upjohn and James Renwick, Jr., who followed the principles of Augustus Pugin, the style in Mobile had a simpler format—a lancet arch, uncomplicated tracery, occasionally a cresting, and in churches a steeple with a spire that was sometimes decorated with crockets and a finial. St. John's Episcopal Church is an example and affords an interesting contrast with the first little Protestant Church on the 1824 map (figures 106a and b and figure 27). St. John's formerly stood on the southwest corner of Monroe and Dearborn in the Church Street East Historic District.[11] It was designed by the architect David Cum-

106a. *St. John's Episcopal Church, 1853, formerly on the southwest corner of Monroe and Dearborn and now destroyed; David Cumming, Jr., architect. Typical Gothic Revival with board-and-batten siding. (Courtesy of the Historic Mobile Preservation Society, Wilson Plates.)*

ming, Jr., who was also responsible for the Italianate Guesnard House on Jackson Street (figure 128). Typical of the style are the basilica plan, the board-and-batten siding, the bays divided by stepped buttresses, and the front entrance tower, with its corner pinnacles topped by small finials. The lancets have simple tracery, and the vestibule opening recalls early fourteenth-century mullions in the English churches, such as All Saints at Sharrington, Norfolk.[12] Old St. John's was destroyed when the congregation's new church was erected in 1956.

Trinity Episcopal, built in 1853, represented a more formal interpretation of the Gothic in brick (figures 107a,b). The building originally stood on the southeast corner of Jackson and St. Anthony streets. When it was moved in 1945, the bricks of all openings were carefully marked for replacement, and the interior framing was reinstated according to the original design (figure 107b).[13] Willis and Dudley of New York were the architects. The spire that was added in 1884 was destroyed by Hurricane Frederick in 1979 and had to be replaced. The large, square tower is not centered but stands on the southwest corner of the facade. Each lancet is filled with stained glass set in mullions with trefoil cusped heads. Trefoils also form the designs in the interstices between the side aisle arches and in the interspacing between the members of the scissors truss in the nave (figure 107b). The exposed common rafters are reinforced by principal rafters that in the chancel rest on corbels.

The St. Francis Street Baptist Church (figure 108) once stood on half the site of the present Scottish Rite Bodies Egyptian Revival Temple. The west wall of the Church, which has stepped buttresses,

106b. *St. John's Episcopal Church, interior. The modified scissors truss of the wooden vault suggests an early English Gothic spirit. (Photograph by Ed D. Poole, courtesy of the University of South Alabama Photographic Archives.)*

The Golden Age, 1850–1860

107a. Trinity Episcopal Church, 1853, originally on the southeast corner of St. Anthony and Jackson streets and moved in 1945–1946 to 1900 Dauphin Street; Willis and Dudley, New York, architects; spire added, 1884, C. L. Hutchisson, Jr., reconstruction architect. (Photograph by Michael Thomason.)

107b. Trinity Episcopal Church, interior. All the original ceiling and trussing timbers were reset during reconstruction. (Photograph by Michael Thomason.)

still stands as the rear wall of the Scottish Rite building. The architecture of the Baptist Church is of eclectic design, with a Romanesque corbel table accenting the cornices of the facade and the tower. A Baptist congregation was organized in 1835, but the denomination suffered serious reverses and had to occupy small rental quarters until it was able to build the Church on St. Francis Street in about 1850.

The Episcopalians were building within the city and also out in the summer colony in Spring Hill. As the western neighborhood evolved from a summer health colony in the 1830s into a place where people lived year round, a school was established as well as a church. At 4051 Old Shell Road, St. Paul's Chapel was constructed under the supervision of John Dawson and Albert Stein (the hydraulic engineer who was responsible for the city waterworks). Other members of the community were also on the building committee, so that the Chapel was a community effort. The small board-and-batten frame building (figure 109) has a square tower at the front elevation, with the altar at the far end of the processional nave, though in the Chapel everything is on a restricted scale. The three-bay porch shades the rounded two-leaf doorway with its shutters shaped to half the arched opening. The windows, while round-headed, have tracery that forms lancets filled with diamond-shaped panes of glass. The liturgical emphasis of the Church is expressed in the symbols placed above each of the windows on the interior—the keys, the pelican, rod and flails, crosier, and so forth. A small balcony supported on iron posts extends across the single nave above the entrance. Tradition has it that the slaves worshiped here, but at

108. St. Francis Street Baptist Church, ca. 1850 (destroyed 1921). The west wall of the Church today forms the rear wall of the Scottish Rite Bodies Egyptian Temple. (Courtesy of the Historic Mobile Preservation Society, Wilson Plates.)

109. St. Paul's Chapel, 1859–1861, 4051 Old Shell Road, north facade and east side elevation. The small board-and-batten Chapel was built for the residents of the Spring Hill area. The work was supervised by John Dawson and Albert Stein. (Photograph by Michael Thomason.)

least in later times the blacks had their own church nearby in Sandtown. Except for a few years during the Civil War when Episcopalian churches were closed, St. Paul served the Spring Hill area until the new building was erected in 1964. It still, however, plays a part in the religious community.[14]

Religious organizations were active during the 1850s in erecting not only churches but also hospitals, schools, and church-affiliated buildings. The Mayor's and Aldermen's Minutes of August 10, 1854, record the purchase of a lot opposite the Old City Hospital on St. Anthony Street for a hospital to be run by the Sisters of Charity. This building was the first of three to be known as the Providence Infirmary, the last one now being called just Providence Hospital. The first building (figure 110), built in 1854–1855, was of brick and was two and one-half stories in height, with a two-story iron gallery extending the full 105 feet of its front elevation. The intimate scale of the design contrasted sharply with the monumental character of the City Hospital across the street (figure 41a). The building provided for sixty beds, with a ward set aside for charity.[15] By 1901 the Infirmary was proving inadequate for the demands made upon it, and a second was built on Spring Hill Avenue.

The Golden Age, 1850–1860

110. *The First Providence Infirmary, 1854–1855, formerly on the south side of St. Anthony, opposite the Old City Hospital (destroyed). The structure was a typical mid-nineteenth-century brick construction of two-story elevation with a cast iron gallery extending the full 105-foot length of the facade. (From Peter Hamilton,* Art Work in Mobile and Vicinity, *1894. Courtesy of the Mobile Public Library, Special Collections Division.)*

Commercial Buildings

During the 1850s the commercial building activity was affected by two improvements in technique. The first was a new brick-making machine that provided bricks of better quality that were more efficiently fired. With this development more and more contracts called for Mobile brick rather than the previously popular Philadelphia or Baltimore products. The second innovation was a vertical saw called the Woodpecker. It was advertised as early as 1852 by the Water Street Phoenix Foundry. Later, in a contract for the lease of a sawmill dated May 20, 1859, a list of machinery included a "cross cut and an upright saw."

The greatly increased number of buildings made it necessary to create some means of identification. On October 9, 1857, the city passed an ordinance for the establishment of a numbering system for buildings, with the provision that a record should be kept of the old numbers to assist in future identification. Unfortunately, the numbers were subsequently changed again, and the old lists have been lost. As the commercial district spread, it became necessary for the Board of Aldermen to modify the old ordinance that prohibited wood buildings within a certain area. On September 12, 1854, an act was passed enlarging the restricted area so that the block-long rows of two- and three-story brick buildings spread farther west along Dauphin, Conti, St. Francis, and Government streets. The buildings formed a continuous facade, with the units indicated by the chimneys and fire walls (figure 111). Common lines of fenestration, story height, and cornice levels were established, and occasionally the facade was enlivened by a cast iron balcony. Individuality was achieved by details of door framing.[16] The new uniformity was deliberate, as is evident from a contract for a store built next door to the south of the Mansion House. The owner, Charles Cullum, asked James F. Hutchisson and A. M. Quigley to build so that the first story

111. Hitchcock Row, formerly on the south side of Government between Royal and Water streets and now destroyed. The row is typical of the commercial buildings of the 1850s. (Courtesy of the Historic Mobile Preservation Society, Wilson Plates.)

112. Three attached commercial-residential buildings. From right to left: the Smith Building, 354 Dauphin (1848); the Chighizola Building, 356 Dauphin (1858); and the McGuire Building, 358 Dauphin (1854). Though of different heights, all have the same story levels and dentil molding below the shallow cornice. The Smith Building originally also had an iron balcony. Only the Chighizola retains the two-entrance arrangement that was common for a commercial-residential building. (Photograph by Michael Thomason.)

of the new building would have the same height and openings as the mansion and also specified that the same "rough cast surface" should be used.[17] While some of the commercial buildings were left without balconies, as in the drugstore on the corner of Royal and Dauphin (figure 100), some had added iron galleries by mid-century. This ornamental iron was still largely imported, as the local foundries were not yet able to produce enough. T. S. James, a popular local builder, was an agent for the Chase Brothers of Boston. The three commercial/residential buildings still standing on Dauphin suggest a typical mid-nineteenth-century street (figure 112). Harmonious relationships are established by the common cornice lines with their dentil moldings and by the similar fenestration. Unfortunately, the first stories of the two end buildings have lost their original design, though an attempt was made to reestablish the early openings in the example on the left during a restoration in 1982. The central building has retained the nineteenth-century form in which two en-

145   The Golden Age, 1850–1860

113. *The La Clede Hotel (1855, 1856, and 1940), 150–160 Government Street; eastern sections, 150–154 Government (1855), for Joseph Peter; central sections, 156–158 Government (1855–1856), for Larimer Price; western section, 160 Government (1940), by Hutchisson and Hutchisson, architects. (Photograph by Thigpen Photography, courtesy of the Mobile City Planning Commission.)*

trances were made, one leading to the store and the other to the residence. The 1848 Smith Building is on the right, at the eastern end of the row. The middle section is the Chighizola Building of 1858, and the western end, on the left, is the three-story McGuire Building of 1854. The same general effect can be seen in the two buildings that were later combined as the La Clede Hotel (figure 113). The corner section was built by Joseph Peter in 1855 for use as a fruit market, with his residence above. The central, taller section of 1856 was owned by Larimer Price. Caleb Price in 1871 united the two parcels to create the La Clede. Not until 1940 were the last 25 feet on the western end added. A 258-foot-long two-story gallery extends along Government Street and wraps around the corner on St. Emanuel, tying together the various sections of the complex, which differ in their floor levels as well as in the height of the roofs. The hotel opened on November 29, 1871, with much fanfare. In 1914 J. H. Wilson acquired the property and continued to operate it as a hotel until 1963.

The early custom of renting a lot upon which a lessee could build and hold a structure for a limited period of time remained common during the middle years of the century. A large store, recently destroyed, that stood on the southeast corner of Dauphin and Claiborne, on what is now the Cathedral Plaza, is a case in point. It was built by James McGanahan on a lot rented from Bishop Portier and served doubly as a residence and a store, with a two-story kitchen in the rear (figure 114).[18] The directories in 1869 listed a bell hanger as living here above his shop. Nearby was a coppersmith, a crockery, and a millinery shop, all in the block-long row of Federally inspired buildings. As yet no Italianate influence appeared in the storefronts.

In the small office of the popular Dr. LeVert in 1856 the Italianate again appeared (figure 115). The coursing of the hard-fired dark red brick is the finest in the city. The mortar joints are extremely thin on the front of the building and on the eastern side. The widely overhanging eaves have rectangular iron-grilled louvres between the brackets that rest on acorn-shaped corbels. Oval louvres vent the attic and are set in a framework of skillfully laid and shaped brickwork. This small building was in continuous use as a doctor's office until 1954. When the extension of the present County Court House

114. McGanahan Store, formerly on the southeast corner of Dauphin and Claiborne streets, now destroyed. Bishop Portier rented the lot to McGanahan so that he could erect a building for his store and residence. (Courtesy of the Mobile City Planning Commission.)

115. Dr. LeVert's office, ca. 1856, 153 Government Street. The office is an early example in Mobile of the Italianate influence. The wide, overhanging eaves are supported by decorative brackets.

was planned, it was decided to build around the historic structure, thus preserving a building important in Mobile history.

When the 1850s began, the hotels of Mobile were doing a thriving business. The Mansion House on the southeast corner of Royal and Conti was being enlarged. On June 26, 1849, James F. Hutchisson signed a contract for the addition of a forty-room, two-story building that would extend along Conti Street for 119 feet.[19] Then, in May 1850, Mr. Cullum contracted with Mr. Hutchisson for a three-story addition, naming A. W. Quigley as the mason.[20] Besides the Mansion House there was the Waverly on the southeast corner of Royal and St. Francis, with the Franklin House next door. There were also other, less well known hotel accommodations. Mobile seemed ade-

147   The Golden Age, 1850–1860

quately supplied, but then disaster struck. First a fire destroyed the Mansion House, and two weeks later the *Mobile Register* of July 20, 1850, described the destruction of the Waverly. The fire began in timbers under the floor of the cupola; while the outer shell and roofing of the buildings were fireproof, the inner partitions and roof timbers were not. The protection of the outer shell and the fire walls kept the flames from destroying the Franklin House, but the Waverly was gutted. Almost immediately after the loss of the two buildings, a company formed, with James Battle, John Battle, Samuel Battle, Judge William Jones, Jr., Samuel St. John, Thomas St. John, Newton St. John, Sanford Cooley, William Dunn, and Jonathan Emanuel as members. Their purpose was to erect a new hotel that would occupy the site of the Waverly and also the Franklin House, which was old and no longer as attractive as the day required. The work was begun on July 20, 1851, and the new hotel opened to the public on December 11, 1852.[21] It was named the Battle House after the men who had led the movement for its construction.

The 1852 building was the first of two to bear the name. It was four stories in height when first constructed, but a fifth story was added before the decade had ended (figures 116a,b). It accommodated 240 sleeping rooms, with parlors, dining rooms, bar, reading rooms, "ordinaries," and all the service rooms necessary to carry on the hotel business. The exterior surfaces were severely plain, and in September 1852, the *Mobile Register* reported that it had been decided to

> place a Verandah before this new hotel—at least on its Royal Street front—and for that purpose the cast iron work is now upon the spot.... The Verandah will not be less ornamental than useful to the establishment. Without it, the house would look more like a cotton factory than the splendid hotel that it is, and the lady dwellers within could never get a peep outside at the barbarians even when the military paraded by day, or the far famed "Cowbellions" at night.[22]

The early engravings in the city directories show the iron balcony only on the Royal Street front. Not until 1881 did engravings depict the veranda on both the Royal and the Conti street elevations.

No one could complain that the interior was not luxurious. A semicircular stairway in the tiled lobby led up to the second story, which housed the main hall, the public rooms, the bar, and the dining room, the first story being used for shops. In announcing the grand opening, the newspapers printed a description of the building, with its forty-foot-square barroom "well supplied with first rate liquids" and dining room ninety-one feet long, forty-two feet wide, and eighteen feet high. An idea of the decor can be formed from the description of the bedrooms: a "parlor, sitting room and chamber united; single and double beds in all splendor of sculptured and gilded finery with the best examples of architecture, painting, upholstery and filmy lace, and rare and beautiful furniture that cultured good taste could apparently devise."[23]

Isaiah Rogers's diary of 1851 states that he was contacted by Mr. Battle to design the new hotel. The building's design is also attributed to him by the *Dictionary of American Architects, De-*

116a. The first Battle House, 1851–1852, fifth floor added in 1857 and iron balcony and gallery in 1870 (destroyed); Isaiah Rogers, architect. As in other hotels designed by Rogers, corner pilasters were used to relieve the severity of the long elevation. A simple Doric architrave formed the original cornice. (Courtesy of the Historic Mobile Preservation Society.)

116b. The first Battle House, night scene. (Courtesy of the University of South Alabama Photographic Archives, McNeeley Collection.)

ceased.[24] Unfortunately no mention was made of the architect in the local accounts at the time of the building's opening. This Mobile Hotel may be compared with the Tremont House in Boston, but the addition of the iron galleries to the former altered the original design.

In 1905 the Old Battle House was destroyed by fire, like so many other local buildings. The second hotel to bear the name was opened in 1908, was extensively remodeled in 1945–1949, and continued to serve the community until the western expansion left the inner city in an economic decline. The building now stands abandoned and is fast deteriorating.

The Golden Age, 1850–1860

Residential Buildings

Dwellings of Wood

During the ten years of the mid-nineteenth century, the cottage evolved into its final form, which remains popular today. Even though the older four-room plan continued to be built, a larger version soon took precedence over the smaller type.[25] Matching wings were added on the sides of the main block, each wing with its own small gallery (figure 118b). The central door framing was elaborated with moldings with eared architraves, as in the Greek tomb shown in figure 121, or with Greek Revival colonnettes such as those in the Marshall-Hixon House (figure 118c). The chaste simplicity of such entrances as seen in the Tardy cottage of 1858 (figure 117) lost popularity, though the transoms continued to extend over both the door and the sidelights. The box Tuscan columns were replaced by those of round section in the Greek orders, especially the Doric (figures 118a–g). Even the site changed, from the informal, natural setting of great moss-laden oaks (figure 119) to the formal garden of the Marshall-Hixon home (figure 118g). A combination of the two site designs can be seen at Stewartfield on the campus of Spring Hill College (figure 120). Here a long avenue of oaks infilled with azaleas terminates in front of the house, encircling a small garden. This avenue once formed the central axis of an oval racetrack where the wealthy neighbors could run their horses and provide entertainment for the guests gathered on the porch. In 1852 Charlotte Page visited the city and wrote in her diary of her visit to the Stewarts: "We went to his bath house and from there to his ten pin alley where we amused ourselves. . . . They live in great style and have their home beautifully furnished."[26] One of the attractions of the home was the semicircular ballroom that was added soon after the house had been completed. Guests reported that the floor "bounced" as they danced, greatly contributing to their enjoyment. A Jesuit teacher remembered that, when he first examined the basement of the building, he had noted no braces between the floor joists, which might have accounted for the floor's resiliency. In 1903 the estate became part of the Spring Hill College campus.

While the raised one-story country home was the most popular during mid-century, two-story dwellings were also built. The finest surviving example is the Bragg-Mitchell House at 1906 Spring Hill Avenue. The fourteen-room dwelling was built by Judge John Bragg soon after he purchased the property. The mid-century design harmoniously combines Classical and Italianate elements. From the latter come the scrolled, bracketed cornice and the slender proportions of the tall sixteen columns with their unusual capitals. Classical influences are seen in the Greek key framing of the interior doors. Sixteen-foot-high ceilings opened the interior space to any cooling breeze (see the frontispiece).

Of all the nineteenth-century Greek Revival one-story dwellings, none is finer than the Marshall-Hixon home, which still stands on its original five-acre parcel (figure 118). A circular drive, with a fountain at its center, leads back to the house, which is hidden from the street by dense plantings. Beautifully proportioned Doric columns extend across both the five-bay veranda and the wing porches. The plan of the house consisted originally of four large rooms, two on either side of the wide hall (figure 118b), with recessed wings of

117. The Tardy cottage, 1858, 104 South Lawrence Street. The transom of the entrance, typical of the decade, continues unbroken across both the door and sidelights.

118a. The Marshall-Hixon House, ca. 1853, 152 Tuthill Lane, Spring Hill. The finest example in Mobile of the transformation of the cottage into a Greek Revival "villa." The west facade has beautifully proportioned Doric columns and refined detailing on the entrance. (Photograph by Michael Thomason.)

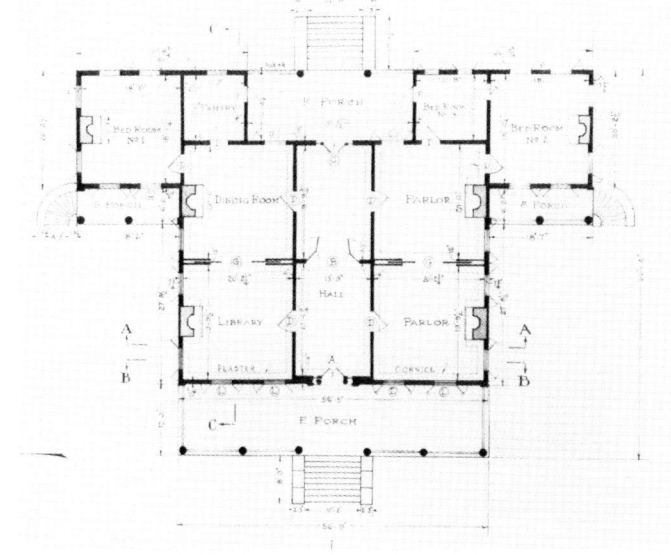

118b. The Marshall-Hixon House. The strictly balanced plan shows side wings with two-bay porches that form a T. (Drawing by H. B. Witherell, courtesy of the Library of Congress, Historic American Building Survey Collection.)

118c. The Marshall-Hixon House, detail of the front veranda, with Doric columns forming the outer colonnade and Ionic colonnettes framing the doorway. (Photograph by Michael Thomason.)

118d. The Marshall-Hixon House, interior doorway leading to the front parlor. The unusual height of the doorway is accentuated by the pronounced batter of the jambs. The eared architrave is slightly pedimented. The hinged transom doors can be opened for better ventilation. (Photograph by Michael Thomason.)

118e. The Marshall-Hixon House. The front parlor south window repeats the framing on the door surround. The crown moldings contain a dentil course. (Photograph by Michael Thomason.)

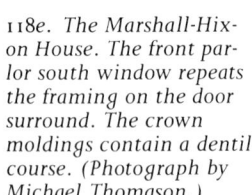

118f. The Marshall-Hixon House. The central hall is divided by a wide doorway with louvres. The same crown moldings continue throughout the hall and parlors. (Photograph by Michael Thomason.)

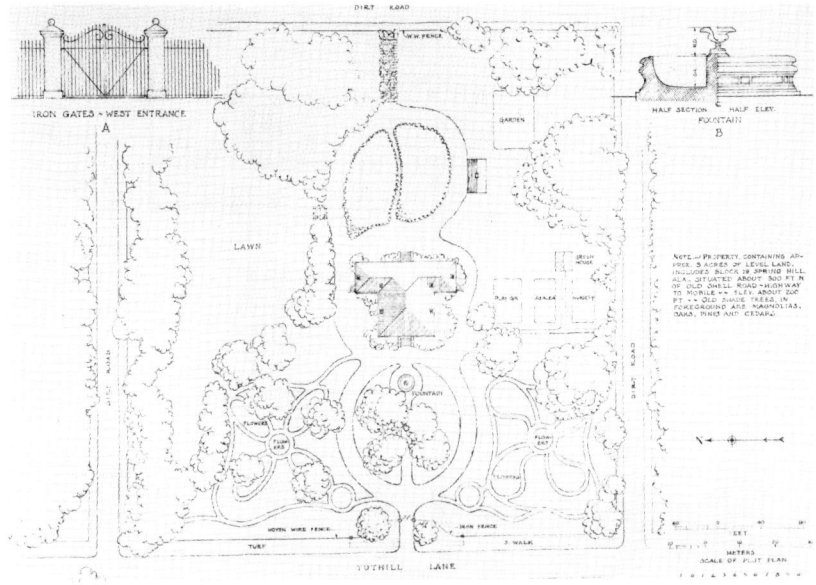

118g. The Marshall-Hixon House, site plan. During McMillan's ownership the original garden layout was reestablished, old paths were excavated, and the fountain was cleaned out. (Drawing by G. C. Chaudron, Jr., courtesy of the Library of Congress, Historic American Building Survey Collection.)

one room adding to the width of the house. The side wings were fronted by a two-bay porch, with steps forming a quarter-circle approach. Succeeding owners made some modifications, but the main fabric of the original home remains intact. One bay on each porch of the side wings was enclosed for bathrooms. The rear gallery was enclosed to accommodate a kitchen and other service areas, and a family room was excavated beneath the rear gallery. The high ceilings, the tall twelve-foot doors with their transoms, and the equally tall windows make the interior spacious. The openings are framed in the Greek Revival style, with pedimented architraves with crossettes (figures 118d, e), and the jambs have a pronounced batter. Louvred doors divide the forty-foot-long hallway (figure 118f). Dentil moldings crown all the main rooms.

The house is important not only because of its architecture but also because it provided a backdrop for various historic events. The home was built for Benjamin Marshall, who came to Mobile from Camden, South Carolina, in 1829. He accumulated a fortune from the cotton trade and in 1852 bought square 19 in section 13 of the Spring Hill area (figure 37). His enjoyment of his beautiful home was short-lived; within ten years he had lost everything, having invested his wealth in the southern cause in the Civil War. The property was acquired by the Eslava family, whose forebears were residents during the Spanish period. Don Miguel Eslava had been keeper of the treasury and collector of customs for the king of Spain. In 1863, his descendants, Jerome and Celestine Eslava, bought the Marshall property, which continued to be owned by the family until 1907. For a few years, from 1908 to 1929, the home was owned by Thomas Byrne and his wife, who undertook some restoration of the building. In 1911 it was bought by the Reverend Leighton G. McMillan, whose heirs still own the property. The McMillans carefully restored the old garden layout, cleaning out the dirt-filled fountain and excavating to reestablish the original garden paths and the circular drive approach to the home (figure 118g). During the various excavations, several grave sites were uncovered. Examination of the Robertson map of 1828 revealed a small church and cemetery on parcel 19.

119. Roberts-Staples House, mid-nineteenth century, 1614 Old Shell Road. The simple box columns were used during both the 1840s and the 1850s but were gradually elaborated by an extra molding below the capital.

120. Stewartfield, ca. 1850, Spring Hill College. The wealthy cotton factor Roger Stewart and his wife, Isabella, built their country home in the best Greek Revival tradition, with fluted Doric columns and Greek key casements surrounding the entrances and slide-by windows above jib doors.

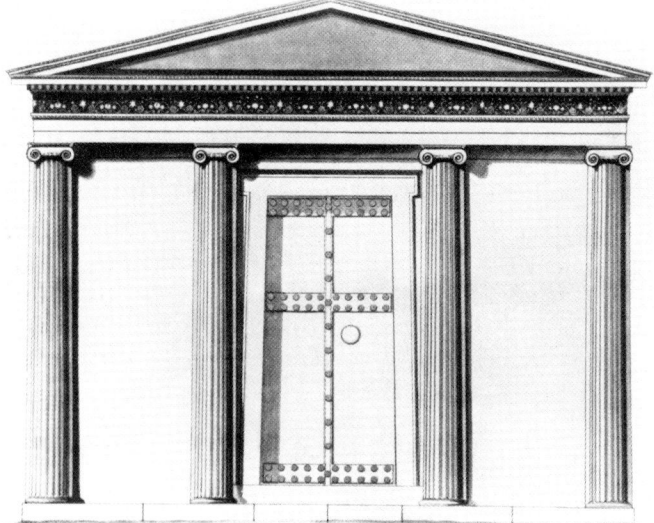

121. Door from the Tomb of Vergina, Greece, ca. 250 B.C. A Greek example of the architrave with the double-mitered ears, or crossettes, and slightly sloping jambs. (Drawing by Rhomaios, courtesy of Manolis Andronikos.)

Within the city limits, frame houses appeared in two forms. The first was a two-story elevation, with the side-hall plan and the gable facing the street. The porch was usually two story, with classical columns supporting each level. The full-height giant columns of the plantation homes were not popular in Mobile until the next century. The Roberts-Abbott House standing at 910 Government Street is a good example of the development (figure 122). The house originally consisted of the central block alone, the right recessed wing being a later addition.[27]

A second variation on the frame dwelling paved the way for the shotgun structure of the next decade. It was half of a double house, being a building about fifteen feet wide by thirty feet deep. Several contracts have survived, including one for an Orange Grove kitchen house built for John Bloodgood by James F. Hutchisson.[28] Though it had two stories, the building lacked a hall, and the rooms, arranged in single file, opened one into the other. The rear gallery in such a house had an outside staircase.[29] These narrow houses of simple tandem room plan grew in numbers until they dominated the street scenes during the years of the 1870s and 1880s in areas where laborers' homes proliferated, north of Beauregard and south of Eslava.[30]

122. Roberts-Abbott House, 1854, 910 Government Street. During the nineteenth century, the large Greek Revival house in Mobile had a two-story porch rather than the portico with full-height columns found in the plantation houses north of thirty-one degrees latitude.

Dwellings of Brick

Regardless of the style of the brick townhouse, the standard plan was the side hall with offset wing for the dining room, as in the Vickery dwelling of 1855 (figure 126). All had either two or three stories (see figures 123 and 124). All the exposed public walls had fine hard-finished dark red bricks bedded in narrow mortar joints with softer, less well formed bricks used in the rear and in private walls. The window heads were formed of straight or jack arches and were exposed (figure 125), stuccoed, or formed of stone, usually marble (figure 126). All windows were double-sash, six-over-six lights unless they were floor length, in which case they were six over nine (figure 135), though occasionally the old jib doors were still used below a six-over-six slide-by.

Variations in the buildings resulted from two different stylistic influences, the one a continuation of the Greek Revival as it had developed locally and the other an increasing use of Italianate details. These qualities can be noted in the massing, in the roof configuration, in the door framing, and in the motifs used in the cast iron of the galleries. During the decade, many brick homes continued the four-square massing of the Federal, the tightly contained box with the gable end hidden on the side by the built-up chimney parapet, and the offset wing set at a strict right angle, as in the now-destroyed

123. *The Gibbons-Torrey brick townhouse, ca. 1856, 60–62 South Conception Street; Richard Redwood, builder. The three-story brick inner-city home became popular in mid-decade. A cast iron balcony once marked the second story. Modern commercial windows altered the street level, but the original door is still intact.*

125. *Detail of the jack, or straight, arch of a lintel of the original Gideon Gee House, 1852 (dismantled and moved in 1969).*

124. *The Elkus House, 1854, 50 South Franklin Street. The compact rectangular block with its side-hall plan was well adapted to the narrow city lot. Here the Federal massing has been modified by the Greek Revival detailing such as that in the framing of the entranceway.*

Vickery House (figure 126). With the Italianate style, the massing became more informal. The offset wing became bowed or polygonal, as in the Richards home (figures 135a–c), gradually evolving into the irregular form of the houses of the 1860s (figure 141). Cast iron designs became more slender and graceful, frequently with organic motifs like those shown in the steps seen in figure 127.

The variation in the roof line is clearly evident in the change from the gable to a lower hip, from the dentiled cornice to the bracketed overhang, as seen in the examples of the Elkus House (figure 124) and the Guesnard (figure 128). With the Italianate style the fascia boards and the soffits were usually paneled, though they were sometimes embellished with reliefs, for example the wreaths in the St. John House (figure 129).

126. The Vickery House, 1855, formerly at 107 North Claiborne and destroyed in 1978; Philip Dougherty, architect; A. M. Quigley and E. Lamb, builders. The jalousie window replacement was not compatible with the fine design of this brick townhouse. Dark red high-fired brick was laid in very narrow mortar joints, and curving marble steps were cut to enhance the graining of the stone.

127. Cluis-Rubira House, 1857, 156 St. Anthony Street. The Italianate style introduced into Mobile decorative brackets as capitals of doorway pilasters, richly colored Bohemian glass in transoms and sidelights, and slender posts and delicate designs in the friezes of galleries. (Photograph by Boucher, courtesy of the Library of Congress, Historic American Building Survey Collection.)

128. The Guesnard House, 1859, 51 South Jackson; David Cumming, Jr., architect; James Hill and James Robertson, builders. Beneath the decorative brackets of the overhanging cornice in this Italianate house, the narrow molding of bricks set at angles gives a new interpretation to the old dentil course.

129. St. John House, 1857, 201 North Conception Street, detail. In addition to the cornice brackets, the soffits are paneled and the fascia is elaborated by wreath designs centered between the brackets.

The Golden Age, 1850–1860

130. The Griffin-Goldsmith home, 1855–1856, formerly on the northeast corner of Conti and Hamilton streets, destroyed in 1969. One of the last examples of the early type of brick townhouse to be built before the Italianate became the dominant style. Within thirty years after the photograph was taken, the house had deteriorated to such an extent that it had to be demolished. (Photograph by E. Russell, courtesy of the Library of Congress, Historic American Building Survey Collection.)

131. The Riley House entrance, ca. 1859, formerly on the east side of Hamilton, first door north of Dauphin, now destroyed. The heavy proportions of the outer surround of the entrance reflect a vernacular adaptation of classical elements. (Photograph by E. Russell, courtesy of the Library of Congress, Historic American Building Survey Collection.)

132. The Chamberlain-Rapier double brick house, 1852, 56–58 South Conception Street. Row or double houses were frequently separated by a carriageway that led back to the stables. (Courtesy of the Library of Congress, Historic American Building Survey Collection.)

133. The Scheffelin double brick building, 1855–1856, formerly on the southwest corner of Conti and Hamilton, now destroyed. With the growth of the city during the 1850s, rental property was in great demand, and investors constructed both single-family dwellings and multiple units. (Courtesy of Historic Mobile Preservation Society.)

134. *The Caulfield House, ca. 1852, formerly at 160 Monroe and destroyed in 1967–1968 during the highway expansion. A large brick two-story home that harmoniously combined elements from several styles. It typifies the homes of the affluent Mobilians who were settling in the area that is now the Church Street East Historic District.*

The door framing varied, depending upon which of the two influences was dominant. If it was the Greek Revival, the street entrance was recessed, with two or more steps leading from the outer plane of the facade to the door itself (figure 124). In this case the outer frame was a rather heavy and simply molded Greek key with battered jambs and an only slightly pedimented architrave. The frame of the recessed door generally had Tuscan pilasters between the narrow sidelights and the single-leaf door, the transom thus being broken into three parts by the extended pilasters (figure 130). This three-part transom was carried over into the Italianate but with the added embellishment of acanthus-scrolled corbels forming the pilaster capitals and Bohemian leaded glass infilling the sidelights, as in the Richards House (figure 135b). In some homes, such as the Riley House, the entrance has heavy proportions in the jambs and dentil course in a vernacular adaption of classical motifs (figure 131).

Double houses in brick were also built, following traditional lines and sometimes including Italianate brackets. These multiple units either were separated by a carriageway, as in the Chamberlain-Rapier building (figure 132), or were just connected by the party walls, as in the Scheffelin rental property (figure 133).

Three houses suffice to illustrate the popular types of the brick inner-city homes of the decade: the Elkus House (1854) at 50 South Franklin (figure 124); the Caulfield House (about 1852), now destroyed (figure 134); and the Richards House (1860), 256 North Joachim (figures 99 and 135a–c). The Elkus House best illustrates the simple massing and the Mobile adaptation of the Federal form, with Greek Revival detailing and wrought iron balcony. The Caulfield House, of a later design, incorporates Italianate features in the bracketed overhanging cornice. The Richards House is the best surviving example of the townhouses built in the late 1850s, both in its general design and in the handsome cast iron of its gallery. The home was built by Charles Richards, a riverboat captain from Maine who used the finest of materials and employed the most skilled workmen. The informal plan with the offset bays is typical of the Italian-

135a. The Richards House, 1860, 256 North Joachim, in the de Tonti Square Historic District. The house is an outstanding example of the Italianate as it developed in Mobile. Widely overhanging eaves hide the low roof. Polygonal bays enlarge the plan, and exceptionally fine Bohemian glass enhances the entrance. The cast iron is the finest in Mobile. (Photograph by Michael Thomason.)

135b. The porch of the Richards House. Decorative brackets cap the pilasters that frame the entrance. Black and white marble tiles cover the floor. Double-sash slide-by windows open a passageway from the porch to the front parlor. (Photograph by Michael Thomason.)

135c. The front hall stairway of the Richards House rises to the second story in a dramatic curve. (Photograph by Michael Thomason.)

ate, as are the bracketed embellishments of the entrance (figure 135b). When the visitor stands at the center of the hall, looking west, the entrance glows with its ruby glass; the view to the east terminates in the sweep of the curving staircase (figure 135c).

Early in the decade one-story cast iron galleries became common (figure 136). Designs were organic, involving leaves, fruits, flowers, and vines, all three dimensional in form (figures 99, 127). As the decade drew to a close, more and more cast iron was used until it dominated entire facades, as in the Lyon House of 1859–1860 (figure 137; contrast figure 124).

Any community has examples of building types that do not follow

136. The Foote House, 1856, 255 North Conception. Many old wrought iron balconies were replaced by galleries with decorative cast iron of elaborate design that altered the original simplicity of the facades. (Photograph by Michael Thomason.)

137. The Lyon House, 1859–1860, 261 North Joachim. By the end of the decade, cast iron galleries had become so popular and were used so extensively that the architectural elements were hidden. (Photograph by Michael Thomason.)

the local traditions. One such is the Murray F. Smith House of 1852, which once stood on the southwest corner of Government and Conception streets, the site of the present Greyhound Bus Company (figure 138). Mr. Smith came from Virginia, established a very successful business in cotton trade, and chose to construct an English Tudor–type home with its crenellated parapet, square-headed hooded windows, and monochromatic stucco surface suggesting stone. The builder is not known but must certainly have been familiar with the early Gothic Revival in both England and the Northeast. There is no oriel or bay, but the hood over the second-story central window conveys the general theme. Missing, too, are the diamond-shaped window panes, but the traditional double-sash six-over-nine lights do not distract from the overall fifteenth-century effect. Much romance surrounds the house because of its association with Murray Smith's daughter, Alva, whose first marriage to William Vanderbilt took her into New York society; after her second marriage to Mr. O. H. P. Belmont, Mobilians watched her activities with great interest. Her daughter, Consuelo, added to the family's romantic history by marrying the duke of Marlborough. The Smith family left Mobile at the beginning of the Civil War, and the house was sold.

161   The Golden Age, 1850–1860

138. Murray F. Smith House, ca. 1852, formerly on the southwest corner of Government and Conception streets, the site of the present Greyhound Bus station. The house was a rare example in Mobile of a Gothic Revival manor style with a crenellated parapet and hood molds over the windows. (Courtesy of the Historic Mobile Preservation Society, Wilson Plates.)

139. The Kennedy House, 1857, 607 Government Street. The house was built by Joshua Kennedy, Jr., and is the only example in Mobile of the Italianate with two-story columns connected by flattened arches and with semicircular-headed windows.

The Kennedy House at 607 Government Street (figure 139) had no precedents in Mobile for its design, nor did it influence subsequent buildings. The *Mobile Daily Register* of June 15, 1857, described it merely as an "elegant mansion . . . approaching completion." The flattened arches of the portico and the semicircular-headed windows are unique in Mobile architecture. The home was built by Joshua Kennedy and remained in the family until 1923. It is now the headquarters of the Lamar Y. McLeod Post No. 3 of the American Legion. Of all the fine homes that once stood on lower Government Street, it is the last surviving example.

During the ten years from 1850 to 1860, Mobile achieved a level of economic prosperity that made the period an architectural golden age. Craftsmanship was excellent, as we see from the many examples that have survived hurricanes and man's vandalism. Well-proportioned designs were enhanced by decorative detailing, all of them constructed by local architects and builders. At this time the community put its own stamp upon the built environment, selecting ideas from various sources and adapting them to local taste.

6 War and the Changing Order, 1860–1870

The prosperity of the 1850s continued into the early years of the 1860s, with considerable building activity. In 1860 the county enlarged the Prison that had been designed by Frederick Bunnell. The east wing was added as originally planned; the work was supervised by Charles T. Liernur, a civil engineer.[1] Also in 1860 the commercial structure owned by Daniels and Elgin was enlarged (figures 140a,b). It is the only example in Mobile of a cast iron facade and one of the few surviving in the state. The manufactured iron elements were expected to prevent the spread of the devastating fires of the century and to furnish prefabricated units that would increase the speed of construction. The 1871 Chicago fire proved that the ferrous substance was not the fireproof material it had been thought. But for about twenty years, from 1850 to 1870, cities such as Chicago, St. Louis, New York, and Baltimore lined their commercial streets with ready-made cast iron fronts shipped by such companies as that of James Bogardus and Daniel Badger.

Catalogues were issued, from which prospective buyers could order individual parts such as columns or hood molds or whole units for bays that could be attached to brick buildings, completely covering the surfaces. The Daniels and Elgin Company studied the Badger Iron Works catalogue and from it selected the design for the enlargement of its two-story store.[2] It is easy to imagine the shopkeepers poring over the catalogue and selecting the design that would allow for larger windows to increase the light into the interior of the establishment. The bay units chosen were designed by J. H. Giles and were prefabricated in New York and shipped to Mobile for installation. Cast iron prepared in this way was an innovation, but the design was based on the waterfront palazzas of fifteenth- and sixteenth-century Venice. The richly arcaded fronts are made of repetitive bays enframed by pilasters, columns, and molded entablatures between the story levels, as seen in the Mobile example. Motifs are similar throughout the design, but details vary subtly from story to story. Crowning the building is the cornice elaborated by the large twinned modillions with three smaller brackets in between. Except for the modern windows installed at street level (figure 140b), the building stands as it was designed in 1860. Of the several owners who

140a. *The Daniels-Elgin cast iron front building, 1860, 2 Water Street, designed by J. H. Giles, fabricated by D. D. Badger and Company, New York, and recorded in the firm's 1865 catalogue. The cast iron elements reflect the Venetian palazza style. (Erik Overbey/Mobile Public Library Collection, University of South Alabama Photographic Archives.)*

141. *The Malaga Inn, 1862, 357–359 Church Street, renovated in 1967. The houses were not originally connected but formed "companion" homes for the Isaac Goldsmith and William Frolichstein families. (Photograph by Michael Thomason.)*

succeeded Daniels and Elgin, the best known was the firm of Frolichstein and Goldsmith, whose twin houses now form the Malaga Inn (figure 141). In 1880 the building was taken over by Brisk Jacobson Clothing, which advertised itself as an "emporium" with the most stylish clothing available.

Other examples of the Italianate style can be seen in housing. The Ketchum House of 1860 (figure 142) and the Butt House of 1861 (figure 143) have the same Italianate antecedents, though they differ greatly in richness of detail. The massing of the Ketchum House is more broken, with every angle accented by the white quoining. The

140b. *The Daniels-Elgin cast iron front building photographed in 1980, showing the modernization of the first-story windows.*

142. *The William Ketchum House, 1860, 400 Government Street. Italian Mannerist in style, this three-story home has the central section raised above the side bays. The elaborate cast iron of the gallery has a complex combination of grape meanders, arabesques, and geometric patterns. (Courtesy of the Mobile City Planning Commission.)*

wide, strongly marked string courses between the stories, the heavy window frames, and the elaborate cast iron of the gallery add to the complexity. In the previous decade the Italianate influence had been limited to the bracketed overhanging cornice and the offset side polygonal wing. With the early 1860s the boxlike quality was replaced by irregular massing. While the Butt House has a bay breaking the facade, it is much simpler than the Ketchum. The contrasts are less sharp because the quoins are the same color as the wall brick. The small recessed porch seen in figure 143 shows the changing orientation as the inner-city houses of the well-to-do increasing-

165   *War and the Changing Order, 1860–1870*

143. *The Butt House, 1861, 254 North Jackson Street, restored in 1966–1967. An excellent example of the Italianate in the early 1860 houses in Mobile. The projecting front bay, the quoining at every angle, the overhanging bracketed cornice, and the small stoop are all characteristic.*

ly substituted a private rear patio for the sociable front veranda. Both of the houses discussed have the overhanging cornice and eaves embellished with decorative modillions, those of the Butt House being painted black in contrast with the white walls. Soffits and fascia are both paneled. Like the exterior, the interior decoration of the Ketchum home has more elaborate detailing than the Butt. In the former the crown moldings are richly designed in floral patterns of camellias and magnolias, and the ceiling medallions are formed of acanthus leaves with the addition of small flowers.

The Butt House has an interesting history of ownership. It was built by C. W. Butt, the son of the architect of Christ Church (figure 45). When the building was being restored in 1967, paint removed from the interior folding door revealed the name of Ira W. Parker, who had been the bookkeeper for Thomas James before opening a hardware store.[3] James was one of the builders of Barton Academy and the Government Street Presbyterian Church. The Kling family of the Mobile Kling Iron Foundry purchased the property in 1899 and held it until 1966. The iron fence is generally believed to have come from their shop. The Butt House is important in the restoration movement in Mobile. In 1967 it was the first major building in the newly established (1961) de Tonti Square Historic District to be selected for restoration and adaptation.

During the years when builders were called architects and were the source of most architectural designs, the twin houses of Isaac Goldsmith and William Frolichstein were constructed on Church Street. These homes with their side-hall plan and offset wings set forth the accepted arrangement for the city dwelling. They are only two examples of some dozen still standing that represent a fifteen-year span of time.[4] The two homes with their side wings facing each other were originally connected by a narrow garden space. In 1967

144. *The Scattergood-Grey House, 1860, formerly at 213 South Jackson Street, now destroyed. The garret windows with their frames of wreaths were unusual in Mobile. (Photograph by Roy C. McAuley.)*

they were joined by a recessed connector, of which the front section forms the foyer of the Malaga Inn. The rear of the main sections of the houses was also connected by a three-story addition that formed the chambers of the inn. Between these two connectors is a fine patio. The facades of the houses retain their original elevations except for the large panes of glass in the first-story windows. The cast iron galleries across both buildings and wings are typical (figure 141).

The Scattergood-Grey House (figure 144) formerly stood at 213 South Jackson Street. It is another good example of the large single-family dwelling of the period. Beyond the obvious architectural elements of the design, there is a pervading sense of locality: this building seems to belong on the Gulf Coast. It reflects the demands of the climate, with the high ceilings and large interior spaces that allow free movement of air and the white exterior walls that reflect the heat of a summer sun instead of absorbing it.

The Advent of War

Even during the early years of the Civil War, Mobile remained prosperous. With the fall of New Orleans in 1862, Mobile was the only Confederate port on the Gulf through which cotton could be exported to procure funds for the purchase of needed military arms and equipment. By 1863 the buildup of military defenses occupied the full attention of the city and county governments. With the tightening of the blockade of the port, nonessential construction came to a halt. Adding to the troubles of the times, on January 31, 1864, a fire from a defective flue destroyed all but the first story of the county court building that had been designed by Alderson in 1852. While

145. *The explosion of the federal munitions magazine, May 25, 1865. The destruction extended along the waterfront, leveling about eight blocks of the newly developed commercial buildings. (Courtesy of Mrs. Carter Smith.)*

the county records were saved, the partially habitable first story was declared unsafe as a repository for the documents. Arrangements were made to rent the 1842 Hagan commercial building standing on the north side of Conti, between Royal and Water streets. After the necessary repairs had been made and vaults had been installed, the building served the county until 1873.[5] Some of the spirit of 1863 is evident in the diary of William Howard Russell, who came to Mobile on May 11, arriving from New Orleans on a boat piloted by Captain Meaher:

> We walked on toward the "Battle House," so called from the name of its proprietor, for Mobile has not yet had its fight, like New Orleans. The quays, which usually, as we were told, are lined with stately hulls and a forest of masts, were deserted; although the port was not actually blockaded, there were squadrons of the United States ships at Pensacola, on the east and at New Orleans, on the west.
>
> The hotel, a fine building of the American stamp, was the seat of a Vigilance Committee, and as we put down our names in the book, they were minutely inspected by some gentlemen who came out of the parlor. It was fortunate they did not find traces of Lincolnism about us, as it appeared by the papers that they were busy deporting "Abolitionists" after certain preliminary processes supposed to—
>
> "Give them a rise, and open their eyes
> To a sense of their situation."
>
> The citizens were busy in drilling, marching, and drum-beating, and the Confederate flag flew from every spire and steeple.[6]

Defeat and catastrophe dealt Mobile a double-barreled charge in the spring of 1865. First, on April 12, after the last of the Confederate army and the blockade runners had withdrawn from the city, Mayor Slough, Caleb Price, and Dr. Ketchum drove their carriage out to the Bay Road to meet the northern forces, carrying with them the white flag of surrender. Then, on May 25, the explosion of the waterfront ordnance depot devastated about eight city blocks, from the river to the west, north, and south of Beauregard Street (figure 145). The situation was further exacerbated by northern soldiers, who occupied homes and controlled the city; by the unemployment and the tide of postwar refugees who poured into the city, hunting work when there was none; and by the loss of revenue from the port (the harbor was blocked by the debris of war). Mobile had hit the nadir of its history, yet the will to survive prevailed once again.

The Postwar Years

While the city and county governments were unable to pursue any building programs during and after the Civil War, some private construction did continue. Two trends developed, the one perpetuating the Italianate style and the other shifting from brick to a small frame board-and-batten Carpenter Gothic. Of the former, the best surviving examples are the Horst House (1867), 407 Conti Street (figures 146a–c); the Osborne House (1868), 500 Church Street; and the Bush-Sands Memorial (1868), 254 St. Anthony (figures 147a,b). Both the Horst House and the Bush-Sands Memorial show a new feature in Italianate detailing—elaboration of the window framing that was not seen in prewar housing. This elaboration employed either cast iron or wood. In the Horst House (figure 146b), the slightly segmental curve of the iron lintels is formed by a leaf-and-dart molding, with a small anthemion rising at the center point. The sills, also of

146b. *The Martin Horst House, detail of a window on the west side. The curved lintel is crowned by an anthemion, and acanthus leaves elaborate the brackets of the sills.*

146a. *The Martin Horst House, 1867, 407 Conti Street; George Cox, master mason; restored as the Moongate Restaurant, 1971–1972. Cast iron window lintels and sills incorporate Greek Revival motifs, adding elaborate detail to the Italianate style. (Drawing by Thomas F. Karwinski, AIA.)*

146c. *The Horst House front entrance on the north facade has an unusual dentil course outlining the doorway. The segmental curve of the entablature is repeated in the profile of the transom lights.*

War and the Changing Order, 1860–1870

iron, have a similar design and are supported by small acanthus-leaf-shaped brackets. Cast iron spans the main entrance (figure 146c) and is decorated with an alternate dentil-and-tongue motif and centered by a cartouche. Also typical of the late Italianate style in Mobile is the low paneled parapet crowning the overhanging bracketed eaves. The interior decor continues the same elegance of detail in moldings and the ceiling medallions. The home was constructed by the master mason George Cox, who also built the Rapelje House of 1865 (figure 148). An interesting letter survives in the Horst family. It is dated January 12, 1868, and was written to a brother in California. In it Martin Horst explained that the cost of his new home had amounted to $26,000, some $7,000 more than anticipated. Young George Cox had come from London to join his brother in Mobile, and over the years he became a prominent mason. His Rapelje House (figure 148) was one of the largest and handsomest to be built in the city. George Rapelje was a New York cotton broker who made a fortune and then lost it all with the end of the cotton boom. In 1869 he sold his home and all its furnishings for $25,000.

When the cotton factor John Bush built his home in 1868, he chose to use wood window framing rather than iron on his brick house (figure 147). Centered above each window and above the door is a

147b. The Bush-Sands entrance has paneled pilasters framing the door. Richly designed Bohemian glass fills the transom and sidelights.

147a. The Bush-Sands Memorial, 1868, 254 St. Anthony Street, was once the home of Dr. Charles Mohr and his wife, Willie Bush Mohr, who inherited the property from her grandmother Sara Bush. A parapet above the bracketed cornice hides the roof and is characteristic of the later Italianate in Mobile.

170   *From Fort to Port*

carved scallop shell. The entrance is one of the best examples in the city of the Italianate style as it developed in Mobile (figure 147b). The richly carved acanthus brackets, the paneled pilasters, and the beveled leaded glass of sidelights and transom attest to the skillful craftsmanship that persisted in the postwar period. The building was long known as the Mohr House; a descendant of the Bush family had married Dr. Mohr, who was the health physician for the city. Many interesting tidbits of medical history are associated with the doctor. He initiated several programs that met not only with resistance but also with outright hostility. After surveying the available literature on causes for the yellow fever and malaria, he ordered that all children be vaccinated, prompting women to line the streets and stone his carriage from a belief that he was harming the children. He also initiated a program to have all houses equipped with screens to keep out the mosquitoes. For this measure he was ridiculed at the time.[7] He was also responsible for inspecting all ships that came into the bay to ensure that no ill seaman brought disease into the city.

The Italianate-style architecture of the 1860s came to an end with the finest house of its kind built in the central Gulf Coast area. The home for Dr. George Ketchum, built on the southeast corner of Government and Chatham, just west of the existing Rapelje House (figure 148), was closer to the asymmetrical country villa than to the formal Roman palazzo. The off-center square tower with the arcaded loggia to one side and the side elevation bays are typical (figure 149). The low-pitched roof extends outward to form the bracketed overhanging cornice. Roundheaded windows, some twinned, are accented by hood molds. The style first gained attention in England in 1802 in Cronkhill, which was designed by John Nash.[8] John Notman introduced it into the United States in the 1830s, and it was popularized by the pattern books of Andrew Jackson Downing, who also spread the influence of the board-and-batten Carpenter Gothic. The 1869–1870 house is now gone, but its memory lingers on in the stories of local residents who recall that the door trim and baseboards of the interior were made of ebony and the crown molds were of gold leaf. Boys used to climb through a trap door in the roof to fly kites from the tower deck. When the estate was broken up, the fountain that once stood in the center of the front circular garden was moved to Montrose.

148. *The Rapelje House, ca. 1865, 1005 Government Street; George Cox, master mason; renovated by George B. Rogers, 1905–1906. The large twenty-nine-room house has ceilings sixteen feet high with great Greek key door frames in the parlors and hall. The house was long known as the Toxey Cawthon home. In the 1906 renovation, the dining room wall was covered with a Japanese paper embossed with oxydized silver figures.*

During the war years some great homes were constructed, but the trend was toward smaller houses. Several reasons can be suggested. The state of the economy discouraged large expenditures for the general population. Then, too, there was a lack of domestic labor to maintain large establishments. Carpenters replaced masons, and the jigsaw art made possible less expensive decorative detailing. The new trend is expressed in the Macy House at 1569 Dauphin, a good example of Carpenter Gothic (figures 150a,b). It was inspired by the board-and-batten cottages of A. J. Downing, whose drawings and engravings were popularized in his publications. Barge boards decorated the edges of the roof lines, designs cut in open patterns that cast interesting shadows on the walls as the sun moved from east to west. Simple hood molds crowned the windows. The plan eliminated the hall as wasted space; the front entrance opened directly into the parlor. In the Macy House a narrow, steep stairway leads up to the second level from a small half-length cross-hall. The center of the attic window is pointed, as was customary in this style, and small diamond-shaped windows are inserted on side elevations. Such small homes were well adapted to a city lot.

A smaller, simpler example is the home at 1161 Old Shell Road (figure 151). In 1856 Franklin Kimball built on adjacent lots five structures that were taxed as kitchen houses, and all had the same value. When his daughter Fannie married W. A. Bass in 1869, he deeded one of the little houses to her. On the 1878 City Atlas, Fannie's house appears larger than the other four, but whether she enlarged the building or built a new one is not known. The style certainly suggests that the structure was built during the end of the 1860s. The massing and construction methods are to be found in many of the homes for blue-collar workmen that were being erected on streets south of Monroe, west of Broad, and north of Beauregard. All were similar in plan, with rooms in tandem and with a three-bay porch extending across the gable-ended facade. They differed in dec-

149. *Dr. George Ketchum House, formerly near the southeast corner of Government and Chatham, now destroyed. The last of the great Italianate homes, the building recalls the country villa style with its square tower, loggia, and asymmetrical massing. (Courtesy of the Historic Mobile Preservation Society.)*

150a. The Macy House, 1867–1868, 1569 Dauphin Street. The best example of the Carpenter Gothic style that has survived in Mobile. Board-and-batten siding is used, and the jigsaw decoration has replaced the classical designs of the Italianate.

150b. The Macy House, west elevation, showing the small hood molds and the decorative barge boards that became common in this type of construction.

151. The Kimball House, ca. 1869–1870, 1161 Old Shell Road. After the Civil War there was a demand for smaller houses that adopted the board-and-batten siding and simple barge board decoration.

orative detailing, some having scalloped, unpierced barge boards, as in the Kimball House, and others having pierced designs. All had board-and-batten siding and small one-inch-by-one-inch hood molds over the windows. As the century advanced, these small homes were replaced by the Victorian cottage. Today only a few examples survive to illustrate an important phase of our built environment.

Commercial Buildings

After the waterfront explosion of 1865, the depressed economy delayed commercial development. One of the first building projects to recover was wharf construction. Mr. Edward Townsend of New York City had John King build a 258-foot-long wharf, complete with double bulkheads, between the State and Congress waterfronts. Warehouses also had to be replaced and old ones refurbished. The *Mobile Register and Advertiser* of May 10, 1866, carried a report of construction taking place along Commerce Street.[9] The A. and B. Moog grocery business built a three-story warehouse extending from Commerce to Water between Dauphin and Conti streets. James H. Hutchisson designed a building for C. P. Page that contained stores on the first floor, offices on the second, and apartments or warehouse space on the third.

On December 18, 1866, the municipal authorities passed an ordinance regulating the construction of fire and party walls. The act was to take effect by January 1, 1867.[10] According to the ordinance, no wall could be less than one and one-half bricks thick; all party walls had to have a projection of no less than three inches where girders and joists were inserted; and there had to be no less than eight inches of solid masonry between the ends of all timbers. All partition walls had to be carried up above the roof for no less than two feet. The results of the ordinance are apparent in the buildings in the Lower Dauphin Street Commercial Historic District. A comparison of the 1862 McGill Building at 254 Dauphin (figure 152) with the 1867 Monin Building, 454–466 Dauphin (figure 153) illustrates the difference in fire wall height, even though the fire wall of the Monin Building is hidden behind a raised parapet. The two also show the difference in window treatment during the prewar and postwar periods. In the 1862 building, the older form with the second-story central window opening on a balcony creates an informal social atmosphere in which the occupants could enjoy watching the activity in the street below. This informality is absent from the more impersonal window arrangement of the 1867 building.

The Antomanchi Building in the Fort Condé section of the Church Street East Historic District survives from 1869. It is located at 200 St. Emanuel and was built alongside Antomanchi's home, which stood to the south (figure 154). Over time the building has been altered; however the basic fabric has survived, including the cast iron egg-and-dart moldings embedded in the north wall that once formed window lintels. The builder, Charles Antomanchi, was one of many immigrants who came to the Gulf Coast and established a small business, prospering with the good times and merely surviving with the bad. Arriving from Corsica in 1839, he became a citizen in 1849 and opened a coffee shop on Government and Water streets at a time when coffee and tea shops played an important part in both the business and social life of the town. In 1869 he was able to build his two brick buildings on St. Emanuel and Monroe, which became rental property after his death. The corner building served as a combined store and apartment for many years, being in succession an upholstery shop, an oyster shop, and a grocery. With the development of the Fort Condé area, the building was restored as an antique shop, and it has recently been purchased by the city.

152. *The McGill commercial building, 1862, 254 Dauphin Street. The slide-by second-story windows characteristic of the prewar elevation once opened onto a gallery overlooking the street. There was originally a third story.*

153. *The Monin commercial building, 1867, 454–466 Dauphin Street. In the postwar elevation, the windows are characteristically set in a repetitive row, creating an impersonal atmosphere because of the loss of the balcony-street relationship. The first-floor windows have been altered with the adaptation of the stores for modern use.*

154. *The Antomanchi store, 1869, 200 St. Emanuel Street. One of the few neighborhood stores still standing within the inner city.*

War and the Changing Order, 1860–1870

At the end of the decade, attempts were made to attract new commercial enterprises, such as the Magnolia Sugar Refinery and the Mobile Fertilizer Manufacturing Company. Most important were the foundries. The Skates Foundry became the Mobile Foundry; and in 1866 the Lang Brass Foundry also produced iron for verandas and shutters.[11] The Park and Lyon Foundry, owned by William Alexander and Horace Hunley, became famous as the site where the first submarine used in naval warfare was constructed. The increase in iron productivity is reflected in the greater use of decorative iron for both galleries and fencing.

The few examples that I have mentioned of buildings constructed for business during the immediate postwar years show little change in the general trends in commercial architecture. The editor of the *Mobile Register and Advertiser* hinted at the reason when he wrote in his column "Progress" on May 10, 1866, "The high cost of material, we are told, is still retarding building operations very materially."

When the decade opened, a building with a cast iron front was being erected in the eastern end of the business district at the southwest corner of Dauphin and Water streets. It is therefore fitting to close this section of the architectural history of the 1860s with a discussion of the Creole Fire Station Number One, which is located at the southwest corner of Dauphin and Dearborn at the western end of the inner city. The fire hall is one of ten such nineteenth-century buildings, of which four are still standing on their original sites (figures 155a,b). In general plan it is typical of all the rest, being a two-story brick building with large exit engine doors at the first level and an open company room on the second. An attached stable still exists on the southern side of the building. The Creole Number One has the finest brickwork of any of the surviving fire company buildings (figure 155b). The complex coursing of the cornice moldings, the parapet, and the hood molds over the second-story windows show remarkable workmanship. The company was founded by John McCluskey in 1819, but the present building was not constructed until fifty years later. The station was designed by James H. Hutchisson, who contributed many fine buildings to the architectural inheritance of nineteenth-century Mobile.[12] When the fire department of the city was established in 1888, the Creole Number One was one of the few volunteer companies that was not closed but became a part of the new department, so that it continued to serve well into the mid-twentieth century.

155a. The Creole Fire Station Number One, 1869, 15–17 South Dearborn Street; James H. Hutchisson, architect. This is the least altered of the four volunteer fire company buildings still standing on their original sites. The Creole Number One was founded in 1819 and continued to serve the community until the City Fire Department was established in 1888, at which time it was incorporated into the city program.

155b. Detail of the brickwork of the Creole Fire Station.

Educational and Religious Buildings

One of the most progressive educational steps taken in Mobile was the founding of the Medical College in 1859. Spearheading the movement was Dr. Joseph C. Nott (1820–1856). Other doctors joining the effort were George Ketchum, J. T. Gilmore, J. F. Heustis, P. A. Ross, William H. Anderson, R. Miller, Jerome Cochran, A. P. Hall, and E. P. Gaines, all of whom became members of the faculty. On May 23, 1859, the Medical College Board purchased the square of land located between State Street, Lawrence, St. Anthony, and Cedar.[13] On January 30, 1860, the state legislature chartered the Medical College of Alabama at Mobile and appropriated $50,000 for a building. While the building was under construction, the faculty and students occupied rented property. They were able to move into their finished quarters by November 1860. The three-story building (figures 156a,b) in design incorporated characteristic aspects of the Italianate style. The elevation was divided by a heavy belt course that separated the ground level from the two upper stories. Each of the bays was framed by a pilaster and was centered by a semicircular-headed window accented by heavy hood molds on brackets. Beneath the cornice and within each bay, three shaped brackets added a decorative accent. The building as it stands today has been greatly modified (figure 156b). The top story has been removed and the second-story windows replaced by windows with square heads and without any hood molds. Side and rear wings have been added, and the old porch has been replaced by one with Neoclassical features. Despite these alterations, the building records an important event in the history of Mobile.

During the late 1860s and 1870s, a program for the education of black people was undertaken. On February 5, 1869, an article of agreement was signed between the Board of School Commissioners and the trustees of the St. Louis Street Baptist Church.[14] In this document the School Board agreed to give $3,500 to help finance the erection of the Church if the Church trustees would agree to reserve the first story exclusively for the education of black children. The contract also stipulated that the lot to the south had to be reserved for a fenced yard to contain two privies. The document was to remain in effect for fourteen years, after which the School Board could renew on a rental basis. The Church was built (figure 157) and was renovated in 1890 and again in 1908, when the architect C. L. Hutchisson, Sr., designed the existing corner tower.

As early as 1865 northern missionary societies sponsored black education through the Freedmen's Bureau. Miscellaneous Book H, dated February 11, 1869, contains a charter for Emerson College. Its statement of purpose includes the sentence, "no one shall be barred on account of race or color." The history of the institution was a turbulent one. The first classes were held in the Medical College building, which had been closed during the war. In 1867 a Government Street building known as the Blue College was acquired. In 1868 an engraving of the building was included in the *Harper's Weekly*. It was an imposing structure of Greek Revival style with a fine two-story portico supported by six Doric columns. Both the College and the Congregational Church with which it was associated were destroyed by fire.[15]

156a. The Medical College of Alabama building, 1860, 550 St. Anthony Street. The Medical School was founded in 1859 under the leadership of Dr. Josiah C. Nott. The community soon provided $25,000 to buy the equipment and supplies necessary to operate the School. On January 30, 1860, the state legislature chartered the School and allocated $50,000 for construction of the building. In 1920 the Medical School was transferred to Tuscaloosa. (Courtesy of the Historic Mobile Preservation Society, Wilson Plates.)

156b. The Medical School building as it stands today has been drastically altered: the third story was removed, the windows of the second story were altered, and wings were added to the east and the rear. The building now serves as Dunbar Middle School.

157. The St. Louis Street Baptist Church, 1869, 1890, 1908, southeast corner of St. Louis and Dearborn. The Church was built in 1869 through the combined efforts of the congregation and the Board of Education, which provided a school on the first floor for black children and a hall for religious services on the second. The present tower was built in 1908 by C. L. Hutchisson, Sr., who replaced the 1890 spire.

158a. The Spring Hill College administration building, 1869; James Freret, architect; Charles Fricke, builder; south facade. The central and end pavilions show French Renaissance influence. Fire and storm twice destroyed the dome; only the base has survived. The concrete galleries replaced the old wooden ones in 1910, after the fire of 1909.

158b. Administration Building, Spring Hill College, north facade, showing the crenellated arcade that continues around the cloister.

For both the black and the white population, educational and religious centers were closely allied even after public school programs were well under way. One such center was Spring Hill College, founded by the Catholic bishop Michael Portier. It has operated continuously ever since its opening, although today it does not occupy the same buildings. February 4, 1869, was a tragic day for the College. Bishop Portier's campus was reduced to ashes by a fire that destroyed all but the little Sodality Chapel and a two-story frame building to the north of the main building. James Freret of New Orleans was asked to design a new building, and Charles Fricke was named contractor-builder. The building was estimated to cost $300,000. Freret's plan called for a longer but narrower building than the former one by Beroujon; the new structure was to be 364 feet long by 40 feet wide, with 12-foot-wide galleries of wood along the southern facade (figure 158a). A dome supported a large brass-plated cupola, which was surmounted by a golden cross. Cupola and cross were both destroyed in the hurricane of 1906. To this main section, wings were added in the 1880s and again in 1909 after a fire in the

180   *From Fort to Port*

east wing. A French Renaissance influence is evident in the breaking of the long plane of the facade by the central and end pavilions. The old wood galleries were replaced in about 1910 by the present concrete slabs and posts connected by iron pipe railings (figure 158a).

On the north side of the Administration Building, the stuccoed wall continues the same general design as on the south, but in place of galleries an arcade continues around the central cloister (figure 158b), forming a covered walkway between the buildings of the quadrangle. To the west of the passageway between the Administration Building and the Chapel is a brick building that incorporates an 1885 kitchen and refectory built by James H. Hutchisson, as recorded in the *Mobile Commercial Register*, trade edition of 1885.[16]

In chapter 3 I mentioned the founding of the Visitation Monastery. Enclosing the cloister were four buildings, of which three remain from the years 1854 to 1899. The north building is the restricted living quarters for the Monastery. On the east are two connected buildings, the northern section also being private quarters of the cloistered order and the southern section containing the public en-

159a. *The Visitation Convent, southeast building of the quadrangle enclosing the cloister, 1860–1864, 2300 Spring Hill Avenue. There is French influence in the design of the three-story building in the central pavilion, the subtle proportions, and the detailing of the entrance. Three of the four Convent buildings still stand, the school building on the west having been destroyed in 1953.*

try and offices for the Visitation Convent, not cloistered. On the west was a building, now destroyed, where lay sisters of the Visitation Order held a school (figures 159a–c). The facade of the southeast building reflects a French Renaissance influence in the central pavilion and in the subtle variation in the dimensions of windows on the different stories. Quoins edge the corners of the main mass and of the pavilion. The soft gray scored stucco gives the walls an Old World atmosphere that seems to transcend time. The central axis of the pavilion is accented by a triangular rhythm established by the pedimented architraves of the first-story side windows and the central window of the second story. The remaining windows have straight-capped architraves, that of the third-story center being enlarged and resting on corbels. All the windows are square headed except the center ones, which are semicircular. The interplay of triangle, straight line, and curve is subtly integrated, suggesting variety without creating disunity. The large entrance is framed by paneled pilasters, and the pediment is embellished with leafy scrolls centered by a cartouche (figure 159b). Leaf-and-dart and egg-and-dart motifs enrich the moldings around the capitals, the archway, and the cornices. The entrance foyer leads into a large public retreat building whose northern facade can be seen in figure 159c. This retreat building forms the southern boundary of the cloister. It was built in 1867 and was enlarged in 1885 by James H. Hutchisson, who also added the clock tower and the three-story galleries on the south facade.[17]

The end of the war not only brought a changed way of life but also turned architecture in new directions. During the period of financial austerity that continued through the 1873 depression, the few buildings that were erected showed little innovation in their designs. The creativity of the builders seemed as depleted as the economy. With the slow recovery ahead, a new type of housing would be needed. It was to be an adaptation of the Victorian style.

159b. Detail of the entrance of the Visitation Convent, east facade of the southeast building. The beautifully proportioned entrance surround has paneled pilasters and moldings enriched by classical motifs.

159c. The Visitation Convent, south building, north facade, overlooking the cloister and the area of the Monastery. The main section was built between 1860 and 1864 and was enlarged toward the west in 1885 following the plans of James H. Hutchisson, who also built the clock tower and the three-story cast iron galleries on the south facade. The monastic building was on the north of the cloister and the Convent building on the south. The less restricted nuns ran a school on the west side. (Courtesy of the Mobile City Planning Commission.)

182   *From Fort to Port*

7 The End of an Era, 1870–1880

Ehrgotte Kreb's "Bird's Eye View of Mobile" of 1873 (figure 160) suggests the geographical spread of the city's development but does not accurately indicate either the economic conditions of the times or the architectural limitations of the decade. In the map the waterfront is lined with wharves servicing the sailing vessels, and steamboats busily ply the river. In reality the harbor was still filled with war debris, which limited commerce until 1808, when a twenty-three-foot channel was finally opened so that ocean vessels could approach the docks.[1] The rows and rows of brick buildings shown on the map, extending from the riverfront west to Broad, dated to earlier, more prosperous days. Not until 1877 was some new construc-

160. Ehrgotte Kreb's "Bird's Eye View" map of Mobile, 1873. The map shows the recovery of the inner city after the explosion of 1865 and the extension of the town development to the west. (Courtesy of the Museum of the City of Mobile)

tion undertaken in the commercial sector. With the depression and panic of 1873, the terrible plague of 1878, the repeal of the city charter, and the change of government in 1879, there was little impetus for large-scale building. With a few exceptions Mobile simply repaired what was at hand. Although the residents regarded the period as a catastrophic stalemate, Edward King, a traveler from Massachusetts, in 1875 perceived it differently. He wrote of the "tranquil beauty—the strange and sleepy air of quiet about the place."

> Mobile is today a pretty town of 35,000 inhabitants tranquil and free from commercial bustle, for it has not been as prosperous as many of its southern sea port sisters.—The streets and shops are large, and many are elegant, but there is no activity; the town is as still as one of those ancient fishing villages on the Massachusetts coast when the fishermen are away.—The port needs much improvement, and the government has for some time been engaged in a kind of desultory dredging out, but has not yet succeeded in affording a sufficient depth of water to allow large vessels to come directly to the wharves; and the lines of artificial obstruction built across the channel of the bay during the war, to impede the passage of vessels, have not yet been removed.[2]

Like other travelers, Mr. King was much impressed with the beauty of Mobile, the homes, the luxuriant gardens, and the "superb oaks" shading the streets.

Civic Buildings

Only one major civic building program was undertaken during the decade, the third County Court House. Since 1864, the county had occupied the old Hagan Store on the north side of Conti between Royal and Water. In 1872, planning for a new building began, and bonds were issued to cover the anticipated expense. The plan submitted by the architect W. O. Pond was accepted on October 1, 1872, and on the same day the building contract was signed with Charles Fricke.[3] The construction was to be finished by October 1, 1873, and was to cost not more than $101,000. The design of the Court House repeated the Neoclassical elements that had typified the first two buildings (figure 161). Fortunately the contract contains specifications, making possible an accurate description of the building. All of the old charred remains of the Alderson Building were cleared down to the foundations, which were then repaired so that they could support the new construction. The building measured 81 feet 6 inches by 146 feet, with the front portico 13 feet deep. With this two-story portico, the temple form was maintained.

At the apex of the brick-filled pediment a stone figure of Justice was installed. A dentil molding outlined both the raking and the horizontal cornices and continued around the overhang of the side elevations. Six fluted Ionic columns that supported the portico entablature tapered from four feet in diameter at the base to three feet three inches at the top. The bases and capitals were of stone furnished by the McDonald, March, and Company.[4] Pilasters of similar design articulated the bays of the wall, with the outer pilasters paneled and the inner ones fluted. All the window and door openings of both the eighteen-foot-high first story and the twenty-two-foot-high second story were roundheaded and the windows had stone sills. Semicircular, too, were the first-story iron doors and window shutters. Interior shutters used in the second story extended only over the lower portion of the openings and did not rise above the transom bar. The interior six panel doors and their framing were of cypress, as was the flooring.

The exterior staircase with its side podia extended the full width of the building and had iron railings around the edges of the podia deck. An iron railing also edged a balcony at the second-story level. The coat of arms of the state of Alabama was incorporated in the center of each balustrade panel. The interior staircase was made of black walnut, and all woodwork was grained to imitate the color and patterning of black walnut. The fireplaces built throughout the building were grained to resemble black marble. No furnace was installed in this third Court House; whether for lack of funds or fear of fire is not indicated. The latter reason may have applied since a defective flue in the attic of the Alderson Building had been proven to have caused the destructive conflagration of 1864. The specifications suggest a building well enough constructed to last for some time, but within three years a newspaper reported that the "New Court House, barely three years old," was already looking dilapidated. It survived only until 1888, when it too was destroyed by fire.[5]

161. *The third County Court House, 1872 (burned in 1888); W. O. Pond, architect; Charles Fricke, builder. The six fluted Ionic columns of the monumental portico continued the classical characteristics of the previous court houses. (Engraving taken from* Mobile: The New South, *1887–88, courtesy of Mrs. Carter Smith.)*

Commercial Buildings

The most important event of 1871 was the opening of the La Clede Hotel. Its opening was heralded by an eight o'clock dinner on the night of November 29, 1871. The building was not a new construction but an adaptive reuse of two older mid-century stores built by Larimer Price and Joseph Peter. Their combined buildings extended about 120 feet along Government, running west from the corner of St. Emanuel, some twenty-six feet shorter than the present building (figure 113). The opening fanfare was described in the November 30 edition of the *Daily Register* as a gala affair. "The parlors were decorated with exquisite taste. The arrangement of the dining room was as perfect as skill and taste could make it, and a repast that would please the most fastidious epicure was spread before us. Mr. Abner Allen bears the palm for the superintendence." A few days later a guest was even more complimentary, saying that the "tables fairly groaned beneath the luxuries of wild game, salads, oysters, desserts, fruits and everything good that one's heart could wish."[6] Mr. and Mrs. J. A. Sample were the hotel proprietors, but the building was owned by Caleb Price, one of the original builders.

Unfortunately the economic conditions of the decade were such that only four years later, in 1875, Caleb Price was forced to sell the La Clede and its entire contents to pay the mortgage. The twenty-one-page list of goods catalogues the furnishings of a hotel at the time. The La Clede was not the only hotel to face bankruptcy. The St. James, located on Royal, the second door south from Dauphin on the site of the present Goldstein Jewelers, also had to dispose of all its furnishings. Even John Forsythe, editor of the *Mobile Daily Register*, found himself obliged to mortgage all the publication equipment of his newspaper to stay in business. Bankruptcy cases are recorded

162. *Warehouse Row, Water Street (destroyed). These well-built brick warehouses served the commercial community for many years, withstanding hurricane and flood. They were destroyed gradually, as modern facilities were needed. The last row was demolished in the 1970s. (Courtesy of the University of South Alabama Photographic Archives.)*

From Fort to Port

on page after page of Miscellaneous Book I/J, which even lists sales of household goods by individuals trying to survive the panic. During these days of tension the Frascati public resort played an important role. It was established on the bay where Brookley is now located. In 1874 land was being obtained for a Bay Shore Rail Road to give people easy access to the recreational area. In 1876 further entertainment was initiated by the mystic societies. In 1876 the Order of the Myths was incorporated to "cultivate a taste for Social historic literature, the fine arts and innocent and refined amusement without profit or remuneration."[7]

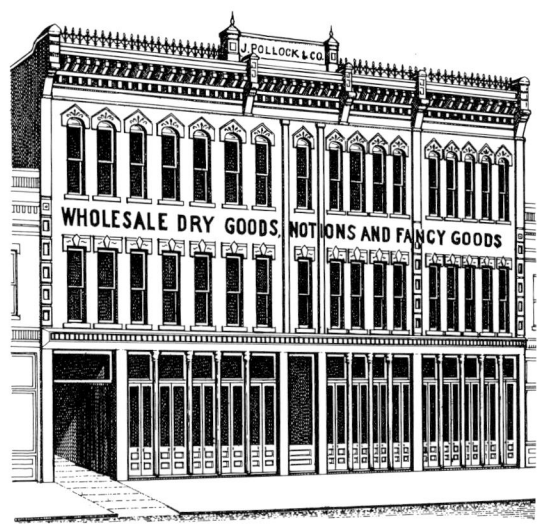

163a. The Pollock and Bernheimer warehouse, ca. 1877, 6–8 Water Street. (Drawing by Thomas F. Karwinski, AIA, based on an engraving made before 1892 in an untitled pamphlet in the files of the Historic Mobile Preservation Society.)

163b. The Pollock and Bernheimer warehouse. Photograph taken about the turn of the century. (Courtesy of the Historic Mobile Preservation Society, Wilson Plates.)

By 1877 things had started to improve, but still the major emphasis was on repair and renovation rather than on new construction. The *Daily Register* of September 9, 1877, concludes a short list of buildings in progress with the summary, "There has not been for ten years such a general refitting and repairing as there is this year."[8] Unfortunately, all the repaired warehouses that once filled the blocks between the river and Water Street have been destroyed, and only old photographs remain (figure 162). The brick buildings, solidly constructed, were three or four stories in height and functional in style, with an occasional decorated cornice to add interest to the

187   The End of an Era, 1870–1880

skyline. Standing next door and to the west of the riverside warehouses were wholesale establishments along the east and west sides of Water Street. One was the early Pollock and Bernheimer Dry Goods Building, in which the hooded windows and elaborate bracketed cornice reflect the last phase of the Italianate style as it appeared in Mobile (figures 163a, b). These old engravings accurately depict the 1870s commercial style for windows and doors. On the first story the nineteenth-century commercial buildings along Dauphin Street have all been altered with modern showcase windows. Some of the upper-story fenestration has survived, however, such as the Grotz Building of the early 1870s and the Demouy of 1878–1879 (figures 164a, b). A comparison of the row of three stores constructed in the mid-1850s at 354–358 Dauphin (figure 112) and the row built in the late 1870s (figure 164) illustrates the change in architectural design within the twenty-year span. The shallow, simple dentil-accented cornice of the former is gone. In its place there is an overhanging roof line, with heavy triangular-shaped brackets beneath that extend between deeply scrolled twin modillions, marking

164a. Three stores forming a block on Dauphin Street: the Demouy, 1878, on the corner, 226 Dauphin; the Demouy, 1878, 224 Dauphin; and the Grotz, 1879, 222 Dauphin. The early twentieth-century photograph shows two-story brick with brick hood molds over the second-story windows and small individual balconies. (Courtesy of the Historic Mobile Preservation Society, Wilson Plates.)

164b. The Demouy and Grotz stores, photographed in 1982 with the windows of the two Demouy buildings infilled with brick and the balconies removed.

From Fort to Port

each party wall division of the row. In addition, the 1879 example has a low parapet above the cornice and a paneled frieze below the brackets. In place of the simple window framing of the mid-century, the later Italianate style has heavy hood molds, with strongly accented keystones heading the windows. While these second-story windows in the example have been infilled in the two western sections, the sills still project. It is only a step from these flat brick hood molds to the three-dimensional, half rounds on corbels that were cast in iron to decorate early Victorian facades. The building at 1 Royal Street (figure 165), which lost its third story during a fire in 1875, is an example of the more elaborate hood molds that became popular during the later years of the century.

The German architect Rudolph Benz in 1877 introduced the high Victorian style to Mobile. His first recorded building was designed for James Turner in 1877 to replace a building that had just burned. It was located on St. Francis Street between Royal and St. Joseph, but no photographs have come to light. Benz seems to have arrived in America in 1870, and he was apparently employed first as a draftsman in a Chicago engineering firm. He came to Mobile in the mid-1870s and advertised in the Mobile City Directory of 1875.[9] At the same time that he was designing the Turner building, he was employed to build two-story quarters for the Franklin Society that would house a library and a reading room. Not until the 1880s and 1890s, however, was the economy lively enough for Benz's exuberant designs to proliferate in the commercial district.

165. *The Burke Building, ca. 1875, 1 North Royal Street. This was originally a three-story building, but the top floor was removed after a fire. The hood molds of the second-story windows rest on decorative corbels. The street-level story has been altered. (Photograph by Michael Thomason.)*

166. *The Blakely House, 1877, 200 North Royal Street. With the economic recovery at the end of the century, small, trim one-story frame houses became popular. Some continued to use Classical porches, while others had simple square posts.*

167. *Worker's cottage, 1871, southwest corner of Dearborn and Monroe. Rows of these cottages once lined the streets north of Monroe as the new laboring class built homes.*

168. *Worker's cottage, once standing at 457 Eslava Street, now destroyed. Though smaller than the preceding example, this cottage has the same basic form, with a steeply pitched roof and the same shotgun plan. (Photograph by Boucher, courtesy of the Library of Congress, Historic American Building Survey Collection.)*

Residential Buildings

Residential construction, although limited, was more active than the civic or commercial. Small one-story frame homes, such as the 1877 example standing at the southwest corner of Royal and Monroe (figure 166), continued to be popular. It too was built during the recovery year of 1877 by James McGill for Emanuel Blakely and was mentioned in the newspaper that year as a "neat cottage house."[10] While these post–Civil War one-story homes with their Neoclassical porch detailing are called cottages, they in no way resemble the traditional Gulf Coast style that evolved from the Creole. With their roof orientation and gable to the street, they were more closely related to the shotgun and, after the shift to Victorian jigsaw work, to the Victorian cottages of the 1890s. Rows of these small homes with their front gardens always impressed visitors to the city. One traveler who saw Mobile in 1877 wrote, "I saw no filthy, crowded tenements, the wretched abode of the lowest class, but many pretty white cottages, with a small [side?] yard with flower beds."[11] The unidentified writer added:

> I can look up Government Street with a vista of two miles, each side of the street lined with handsome buildings; those near the bay being business houses, and those of the western half of the street elegant private residences, for, like all places with any pretensions to wealth, Mobile has its fashionable "West End" where the elite make their homes, and the common herd are crowded out.[12]

This "common herd," the free laborers of the 1870s, built small, simple frame homes such as those recently restored on the southwest corner of Monroe and Dearborn. The rooms were arranged in tandem, like those of a shotgun house, but the massing and the pitch of the roof toward the street ally them with the earlier cottage types (figure 167). They seem to be almost half cottages. The square, unpretentious columns were strictly functional in design, and the porch offered a place to rest and cool off after a hard day's work. The house once standing at 457 Eslava Street was one of many in the vicinity (figure 168) of Church Street East Historic District, a part of the inner city that is once again attracting people from the suburbs.

Rare indeed was the two-story brick house built in the 1870s. The Bernstein home, now the City Museum, was built by Charles Fricke on the design of James H. Hutchisson (figure 169) and was originally simpler than it now appears. In 1890, John Bush, a new owner, had the home renovated, and he may have added the unusual rope molding that surrounds the doorway.[13]

A variation of the Italianate style, locally known as the Bracketed, was introduced in 1870. It was represented by a two-story frame house with a Neoclassical porch formed of tall, square columns that rose the full height of the facade, creating strong vertical lines that were echoed in the twin brackets above each column. The Hellen-Croom home standing on Augusta Street in the Oakleigh Garden District is an isolated example (figure 170), but during the last thirty years of the century, homes that were similar in scale and detail were placed side by side, at equal distances from the public way, setting up a block-long rhythm of repeated vertical lines. Old photographs exist of such street scenes, but only an occasional group can still be found such as the two in the Fort Condé area of Church Street East (figure 171). Also introduced with this style was a new balustrade design in which the balusters were cut from a flat board, so that they formed a two-dimensional silhouette instead of the square section or turned patterns popular earlier.

The close of the decade saw the end of an architectural era. From 1819 to 1880, architecture, while following the nineteenth-century revivals, adapted them in vernacular ways. With the coming of the Victorian period, there was little difference in the style as it appeared in Mobile and in other parts of the county. Only the Gulf Coast cottage continued to go its own way in one long, continuing revival. The Classicism of the architect William Pond yielded to the elaboration of Benz designs. The long and influential career of James H. Hutchisson upon his death in 1887 conferred prestige on his eldest son, James Flandin, who remained active in Mobile until about 1902, when he moved to Chicago after finishing the towers of the Cathedral. Meanwhile, from 1880 to 1900 Victorianism dominated the Mobile architectural scene.

169. *The Bernstein House, 1872, 355 Government Street, now adapted as the Museum of the City of Mobile; James H. Hutchisson, architect; Charles Fricke, builder. This was one of the last of the large brick Italianate houses to be built before the coming of the Victorian period.*

170. *The Hellen-Croom House, 1870, 1001 Augusta Street. In the 1870s a new style of porch was introduced in Mobile. Square columns rose the full height of the facade, giving it a strong vertical line. The balustrades were cut from a flat board in various two-dimensional patterns.*

171. *The Antunez House, 1872, 162 St. Emanuel Street, and the Delacour House, 1878, 164 St. Emanuel Street. Two houses standing side by side are all that remain of the old block-long rows of similar porches that once created a harmonious streetscape with repeating columns.*

8 The High Victorian Period, 1880–1900

The twenty years between 1880 and 1900 made a profound change in the development of Mobile. From a strictly southern Gulf Coast port it grew into a commercial center of some importance nationally. It ceased to be a predominantly cotton-exporting center and became a center for trade of broader scope that included fruit, coffee, and especially lumber. Yellow pine, cypress, and white oak became not only a commercial commodity but also an integral part of the local construction in which the older painted interior woodwork was replaced by hand-rubbed natural finishes.

The last decades of the century were free from the major setbacks that had plagued the city in the previous years. Fires were limited in scale, the largest being one in 1886 that destroyed eight warehouses in the block between St. Anthony, Commerce, St. Louis, and St. Michael. When a fire occasionally destroyed an individual store, it was replaced immediately by a new one of Victorian design. The hurricane of October 2, 1893, which produced a water level eight feet eight inches above mean tide, did not greatly damage the town, though winds of seventy-five miles an hour drove the water as far as Royal Street, inundating Water and Commerce streets. Even the 1897 yellow fever epidemic was not as devastating as previous outbursts.[1]

With the economy recovering, improvements in community services were undertaken. The old horse-drawn trolleys were replaced in 1893 by electric cars. Gas lighting was replaced by electric fixtures when the Mobile Lighting Company and the Progress Light and Motor Company were established in the 1880s.[2] An increased number of architects trained in the Victorian tradition were altering the Mobile streetscapes. Yet in spite of these obvious changes, much of the old Mobile remained that always appealed to visitors to the city.

A Kansan wrote in his 1892 home paper that he was much interested in the local market with its oyster shuckers and had greatly enjoyed a drive along the Bay Shore Old Shell Road, which resembled "a long wavy ribbon of white, now visible, again hidden from sight by the stately magnolias or cypress." He made no comment on the fine Greek Revival buildings along Government Street, either Barton Academy or the Government Street Presbyterian

Church. He reserved his observations for the old dilapidated Guard House and for the cast iron galleries of the larger homes. As late as 1893, a traveler from Detroit saw in Mobile a kind of "Arcadian retreat" and wrote in the *Mobile Weekly Register* that the architecture reminded him of a European city, that many of the gable-roofed buildings were identical with those of Normandy.[3] He was especially delighted with the "verandas on the second floor of the stores that provided shade for the passer-by." Thus the new Mobile was interlocked with the old even as the architectural history of the city changed (figure 172).

Civic Buildings

Once again a fire triggered the construction of a major civic building, this time the fourth County Court House. On January 20, 1888, the 1872 Neoclassical-style Court House designed by W. O. Pond was destroyed by fire (figure 161). Seven fire companies of the city responded to the 9:00 A.M. call, the Hook and Ladder Number Three and the Salvage Corps, the Creole Number One, Merchants Number Four, Neptune Number Two, Torrent Number Five, Mechanics Number Seven, and the Washington Number Eight. Apart from problems with the equipment, the fire's location between the second-story ceiling and the roof made it difficult for the men to control the flames, and all but parts of the first story were lost. The *Mobile Daily Register* reported, "The flames had spread over the entire ceiling of the second floor and the new ceiling of oiled yellow pine recently put

172. *Mobile, 1884, engraving from* Harper's Weekly, *February 2, 1884. At left center is the third County Court House building designed by Pond. In the center foreground stands the Old Guard House. In the lower right corner is the rear of the La Clede Hotel. In the center left foreground is the Eslava-Zaphiris Building before the addition of the rear wing in 1889. In between stands Christ Episcopal Church with its tower, which was destroyed in the hurricane of 1906. (Courtesy of Mrs. Carter Smith and the Mobile City Planning Commission.)*

in furnished fuel for the fire." Before long the roof collapsed, and the parapet with its sandstone figure of Justice crashed to the "mud of Government Street smashing into a thousand pieces."[4]

Fast work on the part of the county officials saved the records from the first floor, but the law library on the second story was largely destroyed. Again the county had to seek temporary quarters, this time in the old hotel that can be seen to the rear of figure 173. The insurance companies settled immediately, and plans were quickly formulated for a new building. Several designs were submitted, including one by James F. Hutchisson, son of the long influential James H. Hutchisson, who had died the previous August. Rudolph Benz won the vote of the council, and on March 26, 1888, a contract was signed with him. The builder, Louis Monin, received the contract for construction with his bid for $60,763.00.[5]

The construction proceeded rapidly, and on July 9, 1889, the building was turned over to the county council. Upon close examination the major forms of the third and fourth county court houses prove to have the same basic temple plan, but they also illustrate the change that fifteen years had brought in Mobile's taste (figures 161 and 173). Both structures use Ionic columns but in a different arrangement. Instead of the earlier prostyle elevation, with six columns extending across the whole facade, the Benz plan calls for a portico stepping forward from the plane of the wall, with four columns rising to the gable. Replacing the central stairway with its side podia, there are end steps separated by the basement wall, forming a support for the deck. Benz retained the dentil-outlined gable but filled the pediment with relief sculpture of two eagles enframing a coat of arms of the state of Alabama. Three allegorical figures above the pediment de-

173. *The fourth County Court House, 1889; Rudolph Benz, architect; Louis Monin, builder. Victorian detailing has been added to the basically classical format. The 1907 photograph shows the building before the addition of the rear wing, which was built on the site of the old Royal Street Hotel. (Courtesy of the Historic Mobile Preservation Society, Wilson Plates.)*

The High Victorian Period, 1880–1900

clare the purpose of the building: Law reclining on the left with a book, Unity in the center, holding the fasces of the republic, and Wisdom on the right with an owl.[6]

The skyline breaks with all previous Mobile traditions. Three corner towers and one large central tower are all of complex Victorian design, belonging to the French Second Empire (1852–1870). The high, top-heavy roof configuration suggests descent from the design of François Mansart or from the 1852–1857 wing of the Louvre. The smaller corner towers reach 94 feet into the air, and the central one, 186 feet high, will dominate the skyline for the next quarter century.

The side elevations retain more of the earlier design features of the Pond building. The roundheaded windows are the same in the 1888 elevation. The exterior shutters on the first story and the interior ones on the second story repeat the 1872 details. Even some of the interior structural arches were reinforced and readapted.[7] But the decor as described in the local newspaper of the time illustrated the change from the Classical to the Victorian mode. Richer colors were used. The floor of the lobby was tiled with red, cream, and gray marble. The wainscoting was paneled in alternate designs of grooved and plain surfaces, both of yellow pine with a rubbed oil finish. Art glass filled the windows of the staircase landing, and the circuit court room was paneled in yellow pine accented by the brass of the fixtures. Within a short time the old hotel which had served the courts during the construction of the new building had been torn down, and an addition had been made on the south end of the Benz building. This is the Court House remembered by older Mobilians and so often made the subject of photographs. The building survived the 1906 hurricane with damage and the loss of statues, but it continued to be a part of the lower Government Street scene until 1958, when the present Cooper van Antwerp Court House was constructed (see appendix 6).

The city did not undertake as large a building program as the county, but it did authorize some construction. In 1886, when the alderman form of government was reestablished, Richard Bower, the new mayor, embarked on projects needed for the general improvement of the community. The results of this initiative can be seen in the 1888 Matzenger map, in which new streets led out to platted suburban areas. Communities were developed along Davis Avenue, with the blocks established out as far as Rylands on the north (figure 174). On the west the city boundary extended to beyond Monterey, with connecting streets between the main arteries of Dauphin, Spring Hill, and Old Shell. On the south, developments stretched to the Mandeville Tract. Most of the streets were left with a dirt surface, but some were topped with shell, and a few important ones in the inner city were paved with cypress blocks driven into the roadbed.[8] Cobblestones were reserved for the streets between Royal and Water, where heavy commercial traffic was carried on near the waterfront.

The major building program undertaken by the city was the construction of the new Jail and Police Station (figure 175). The picturesque old Guard House (figure 77c) was no longer adequate for its task. Though the new building was heralded enthusiastically, the loss of the old was mourned. On September 1, 1895, the local press reported that the "antique looking building, formerly occupied by the police authorities and behind the massive walls of which so

175. City Jail and Police Station, 1895–1896, now destroyed; Rudolph Benz, architect; Pauly Jail Company (St. Louis), contractors; D. B. and W. S. Hull of Dallas, Texas, builders; cost, $27,000. The building faced on both St. Emanuel and Conti streets and formed an L-shaped plan. Benz chose a Victorian design in dark red St. Louis brick with rusticated stone trim. (Erik Overbey/Mobile Public Library Collection, University of South Alabama Photographic Archives.)

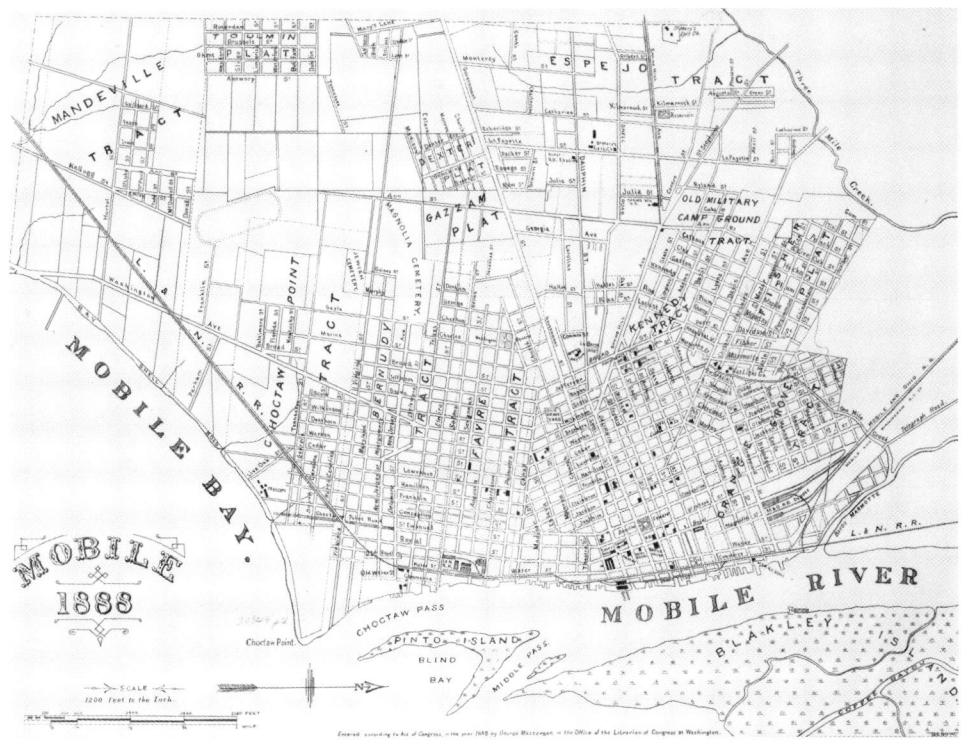

174. The Matzenger map of Mobile, 1888. The western boundary of the city has been extended just beyond Monterey Street. The northern boundary includes the platting of the Davis Avenue neighborhood. The south boundary includes Mandeville and extends not quite as far as the modern Brookley Field. (Courtesy of the Library of Congress.)

The High Victorian Period, 1880–1900

many have pined in durance vile, are no more."⁹ In its place, Rudolph Benz designed a two-story building of irregular plan, with two wings meeting at a ninety-degree angle. The mayor's office, the courtrooms, and the lockup room occupied the larger wing facing on St. Emanuel with 63 feet of frontage and a depth of 108 feet. At right angles, facing on Conti, was the Police Department and the rooms for the patrol, which also had an attached wagon room and a stable. The wing facing Conti had a front of 36 feet and a depth of 69 feet. The two wings wrapped around the German Relief Hall on the corner. Dominating the whole mass was the 80-foot-high Victorian Romanesque tower located on the southwest corner. The contractor for the jail was the Pauly Jail Company of St. Louis, and the builders were D. B. and W. S. Hull from Dallas.¹⁰ The dark red St. Louis pressed brick made a colorful textural contrast with the rusticated stone trim used to accent the heavy Richardsonian arch over the entrance and the lintels of the first-story windows. The same rough stone formed slender string courses marking the stories and forming the arcade in the tower. The two Benz buildings, the 1888 County Court House and the 1895–1896 City Jail, illustrate the variety of architectural types included within the broad term "Victorian."

The German Relief Hall (figures 176a–c), designed by Benz, and the YMCA, done by Watkins and Johnson, are representative of the buildings erected by civic organizations. They represent the different trends to be found during the last five years of the century. The German Relief Hall (figure 176b) is a prime example of Mobile Victorian. As it stands today (figure 176c), the building has lost all of its characteristic detailing except the cornice and corner tower, but the present plans are to restore the elevations, following early engravings of the structure as it appeared in 1896.¹¹ The German Relief organization was founded in 1870 and had occupied quarters on part of the site of the later building (figure 176a). The organization's increased membership and the many social functions held in the various accommodations made it necessary to build a larger structure, so Rudolph Benz was employed in 1895 to design an addition that would occupy the corner facing on both St. Emanuel and Conti. His building was dedicated on October 17, 1896. The frontal planes of this large quadrilateral mass were broken by the curve of the corner tower and by wide central bays facing on both streets. Side gables rising from cornice level broke the slope of the steep hip roof, along whose ridge ran an iron cresting.¹² The curved heads of the windows were filled with stained glass, and the door transoms repeated the design, as did the infilling of the gables. On the left, in the Conti Street facade, the old configuration can still be seen, though the openings have been infilled with modern materials. The division between the first and second stories was once marked by a cast iron balcony that extended down both the north and the west facades. Three main entrances led into the building, one centered on each side of the building and one at the corner. The corner door was enframed by stone voussoirs forming the arch and marble columns on each side of the recessed entrance. The corner tower was given the most elaborate Victorian detailing. The drum with two bands of decoration supports a truncated roof projecting over heavy brackets, suggesting the medieval machicolations of a castle. An iron crest encircles the top of the tower, from the center of which a flagpole once rose.

The building may look Victorian and nineteenth century, but

176a. The German Relief Hall, 1896; Rudolph Benz, architect; John McAdory, contractor. The first German Relief building was located on the corner, next door to the north of the old jail, with its entrance on St. Emanuel. It was enlarged by Benz with the addition of the cornice elaboration. (From Mobile, Alabama, in Photogravure, by the Zadex Jewelry Company, 1892, courtesy of the Historic Mobile Preservation Society.)

176b. The German Relief building as enlarged and renovated by Rudolph Benz, 1896. (Erik Overbey/Mobile Public Library Collection, University of South Alabama Photographic Archives.)

176c. The German Relief Hall, 1983. With the windows and doors infilled and plastered, only the main massing and the remarkable cornice remain in their original condition. The building has been purchased for restoration. (Photograph by Michael Thomason.)

structurally it belongs to the twentieth. It was made of cement, not brick or stone, and the corner tower was of steel. Steel was also used for the roof framing of the twenty-four-foot-high second-story auditorium, though the traditional wood ceiling was used in the first-floor banquet hall, in which six iron columns supported the weight above. An innovative idea was also incorporated in the use of temporary partitions formed by sliding doors hung from the ceiling, thus making possible the division of the forty-five-by-seventy-foot room into smaller units as needed.

201   *The High Victorian Period, 1880–1900*

The 1897–1898 YMCA building, standing on the northeast corner of Government and Conception streets (figure 177), contrasts with Benz's German Relief Hall. The architects, Watkins and Johnson, occasionally worked in a restrained Victorian mode, but usually they followed a Neoclassical style, a tradition that had been a trademark of the James H. Hutchisson designs. The strictly rectangular massing of the YMCA building is broken only by the low gables above the central axis of both the Government Street and St. Emanuel Street facades. The bays are clearly articulated by a balance of vertical and horizontal lines, further accented by color contrasts between the brick and the white belt courses. The semicircular-headed windows of the first story above the basement suggest a Renaissance arcade.[13] Four pilasters frame the central bays of the second story, rising from a string course that surrounds the building and marks the level of the stories. The smooth surfaces of the pilasters and walls contrast texturally with the rustication of the piers supporting the arcaded windows. The main entrance on the Conception Street side, on the left, has a canopy supported by elaborately cast scrolled brackets and a balustrade that encloses the deck. The main walls are of a buff Roman brick, with the basement level of stone. As originally planned but not as it developed, the roof was to have been a truncated hip, with the flattened top made into a roof garden enclosed by a balustrade. The interior of the building was well planned to serve the various programs of the YMCA: it had study halls, lecture rooms, parlors, reception rooms, banquet halls, a gymnasium, a track, an auditorium, a restaurant, some sleeping accommodations, and even a bicycle storage area. In 1907 a new auditorium greatly increased the seating capacity for popular events.[14] The building served the community until 1969, when the association felt that a new location was needed for parking space.

177. *YMCA Building, 1897; Watkins and Johnson, architects; Knoxville Building Company, contractors; cost, $60,000. Architect Watkins exerted an understated and elegant classical influence on Mobile architecture. (Photograph by Michael Thomason.)*

Religious Buildings

Both white and black congregations were active in building churches during the twenty years from 1880 to 1900. Two from the white community are the 1890 Gothic Revival Government Street Methodist Church on the southwest corner of Government and Broad streets (figure 178) and the St. Francis Street Methodist Church of 1895 (figure 179). The Gothic Revival structure on Government and Broad was enlarged and was completely altered in design by George B. Rogers in 1908 (figures 178 and 215). The black congregations included the State Street A.M.E. Zion (1884, 1896; figures 180a,b), the St. Michael Street Emanuel A.M.E. Church, of which the facade was built in 1890–1891 by James F. Hutchisson (figure 181), and the 1895 Big Zion A.M.E.Z. Church standing on the northwest corner of Bayou and Church streets. Among those destroyed are the Broad Street Methodist Church at the corner of Broad and Elmira (1895), and the Bethel A.M.E. on the west side of Franklin between Monroe and Eslava (1896). The Baptists were also active, building the Union Baptist at Warren and St. Anthony (1890), the new facade and tower for the St. Louis Street Baptist Church (1890), and another church on Dearborn and Palmetto.[15]

179. *St. Francis Street Methodist Church, 1895–1896, 251 St. Francis Street; Watkins and Johnson, architects; J. P. Emrich, contractor; $30,000. The 1916 hurricane destroyed the upper half of the 148-foot-high spire. The building is the last of the unaltered Victorian churches to survive in the city. (Photograph by Michael Thomason.)*

178. *The Government Street Methodist Church, 1890–1891, at the southwest corner of Government and Broad, now destroyed; B. D. Price, architect; W. S. Foster, contractor. A Gothic Revival design in pressed brick with stone trim was soon replaced by the present Spanish Revival building. (From* Mobile, Alabama, in Photogravure, *by the Zadex Jewelry Company, 1892, courtesy of the Historic Mobile Preservation Society.)*

203   *The High Victorian Period, 1880–1900*

180a. The A.M.E.Z. State Street Methodist Church, 1884, 1896, 502 State Street; James H. Hutchisson, architect of the facade and the 1884 construction; Watkins and Johnson, architects of the sanctuary end and enlargement, 1896. (Courtesy of the Historic Mobile Preservation Society.)

180b. The A.M.E.Z. State Street Methodist Church, interior. The delicate cusping of the trussing and brackets is illuminated by windows on three levels of the interior elevation. (Courtesy of the Historic Mobile Preservation Society.)

181. *St. Michael Street A.M.E. Church, 1890–1891, St. Michael Street, two doors east of Washington; James F. Hutchisson, architect; cost, $10,000. Hutchisson added the Gothic facade to an earlier church.*

In addition to the Methodists and the Baptists, the Catholics were occupied with erecting neighborhood churches and with finishing the Cathedral. The facade was completed in 1890 by James F. Hutchisson, following the work of his late father, James H. Hutchisson, who had been retained as architect in 1873 to construct the portico. James F. Hutchisson completed the corner towers in 1895 (figure 182). Another very important Catholic church built during this time was the Richardsonian Romanesque Chapel at the Visitation Monastery (figure 183). Apart from the church buildings, auxiliary structures were increasing in number. One such building was the Christ Church Vestry facing on St. Emanuel Street, the last design by James H. Hutchisson before his death.[16]

Three of these religious buildings may be regarded as representing the variations and development of ecclesiastical styles at the close of the century: the State Street A.M.E. Zion, the St. Francis Street Methodist, and the Chapel of the Sacred Heart at the Visitation Monastery. The exterior of the State Street A.M.E.Z. Church illustrates the vernacular adaptation of the eighteenth-century churches inspired by Sir Christopher Wren, with the two-story rectangular massing and the tower with the spire over the entrance (figure 180). The interior (figure 180b) of the auditorium and sanctuary has cusped trussing of Gothic Revival derivation. It is similar in style to Trinity Episcopal on Dauphin Street (figure 107b), though the members are more slender and elaborated, with minor cusping edging the main motifs. The interior is lit by windows on three levels—the side aisle, the balcony, and a clerestory that breaks into the wall above the gallery roof. The auditorium was designed by Watkins and Johnson, according to the newspaper account, but whether it was a new building or an enlargement of the 1884 construction by James H. Hutchisson is still a question.[17] The descriptions of the 1884 facade and vestibule make it appear that the Hutchisson design was retained for the front bay and the 1896 auditorium of Watkins and

Johnson was attached to it. The Church not only is a good example of other similar buildings in Mobile but also symbolizes the activities of the black community.

The only nineteenth-century Victorian church surviving in its original state is the St. Francis Street Methodist Church (figure 179). It too was a design of Watkins and Johnson, though through some error a newspaper reporter credited it to Benz. The building replaced an earlier one of 1842 that had developed from a division of the "mother" Church known as the "Bee Hive." As in the State Street A.M.E.Z. the auditorium is on the second story. The slightly projecting front and side pavilions and the rear wing forming the apse are embellished with fine nineteenth-century stained glass windows, those on the front and rear being circular, forming rose windows. The single tower is located on the facade's northeast corner and originally supported a spire that rose 148 feet above the street below. When the 1916 hurricane removed the upper half, the spire was left truncated, as it is at present, and a cross was placed on the top (figure 179). The dark red of the Nashville brick used in construction was set in black mortar and contrasted strongly with the white of the stone trim.[18]

The trade journal of the *Mobile Daily Register* carries a description of the building at the time of its dedication in 1896. There have been no changes in the elevations of the building. Six stone string courses mark various levels of the doors, windows, and story divisions. The roof is partially hidden by large gables that rise over the front and side pavilions. Roundheaded windows are used throughout, either single or twinned, and in the sanctuary with a transom in the design of half a wheel. While the exterior design is controlled for a Victorian building, the description of the interior at the time of the dedication tells a truly Victorian story. The ground-level Sunday school walls were finished in a salmon pink color, graded to a light terra cotta, with a gray and gold crown molding. The color was repeated in the opal stained glass of the windows. Two oak stairways led to the second-level vestibule. The walls of the auditorium were painted to resemble paneling, with the color grading from dark at the bottom to light at the top and frames painted in a trompe-l'oeil fashion. Corinthian pilasters finished in gold articulated the bays, and a gold and amethyst arch framed the windows. The large memorial windows centering on the sides of the auditorium measure eighteen and one-half feet high by thirteen feet wide, creating a multicolored surface. A costly organ also finished in gold was located just below the western rose of the sanctuary, the stained glass of which showed figures of cherubs looking out from clouds. When the interior was illuminated by the great chandelier with its thirty-four gas and twenty-four electric jets, it must have thrilled the Victorian sensibility.

The Chapel of the Sacred Heart at the Visitation Monastery is one of the few stone buildings in Mobile, stone being a rarity along the coast. The Richardsonian Romanesque building (figure 183) was designed by two New Orleans architects, B. M. Harrod and Paul Andry, who were also involved with the selection of plans for Tulane University. The supervising architect of construction was Hermann Brunns, also of New Orleans, and the contractor was M. T. Lewman and Company of Louisville, Kentucky.[19] The massive walls are made of rusticated limestone and granite, richly ornamented with floral carvings in the flattened coloristic style of the Byzantine. Gargoyles peer down from the outer angles of the gable pediment and a heavy stone cross crowns the apex. The main plan is roughly a Greek cross, with the two-story west arm elongated to form an area for the cloistered sisters. This section was originally curtained off with both grilles and shutters. Provisions were also made that members of the order in the infirmary could hear the mass. The present interior decor has a quiet simplicity given vitality by the color of the stained glass windows and the lighting in the sanctuary over the altar. The windows departed from the usual subjects in that they included, together with Christ the Good Shepherd and Christ Carrying the Cross, one scene with a nun and another with a priest. The front central panel contains the figure of the Virgin and a member of the Visitation Order. The half wheel above the door is colorfully infilled with floral patterns surrounding a dove. At the time when the Chapel was

182. *The Cathedral of the Immaculate Conception. The facade of the Cathedral was constructed between 1873 and 1890 by the architects James H. and James F. Hutchisson. The towers and domes were finished in 1895 by James F. Hutchisson.*

183. *Chapel of the Sacred Heart, Visitation Convent, 1894; Harrod and Andry, architects; M. T. Lewman and Company, Louisville, contractors; cost, $35,528. The finest example of Richardsonian Romanesque in Mobile.*

The High Victorian Period, 1880–1900

constructed, a kiosk was built so that it formed a gate in the front wall marking the boundary of the Visitation Monastery property.

Educational buildings as well as churches played an important role in the increased number of constructions of the period. In 1884 a three-story building designed by Freret of New Orleans was added to the Spring Hill campus. It was located on the east line of the north yard. The second story was intended as an exhibition hall and the third as a chapel. The next year James H. Hutchisson designed a two-story refectory and a one-story brick kitchen located on the west of the quadrangle.[20] Embedded in the interior east wall at the south end of Moore Hall are some exposed relieving arches that may well be part of another Hutchisson building constructed as an infirmary. The most impressive of the educational buildings was the McGill Institute, the result of the enlargement of the old Chandler House at 252 Government Street (figure 184). The facade of the original two-story house included only the three western bays and, on the left, four Tuscan Doric columns standing to their full height. The fifth column on the right and the recessed wing with the main entrance and the continuation of the colonnade were added when the building was renovated for the boys' school. Before his death in 1895, Arthur McGill and his younger brother, Felix, purchased the Chandler House and the vacant lot next door on the east so that the building could be enlarged. When the institution was established, a board of directors was selected, with Bishop O'Sullivan as president.

For more than fifty years the imposing eclectic Greek Revival building contributed to the architectural scene of Government Street, making an interesting contrast with the 1830 applications of the style as in the Barton Academy. The facade, 44 feet high by 160 feet long, was crowned by an entablature that was embellished by Greek motifs, for example the triglyphs and metopes, but used without attention to the classical subtleties or harmonious proportions of the earlier revival period. The bracketed cornice, the roof parapet, and the elaborate entrance detail belong to a late Italianate influence. All these various influences are harmoniously combined in the facade. The 1896 account described the interior in detail, with the

184. *McGill Institute, enlarged in 1896 and now destroyed, formerly at 252 Government Street. The old Chandler home was enlarged by Harrod and Andry, who lengthened the facade by a fifth column and a recessed east wing. (Courtesy of the Historic Mobile Preservation Society, Wilson Plates.)*

208   *From Fort to Port*

necessary classrooms, offices, refectory, assembly hall, and sleeping accommodations on the second and third stories. The building served the school until 1952, when a new facility was erected. By 1955 the old building had been destroyed.[21]

Commercial Buildings

Progress in commercial development from 1880 to 1900 was rapid and diversified, resulting in many architectural demands. Old warehouses were enlarged and new ones constructed (figure 186). A comparison of the three Pollock Company buildings (figure 163, 1877; figure 186, 1897; the central building in figure 187, 1903) shows the stylistic evolution from early Italianate through the Victorian to the early twentieth century. Industry was also coming into Mobile, requiring an architecture not found in the area previously. Two of the most interesting of these buildings were the 1892 brewery and the large grain elevator of 1896.[22] Both were designed by A. Maritzen of Chicago. The brewery (figure 185) was an imposing Victorian building with a massive front tower topped by a crested Mansard roof and by a Byzantine-type dome that crowned the center of the mass. It was enthusiastically proclaimed to be the most progressive brewery in the United States. The late nineteenth-century method of storing and moving large quantities of produce is illustrated in the grain elevator that once stood on the block bounded by Water, Commerce, Bloodgood, and Earle streets. In importance it can be compared with the present Alabama State Docks container facility. As pictured and described in the *Mobile Daily Register* trade journal for 1896, the 130-foot high elevator required a foundation of 600 pilings to support the load of the 250,000 bushels of grain that the building could house.

Other, less ambitious programs were undertaken, for example the carriage factory that once stood on the south side of Theatre Street between Royal and St. Emanuel, the site of the modern Rousseau's

185. *The Mobile Brewery, 1892, formerly on Water and Adams streets. This eight-story Victorian building used brick over a steel frame and was designed by the Chicago architect August Maritzen. (From* Mobile, Alabama, in Photogravure, *by the Zadex Jewelry Company, 1892, courtesy of the Historic Mobile Preservation Society.)*

186. The Pollock and Bernheimer Building, 1897, formerly on the east side of Water Street, across from the earlier warehouse; Rudolph Benz, architect; Collier and Weeks, contractors; cost, $16,000. (From the Mobile Daily Register, September 1, 1897.)

187. View of the south side of Dauphin Street between Royal and Water streets. On the left end of the block, a cast iron building (1860). Next to the west, the Baerman Building, Dreaper and Burns (1893), the six-story Pollock and Bernheimer Store (1903), the Felrath Building, and, last on the right, the Rhodes. (Courtesy of the University of South Alabama Photographic Archives.)

210   From Fort to Port

Restaurant. The shop and two related houses on Royal were designed by James H. Hutchisson in 1885.[23] A drawing of the entrance to the carriage factory appears in the First National Bank publication *Where Time Bears Witness to Sound Building*. The two-story brick building faced on Theatre Street. On the left of the facade, a wide double-leaf door, under a relieving arch, formed the entrance to the shop. A second relieving arch once provided an opening for a passageway that gave access to the rear yard. On the right, extending over the sidewalk, was a two-story gallery, with the upper deck roofed and framed by cast iron.

The Kling company that was responsible for so much of the ironwork in the city erected a new foundry in 1884, another building designed by Hutchisson. The lighter side of Mobile life was not forgotten. A $10,000 skating rink was built in 1886 at the corner of Royal and St. Louis, which was later transformed into the Princess Theatre in 1895. In 1899 the Pollock Company combined an office, commercial facility, and theater all in one building, an idea whose time would not come for another half century. It was designed by Thomas Sully of New Orleans.[24]

The retail business received the most attention as storefront after storefront was renovated or rebuilt. The scene on Royal, Dauphin, and Conti streets was changed by the shift to a Victorian style. An early twentieth-century photograph of the eastern end of Dauphin on the south side shows the evolution from the Italianate cast iron storefront on the left corner to the ornate Victorian on the right (figure 187). Of this row, only one building is still standing in toto, the Daniels-Elgin cast iron store (figure 140) and the first three stories of the tall Pollock-Bernheimer Building mid-block. Of the six buildings in the photograph, the third from the left, the Dreaper and Burns of 1893, is an excellent example of the developing storefront (figure 188).[25] In it, the Chicago art glass of the cabinet windows,

188. *The Dreaper and Burns Building, 1893, formerly at 55–57 Dauphin, George Watkins, architect; Heuston and Richards, masons; cost, $3,350; McDonald, March, and Company, stonework. The structure represents a transitional design between the older flat facades of the Federal and Italianate and the high Victorian broken massing of R. Benz. One of the first uses of the cabinet-style store windows. (Drawing by Thomas F. Karwinski, AIA, from an old newspaper sketch.)*

211 *The High Victorian Period, 1880–1900*

the decorative lintels of the second-story fenestration, and the segmental arches of the third story are Victorian but were treated with a light touch typical of the architect George Watkins, who designed the building. The black-and-white drawing by Thomas Karwinski of the American Institute of Architects delineates the building but does not suggest the color. A newspaper account of 1893 described windows made of "fine French plate glass set in frames of highly polished quarter sawed oak, enriched with mouldings of copper. The upper part of the show windows are ornamented with wide panels of Cathedral glass studded with brilliant jewels of various colors." The layered planes of the recessed entrance and the projecting windows broke with the older Mobile storefront tradition.

The contrast in the aesthetic values is evident from a comparison of the Dreaper-Burns with the McCaw Italianate store of 1885 (figure 189), which still retains its original upper story. The Lower Dauphin Street Commercial Historic District has a valuable collection of store facades covering the last half of the nineteenth century. While most of them have had the first stories altered, the upper levels retain their original configuration. In figure 190, the 1879 Grotz Building at 222 Dauphin and the 1891 Spira Building on the right share party walls but not style. In the last twenty years of the century, many of the stores were being designed by popular local architects such as James F. Hutchisson, Rudolph Benz, and George Watkins. Benz did the Scheuerman Building at 203 Dauphin Street (figure 191).[26] He incorporated the textural contrasts of the Queen Anne style in the rusticated stone trim, the polished columns, and the smooth brick. He enriched the surfaces by carving arabesques in the half circles above the windows on the upper side and acanthus scrolls in the interstices above the semicircular central window. Acanthus and palmetto leaves form the brackets below the cornice. The street-level windows have been completely changed.

189. *The McCaw Building, 210 Dauphin Street, 1883, R. Benz, architect; McGuire and Lyndall, contractors; cost, $3,000. The structure is late Italianate in style. The first story has been altered, but the second story retains its original configuration.*

190. 220 Dauphin, 1891, the Spira Building (right); 222 Dauphin, 1879, the Grotz Building (left). Standing side by side, an Italianate structure and a Victorian illustrate the change in taste between 1879 and 1891. The Spira was designed by Benz and was constructed by C. C. Griffin at a cost of $4,500. (Photograph by Michael Thomason.)

191. The Scheuerman Building, 203 Dauphin Street, 1893; R. Benz, architect; Sossaman Brothers, contractors; cost, $3,500; McDonald, March, and Company, stonework; Henry Kearns, mason; A. Kling, ironwork. This Victorian design in Philadelphia brick has trim of Alabama stone and granite columns framing the large central semicircular-headed window. (Photograph by Michael Thomason.)

213   *The High Victorian Period, 1880–1900*

192. *The J. H. Masson Building, 204–206 Dauphin Street, 1897; the Knoxville Building and Construction Company; cost, $5,000. The second-story architectural features are original; the first story has been altered. The rectilinear patterns of the second-story decoration relate more to the new Art Moderne than to the contemporary Victorian.*

193. *The Spira and Pincus Building, standing at 171 Dauphin Street, 1899; Rudolph Benz, architect; J. McAdory, contractor; McDonald, March, and Company, stonework; cost, $12,000. Bedford limestone was used to cover the exposed walls. The design was planned for use by Gayfer's Department Store and is unusual for Rudolph Benz, who typically worked in the Victorian mode.*

The rather heavy treatment of the Scheuerman Building contrasts with the flat linear design of the 1897 Masson Building at 204–206 Dauphin (figure 192). Here the rectilinear motifs and the thin shadow lines of the architectural coursing have broken away from the three-dimensional decor and deep shadows of the Victorian. The final step into the twentieth century was taken in the Spira and Pincus Building of 1899, which was constructed to replace the 1886 building that had burned (figures 193 and 197).[27] In the 1899 version, though it was only three stories in height, the street-oriented first story with the layered series of windows above foreshadows the commercial establishments of the twentieth century. Merely by multiplying the number of stories Mobile will bury its nineteenth-century heritage.

Four of Rudolph Benz's buildings, two from the 1880s and two from the 1890s, illustrate the Victorian movement in Mobile. In 1886 he designed the so-called English Block (figure 194) and the building that houses both the Cotton Exchange and the Chamber of Commerce (figure 195), which was built with Zanesville brick set in red

194. The English Block, formerly on the southeast corner of Dauphin and Water Street, built in 1886 and now destroyed; Rudolph Benz, architect; Monin and Farley, contractors; cost, $18,000. (Engraving taken from Mobile, The New South, 1887–88, courtesy of Mrs. Carter Smith.)

195. The Mobile Cotton Exchange and Chamber of Commerce Building (1886); formerly on the northwest corner of Commerce and St. Francis streets; Rudolph Benz, architect; Charles Farley, contractor and mason; cost, $32,000. The fairly regular massing of the Victorian design is typical of the work of Benz in the 1880s, differing from his more complex buildings of the 1890s. (T. E. Armitstead/Museum of the City of Mobile Collection, University of South Alabama Photographic Archives.)

215 The High Victorian Period, 1880–1900

mortar. Both have Mansard roofs broken by dormers and pediments with decorative finials and sculpture. In the English Block a dragon with outstretched wings symbolizes protection, and in the Cotton Exchange the Goddess of Industry stands with her right hand holding a wreath and her left resting on an anchor, symbols of Mobile's commerce by sea and by land. Neither building has the deeply broken Victorian masses, but each retains the integrity of the plane of the wall. Each has the bays delineated by pilasters. In both, contrasting textures or colors give the windows decorative treatment. Not so with the 1890 buildings. In the Pincus Building on the corner of Dauphin and Royal (figures 196a,b) and the one on the southeast corner of Dauphin and Conception (figure 197), the rectilinear mass is broken by rounded corner towers and turrets that dominate the skyline. The roof lines are subordinated in visual importance to the dormers and the conical spires. The linearity of the 1880 designs has given way to a greater use of form. In these last two buildings Mobile's commercial Victorianism reached its final state.[28]

196a. The Pincus Building, 1 South Royal, exterior. (Photograph by Michael Thomason.)

197. The Spira and Pincus Building, 1896, formerly on the southeast corner of Dauphin and Conception and now destroyed; R. Benz, architect; D. G. Harrison, contractor; McDonald, March, and Company, stonework. This building was destroyed by fire on March 30, 1899, and was replaced by a new building by Benz in 1899. The first story was occupied by Gayfer's Department Store, the upper stories by the Fidelia Club. (Courtesy of the Historic Mobile Preservation Society, Wilson Plates.)

196b. The Pincus Building, 1 South Royal (1890); Rudolph Benz, architect; cost, $17,000. The photograph was taken in about 1900. The building was originally occupied by the Zadex Jewelry Company. A Victorian design in brick and terra cotta, with cast iron columns and balcony. (Courtesy of the Historic Mobile Preservation Society, Wilson Plates.)

The High Victorian Period, 1880–1900

198. *The Scott cottage, 209 Cedar, 1889, moved for restoration from 105 Jefferson; J. F. Hutchisson, architect; V. Overton, contractor; cost, $800. The building is a typical Victorian cottage with simple detailing.*

199. *The Gonzales cottage, 204 Royal, 1882; R. Benz, architect. This example shows a more elaborate treatment of the details, with the textural variations in the surfacing of the gable end.*

200. *View of the west side of Cedar Street between Monroe and Eslava, showing cottages ranging in dates from 1887 to 1905.*

Residential Buildings

The 1880s were years of great activity in the construction of Victorian cottages. They appeared in all degrees of elaboration; some had only a few simple porch brackets (figure 198); others had complex decorative treatment (figure 199). The newspaper reported on August 31, 1884, "The houses being erected during the past year, are, in the main, small and comfortable cottages such as are built by the laboring men and the poorer class of people, whose limited means do not allow them a gaudy Eastlake or Queen Anne structure." In 1882, seventeen of the twenty-two building permits for housing were for cottages.[29] A row of these small homes lining the second block of Cedar Street has been restored, and the buildings are in great demand; the inner city is coming back to life through the efforts of the Community Development Program and the work of the Mobile Historic Development Commission (figure 200). Unlike the shotgun structures with their single front six-over-six-light window, some cottages have two floor-length windows opening from the porch, with the lower sash a slide-by to give more circulation of air throughout the rooms (figure 198). Windowpanes are now either two over two or two over four lights, and the panes of glass are cut larger. Doors have small transoms that increase the air flow, and many cottages have an offset wing for added space (figure 198). An infinite variety of columnar types and architectural detail is achieved by the clever use of the jigsaw and the lathe, and the shadows cast by the pierced work make ever-changing patterns on the walls (figures 201, 202). These cottages may have been built by the less affluent classes, but they are not examples of poor architecture, and many were designed by the architects of the large mansions, J. F. Hutchisson and Rudolph Benz.

202. *The Mitchell House, 107 Dearborn Street, 1895. Part of the effectiveness of the design is the play of shadows cast by the varied decorative elements. (Photograph by Michael Thomason.)*

201. *Victorian cottage, 210 Cedar Street, built in about 1887, with later additions. Designs of turned columns, brackets, and friezes show endless variety in the Victorian cottages.*

203. *The Scott House, 207 Cedar, 1889; J. F. Hutchisson, architect; V. Overton, contractor; cost, $2,500. A two-story house formed by superimposing one cottage plan on another. In the restoration, Victorian colors were selected that would enhance the detailing of the decorative elements.*

204. *The Kilduff House, 200 George, 1891; J. F. Hutchisson, architect; B. Sossaman, builder; cost, $1,800. Here the decor is sturdier and less pierced than in the Mitchell House. The elements of the Gothic Revival are emphasized.*

Standing between the extremes in size were such homes as the 1889 Scott House, now restored at 207 Cedar Street. In designing it, J. F. Hutchisson superimposed one cottage on top of another, creating a two-story dwelling (figure 203). The doubling of the masses is repeated in the two-level treatment of the gable end in which the lower half is covered with fish-scale shingles, known as an imbrication, while the upper half projects over brackets. The upper half has a pierced design that includes the date of construction. The plant-sized second-story balconies on the south side, unusual in Mobile, increased safety when the floor-length windows were opened. During the house's restoration these balconies had to be rebuilt, as the originals had been destroyed. Their location was indicated in the foundation walls and in early Sanborn maps. To design them the architect used the porch balustrade and brackets as a pattern. Another example of the larger cottage is the Kilduff House (figure 204). It too is a Hutchisson design that gains space by spreading out horizontally rather than by forming a second story vertically. It is a harmonious combination of elements taken from the late Gothic Revival and the Victorian without the open spindle work found in later porch detailing.[30]

Mobile has a rich inheritance of these nineteenth-century "everyman" homes. They are not readily appreciated from a swiftly passing automobile. They belong to an age when people took the time to walk by and to enjoy their varied columns and brackets. While a row of great Neoclassical-style houses can be enjoyed in a quick passage, the Victorian cottages must be taken individually and invite more intimate contact.

The cottages dominated the constructions of the 1880s, but by 1890 the large high Victorian and Queen Anne homes had also appeared. From Hamilton Street to the area west of Ann, Government Street once bristled with towers, bays, porches, complex roof lines, and elaborate detailing of windows and doors. Now fewer than a half dozen remain. One of the grandest of those lost was the 1883 Dunlap home, built on the site of the burned Blue College, on the south side of Government two doors east of Ann. Only a few photographs exist of it (figure 205). The *Mobile Daily Register* of September 1, 1883, described it at the time of its completion. The house was built using the best of materials throughout, with stylish detailing. The interior woodwork was rubbed curly yellow pine. The grand staircase, rising to a central landing from which the steps divided, was ornamented with a large stained glass window above which was a nine-foot oriel. Statues holding gas lamps stood on the pedestal newels. One of the unusual features was the Truill gas-making machine, built underground, that furnished the gas for the lighting. The designs of the parquetry floors used oaks of different color.

205. *The Dunlap mansion, 1883, formerly on the south side of Government, two doors east of Ann; Charles T. Liddel, architect and builder; cost, $20,000. This beautifully situated Victorian mansion was one of the few examples in Mobile of the Mansard roof, which was not well suited to the torrential rainfall of the Gulf Coast or to the hurricanes. (Courtesy of the Historic Mobile Preservation Society, Wilson Plates.)*

In spite of the grandiose quality of the Dunlap home, the M. Forcheimer House of 1892 best expressed the high Victorian style in Mobile (figure 206). Here the basic rectangular block of the building has been completely lost in the broken projections, the bays, porches, balconies, towers, and deeply overhanging cornices that cast heavy shadows on the walls. The building incorporates elements from the entire Victorian vocabulary, including the elaborated window heads, the shaped balusters and brackets, the gable decor, and the crested square tower, all breaks in the planes accented by contrasting color.

A house standing in a transitional position between the Victorian and the Queen Anne styles was the McCoy House of 1883 (figure 207). From the Queen Anne comes the interest in the textural variations of the surfacing more than in the deep breaks in the massing. While porches, bays, gables, and overhangs continue in the McCoy

206. *M. Forcheimer House, formerly on the south side of Government between Chatham and George, 1892. An outstanding example of Mobilian high Victorianism. Here the heaviness and strength of the style have not yet been lightened by the grace and delicacy of the Queen Anne decor.* (From Mobile, Alabama, in Photogravure, *by Zadex Jewelry Company, 1892, courtesy of the Historic Mobile Preservation Society.*)

207. *The McCoy mansion, 1883, formerly on the southwest corner of Government and Washington, site of the present Mobile Public Library, now destroyed; Rudolph Benz, architect; cost, $15,000. The massing of the McCoy House is Victorian, but the varied treatment of the surfaces anticipates the Queen Anne. (Courtesy of the Historic Mobile Preservation Society, Wilson Plates.)*

222   *From Fort to Port*

House, the weatherboarding was varied, using some horizontal siding, some imbrication, and some panels. The final step into the Queen Anne is more evident in the Festorazzi House of 1893 (figure 208), in which the surfaces of the walls attract as much attention as the skyline broken by the roof dormers and turrets. Again, in our imaginations we may add color: the house was yellow with copper-brown contrasting trim. The small square panes above the windows were colored glass. The Government Street scene of the 1890s differed from the pristine white of the present Neoclassical facades built early in the twentieth century. And different too were the interiors, with their natural rubbed oak and cherry, the chosen materials for mantels that rose to ceiling height. In place of the classical moldings that decorated the arches between parlors, there were grilles of Moorish inspiration and latticework formed of slender spindles. Older homes such as the one-and-a-half story Hopkins place on the

208. *The Festorazzi mansion, 1893, formerly on the southeast corner of Government and Hamilton streets; Rudolph Benz, architect; James Bride, contractor; cost, $8,500. The rounded corner towers with the imbricated siding and the general decor are typical of the Queen Anne. The Spanish Plaza now occupies the site of the Festorazzi House. (Courtesy of the Historic Mobile Preservation Society, Wilson Plates.)*

209. *The Shepherd House, 1897, 1552 Monterey Place; Rudolph Benz, architect; J. P. Emrich, contractor; cost, $3,115. The delicate spindles and other decorative elements characterize the Queen Anne style as it developed in Mobile.*

The High Victorian Period, 1880–1900

210b. Tacon-Tissington House, interior, showing the grand staircase with the dark rubbed wood enriched by paneling and a stained glass window on the landing. (Photograph by Michael Thomason.)

north side of Government, five doors west of Charles, were renovated in the new style.[31]

Of the half dozen such buildings that have survived, two must be mentioned: the Charles Shepherd home (1897), at 1552 Monterey Place (figure 209), and the Tacon-Tissington home (1901), at the northeast corner of Government and Georgia (figures 210a–d).[32] The delicacy of the spindle work on the Monterey Place house is exceptional, as are the brackets and the other surface detailing. The Tacon-Tissington House retains all of its original detailing, even to the 1901 wallpaper. The black-and-white photograph of the wallpaper (figure 210c) is harsher than the actual design, with an effect that is somewhat softened by the maroon color with the gold-embossed patterns. The grand staircase rising in the corner of the front east reception room is richly paneled. On the landing is the typical stained glass window, casting dancing flecks of colored light on the dark woodwork. The reception room is wainscoted in the same dark wood, with a brown marble mantel, though the parlors have white trim (figure 210d). Three other houses of the same period are well worth a visit: the Sprague House (1890), 203 Charles Street, the second Forcheimer House (1898), at 950 Government and the Abba

210a. The Tacon-Tissington House, 1901, 1215 Government Street; the last of the great Victorian–Queen Anne mansions to be built along Government Street. The home has been carefully preserved inside as well as outside. (Photograph by Michael Thomason.)

Temple, and the old Hearin home at 1050 Government, which has strong Neoclassical detailing.

The Captain John Quill House, now destroyed (figure 211) brought the century of residential development to a fitting stylistic close. The stone front of this 1899 Richardsonian Victorian house is both an architectural statement of its time and a record of turn-of-the-century prosperity. Ninety-nine years earlier, Mobile had been an unimportant French coastal settlement maintained by the Spanish. Now it was an important commercial center. A reporter in 1899 observed, "Never before in the history of Mobile has there been such activity in the line of erecting buildings. In all parts of the city there are heard the sound of the carpenter's hammer and the brick mason's trowel and everywhere the odor of pine planking pervades the air."[33]

210c. The Tacon-Tissington parlor wallpaper of 1901. The design extends up the wall, over the cove, and across the ceiling. The colors, a soft maroon with gold embossed design, are less startling than they appear in the black-and-white photograph. (Photograph by Michael Thomason.)

210d. An interior view of the Tacon-Tissington House, from the front reception room looking toward the west front parlor. (Photograph by Michael Thomason.)

211. The Quill House, 1899, formerly at 927 Government Street, now destroyed. Both the material and the style of architecture of the Quill House were unusual for Mobile. The rusticated stone and the heavy Romanesque-inspired tower strikingly contrasted with the delicate spindle work of neighboring Queen Anne homes. (Courtesy of the Historic Mobile Preservation Society, Wilson Plates.)

The High Victorian Period, 1880–1900

9 The Early Twentieth Century, 1900–1918

From the opening of the new century to World War 1, architecture was a house divided unto itself, with one foot anchored in the past and the other struggling to free itself to meet the challenges of a new technological age. From the past came the grandiose designs of the Beaux Arts style that drew its inspiration from the 1893 Chicago Exposition. Great coupled columns, arched openings, end pavilions, and rich decorative detailing characterized the facades that lined the streets of the big cities. Opposed to this were the technological visions of the early Chicago School of architects: William Le Baron Jenney, John Willborn Root, Louis H. Sullivan, and Frank Lloyd Wright. While Mobile stood outside the mainstream, the influence of these men was felt with the rise of a group of young architects who either moved to Mobile or worked in the city while maintaining offices elsewhere. The men who had dominated the nineteenth-century architectural scene were retiring or were no longer living. Rudolph Benz died in 1906, George Watkins in 1907. James F. Hutchisson left Mobile for Chicago about 1902 and died there in 1926. The new leaders included C. L. Hutchisson (1872–1953), the youngest son of James H. Hutchisson, and George B. Rogers (1869–1945), who came to Mobile at the turn of the century and built Mobile's first skyscraper in 1906–1908. Others were Joseph A. Garvin, who was in partnership with C. L. Hutchisson, Sr., from 1907 to 1910, and W. L. Denham, also a partner of C. L. Hutchisson, Sr., from 1914 to 1917, who designed the St. Joseph Chapel at Spring Hill College together with Andrew Downey of New Orleans. W. H. Hammond was responsible for the large Catholic Boys Industrial School, and A. McCrary designed the First Christian Church in 1904.

With the increasing opportunities for work in Mobile, architects from other cities began to establish branch offices in the city. Pearson and Ashe of Raleigh, North Carolina, sent one of their staff to erect the Fidelia Club (figure 219). The Stone Brothers of New Orleans carried out many commissions in Mobile between 1902 and 1907, such as the Masonic Temple (1902), the Southern Hardware Company (1902), Piser and Company (1902), the Lowenstein Bank (1903), and the new Lyric Theatre (1906). Paul Andry, also of New Orleans, filled contracts in the city, as did Andrew Downey. C. L.

Noraman, an Atlanta architect, designed the Bienville Hotel (1900), and Frank Andrews of New York and Cincinnati did the new Battle House in 1906. Philip Thornton Marye from Atlanta was the architect of the Spanish-influenced Gulf, Mobile, and Ohio Railroad Terminal. Reuben Harrison Hunt of Chattanooga designed the First Baptist Church on Government Street.

Not only were the architects increasing in numbers, but new building materials were being introduced and old ones used in new ways. The first brick veneer house was built in 1908 by George B. Rogers for the Ralph Richards home on Michigan Avenue. Gray brick replaced the old red in popularity. Stucco was combined with shingle by Hutchisson and Garvin in a house for Mrs. Dickens on Government Street. The same architects built a home covered completely with shingles for B. H. Davis in Ashland Place.[1] In commercial construction, steel and concrete became important for stores and warehouses.

While the individual buildings of the inner city were incorporating new ideas, the city boundaries were spreading to the west. In 1904 fifteen new blocks beyond Georgia Street opened up. The Fearn Company developed a large area around Monterey and the old Edward Hall property near the junction of Dauphin and Catherine. In the Monterey area more than a dozen homes had been built by 1909, many designed by Downey and Denham or by McCrary and Slater. By 1906, Ashland Place had been platted. Some thirteen homes designed by C. L. Hutchisson, Sr., still stand there. Flo-Claire was carved out of the old McDonald tract in 1908. To the south of the city, along Tennessee, Virginia, and Washington streets, workingmen's houses were going up and to the north in the Davis Avenue community, blocks along Rylands, Cuba, Lyons, and Congress streets were being developed, 90 percent of the buildings being constructed by black citizens.[2]

By 1910 all the streets of the inner city had been paved. Paved sidewalks were installed even around Washington Square in the Oakleigh Garden Historic District.[3] By 1914, Mobile thus had a modern appearance.

Civic Buildings

The city's major expenditure on capital investments during the early twentieth century was the extension of the plan and the necessary services. Architecturally, public monies were used to add to existing buildings rather than to undertake new construction. A rear wing was added to the City Hospital in 1910, and the same year $30,000 was spent on improvements to City Hall.[4]

In 1907 the county initiated two programs. Rudolph Benz was employed to design a large rear wing for the Court House that would cover the rest of the block to Church Street, and Watkins and Hutchisson were given the commission for Leinkauf School (figure 212).[5] In enlarging the Court House, Benz continued the same general design he had used in the main building. In planning the school, Watkins and Hutchisson used bricks in a skillfully laid coursing with Romanesque antecedents in the corbel tables, the hood molds above the segmentally headed windows, and the decorative treatment of the cornices, all of which were kept flattened and shallow so that the integrity of the wall was maintained. The design is clearly defined and symbolic of the purposes of an educational institution. Its rhythms of both form and shadow are controlled, and even the broken roof lines are ordered.

212. *Leinkauf School, 1904, 1907, 1911, 1451 Church Street; Watkins and Hutchisson, architects. Bricks are skillfully laid to form corbel tables over the windows of both stories, suggesting the strength and security of a Romanesque fortress. (Erik Overbey/Mobile Public Library Collection, University of South Alabama Photographic Archives.)*

213. *The U.S. Post Office, 1916 (destroyed in 1968), formerly on the northwest corner of St. Joseph and St. Michael streets; James Knox Taylor, architect; Berryman, superintendent of construction; cost, $200,000. The fifteenth-century Italian Renaissance was the inspiration for the arcaded loggia in white Alabama marble and for the coffered ceiling of the main lobby. (Erik Overbey/Mobile Public Library Collection, University of South Alabama Photographic Archives.)*

As the Lombard Romanesque influenced the corbeling of the Leinkauf School, so the Italian Renaissance inspired the design for the Mobile United States Post Office of 1916 (figure 213). Brunelleschi's Florentine Foundling Hospital (1419–1421) was the source for the design of the Post Office's St. Joseph Street facade and for other similar arcades. James Knox Taylor, who was the acting superintendent of architecture in Washington from 1897 to 1912, seems to have been responsible for the building. Alabama marble was used as a veneer on the exterior of the walls as well as for interior surfaces. It was of the same pure white, clear texture as that found in the Sylacauga quarries.[6] On the exterior the architect used deep color. The gold in the overhanging cornices and in some of the interior trim caused much comment when the building was dedicated.

Other important civic buildings of the early part of the century were the hospitals. The Mobile Infirmary, designed by Hutchisson and Garvin, was constructed in 1910, and the four-story Providence Infirmary, on the north side of Spring Hill at Catherine Street, was built in 1903 following designs by R. L. Mulligan of St. Louis.[7] Both buildings have been replaced by new construction.

Religious Buildings

More than a dozen major churches were constructed during the first ten years of the century. All were revivalist in style. Of these, four churches and one chapter house may be regarded as representative.

The earliest of the group was the Sha'arai Shomayim Temple, which formerly stood on the southeast corner of Government and Warren streets (figure 214). It was begun in 1906, was dedicated in 1907, and was destroyed in 1956.[8] The building was made from Indiana limestone, Georgian granite, and light-colored pressed brick. The architects, Watkins and Hutchisson, created an unusual design, inspired by the French Romanesque, in which the multiple-arched deeply splayed doorways of the medieval facade have been flattened to become linear patterns of decorative moldings supported not by colonnettes but by vertical pilaster strips. Only the cavelike entrance recessed between the corner towers has retained the shadowed depth of the early inspiration. A secondary entrance was located on the Warren Street side of the added educational wing.

In 1908 George B. Rogers was retained by the Methodists to enlarge

214. *The Sha'arai Shomayim Temple, 1906, formerly on the southeast corner of Government and Warren; Watkins and Hutchisson, architects; Nicol and Legee, contractors. The building was sold in 1952 and was destroyed a few years later. The deeply splayed windows of medieval origin with their colonnettes and multiple moldings are here flattened into linear patterns in a highly decorative treatment of the tower walls. (Courtesy of the Historic Mobile Preservation Society, Wilson Plates.)*

their Gothic Revival building of 1890 (figure 178). As frequently happened with Rogers, he not only enlarged but also completely altered the original design. In the Church shown in figure 215, Rogers drew from the Spanish-Mexican missions, influenced by the work of the Churriguera family in Spain. The richly sculptured detailing of the central bay abounds with Christian symbols. Above the door is the Christogram, based on the Chi Rho, formed of the Greek letters that signify Jesus Christ. Above the window is a medallion showing a crown placed against the rays of the sun. Even the pilgrim's cockle shell is given prominence at the base of the twisted columns.

In the same year that the Methodists altered their building, the Baptists began a new church on the corner of Government and Jefferson (figure 216).[9] Here the architect, Reuben H. Hunt of Chattanooga, designed a hexastyle Doric temple with greater archaeological accuracy than was found in the 1830 revivals. Except for the stepped stylobate around the whole building, which was precluded by the limits of a city block, the divisions of the temple elevation have been carefully observed. The columns have no bases, and their

215. *The Government Street United Methodist Church, 1908, 905 Government Street; George B. Rogers, architect. The most elaborate of the Spanish Revival buildings in Mobile. Rogers not only used the highly decorative elements of the Churrigueresque but incorporated many Christian symbols as well.*

216. *The First Baptist Church, 1906, 806 Government Street; Reuben H. Hunt, architect; Jett Brothers, contractors. Though the style belongs to the second period of the Greek Revival, it uses reinforced concrete for the foundation and Bedford stone over bricks for the walls. The interior is more freely designed than the exterior, which represents a stricter, academic interpretation of a Greek temple.*

flutes meet in a sharp line known as the arris. The entablature has the "proper" arrangements in the architrave and frieze; the pediment has the correct angularity. The large central entrance has the rosettes along the surround and the bracketed lintel that resembles the one on the north door of the Erectheum. The three doors have been framed in iron, however, and not in cut stone. Even the negative spaces formed between the shafts of the columns approach the shaping of the Greek prototype. The Spanish Church by Rogers and the Greek Revival Church of Hunt, situated so close together, make an interesting record of two popular revivals in the early twentieth century.

The last of the four churches is St. Joseph, at Spring Hill College, which was designed by Downey and Denham (figure 217). Built in brick with a yellow stucco surface, it is of the late Gothic Revival style. The decorative elements are flatter and the towers project less from the frontal plane than in the earlier period. This 1909 interpretation of the English Perpendicular style has created linear patterns from the three-dimensionality of the true Gothic. The slight shadows cast by the shallow moldings are only grace notes within the larger context of the whole design. Thus, while Downey and Denham chose a traditional style for their chapel, they gave it the stamp of the twentieth century and of their own personalities.

Several churches erected chapter houses or rectories during these years. In 1900 Christ Church built its rectory. In 1909 the Big Zion on Bayou added one that had been designed by George B. Rogers. Hutchisson and Denham in 1916 added the small Robinson Memorial of Trinity in de Tonti Square (figure 218). When the church was

217. *St. Joseph's Chapel, 1909, Spring Hill College; Downey and Denham, architects; Jett Brothers, contractors. The Chapel is an adaptation of the late English Gothic style that influenced academic and ecclesiastical construction during the early years of the twentieth century. The massing was less complex and the detailing more linear than in the nineteenth-century interpretation.*

218. *Trinity Church Parish House, the Robinson Memorial, dedicated December 1916, 257 State Street; Hutchisson and Garvin, architects; a simple rectangular hall that was made monumental by the skill with which the Baroque entrance was designed. After fire and vandals had caused considerable deterioration, the architectural firm of Knodel and Thomas restored the building for use as offices.*

moved to Dauphin Street, the parish house was left behind. It was almost destroyed by vandalism and fire before it was rescued by the architectural firm of Knodel and Thomas. The building was begun as a simpler structure in about 1912, but with the establishment of the Robinson Memorial, the plans were enlarged. The scale of the Baroque facade is so skillfully treated that its monumentality belies its small size. The texture of the stuccoed surface contrasted with that of the stone trim balances the complexity of the central bay. In the adaptive restoration, the architects retained the integrity of the original yet incorporated the necessary elements such as adequate lighting. The frame trellises used for the ceilings of the separate offices preserve the open spaces of the chapter hall as well as the visual effect of the trussing.

Social Buildings

As with other building programs, the social clubs were busy erecting new headquarters throughout the downtown area. An inventory and study of them all would fill a small book, and so representative examples alone will be considered here.

The Fidelia Club was the most conservative in its architectural selection (figure 219). It was designed by Pearson and Ashe of Raleigh, North Carolina. Before the building was completed, Mr. Ashe died, and his partner, Pearson, established an office in Mobile. The architects chose the Italian Renaissance palazza style, as seen in the window trim, the third-floor loggia, the quoining, and the bracketed cornice. The architectural details, such as the string courses marking the story levels, served as the decoration and gave the building a clean, dignified appearance. The twin windows provided adequate interior lighting. Elegant interior detail was carried out in the decor and in the furnishings. The ladies' parlor had satin damask fabrics and gilt furniture. Gray marble wainscoting lined the stairway. Parquetry floors were laid in geometric designs.[10] On the roof was a garden, and every conceivable form of recreational area was provided—a bowling alley, a billiard room, a card room, a reading area, a bar, a ballroom with a stage, and private drawing rooms.

Very different in construction is the Masonic building on St. Joseph Street facing Bienville Square. It was built only one year later but was one of the first of the so-called slow-burning types that used steel skeletal framing. Its survival supports the reliability of its claim (figure 220). The elevation, marked by the break in the design between the street story and the upper floors, is a direct offshoot from the early Chicago School as developed by Sullivan. The upper rooms are united by the vertical lines of the pilasters that rise unbroken to the flat roof. There is more glass than not in the facade. The new, progressive style is partially hidden by the more traditional decoration, the detailing of the capitals, and the use of the wreaths with the emblem of the Masonic order at the center. The steel skeleton is encased by light-colored brick, Bedford limestone, and terra cotta.[11] Unfortunately the street story has been bastardized with modern glazed panels. The foundation for this building in 1901 set a precedent for future tall construction. A concrete bed fifteen inches thick was reinforced with steel rods and beams. Upon it were laid brick piers serving as the substructure for the steel skeleton.

219. The Fidelia Club, 1900 (destroyed); formerly on the southeast corner of Government and Conception streets; Pearson and Ashe, architects; Zachary and Zachary, contractors; cost $26,000. This Renaissance-derived building with its recessed third-story loggia was once the center of much social life in the city. It stood on the corner upon which the new County Court House addition has been constructed. (Erik Overbey/Mobile Public Library Collection, University of South Alabama Photographic Archives.)

220. Masonic Temple, 1901, 8 St. Joseph Street; Stone Brothers, architects; Jett Brothers, contractors; cost, $50,000 exclusive of site. It was the first steel frame building to be constructed in Mobile, but the modern construction was hidden by Bedford limestone and terra cotta. (Photograph by Michael Thomason.)

The Early Twentieth Century, 1900–1918

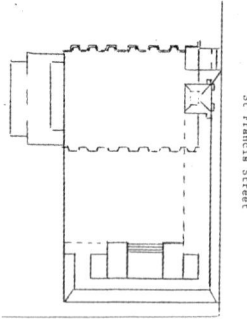

221b. The outline of the Scottish Rites Temple superimposed over the St. Francis Street Baptist Church, retaining the west wall of the older Church for the rear west wall of the temple.

221a. The Scottish Rite Bodies Egyptian Temple, 1920–1921, 351 St. Francis Street; George Rogers, architect. The only Egyptian Revival building in the city, it was among the last of the purely revivalist designs to be constructed. (Photograph by Michael Thomason.)

Unlike the Fidelia Club, which was strictly a social gathering place, the Masonic building had a number of uses. The lower three floors served commercial purposes, and the upper two offered quarters to the various lodges, the fourth floor being for the Blue Lodge and the fifth for the Knight Templars, the Scottish Rite Bodies, and the Royal Masons.

The last building selected from this group falls outside the indicated time frame but has been included because of its unusual design. In 1920–1921, George B. Rogers was employed to plan the new Scottish Rite Bodies building that was to occupy the site of the former Methodist parsonage, next door to the east of the St. Francis Street Baptist Church (figures 108, 221b). As was his custom, he used what he could of the old Baptist Church, incorporating the west wall with its stepped buttresses into the rear wall of his new temple. He also saved the Sunday school rooms that had been formed against this wall. To the east he added a massive Egyptian Revival building, its battered walls rising a sheer sixty-five feet from the sidewalk (figure 221a). Cavetto cornices crown the structure, and the pylon-shaped entrances complete the theme. Miniature obelisks define the limits of the roof terrace, which once had a promenade and a raised platform. Over this raised terrace was suspended a brilliant awning.[12] While the architect designed the building with serious intent to suggest the permanent, timeless qualities of the Egyptian architecture, the twentieth-century sculptor, with his tongue in his cheek, carved two very busty sphinxes that somewhat relieve the solemnity of the edifice they guard.

The interior spaces and details continued the Egyptian style. The fifty-two-foot-long lobby contained two sets of stairs leading to the mezzanine and the upper floors. Doors opened from the lobby into a large auditorium 78 feet wide and 120 feet long. Club rooms and offices occupied the mezzanine, and two large lodge rooms were partitioned off on the second story. During World War II, the building was partially occupied by the United States Army Aviation Interceptor Center, which used the large auditorium to spread out the maps that tracked the movement of planes in the southeast area.

Commercial Buildings

As the century opened, smaller builders continued to erect two- and three-level storefronts along streets such as Dauphin, using the same general scale, fenestration, and construction methods that had been employed during the previous century. Some old buildings were given a face-lift, some buildings were replaced after they had burned down, and some were new. One 1900 construction is the Crawford store, standing at 417 Dauphin on the corner of Hamilton. While the general massing is compatible with the older store next door to the east, the details of the design have definitely changed (figure 222). There must originally have been a balcony beneath the floor-length second-story windows. Even so, the clean-cut lines of the cornice, the decoration around the segmental arches of the windows, and the textural variations in the surfacing of the two stories herald a new age. The large showcase first-story windows seem appropriate here, while they are out of place on the older building next door to the east.

222. *The Crawford Building, 1900, 417 Dauphin Street. As the nineteenth-century stores along Dauphin Street either burned or were demolished, a new style of storefront was developed, though the old two- and three-story elevations were retained.*

The Early Twentieth Century, 1900–1918

The larger commission, which employed architects, determined the direction that the architecture would take, whether revivalist or in line with the new Chicago School. The most elaborate in the former category is the imposing Mobile and Ohio Railroad Station of 1908, which is Spanish in derivation (figure 223). It was designed by the Atlanta architect P. Thornton Marye, who used modern reinforced concrete walls encased in gray brick veneer with terra cotta for the cornice, brackets, lintels, and medallions. The horizontal lines of the 196-foot-long facade are further emphasized by the arcaded passageway, whose undulating cornice curves repeat the treatment of the end bays in the main building. The flattened decorative elements of the central bay are closer to the seventeenth-century Spanish Plateresque than to the eighteenth-century Churrigueresque. The central dome, 100 feet high, unifies the design as well as bringing light into the originally square waiting room,[13] which has unfortunately been partitioned to create small offices and storage areas.

As the economic conditions improved, banks grew in numbers, and between 1902 and 1906, a half dozen were either constructed or renovated. The Stone Brothers of New Orleans planned the three-story Lowenstein Bank on St. Francis Street. Its rectangular mass and balustraded parapet continued the Renaissance influence. In 1903 the New Orleans firm of Andry and Bendernagle joined with George B. Rogers to design the seven-story narrow City Bank and Trust on Royal Street. While its tall proportions and the treatment of the stories suggest the new trend, the heavy overhanging cornice looks backward rather than into the future.[14] George B. Rogers designed the Bank of Mobile on St. Michael Street in 1904, and in 1906 Watkins, Hutchisson, and Garvin planned the First National Bank

223. *The Gulf, Mobile, and Ohio Railroad Station, 1908, Beauregard and Royal streets; P. Thornton Marye, architect; Oliver Sellitt Company, contractor. The whole complex cost $1,540,000, of which the station represented $575,000. The monumental building incorporated stuccoed walls embellished with flattened Plateresque carving and a first-story arcade with undulating cornice lines, all showing Spanish influence. The interior has been altered by the present owners, the Southern Railroad Company, but the exterior remains as it was designed in 1906. (Erik Overbey/Mobile Public Library Collection, University of South Alabama Photographic Archives.)*

on the north side of St. Francis Street, between Royal and Water. This last building may be regarded as representative of the group. The design was one of the last big commissions awarded to the firm of Watkins, Hutchisson, and Garvin while Watkins was still alive. He died in 1907. The banking company was an old one, having been organized in 1865. It wanted a design that would symbolize dependability. Accordingly, the architects developed a vertically proportioned temple facade, which was placed against a larger horizontal rectangle, somewhat in the manner of sixteenth-century Italy. The central bay was framed by a tall, white terra cotta Ionic column, which was set on the same granite base as its companion pilaster (figure 224). The pediment above is accented by both a dentil course and a heavy, blocky row of brackets. Terra cotta forms the lintels of the windows of the second story, with their enlarged end voussoirs and keystones.[15] The two side entrances are crowned by a Baroque broken pediment and are further embellished by a terra cotta swag set against a panel placed between the stories. The interior was as elegant as the exterior, with gold-stenciled green burlap covering the walls above a seven-foot-high marble wainscoting and a green marble base. The ceiling of the director's room was painted by Mr. Felleg of St. Louis. In spite of the historic detailing, the structure belongs to the twentieth century, with its steel beams and reinforced concrete floors.

224. *The First National Bank, 1906, 68 St. Francis Street; Watkins, Hutchisson, and Garvin, architects; Interstate Construction Company, contractors. White brick, glazed terra cotta moldings, reinforced concrete floors, and steel structural members combine the old and the new in this Renaissance-inspired design. (Photograph by Michael Thomason.)*

The Early Twentieth Century, 1900–1918

Mobile had its Coney Island and Atlantic City in Monroe Park, located on the waterfront near present-day Brookley Field. It was developed on the old Mandeville Tract between the water and the extension of Broad Street, with Van Doren on the south. A streetcar line ran out to the site, and all Mobile gathered there to sample the many recreational facilities, one of the most popular being the casino where ice cream and other enticements were served. In 1890 Howard Wilson acquired the land and developed the park that flourished until 1906, when the hurricane demolished much of it.[16] The casino was rebuilt in 1906, a light airy pavilion whose wide-cusped triple arches suggested some kind of exotic Moorish ancestry (figure 225). It was a place of relaxation and fun, as its style indicates.

Mobile's commercial architecture took its final steps into the twentieth century with the building of hotels and department stores. Both forms grew from the low, galleried homelike buildings into more impersonal cellular beehives that occupy whole blocks. This trend could first be noted in the six-story Bienville Hotel of 1900, which was designed by G. L. Noraman of Atlanta, was built on the northwest corner of St. Francis and St. Joseph, and was later destroyed. In mass the Hotel consisted of two large rectangular blocks connected by a lobby and court so arranged that all hotel rooms received direct light and air. While some new design elements were present, the structure retained the traditional brick and wood. Not so the 1906 Cawthon Hotel (figure 226), which was made of steel framing, had reinforced concrete floors, and was veneered with granite on the first story and with gray brick in the upper levels.[17] It was originally a six-story elevation, with a seventh story added later. The architects Watkins, Hutchisson, and Garvin drew inspiration from the 1880 Chicago commercial style, which differentiated markedly between the design of the first story and that of the fenestration of the upper levels of the facade. While the structural members and the overall design were moving into the new century, the decorative elements were still those of the past, giving the building an atmosphere that harmonized with its surroundings: the classic treatment of the entrance, the swags carved against the panels above the bay windows, the window lintels, with their accented keystones and end voussoirs, and the bracketed, overhanging cornice. This combination of elements gave the Cawthon an individuality, an identity, that later hotels, with their uniform surfaces, would lack. The decline of the inner city and the westward movement of hotels and motels brought hard times for the Cawthon, and it, too, was demolished, leaving a parking lot in its place.

On February 12, 1905, the historic Battle House burned (figure 116). Ever since 1852 there had been a Battle House in Mobile, and it had become the center for the city's social events. Within a year a replacement was under way, planned by Frank M. Andrews of New York and Cincinnati (figures 227a–c). It was to be the most elegant hotel in the area, from its glass-domed lobby to its roof garden. No aspect of the patron's comfort went unconsidered. There were several different types of dining areas, including a cafe in the basement, the Trellis Room for more formal lunches, and a grand dining room, which had tapestried walls. For guests who wanted à la carte service, there was the roof terrace. A variety of entertainment rooms were provided for billiards, reading, lounging, and writing—and of course there was the Crystal Ballroom.[18]

225. Monroe Park Pavilion, rebuilt in 1906 and now destroyed, formerly located near what is now Brookley Field; Rudolph Benz, architect. This light, open, exotic pavilion replaced one that had been destroyed by the hurricane of 1906. From the early 1890s onward, Monroe Park at the end of the car line was the seaside entertainment center for city-weary Mobilians. (Courtesy of the Historic Mobile Preservation Society, Wilson Plates.)

226. The Cawthon Hotel, built in 1906 and now destroyed, formerly on the southwest corner of St. Francis and Conception streets; Watkins, Hutchisson, and Garvin, architects; Jett Brothers, contractors, cost $265,000, not counting site and furnishings. Though the Cawthon was modern in its reinforced concrete and steel construction, its bays and delicate decorative detailing relieved its austerity. The top story was not part of the original design. (Erik Overbey/Mobile Public Library Collection, University of South Alabama Photographic Archives.)

Just as nothing had been omitted for the physical comfort of the guests, so the decor was planned to please the eye. The sixty-foot-square entrance lobby was illuminated by a crown of lights at the base of the dome (figure 227b). Each side of the square served as the center for some service or important entrance, for example the registering station or the door to the dining room. And each was framed by a great arch springing from stone piers that together supported the glass dome above. Scrolled and leafy reliefs decorated the arches and the pendentives between. The mezzanine spaces above were variously allocated. One was the ladies' lounge; another was a writing area. On festive occasions, musicians could use one of the spaces.

227a. The new Battle House, 1906–1908, 26 North Royal Street; Frank M. Andrews, architect; General Supply and Construction Company, contractors; cost, $1,150,000. The new Battle House was the last great hotel built in downtown Mobile. It replaced the other building that burned in 1905 and, like its predecessor, was the center of Mobile's high society. It has long been vacant, and its beauty is now slowly being eroded by mildew and decay. (Erik Overbey/Mobile Public Library, University of South Alabama Photographic Archives.)

227b. Lobby of the Battle House. The decorative dome of the lobby rests on square piers and sweeping arches that frame the centers for various hotel functions. (Erik Overbey/Mobile Public Library Collection, University of South Alabama Photographic Archives.)

The Grand Dining Room faced on the St. Francis Street side, with a large stained glass window catching the daylight. Its tapestry-covered walls made the general effect quite formal. The Trellis Room was lighter and had a skylight centered in the ceiling vault. Shallow pilasters formed bays that were decorated with recessed panels except at the midpoints, where the central bays were painted with a flowing, formalized design of winged victories supporting a central cartouche (figure 227c). A fountain was recessed in the wall opposite the entrance, and at one end the musicians' balcony was skillfully incorporated into the general decorative effect. For years the Battle House was the center of the city's social life, but when the

227c. *The Trellis Room of the Battle House, a delightful dining area made light and airy by the skylight in the ceiling vault. The Italianate fountain on the side wall and the musicians' balcony at the end add to the charm of the room. (Erik Overbey/Mobile Public Library Collection, University of South Alabama Photographic Archives.)*

shift to the west really developed, the Battle House too lost its popularity. It is still standing, long vacant, neglected, and with mold and decay slowly destroying all its former glory.

Two commercial buildings that once almost faced each other on Royal Street most vividly illustrate the changes in architecture that took place between 1901 and 1906, Hammel's Store (1902; figure 228) and the Van Antwerp Building (1906–1908; figure 229). Hammel's was designed by the Stone Brothers, and while it had some features that belonged to the new century, such as the large number of glass surfaces in the facade, its dependence upon the heavy decorative elements of Renaissance origin made its relationship with the past more prominent. The wide horizontal emphasis above the second story destroyed the sense of the vertical that could have been achieved by continuous pilasters. Even the idea of the covered walkway of the entrance continued the idea of the nineteenth-century gallery, differing in that the old cast iron had been replaced by reinforced concrete and a glass barrel vault.[19]

Five years later George B. Rogers, in the Van Antwerp Building, reached for the goal sought by Sullivan and the men of the Chicago

228. *Hammel's Department Store, 1902, now destroyed, formerly on the east side of Royal between Dauphin and Conti; Stone Brothers, architects; Cook and Laurie, contractors. With its large windows and reinforced concrete construction, the building has moved into the twentieth century, but it has retained revivalist detailing and thus embodies a transition between the old and the new. (Erik Overbey/Mobile Public Library Collection, University of South Alabama Photographic Archives.)*

School. Rogers maintained a delicate balance between horizontals and verticals that culminated in the upward sweep of a tall building. Although it was only ten stories high, Mobile had its first skyscraper.[20] There is terra cotta decoration beneath the widely overhanging cornice, but it was subordinated to the overall design, so that it merged with rather than distracting from the overall unity. The four pilasters of Hammel's Store define a facade, a front. The corner piers and the spandrels of the Van Antwerp Building enclose a box expressing the steel skeleton that forms the framing. It was Mobile's answer to the need for a fireproof building: reinforced concrete in white-enameled terra cotta. Even the windows were so hinged that they could be turned around for easy cleaning. Commercially the city was entering a period of national identity and was leaving behind its vernacular Gulf Coast inheritance.

229. The Van Antwerp Building, 1906–1908, 103 Dauphin Street; George B. Rogers, architect; Interstate Construction Company, contractors; estimated cost, $200,000 without the lot. Mobile's first skyscraper in both structure and design belongs in the early twentieth century. (Erik Overbey/Mobile Public Library Collection, University of South Alabama Photographic Archives.)

230. *Queen Anne Row, 1902, 505, 507, 509 Church Street. Many middle-income homes continued to use a modified Queen Anne form even though they were built in the early twentieth century. The three buildings are located in the section of the Church Street East Historic District that was rehabilitated under the sponsorship of the Community Development Program.*

231. *206 Dearborn Street, 1910, in the Church Street East Historic District. Workmen continued to build single- and double-family units as late as World War I.*

232. *213 Lanier Avenue, 1921, C. L. Hutchisson, Sr., architect. Just after World War I, the cottage was replaced by the bungalow, which had a plan that offered greater flexibility.*

Residential Buildings

Buildings in the residential areas were more varied than in the commercial. They differed not only in style but also in the affluence of the families they were built to house. The wealthy continued to build their classically inspired mansions along Government Street (figures 233, 234, 235). Within the inner city, middle-income families continued to prefer the Queen Anne, for example on the row along Church Street between Lawrence and Cedar (figure 230). The Spanish Revival became most popular in the newer subdivisions, such as Flo-Claire and the Houston Street area, near Old Government (figure 236). The American "four square," a new style with a name introduced by the *Old House Journal*,[21] soon dominated the Georgia Avenue section of Oakleigh as well as other areas (figures 237, 238). Low-income single and double cottages continued to be built (figure 231), but by the time of World War I they were being replaced by bungalows (figure 232). Limitations of space permit me to consider only a few developments within this range.

In turning from the cottage to the bungalow, Mobile moved farther from its inheritance and closer to street scenes found throughout the United States. It is easy to understand the popularity of the type. It was comfortable, the plan was flexible, the wide porches protected by the overhanging roof were attractive, and the lack of decorative detailing reduced the initial cost. Building crews could erect rows of the homes in record time by a sort of assembly-line technique that also kept down the price (figure 232). With the tremendous increase in the working class, especially during the years of the Great War, the little houses were in great demand. They lined streets such as Old Shell west of Houston, Bienville, and Demouy

233a. *The J. F. McGowin House, 1903, 1151 Government Street; T. J. Smith, architect, from Montgomery. A beautifully designed house showing two architectural influences. In style it drew inspiration from the decorative detailing of the French eighteenth century, but the construction material was modern, being concrete block veneer on frame. (Erik Overbey/Mobile Public Library Collection, University of South Alabama Photographic Archives.)*

The Early Twentieth Century, 1900–1918

and could be found in both the southern and the northern sections of the city.

While the building and investment companies were busy erecting mass housing, the architects were occupied with designing the homes of the wealthy. In 1903 the architect T. J. Smith of Montgomery was engaged to plan a house for Joseph F. McGowin on the southwest corner of Government and Roper (figures 233a–c). On both the interior and the exterior it is one of the most impressive mansions standing on Government. The Baroque use of curves in the plan, the thrust of the semicircular porch with its widely spaced Ionic columns, which is countered by the recessed loggia above—these elements are not common to Mobile. The balustraded deck does not quite reach across the entire front but is broken off, to be picked up again in the west porch and the east porte-cochère. The play between opposites is, however, carefully controlled by the repetition of the pedimented windows and the strong, vertical lines of the white columns. While a Baroque influence is present in the design, the structure points to the modern in the use of concrete-block veneer over a traditional frame of wood.[22]

Classicism also dominated the interior. The entrance to the stairhall had a double set of doors, the first of polished cherry and the second of mahogany. The woodwork of the hallway was painted in a white enamel and was ornamented with richly formed moldings, with the supporting members resting on wall brackets and Ionic columns as necessary for extra reinforcement (figure 233b). The reception room to the right brought the grace of the style of Louis XV to Mobile in the blue and gold of the decor and the furniture, the onyx fireplace, the carved mantel, and the elaborate mirror (figure 233c).

Just a block west, on the same side of the street, three large homes were built at about the same time, in 1906–1908. The Old Rapier one-and-a-half-story house was enlarged and was given a monumental portico by C. L. Hutchisson, Sr. Next door to the west, at 1209 Government, the Burgess home was built (figure 234) in 1906, and one year later the G. C. Clarke House was added at 1211 Government. Around the corner on Rapier stood the large Lott House of 1908, planned by Hutchisson and Garvin. In planning the Burgess House, George B. Rogers turned to the Italian Renaissance, using a Palladian window in the central bay of the second story. He popularized the use of the twin columns and the wraparound porch with the rather heavy balustrade forming the long horizontal line across the front and the sides of the building. The floor of the eighty-four-foot-long porch was tiled in a Venetian style. As in the McGowin House, the interior decor varied from room to room, a feature typical of many of Rogers's buildings. The Burgess hallway favored a Georgian style, with a stair that rose the full three stories around an open rectangular space. Each tread supported three differently shaped balusters. The reception room walls were embellished with carvings in low relief, interspersed with painted decoration. In the circular-walled dining room, above the mahogany wainscoting, mahogany pilasters framed painted panels of cherubs dancing with festoons of flowers. The fireplace had a Rookwood ceramic surface. In both the McGowin and the Burgess houses, the architects succeeded in expressing the taste and the wealth of the new century.

The last of the mansions of the early twentieth century that I will

233b. The McGowin House entrance hall. The white woodwork of Classical columns and moldings contrasted with the rich red of the wall surfaces. At the landing a stained glass window contained representations of industry, art, and music. (Erik Overbey/Mobile Public Library Collection, University of South Alabama Photographic Archives.)

233c. The McGowin House reception room. In contrast to the hallway, the reception room has the lightness and grace of the French Rococo style of Louis XV. In 1903 the decor was in white with blue and gold touches in both room and furniture. The ceiling was hand painted. (Erik Overbey/Mobile Public Library Collection, University of South Alabama Photographic Archives.)

discuss is the G. C. Clarke House (figure 235) at 1211 Government. It is the last of three houses built by members of the Clarke family on the same street, another that is still standing (though altered) being the now vacant YWCA. The Clarke House is one of many homes built on city lots in Mobile at this time and manifesting a revival of the old "White Pillars of the South." It was a style adapted for and first built in an agricultural economy rather than in a commercially compact area, and hence it was foreign to Mobile history. Down went many of the fine dark red brick townhouses and the row buildings with their early Greek Revival detailing. Down, too, went the Victorian and Queen Anne styles, whose towers had bristled along the major residential streets. Up went the "plantation houses" with

234. *The Burgess House, 1906, 1209 Government Street; George B. Rogers, architect; E. S. Ward, contractor; murals by Thil Wilbergand; interior design by William F. Behrens of Cincinnati. Each room has a different style of decor. The building is of gray brick, with Indiana limestone columns and terra cotta trim. (Erik Overbey/Mobile Public Library Collection, University of South Alabama Photographic Archives.)*

their majestic columns, their graceful second-story balconies, and their formal facades. This was a revival of a revival. The Clarke House (figure 235) is an excellent example. It is not a slavish copy of the original type. The architect showed some freedom in his treatment of some surfaces, for example in the diamond pattern that infills the pediment. But the four great Ionic columns of the portico, the regular fenestration, and the bold lines of the design give the house a monumentality found in the pre–Civil War period. It comes as almost a shock to find that the house was constructed of concrete blocks, though large to be sure—they measure eighteen inches by thirty-six inches—which were then stuccoed and scored to resemble stone, with the corners accented by quoining. It is the first known example in Mobile of the use of a solid concrete-block wall in a large home.[23]

In the western suburbs of Flo-Claire and around the junction of Old Government and Houston, the Spanish Revival took precedence over the classical styles. Standing as sentinels on either side of the entrance to McDonald Street are two examples from this period. A few blocks farther west, the Fearns built a tile-roofed Mission-type house in 1904 and by 1910 their second example at 1806 Old Government, now listed as Airport Boulevard (figure 236). This latter home is a good example of the Spanish influence as it developed in Mobile, having the stuccoed wall, picturesque double-curving parapet, the shadowed entrance, and the red tile roof.

Revivalism continued to be a strong influence in Mobile architecture, but the future direction that it would take is to be found in the American four square, which would eventually be overthrown in turn by the ubiquitous brick ranch house as suburbs farther and farther west developed. The houses were advertised in the newspapers

235. *The G. C. Clarke House, 1907, 1211 Government Street. This mansion with full-height columns in the style of the old plantation South was constructed of large concrete blocks during the romantic revival of the early twentieth century. With the return to the Classical mode, Victorian colors that had enlivened Government Street for a quarter century were abandoned for a street scene of white.*

236. *1806 Airport (Old Government Street), the second suburban development of the Fearn Company between 1904 and 1910. In the new western suburbs a Spanish influence became popular, and several fine examples of the Mission style still survive.*

237. *M. T. Vicker's House, 1910, 601 Church Street, within the Church Street East Historic District. By 1910 the Americanization of Mobile was virtually complete, and the widespread "foursquare" two-story house with its comfortable front porch became the style preferred by middle- and upper-income homeowners.*

238. *162–164 South Georgia, 1904 and 1906. A row of typical American four-square homes lining the street in the Oakleigh Garden Historic District creates a pleasing streetscape by repeating the one-story columns.*

with offers for sale on a monthly rental basis. The standardization of framing, of door and window openings, and of fixtures and fittings all helped to make the large, two-story square house the main structure in the new city (figure 237). The homes were spacious and were easily adapted to family needs. When they were located along a shady street, the repetitive lines of their one-story porches made as pleasant a streetscape as could be found anywhere (figure 238).

The World War I years close this study of the architectural development of Mobile. From its inception as a French Colonial fort to its integration into the national community as a great Gulf port city, Mobile in its buildings and building practices has reflected the tastes and skills of its people. All structures, from the monumental to the most humble, make up a city's character. A study of the architecture of any locality requires the consideration of the carpenter-builder cottages as well as the architect-designed court houses. In Mobile, this broad consideration encompasses the changes brought about through 207 years of history, when a colony became a national entity, when a slave-supported economy was replaced by one involving a free working class. The buildings that have survived and those that have not bear witness to a past of which Mobile can be proud.

APPENDIX I

Text of the 1711 Chevillot Map and the 1734 Devin Map

1711 *Chevillot Map*

fort Louis, fortiffié suivant la Longueur de Son[1] Coste exterieur d'une pointe de Bastion a L'autre ayant 90 Toises et par cette longueur Lon a donné aux faces des Bastions Vignt trois toises et demie. aux flane douze toises et demie aux Gorges Cinq toises et aux Courtines quarantes toises.

Le fort est Construit de pieux de Bois de Cédre ayant treize pieds dhauteur dont deux et demies entre en terre, et de quatorzes pouces en quarrées de paisseur, plantées, jointement les uns Contre Les autres. Ces pieux ce terminent par leurs Bout denhaut enpointe Comme des palissades; interieuremant aux Long de ces pieux il règne une espece de Banquette ayant deux pieds de hauteur en talus Sur, un et demie de Longeur—

Il ny a pour tout Logement dans ce fort que La maison du Gouverneur. Le magazin ou Sont les effets du Roy, et un Corp de Garde Succintement; Les officiers les Soldats & les habitans ont tous leurs Logements hors du fort Comme cy est marquez, extant disposez de maniere que les rues ont Six toises de Largeur et toutes paralleles les unes aux autres. Les isles de maison ont Cinquante toises—en quarrées hors ceuze de Vis a Vis le fort qui ont Soixante toises de Largeur Sur Cinquante de profondeur, et Les plus proches de La riviere ont Cinquante toises de Largeur Sur Soixante de profondeur—

Les maisons que Lon Batties Sont Construittes de Bois de Cedre et pin Suportées par un fondemens d'une quantité de pieux de Bois qui éxédent de terre d'un pied, qu'on pourroit Nommer pillotis parceque ce terrain se trouve inondées comme vous Le Voÿez marquez dans le Plan dans quelques androits, dans les temps de Pluye; quelque uns ce Sont Servis, pour Suporter leurs maison d'une pierre qui est Comme un Espece de tufle, qui est tres douce et qui Seroit merveilleuze á faire de Beaux Éddifices. Cette pierre ce prand á dix huit Lieux audossus du nouvelle éstablissement Les Long des Bord de la Riviere de La Mobille.—Les Maisons ont 18,20 á 25 pieds auplus de hauteur, il y en á quelques unes plus Basses Construittes d'un mortié fait avec de la terre et de La Chaud,—

Na cette Chaud est faitte de Coquille d'huistre que lon trouve á

Lentré de la Riviere Sur des petittes illes qui en porte le nom, & Lon donne á ceuze qui Veute Sétablir dans Cette endroit, de terrain douze toises et de Mie de Largeur, Sur la face d'une rŭes Sur Vignt Cinq de profondeur;—

Lapierre dont Lon Se Sert pour Supporter les maisons, est Rare et Non commune faute des Voitures qu'il Seroit Necessaires davoir par eaux, Comme des Batteaux plats qu'il ny a pas, ny dont personnes nen veut faire La dépence, ce qui Seroit d'un grand Secours, car ceuze dont les maisons ne Sont Soutenues que de pieux de Bois Sont obligez de Les Changer tous les trois á quatre ans parce qu'il pourisse dans La Terre. & c.

B. Maison du Gouvernueur
C. Magazin du Roy
D. Pondriere ou magazin á Poudre
H. Bastion dans Le quel est une Cloche nayant point de Chapelle dans le fort.
E. Corp de Garde
F. Prizons
G. Bastion dans le quel on met le pavillon

1734 Devin Map

1. House of wood, covered with bark, being used as a forge and serving as house for the ironmonger. Falling into ruins.
2. House of wood, covered with bark, serving the Church as a lodging for the priest. Also in ruins.
3. House of wood, covered with bark, serving for the captain of the Swiss Guards.
4. House of wood, covered with bark, falling into ruins, as well as the huts which are serving to house the blacks of the king.
5. Small bark house, lodging for interpreter.
6. Lodging for the governor, built of wood with roof of shingles, one story, gallery all around, the best of the houses standing today which belong to the king.
7. House of wood, covered with bark, lodging for the major, largely in ruins.
8. Wharf [some words indecipherable] discharge wharf on which a hut is constructed as lodging for the king's sailors, and it would be necessary to have it rebuilt.
9. Hospital of wood covered by shingles which is not sufficient for the post, which is very small and will not last for long.

(Portions of the legend identifying buildings on the map are indicated by letters but have not been translated here because the buildings to which they correspond are not visible in figure 12.)

APPENDIX 2

Report in the *Mobile Commercial Register* for May 27, 1822

MOBILE

Monday Evening, May 27, 1822

Wm. Tabelé is a Candidate at the next General Election for the office of Sheriff of Mobile County.

Wm. Tabelé est candidat pour la place de Sheriff du Comté de la Mobile à la prochaine Election.

Improvement—We notice with much satisfaction, the progress now making in the way of building in this City. The walls of no less than Nine Brick Stores have risen up, as if by magic. The spot which, but a few weeks since, exhibited a scene of smoky ruins, is now completely covered with five brick tenements, the roofs of which are now going up. We consider it a tribute due to public spirited enterprise, to state that the fire proof buildings are erecting by Henry Stickney, Addin Lewis, Holman & Brown, and Joshua Armstrong; whose present labors and example we consider intimately connected with the future history and present advancement of our city, while they are well calculated to advance their own fortunes, being engaged in the most durable, and far from the most expensive, mode of building: and consequently profitable, safe and ornamental. We hope this spirit may continue to spread, to the continued increase of our commercial importance. In addition to the above, there are ten or twelve new wooden stores and warehouses, of respectable appearance completed and completing. The erection of several other brick buildings will, we understand, commence as soon as materials can be obtained. Vessels sailing from the north for this port, would do well to take bricks, lime, stone, &c. for owners' account, particularly when outward freights are scarce.

While on the subject of improvement, we cannot suffer to pass unnoticed the completion of our beautiful little Church. This building is not perhaps surpassed in convenience of plan, tastefulness of execution, and neatness of appearance, by any house of public worship, built of wood, of similar dimensions, in the Southern States: And although a temple has been erected, and "dedicated to the living God," it is a source of satisfaction to the friends of society to know that it was destined for a worthier purpose than mere show, having settled a clergyman the moment the work was finished, one who will not shrink from his duties on account of season, or desert his flock in time of distress, on account of climate, but cheerfully enlists in their interests, ever to be ready to administer comfort to afflicted, or if occasion should require, to perform the last offices of humanity.

The order of the edifice, as mentioned on a former occasion, is somewhat of the Gothic, and taking it altogether, it reflects equal credit upon its architect and liberal founders—while the building committee justly claim the grateful thanks of all, for their indefatigable zeal and unwearied exertions in effecting so laudable a purpose.

APPENDIX 3

The Fire of 1839: Report in the *Mercantile Advertiser*, October 9, 1839

THE GREAT MOBILE FIRE

THE RECORDS OF OUR PAST.

A friend has kindly furnished us with a synopsis of the principal conflagrations on record in early and later times, but he had already been anticipated by our scissors. In the catalogue furnished to us, and in that which we have copied, as in all others which we have seen, two remarkable fires are omitted. One is that of Rome, in the time of Nero, probably the greatest civic conflagration on record. Of this we supply an account, clipped from one of our exchanges. The other is the Mobile fire of 1839, for the story of which we refer to our own files. This, like the Chicago fire, was a double conflagration. The paper of October 8, gives an account of the first fire, but the breaking out of the second delayed the publication, a brief account of which appears in the form of a "Postscript" in the same issue. Owing to the prevalence of the dreadful yellow fever of that year, the publication of the Mercantile Advertiser—C. C. Langdon, editor, (the only paper in our possession of which the file for that period is not defective,) had been reduced to a weekly issue. The number of the Advertiser now before us, mentions the illness of its foreman and pressman, and the reduction of the force to one compositor.

We have spoken of a first and a second fire, but there had been fires before. We copy from the Mercantile Advertiser of Tuesday, October 1, 1839:

F I R E !—On Saturday night last, between the hours of eleven and twelve o'clock, a fire broke out in Dauphin street, between Hamilton and Lawrence, which proved very destructive. On that square, all the buildings on Dauphin street were destroyed, and about half of those on Hamilton and Lawrence—in all about twenty' buildings. The aggregate amount of loss is not large, the buildings having been mostly old and small, and composed entirely of wood; but the individual suffering, notwithstanding, is severe—several persons having lost their *little all*. The present is a very unfortunate time for a fire in our city, as but few, comparatively, of our citizens stay in the city during the night, and our *main reliance* on such occasions, *the Fireman*, are reduced to a mere handfull in numbers. We learn, however, that great credit is due to Mr. J. F. Hutchinson, Assistant Foreman of the Department, who took command on Saturday night, for the coolness, skill, and energy he displayed on the occasion. It is said that it was owing principally to his intrepidity and judicious management, that the fire was arrested in its progress, and one half the square preserved from destruction.

ANOTHER!—About 11 o'clock on Sunday night, the carpenters shop belonging to Mr. J. F. Hutchinson, situated in the lower part of the city, was entirely consumed with all its contents, consisting of a large quantity of lumber, tools, &c. We have not heard the amount of the loss. It was evidently the work of an incendiary. Mr. H. has been burnt out once before within the past year. Strange there should exist a monster in human shape, who could thus seek to gratify private revenge.

Even this was but the first note of the prelude to what has ever since been known as as The Fire of 1839.

We now proceed to copy in their order the accounts, premising that the population of Mobile, by the census of 1840, was 12,672:

[From the Mercantile Advertiser, Tuesday Morning, October 8, 1839.]

DESTRUCTIVE FIRE!—Our city seems doomed to destruction. On Wednesday night last, at about half-past 10 o'clock, a fire broke out in the workshop attached to the Furniture Store of Messrs. Gwinn & Brant, on Dauphin street, destroying that building, then extending southward to the out buildings of the City Hotel, and the warehouse of B. & J. Newhouse, and northward to the furniture store of Gwinn & Brant, the Grocery of Geo. Davis, Jr., and the Drug store of Owen & Gould on Dauphin street, all of which were entirely destroyed. Here the progress of the flames was arrested, and the people began to disperse for their homes, when suddenly the flames was discovered bursting from the roof of the City Hotel, on Royal street, and all efforts to save it proved unavailing. The printing office of the Commercial Register was in imminent danger, and was only saved by the liberal application of water from the engines. The Register gives the following list of sufferers:

Gwinn & Brant, cabinet makers store and workshop, owned by Jotham Clarke—insurance $8,000.

B. & J. Newhouse, warehouse, insured.

George Davis, jr., grocery store, insurance $8,000—owned by Mr. Pian.

Owen & Gould, drug store, owned by G. Chicghasola; stock valued at $10,000—insurance $10,000.

City Hotel, owned by Mrs. Robb, occupied by Mr. Field—building insured for $25,000; furniture $7,000. In the basement story, there was a bar room kept by Mr. Gosling, a barber shop, by Elam Page, and the music store of Bromberg & Koone—all of which, and the out buildings, were totally destroyed.

The total loss is estimated at about 120,000 dollars, 72,000 of which is covered by Insurance, which is divided among the following offices: Alabama Life and Trust Company, $17,000—Mobile, $10,000—Fireman's, $4,000—Merchants, $1,500, all of this City. New Orleans Ocean, $10,000—Georgia Insurance and Trust, at Augusta, $16,000—Charleston Life and Trust, $5,000—Howard, N. York, $5,000—and Hudson, New York, $3,500.

The fire was without doubt the work of incendiaries. It continued during nearly the whole night, all of which time, refreshments were liberally furnished by Mr. James F. M'Bride, at his residence on Dauphin street.

AWFUL CONFLAGRATION!!
ELEVEN SQUARES DESTROYED BY FIRE!!!

We have only time this morning, before going to press, to announce the occurrence of the most awful and destructive fire which ever before occurred in our unfortunate and ill-starred city. Last night, at about eight o'clock, when the wind was blowing almost a gale from the South East, the fire broke out in an old wooden building in the rear of the house on the South East corner of Dauphin and Conception streets, owned by Mr. Pinto. The adjoining buildings being all of wood, the fire was soon communicated to them, and in a few minutes crossed Conception street. Here it had full sweep—the buildings being very compact, and all of wood, and the wind south east—the fire swept over the two squares west of Conception, from Conti, on the south, to St. Francis, on the north, with unexampled and terrific rapidity. Proceeding west, it crossed to St. Joachim street—then Jackson—where it extended one square further North to St. Michael street—and then, three solid squares abreast, all in one grand terrific flame, it swept onward to Claiborne street, and crossed it, sweeping everything, to Franklin. Here, at about twelve o'clock, the wind fortunately abated, in consequence of which, and the blowing up of several buildings on the west side of Franklin street, the progress of the devouring element was stayed. Not, however, until six or eight buildings on the west side of Franklin had been destroyed. The dwelling of Duke Goodman, Esq., on the corner of Dauphin and Franklin, was blown up.

Thus all the buildings on the north side of Conti, from Conception to Franklin, a distance of four squares—all on both sides of Dauphin, to the same extent—on both sides of St. Francis to same extent, with the exception of three buildings on each side at the corner of Conception—all the buildings on the south side of St. Michael, from Jackson to Franklin—all on the cross streets of Conception, St. Joachim, Jackson, Claiborne and Franklin, within the limits described above, and probably twenty to thirty buildings besides, in the vicinity—numbering, it is supposed, about FIVE HUNDRED BUILDINGS—have suddenly been reduced to ashes! By this awful calamity, probably two hundred families are turned into the streets, many of whom are poor and penniless, and will depend entirely upon public charity for a place to rest their heads, and for bread to appease their hunger. The flames extended with such rapidity, that but little property could be saved, and many, very many, have lost their all. We are unable this morning to descend to particulars. It is impossible to convey any idea of the distress produced. The removal of the sick and the consequent exposure, excitement and alarm, we fear will in many instances be productive of fatal results.

The origin of the fire is attributed to incendiaries; and we understand that two persons were seized on suspicion and lodged in jail. Can it be possible there can be found in human shape, such base, fiendish monsters? Mobile seems indeed a doomed city. Have we not drank deep enough of the bitter cup of adversity and affliction? When and where will our calamities end? Alas! Heaven only knows!

POSTSCRIPT
Wednesday Morning, Oct. 9th, 1839
STILL ANOTHER TREMENDOUS CONFLAGRATION!!

The Planters' and Merchants' Bank—The Mansion House—The New Hotel—all destroyed.

With the most painful and melancholy feelings we again announce the recurrence of another most awful and destructive conflagration in our devoted city. At two o'clock this morning, that long known and splendid establishment, the Mansion House, was discovered on fire, and to such an extent that it was impossible to extinguish it. We have only time to say, that from the Mansion House the fire was communicated to the magnificent new Hotel, adjoining on the south, which was yet in an unfinished state, and to the Planters' and Merchants' Bank, that new, beautiful and splendid edifice, both of which were reduced to ashes. From the new Hotel the fire crossed Royal street, and the greater portion of the square west of the new Hotel and Mansion House is already destroyed, and while we write (7 o'clock), the fire is still raging.

The residence of Mr. Cunningham, adjoining the new Hotel on Government street to the South, is also consumed as well as the vegetable market House, and the fire is still extending downward toward the water. Where it will end, God only knows. The loss by fire this morning already cannot be less than HALF A MILLION OF DOLLARS!! Charles Cullum, Esq., the worthy philanthropic and public spirited PROPRIETOR of the Mansion House was insured $67,000, but his loss besides will be very great. We have ascertained no other particulars. All is horror and confusion—and on every countenance is depicted feelings of the deepest melancholy and gloom.

Within the last ten days property to the amount of upwards of a million of dollars has been destroyed by fire; and hundreds of worthy citizens are left without a dollar, or even a roof to shelter them from the pitiless storm. And what is worse, all is attributed to the fiendish spirit of incendiarism! Ruin, inevitable ruin, seems to be our doom! At this moment we see from our window that the fire is extending from the Planters' and Merchants' Bank, down Conti street. Gracious heaven! where will it end, and what are we coming to?

We omitted to mention above that the Post Office is destroyed.

The Mercantile Advertiser of the 15th reports the proceedings of a public meeting, (W. R. Hallett, chairman,) held on the 10th, by which a Committee of Safety (Jeremiah Austill, Charles A. Henry, John K. Collins, John Ticknor, Philip McLoskey, Henry Chamberlain and H. B. Gwathmey; with the addition of the chairman, and Wm. Magee, Sheriff,) was appointed, measures of relief were instituted, etc. The vaults of the Planters and Merchants' Bank are reported to have proved fire-proof. Reports of Lynch law are contradicted—"Not a single act of violence has been committed—in not a single instance has the sanctity of the law been invaded." A relief meeting at New Orleans—James H. Caldwell, President—is reported, etc. In the paper of October 22, we find the losses by fire during the month estimated at $1,500,000. We find no estimate of the number of buildings destroyed, but we believe it was above 1,300. The buildings themselves, in those days were generally of a cheap character, and owing to the depletion of business, there was comparatively a small stock of merchandise in the city, otherwise the losses would have footed up a much larger amount.

APPENDIX 4

Toulmin's *Digest of the Laws of the State of Alabama*

An Act to Incorporate the City of Mobile—Passed December 17, 1819.

Sec. 1. Be it enacted by the Senate and House of Representatives of the State of Alabama, in general assembly convened,

That the inhabitants of the town of Mobile be constituted a body politic and corporate, by the name of the Mayor and Aldermen of the city of Mobile, and by their corporate name may sue and be sued, implead and be impleaded, grant, receive, and do all other acts as natural persons, and may purchase and hold real, personal, and mixed property, not exceeding at any one time fifty thousand dollars, or dispose of the same for the benefit of the said city, and may have and use a city seal, which may be broken or altered at pleasure.

Sec. 2. And be it further enacted,

That the limits or boundaries of the city of Mobile shall be as follows: Commencing at Choctaw Point, and running in a straight direction to the western banks of the Bayou Chotage, at a point lying two hundred yards above the place on said Bayou Chotage called the Portage; thence down the western bank of said Bayou to its mouth, thence in a straight line to the west bank of the island in front of Mobile; thence along the margin of said island to the south point of said island, and thence in a straight line to the place of beginning.

Sec. 3. And be it further enacted,

That the said mayor and aldermen shall have full power to appoint a clerk to the corporation, a treasurer, an inspector or inspectors of streets, lanes, and alleys, fences, yards, and all out-houses, three police constables, an assessor, a collector of taxes, an attorney to the corporation, and all other officers necessary to carry into effect this incorporation.

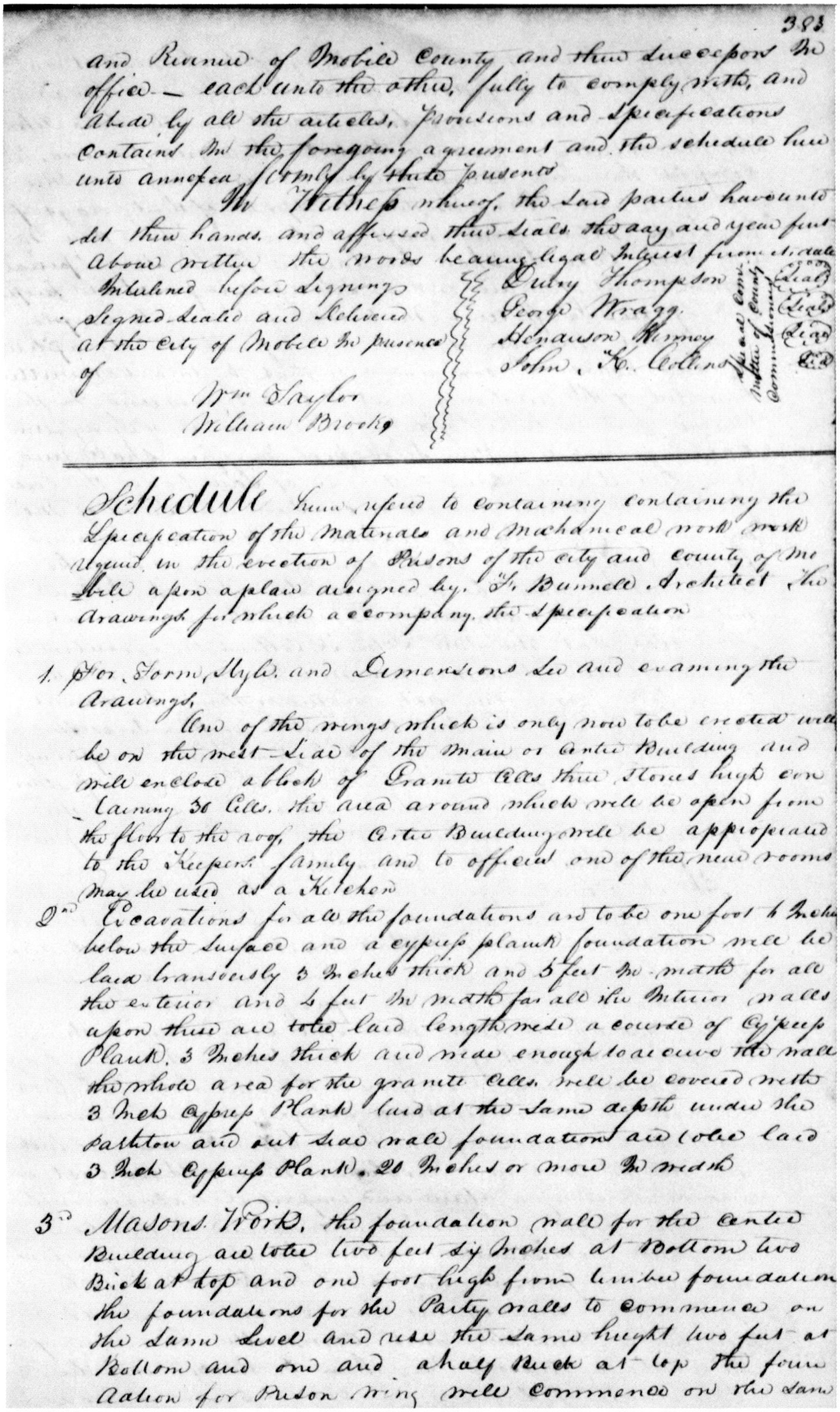

239. *A sample page from Miscellaneous Book C, pp. 383–87, showing a contract dated August 31, 1839, for a county prison, to be located on the rear of the Hospital lot; F. Bunnell, architect; J. Collins, builder; cost, $25,000.*

[Handwritten manuscript page, numbered 383 at top right. Text reads approximately:]

and Revenue of Mobile County and their Successors in office — each unto the other, fully to comply with, and abide by all the articles, provisions and specifications contains in the foregoing agreement and the schedule hereunto annexed formly by these presents

In Witness whereof the said parties have hereunto set their hands and affixed their seals the day and year first above written the words bearing legal interest from this date interlined before signing

Signed sealed and delivered
at the city of Mobile in presence of

Wm Taylor
William Brooks

Duley Thompson [seal]
George Wragg [seal]
Henderson Kinney [seal]
John K. Collins [seal]

Schedule herein referred to containing containing the Specification of the Materials and Mechanical work required in the erection of Prisons of the city and county of Mobile upon a plan designed by F. Bunnell Architect the drawings for which accompany the Specification

1. *For Form, Style, and Dimensions* See and examine the drawings.

   One of the wings which is only now to be erected will be on the west side of the Main or Center Building and will enclose a block of Granite Cells three Stories high containing 36 Cells, the area around which will be open from the floor to the roof, the Center Building will be appropriated to the Keepers family and to officers one of the rear rooms may be used as a Kitchen

2. Excavations for all the foundations are to be one foot 6 inches below the Surface and a Cypress plank foundation will be laid transversely 3 Inches thick and 5 feet in width for all the exterior and 4 feet in width for all the interior walls upon these are to be laid lengthwise a course of Cypress Plank 3 Inches thick and wide enough to secure the wall the whole area for the granite Cells will be covered with 3 Inch Cypress Plank laid at the Same depth under the partition and out side wall foundation are to be laid 3 Inch Cypress Plank 20 Inches or more in width

3. *Masons Work.* the foundation wall for the Center Building are to be two feet six inches at bottom two Brick at top and one foot high from timber foundation the foundations for the Party walls to commence on the Same Level and rise the same height two feet at bottom and one and a half Brick at top the foundation for Prison wing will commence on the Same

262   Appendix 4

APPENDIX 5

Sample Contract for a Frame House

Contract: house, two-story frame; with basement of brick and garret.

Misc. Book C/165–166; June 16, 1838. C. Shaw, I. S. Vaughn and B. H. White, builders, for Patrick Henry.

In the country, near the Race Track.

The house to be thirty four (34) feet square with a front and rear gallery of eight feet in the Clear. The back Gallery to be enclosed with two rooms of eight by ten feet, the Center part of the House to be open with two doors to the main body of the House and two doors leading into the back Gallery and rooms, all of which doors to be six pannel each, the principal Story to be ten feet in the clear with two Chimneys, one on each end, the said Chimneys to be built in the inside of the House, there will be two doors and two windows in front, two windows on the end on each room, one door leading to each room, So there will be three windows in each front room and five doors in the both rooms, there will be one door and two windows in each room on the back Gallery, the size of the glass in principal Story will be ten by fifteen (10 by 15), the doors to be six pannel except the two front doors which will be eight pannel with transom sash over each—

—the two large rooms to be divided by the center partition, each of these front rooms to be plaistered with good three coats plastering, hand finish, the balance of the house to be good two coats work except the front and upper part of the Gallery which will be the same as the front rooms. The Stair leading to the Garrett will run from the open span between the back gallery bed rooms, the same Stair will have turned Collums and Bannisters the same as on the front steps. The Garrett will be divided in two rooms with a good Batten door-groved and tounged, 3 by 7 feet leading to each—the

Garrett will be Studded, Beamed [?] to support plastering—that will bring the rooms nearly square, the plastering of the Garrett to be good two coat work—

—the two front doors to be painted Oak Colour, the last of the doors in the principal Story to be painted Mahogany Colour, the two mantle pieces to be painted Marble Colour or imitation, the Basement Story to have two fireplaces on each end leading in the main chimney—this Story will be seven feet in the clear, the body of the house Basement to be built with brick with two rooms, four windows and two doors in each room and one door leading to each room

—the stairs in front and back leading to the Principal Story to be well finished with turned Collums, handrails and Newells—and there will be a good base around each and every room in the House, all the doors to have good hinges and locks patent, Brass nobs. There will be blinds well painted green—

—all the carpenter work to have two good coats of white paint inside and out. The floors in the principal rooms and the Gallery to be six inches, one and a quarter inch thick, groved and tounged, likewise the floor of the garrett to be tounged and groved, likewise the floor of the basement—

—the sills to be sypress or cedar, the front Collums to be Sypress and well turned round with Caps—all the front Gallery Newells, handrails and stairs to be Sypress—

—the front Gallery and Stairs to be painted Yellow, two good coats—

—also to make a kitchen—and place it on brick pillars two feet high in the clear and have the Kichen in the same repair as when found it except the chimney which the party of the first part will do at his own expense. The above work to be finished on or before the first day of December next 1838. If the party of the second part doth not have the said house finished by the above said time then agrees to allow the party of the first part five dollars for each and every day until the same said house is finished

$2100.00

APPENDIX 6

Building History of the Mobile County Court Houses

Source	Date	Transaction
		First Court House, 1825
MCR	2/7/22	Statement that permission had been granted to build a county court house.
Misc. Bk. B, pp. 42–44	8/30/25	Contract between the county government, Peter Hobart, and Lewis Judson, stating that Hobart was to construct the new building.
		County commissioners: W. Hale, Benjamin Smoot, S. H. Garrow.
		Description: 2-story brick on a 5-foot basement. White marble lintels and sills. Front "piazza" 20 feet long by 8 feet wide. Building 50 feet wide. Giant columns rising from top of basement level. Divided staircase leading to piazza deck. Main courtroom on second story.
		Cost: $13,000
		Destroyed by fire. Date not known but believed to be in October 1851, when the court moved to the Alhambra.
		Second Court House, 1853
Misc. Bk. F, pp. 72–74, 88–105	4/16/53	Contract between county government and James Barnes, builder. Architect and superintendent of construction, William S. Alderson.
		County commissioners: Jacob Magee, president; D. W. Goodman; I. C. Smith; James Alder; I. I. Gliddon.
		Description: 3-story brick with rough stucco, classic columns, pilasters, and entablature; window and door trim of white

APPENDIX 6 (Continued)

Source	Date	Transaction
		marble; capitals and bases, also water table, of Tennessee blue marble. Groin-vaulted courtrooms. Hot air furnace with iron pipes set in double brick walls. Shutters, sheet iron.
		Cost: $70,289.08
MCR	1/31/64	Destroyed by fire 1/31/64.

INTERIM COURT HOUSE, 1864–1874

Source	Date	Transaction
CD	1864–1874	County court house located on Conti.
CD	1874	County court house located on southwest corner of Government and Royal.
CCM, Bk. 3, p. 311	9/20/64	Rental contract with Hagan's Store, located on the north side of Conti between Royal and Water.
CCM, Bk. 3, p. 351	3/7/65	Bills paid to Scattergood, Burfoot, Orfellas, Partridge, and Spence for repair work on leased building and vaults for records. Total, $6,830.
CCM, Bk. 4, p. 110	8/3/68	Court committee reported having ordered that plans be drawn up for a building to replace the burned structure.
CCM, Bk. 4, p. 146	3/8/69	Lot behind court house purchased.
CCM, Bk. 4, p. 151	4/21/69	Contract with Cahill and others to remove remaining material of burned building, rebuilding outhouses and walls and paving courtyard. (The records do not differentiate between repairs made to the rented building and work done on the new site. Cahill was also hired 12/68 [p. 137] to build a poorhouse at a cost of $1,000.)
CCM, Bk. 4, p. 310	7/16/72	Advertisements for proposals for new building.
CCM, Bk. 4, p. 321	9/26/72	Bonds issued for construction costs.
CCM, Bk. 4, pp. 322–27	10/1/72	Contract with Charles Fricke for construction, $101,000.
CCM, Bk. 4, pp. 327–45	10/1/72	Contract with W. O. Pond as architect. Includes specs.
Misc. Bk. H, p. 501	10/10/72	Contract between Fricke and subcontractor McDonald, March, and Company, stonework, $16,850.
CCM, Bk. 4, pp. 322–27	10/10/72	Fricke contract calls for building to be finished on or before 10/1/73.

APPENDIX 6 (*Continued*)

SOURCE	DATE	TRANSACTION
		THIRD COURT HOUSE, 1873
		Description: classical style, 6 giant Ionic columns rising above high podium base. Monumental entrance stairway with high cheeks on either side. Balcony between columnar shafts at second-story level. Dentils accenting both horizontal and raking cornices.
MCR	1/21/88	Destroyed by fires, 1/20/88
		FOURTH COUNTY COURT HOUSE, 1889
CCM, Bk. 7, p. 353	1/27/88	Minutes state fire occurred 1/20/88.
CCM, Bk. 7, p. 354	1/27/88	Meeting with insurance company, loss settled at $23,906.78.
		County government moved to Royal Street Hotel, west side of Royal, behind the burned building, between Government and Church.
MCR	3/13/88	Newspaper account of 3 sets of plans submitted for the new building. No architects named.
CCM, Bk. 7, pp. 382–84	3/26/88	Plans of Rudolph Benz accepted.
CCM, Bk. 7, p. 414	7/2/88	Contract with Louis Monin (also spelled Monnin) as contractor with bid of $60,763.
CCM, Bk. 9, p. 255	7/9/89	Building turned over to commissioners.
MCR	9/1/89	Newspaper photo of Benz building and spread of description.
		FIFTH COUNTY COURT HOUSE, 1958
Virginia Lott Report	5/81	Cooper van Antwerp, architect; cost, $4,717,413.
		ADDITION TO COURT HOUSE, 1977
Virginia Lott Report		Laraway and Grider, architects; cost, $1,600,000.

Note: Unless otherwise indicated, all years are nineteenth century. Before the first Court House was built, the county government rented the house of Catalia Mottus. The receipt for rent paid in 1822–1823 is in the county probate records. For the interim Court House (1864–1874), the county government rented the Hagan Building on the north side of Conti Street, between Royal and Water streets.

Abbreviations

AIA	American Institute of Architects
ASP	*American State Papers*
CCM	County Council Minutes, Mobile County Board of Commissioners
CD	*City of Mobile Directory*
CPC	County Probate Court, Mobile County
DB	Deed Books, Probate Court, Mobile County
FHQ	*Florida Historical Quarterly*
HABS	Historic American Building Survey
HMPS	Historic Mobile Preservation Society
LC	Library of Congress
LHQ	*Louisiana Historical Quarterly*
MAM	Mayor and Board of Aldermen, Minutes, City of Mobile
MCC	Minutes of the Common Council, Mobile City
MCR	*Mobile Commercial Register*, including the same paper published under slightly different names during the first sixty years
MCPIC	Mobile City Planning Commission
MHDC	Mobile Historic Development Commission
Misc. Bks.	Miscellaneous Books, County Probate Court
MPA	*Mississippi Provincial Archives*
MPL(SC)	Mobile Public Library (Special Collections)
MTP	*U.S. Territorial Papers*, vol. 5, *Territory of Mississippi*
USTP	*Territorial Papers of the United States*
USA PhA	University of South Alabama Photographic Archives

Notes

1. Inheritance: The Colonial Years, 1711–1813

1. P. Jay Higginbotham, *Old Mobile: Fort Louis de la Louisiane, 1702–1711* (Mobile: Museum of the City of Mobile, 1977), p. 451.

2. One toise equals six French feet; one French foot equals 12.78933 English inches. For a complete transcription of the legend on the 1711 Chevillot map, see appendix 1.

3. A transcription of the legend on the 1734 Devin map appears in appendix 1.

4. Willard B. Robinson, "Military Architecture at Mobile Bay," *Journal of the Society of Architectural Historians* 30, no. 2 (May 1971), pp. 119–39. Ronald Barker collected and translated recent important documentation on the history of the Fort while serving as resident archivist there. A copy of some of this material is on file in MPL(SC).

5. Charles E. Peterson has extensively researched the origins of the French dwellings in the Mississippi valley. A summary of this research is included in "The Houses of French St. Louis," in *The French in the Mississippi Valley*, ed. John F. McDermott (Urbana: University of Illinois Press, 1965), pp. 17–40.

6. "Inventory of the Property of Joseph Bock, Mobile, April 4, 1762," *LHQ* 23, no. 3 (July 1940), pp. 917–18 (reprinted from the *Records of the Superior Council of Louisiana*, no. 8131, p. 9).

7. Ibid., p. 918.

8. Peter J. Hamilton, *Colonial Mobile*, 3d ed. (1897; reprint, Mobile: First National Bank, 1952), p. 160.

9. Peterson, "Houses of French St. Louis," pp. 17–40; C. Johnson, "Missouri French Houses: Some Relict Features of Early Settlements," *Journal of the Pioneer American Society* 6, no. 2 (July 1974), pp. 1–12; Carolyn Ramsey, *Cajuns on the Bayous* (New York: Hastings House, 1957), p. xii; Sidney Marchand, *Acadian Exiles in the Golden Coast of Louisiana* (Donaldsonville, La.: Ascension and St. James Parishes, 1943), pp. 21; Peter N. Moogk, *Building a House in New France* (Toronto: McClelland and Stewart, 1977), pp. 24–32. In seventeenth-century Acadia, *poteaux en terre* (posts in the earth) were common in construction. In Quebec *poteaux sur*

sole (posts on a sill) were common. There was often a filling between the posts of small stones and mortar known as *maison en colombage*. By the eighteenth century, stone construction had become popular and also walls solidly built up from wood posts that were dressed on two sides and squared. The posts could be set on the vertical or on the horizontal and became known as *pièces sur pièces*. While later forms developed during the eighteenth century, the emigrating French carried the earlier forms down the Mississippi.

10. Even in this crude dwelling, the pitch of the roof forms a well-defined concave curve as it descends from the ridge to the edge of the gallery. Later cottages of the nineteenth century straightened this curve to form a straight plane covering both cottage and porch.

11. Gregory Franzwa, *The Story of Ste. Genevieve* (St. Louis: Patrice Press, 1967). The author includes a history of the town as well as a catalogue of the buildings and on pp. 101–5, the history of the Bolduc House. Also see P. Jay Higginbotham, *Pascagoula, Singing River City* (Mobile: Gill Printing and Stationery, 1967), p. 4. The 1971 winter edition of the unpaginated journal of the Mississippi Agricultural and Industry Board has a short article on the Old Spanish Fort; no author is given. Regarding the hurricane, see Albert J. Pickett and Thomas McAdory Owen, "History of Alabama and Incidentally of Georgia and Mississippi from the earliest Period" and "Annals of Alabama (1819–1900)," 2 vols. in 1 (1900; reprint, Spartanburg: Reprint, 1975), pp. 326–27.

12. Pickett and Owen, *History of Alabama*, p. 326.

13. Dunbar Rowland, ed., "Letters and Enclosures to the Secretary of State from Major Robert Farmer and Governor George Johnstone of West Florida," *MPA* 1, "English Dominion, 1763–1766" (October 1911), pp. 78–79.

14. Ibid., p. 79.

15. Hamilton, *Colonial Mobile*, p. 253.

16. *ASP* 5:707.

17. Pickett and Owen, *History of Alabama*, pp. 185–86, 228. German emigrants were brought into the territory in 1722 under the direction of the Chevalier d'Arensbourg. Also see Hamilton, *Colonial Mobile*, p. 206 (Governor Johnstone's report of 1708).

18. *Mémoire Justificatif du Chevalier Montault Monberaut, 1763–1765*, trans. Milo B. Howard, Jr., and Robert R. Rea (University: University of Alabama Press, 1965), pp. 21–22.

19. Dunbar Rowland, ed., "Extract from the Text of the Cession of Mobile, submitted by Peter Hanibal Develle, Chevalier of the Royal and Military Order of St. Louis, King's Lieutenant and Commander of the Port of Mobile and René John Gabriel Fezende, doing the duty of Commissary of Marines of the same Port, submitted to Mons: Robert Farmer named by his Britannick. Majesty to command the Post of Mobile," in *MPA* 1, "English Dominion, 1763–1766" (October 1911), pp. 77–79.

20. Ibid., "Report of the State of Fort Charlotte by Robert Farmer," November 30, 1763, and recorded in a letter of January 24, 1764, pp. 19–20.

21. Dunbar Rowland, ed., "Letter from Major Farmer to Lord Egremont," January 24, 1764, in *MPA* 1, "English Dominion, 1763–1766" (October 1911), pp. 137–38.

22. Dunbar Rowland, ed., Manifesto Issued by Major Farmer, October 20, 1763, in *MPA* 1, "English Dominion, 1763–1766"

(October 1911), pp. 61–63, 121ff. The manifesto lists the names of the French taking the oath of allegiance to the English crown as they were submitted by Major Farmer, October 2, 1764.

23. *ASP* 1:756 (November 1, 1765).

24. Clinton N. Howard, *The British Development of West Florida, 1763–1769*, University of California Publications in History 34 (Berkeley: University of California Press, 1947), pp. 9, 16; *ASP* 1:584 (August 6, 1778).

25. Howard, *British Development of West Florida*, pp. 13–14.

26. Hamilton, *Colonial Mobile*, pp. 272–73; *Mémoire Justificatif du Chevalier Montault Monberaut, 1763–1765*. According to Hamilton, *Colonial Mobile*, pp. 227–38, Monberaut had his estate on Bull Island. He was of noble birth and had emigrated to Louisiana in about 1793, when he was stationed at Fort Toulouse.

27. Lord Adam Gordon, "Journal of an Officer, 1764–1765," in *Travels in the North American Colonies and the West Indies, 1764–1765*, ed. Newton Dennison Mereness (1916; reprint, New York: Antiquarian Society, 1961), p. 388.

28. Howard, *British Development of West Florida*, pp. 36, 44–45. The request was divided into two classifications, the needs of the military and the needs of the colony, with allowances for the poor and for opening up new waterways. Also see Hamilton, *Colonial Mobile*, p. 272.

29. Dunbar Rowland, ed., Major Farmer's Contingent Account, *MPA*, 1, "English Dominion, 1763–1766" (October 1911), pp. 65–74 and 116–17. See also Howard, "Interval of Military Government in West Florida," *LHQ* 22 (April 1939), pp. 19–20.

30. Hamilton, *Colonial Mobile*, p. 253; Peter Hamilton, "British West Florida," *Mississippi Historical Society* 7 (1903), p. 409.

31. Lord Adam Gordon, "Journal," p. 388.

32. Rowland, "Correspondence between Governor Johnstone and John Pownall," *MPA* 1, "English Dominion, 1763–1766" (October 1911), p. 169.

33. Howard, *British Development of West Florida*, p. 13; Pickett, *History of Alabama*, p. 324.

34. Howard, *British Development of West Florida*, p. 15; Pickett, *History of Alabama*, pp. 324–25; Hamilton, *Colonial Mobile*, p. 253.

35. Peter Brannon, *The Southern Indian Trade* (Montgomery: Paragon Press, 1935), pp. 25–32, 33–35. The two-story porch can be seen in the southern Atlantic states, for example on the Brewton-Pringle House in Charleston.

36. Pickett, *History of Alabama*. The history of the McGillivrays appears on pp. 342–51. Alexander's mother was a member of the tribe of The Wind, the most powerful of all the Creek tribes. Another account appears in Lyle McAlister, "Pensacola during the Second Spanish Period," *FHQ* 37, nos. 3 and 4 (January–April 1959), p. 295.

37. "Minutes of the First Session of West Florida Assembly, 1766–1767," *LHQ* 22 (April 1939), pp. 1–40.

38. Howard, *British Development of West Florida*, pp. 50–101; the quoted statements appear on pp. 90, 80, and 14 (quoting Lord Adam Gordon).

39. Ibid., pp. 52, 100. The grant was issued to a committee of citizens who were to select a site for the Church. The quoted statement appears on p. 28.

40. Ibid., pp. 116, 121.

41. Hamilton, *Colonial Mobile*, p. 264n.

42. Howard, "Interval of Military Government in West Florida," pp. 18–30; William Bartram, *Travels through North and South Carolina, Georgia, East and West Florida* (1791; reprint, New York: Dover, 1928), pp. 323–24.

43. *ASP*, 5:713 (May 24, 1796). Andrew Ellicott executed the commission that was authorized in the names of Ellicott and Freeman; 1,658,880 acres of land were recorded south of the thirty-first degree latitude and were retained by the Spanish. The Ellicott stone marking the old boundary still stands about one-quarter mile east of highway 43, about twenty-one miles north of Mobile. On its south side, the stone reads, "Dominios de S. M. Carlos IV, Lat. 31°, 1799." On the north side is the inscription, "U.S. Lat. 31°, 1799." Regarding agriculture, see Donald Dodd, *Historic Atlas of Alabama* (University: University of Alabama Press, 1974), p. 40. For more on the introduction of cotton, see Lyle McAlister, "Pensacola during the Second Spanish Period," *FHQ* 37, nos. 3 and 4 (January–April 1959), p. 281. The first cotton gin was imported by Panton and Leslie in 1802 (p. 301).

44. Jack D. L. Holmes, *Alabama Colonial Settlers: Spanish Period, 1780–1813*, Louisiana Collection Series 2 (New Orleans: Holmes, 1970), Microfilm of Spanish Documents, University of South Alabama, p. 170 (Letters between Gálvez and Durnford); John W. Caughey, *Bernardo de Gálvez in Louisiana, 1776–1783* (Gretna: Pelican, 1972), p. 182. Helen Parkhurst, "Don Pedro Favrot, A Creole Pepys," *LHQ* 28, no. 3 (July 1945), p. 701 (quoted); Lyle McAlister, "Pensacola during the Second Spanish Period," p. 294. In *Colonial Mobile*, Peter Hamilton wrote that in 1787 Irish priests from the College of Salamanca had been sent to serve the English-speaking subjects (p. 366).

45. *ASP* 3, no. 234: 18, 7, 12, 77. Forbes and Company owned land in Mobile at Choctaw Point and on the Bayou Chatogues, listed in *ASP* 5:329; its lots in Mobile are listed in *ASP* 3:8. The Mobile city tax record of 1829 valued its holdings at $62,000. Also see McAlister, "Pensacola during the Second Spanish Period," p. 303.

46. The map drawn by Dan Geary for the years 1802–13 has not been used. Some of the property owners listed are not those given in the *ASP* records. About Judson's warehouse, see *ASP* 3, no. 234:32 (December 22, 1815–May 26, 1824).

47. Parkhurst, "Don Pedro Favrot," p. 699; I have quoted from General Louis Milfort, *Mémoire; ou, Coup-d'Oeil Rapide Sur Mes Différents Voyages et Mon Séjour Dans la Nation Creek* (Paris, 1802); Levi Lengel Leland, "Keeper of the Peace in the West Florida Controversy: Harry Toulmin, 1805–1813" (master's thesis, Duke University, 1962), pp. 17–18; *American Gazette* (London), 1798 (clipping in the private collection of Mrs. Sydney Smith, Mobile); Thomas Hutchins, *An Historical Narrative and Topographical Description of Louisiana and West Florida, 1784*, Floridiana Facsimile and Reprint Series (1784; reprint, Gainesville: University of Florida Press, 1968), pp. 69–70; Ephraim Kirby, "Letter to the President, May 1, 1804," in *MTP*:325. Misc. Bk. E, p. 467 (letter from Josiah Blakeley to his niece, 1812).

48. Herbert J. Doherty, Jr., "Ante-Bellum Pensacola, 1821–1863," *FHQ* 37, nos. 3 and 4 (January–April 1959), p. 340. McAlister, "Pensacola during the Second Spanish Period," in the same issue of *FHQ*, pp. 281–327, has several drawings of early Spanish houses. The one illustrated on p. 326 has an elevation

49. Map of proposed plan for Mobile: "Plano de la Nueva Movila," Archives General de Indies, Seville. There is a copy of this map in the Mobile City Planning Commission files.

50. The volumes of *ASP* have pages of property confirmations made when the Americans took over the territory. In 1807 the Kennedys were living in their home on a lot near the Fort. Lewis Judson had his home by 1812. Other individuals are listed as having established their homes during the Spanish period.

   like that of the Old Spanish Jail in the Doherty article. It has two stories, with an overhanging full-width, five-bay balcony made of wood. It also appears to have wood siding.

2. Americans Begin Building, 1813–1830

1. *The American Heritage Pictorial Atlas of United States History*, ed. Hilde Heum Kagan (New York: American Heritage, 1966), p. 76; Alexander B. Meek, *Romantic Passages in Southwestern History* (1857; reprint, Spartanburg: Reprint, 1975), p. 51.

2. Judge Harry Toulmin, *Digest of the Laws of Alabama*, comp. John G. Aiken (Cahawba, N.Y.: Ginn and Curtis, 1823), p. 781 (December 1, 1814). A second boundary determination appears on p. 784 (December 17, 1819): "Commencing at Choctaw Point, and running in a straight direction to the western banks of the Bayou Chotage, at a point lying two hundred yards above the place on said island called the Portage; thence down the western bank of said Bayou to its mouth, thence in a straight line to the west bank of the island in front of Mobile; thence along the margin of said island to the south point of said island, and thence in a straight line to the place of the beginning" (see appendix 4).

3. Hamilton, *Colonial Mobile*, p. 445. The wharf was built by James Wilson and was described as twenty-five feet wide, with wings at the water's edge, extending to a depth of nine feet in the river. Also see *CD* 1844. The historical section includes on p. lvii a table describing the cotton trade of the early years.

4. Hamilton, *Colonial Mobile*, p. 471; Toulmin, *Laws of Alabama*, pp. 73, 404, 74, 75.

5. Hamilton, *Colonial Mobile*, p. 444 (quoted); *ASP* 3, no. 322: 398 (December 22, 1815–May 26, 1824).

6. Misc. Bk. A, pp. 13–14. Misc. Bk. A has several contracts that shed light on the building practices of the times. See the record (p. 10) of a building by S. H. Garrow, located on Water Street, dated April 17, 1819, and "not to exceed $1500.00." Another (p. 17, dated January 18, 1817) describes a store built on Royal Street that measured thirty feet by thirty feet, was two stories high, and was "weatherboarded without and ceiled or plastered within."

7. Misc. Bk. A, pp. 136–37, dated March 30, 1824. The Hale building, built by Ward and Starke, called for lathed and plastered walls. This is the first such detail to have been noted in the contracts.

8. Misc. Bk. A, p. 17; contract dated January 18, 1817, signed by James Innerarity, John Johnson, and John Conolly. The 30-foot-wide building filled the width of the lot, 30 feet by 120 feet deep, the lot size noted in *ASP* 3:398. The business lots in the inner city were all narrow. Frontage ranged from 22 feet to about 30 feet, with 27 feet the average. Lot depths ranged from 80 feet to 126 feet. All are noted in *ASP* 3.

9. Toulmin, *Laws of Alabama*, pp. 109–10. The act was to "fix the permanent Seat of Justice for the County of Mobile in the town of Mobile and to authorize the erection of a Court House and Jail." The same act appointed commissioners to locate and construct the buildings.

10. Ibid., pp. 45–62. The Banking Act set the rules for governing the bank, the limits on capital, requirements regarding the Board of Directors and stockholders, and so forth.

11. *ASP* 3:398.

12. Misc. Bk. A, p. 51 (May 21, 1817). Volume A has many other rental-of-land contracts for construction purposes.

13. Toulmin, *Laws of Alabama*: "Sec. 1, an Act by the Senate and House of Representatives of the State of Alabama for the incorporation of the City of Mobile, with a Mayor and Board of Aldermen" (p. 784; December 17, 1819). The law also sets forth the responsibilities of the officials.

14. *MCR*, February 7, 1822, p. 5 ("Mobile").

15. Ibid., p. 3 ("Mobile").

16. Ibid. Toulmin, *Laws of Alabama*, pp. 791, 422, 441. *MCR*, November 28, 1822, lists the road expenditures for both 1820 and 1821; Toulmin, *Laws of Alabama*, pp. 422, 441. MAM, 1824–29, have many records of street development, such as grading, ditching, infilling, and even bridges to cross drainage canals.

17. The legislative act of 1818 decreed that the Fort should be demolished, but demolition was not carried out until the early years of the 1820s. *MCR*, February 7, 1822, notes: "The Fort, situated a little south of the center of the city was built something more than one hundred years ago. It was a work of immense labor, ably planned and well constructed, and if it did not obstruct our most interesting views, occupying some of the most healthy and eligible ground, and was not required to fill up the low and disagreeable places, we would be sorry to see this venerable monument to ingenuity, industry and expense (as is now the case) demolishing" (p. 3).

18. Toulmin, *Laws of Alabama*, p. 792.

19. There are references to establishing drainage canals in MAM, as on March 10, 1825, p. 85. The main canal was in the south part of town and followed what is now Canal Street. It was seven feet wide at the top and eight feet deep to "carry off the vast quantity of water collected."

20. Robert Goodacre, "Report on Mobile," *MCR*, February 19, 1828 (reprinted from the *Nashville Whig and Banner*).

21. *MCR*, December 15, 1828. Report on Resolutions of the Mayor and Board of Selectmen.

22. *MCR*, December 20, 1821 (advertisements for sale).

23. Ibid., January 13, 1823 (advertisements for sale); January 17, 1824 (advertisements for lumber for sale).

24. Various documents spell the name differently, and the handwritten records are often difficult to decipher.

25. Misc. Bk. A, pp. 85–86. John Lepetre and Thomas Townsley were investors from New Orleans, as stated in the slave sale claim with Asher Stone that is recorded in Misc. Bk. B, August 5, 1826, p. 30. Mr. Stone became a partner in 1823.

26. Bernhard, Duke of Saxe-Weimar Eisenach, *Travels through North America, 1825–1826*, vol. 1 (Philadelphia: Carey, Lea and Carey, 1828), p. 40.

27. The *MCR*, March 7, 1822, reports on the fire that started in a shed attached to the new wharves belonging to Holman and Brown. It was stopped by pulling down a house that belonged to Judge Chamberlain. One store that burned had been occupied by five different concerns. The report refers to a previous fire in 1820, when the city had purchased a fire engine at the cost of $461.66 and had built two engine houses for $130. The items listed in the expenses for that year appear in *MCR* for November 28, 1822.

28. Toulmin, *Laws of Alabama*, pp. 46–52.

29. *MCR*, March 20, 1823.

30. *MCR*, November 12, 1828, October 14, 1849.

31. According to the La Tourrette map of 1838, the Court House was located on the southwest corner of Government and Royal streets. The comment appeared in *MCR*, November 12, 1828.

32. I have a list of the 1820 contracts that I found in the Misc. Bks. Photocopies have been made of those for nine stores, both wood and brick, two civic buildings, five wharves, and ten houses, both wood and brick. I have also compiled a list of the builders of the decade. Misc. Bk. B, May 24, 1828, pp. 176–78 (contract between the builders Garrow and Center for Robertson and Barnwall); Misc. Bk. B, January 14, 1828, pp. 130–32 (contract by the builder William L. Little for Robertson and Barnwall).

33. Robert Goodacre, "Report on Mobile," *MCR*, February 19, 1828.

34. Misc. Bk. A, July 16, 1824, pp. 154–58 (contract between the builder John Ward and Philip McLoskey and J. Hogan).

35. Misc. Bk. B, p. 104. The property was described as bounded on the west by Royal and on the north by Dauphin, with sixty-four feet on Royal and sixty feet on Dauphin.

36. Misc. Bk. B, December 1, 1827, pp. 166–68 (contract between a Boston investor, Charles Brown, and his Boston workmen).

37. *MCR*, October 28, 1822.

38. *MCR*, June 1, 1828. MAM for the 1820s include pages of references to agreements for infilling the land along the waterfront.

39. *MCR*, October 29, 1823.

40. Misc. Bk. A, June 27, 1825, p. 245. In Toulmin's *Laws of Alabama*, p. 869, is recorded the act of December 23, 1822, for the establishment of a Board of Wardens for the Port of Mobile, to consist of "five discreet persons, one as harbour master," to keep accounts, to have the right of granting licenses to pilots and deputy pilots, to regulate and station all ships, to control the movement of ships, and to inspect the hatches and damaged goods. The same source, for December 31, 1822, p. 868, indicates that the official regulatory weight scale for selling and purchasing cotton and other merchandise was established. In MAM, 1824–29, there are many references to the release of land for wharves and to laws for controlling their length. Regarding the warehouses and stores, see *MCR*, December 27, 1821, and *MCR*, November 12, 1823. Also see Misc. Bk. A, June 30, 1825, pp. 281–82. There is a contract for a wharf next to Hallett's. It was built by L. B. Butler, a New York investor; see Misc. Bk. A, December 1, 1823.

41. *MCR*, May 2, 1822; also MAM, August 5, 1824, pp. 19, 24, 40; *MCR*, December 2, 1822, and February 24, 1823; Talbot Hamlin, *Greek Revival Architecture* (New York: Dover, 1964), p. 111. The building's attribution to Rogers has been further

documented by the discovery of Isaiah Rogers's diary and by the research of Denys Peter Myers, reviewed in the Columbia University publication *Columbia Library Columns* 16, no. 1 (November 1966), pp. 25–31. Mrs. Harry Toulmin of Daphne, Alabama, has been investigating the history of Mobile's early theater. Her research, when it is finished, will add much to our knowledge of the theater in Mobile. Also see *MCR*, January 24, 1824, which notes the structure's completion.

42. *MCR*, February 3, 1824.
43. Ibid.; *MCR*, February 27, 1823.
44. *MCR*, December 24, 1828.
45. Bernhard, Duke of Saxe-Weimar Eisenach, *Travels through North America*, 1:39; *MCR*, November 12, 1828; *MCR*, April 7, 1823.
46. *MCR*, November 22, 1838.
47. Hamilton, *Colonial Mobile*, p. 447; Misc. Bk. A, February 26, 1821, p. 42.
48. Misc. Bk. A, December 1, 1820, p. 55.
49. *MCR*, October 28, 1822.
50. *MCR*, November 12, 1823.
51. The fire and the reopening are recorded in the *MCR* for June 26, 1823, and November 12, 1823.
52. Captain Basil Hall, *Travels in North America in the Years 1827–1828*, vol. 3 (Edinburgh, 1829), pp. 316–17; Caldwell Delaney, *The Story of Mobile* (Mobile: Gill Printing and Stationery, 1962), p. 85. Mr. Delaney states that the Franklin was owned by Mr. White, who brought the building from Cahaba. Also see Mrs. Basil Hall, *The Aristocratic Journey: Letters Written . . .* , ed. Una Pope Hennessy (New York: Putnam, 1931), p. 246.
53. The Tax Record for 1829 states that the owner of the City Hotel was Isaac Meeker and that the building was valued at $20,000.
54. A city market had been in existence for some time prior to the erection of the building on the Haire and Goodwin map. An ordinance passed on January 21, 1822, permitted the Market to be open from daylight to 9:00 A.M., a schedule wisely chosen in the days before refrigeration. The Market was probably the one built on Dauphin Street at the end of the Spanish period.
55. Misc. Bk. A, November 14, 1823, pp. 130–31.
56. *MCR*, February 7, 1822.
57. *MCR*, May 27, 1822 (see appendix 2).
58. Robert Goodacre, "Report," *MCR*, February 19, 1828; *MCR*, May 7, 1823.
59. *MCR*, February 7, 1822. Also in Toulmin's *Laws of Alabama* is recorded an act of November 1821, authorizing the Catholic congregation to sell certain real estate, including "a certain lot of ground situated on the east side of Royal—on which the Church or Chapel—was long since erected and which is now in a state of complete dilapidation, the proceeds arising from the said sale to be applied to the suitable erection or construction of a new Church or Chapel on another lot" (p. 560). Bernhard, Duke of Saxe-Weimar Eisenach, *Travels through North America*, pp. 39–40.
60. Misc. Bk. B, December 28, 1826, pp. 212, 214; it was "bounded

on the north by Dauphin for 426 feet; on the west by Franklin, 200 feet; on the south by Conti, 400 feet; on the east by the ground belonging to Jack Chighizola 200 feet. A second lot separate from the above by Conti Street bounded on the north by Conti Street, 400 feet; west by Franklin, 100 feet; south by unknown, 400 feet; east also unknown, 100 feet" (p. 213). Also see Oscar Lipscomb, "The Administration of Michael Portier, Vicar Apostolic of Alabama and the Floridas, 1825–1829, and the First Bishop of Mobile, 1829–1859" (Ph.D. diss., American University, 1965, microfilm), p. 118.

61. In the archives of the County Court House is a receipt from 1822–23 stating that $375 (minus an unexplained $115) was paid to Catalina Mottus for one and a half years' hire of a house for the use of the county circuit court. *MCR*, February 7, 1822, and April 11, 1822; Misc. Bk. B, August 30, 1825, pp. 42–44 (contract between the county government and Peter Hobart and Lewis Judson).

62. There has been confusion about the location of the first County Court House, but there is no reason to doubt the accuracy of the La Tourrette map, which shows the Court House on the southwest corner of Royal and Government. The building designed by Hobart was the Court House until it burned early in the 1850s and must therefore have been the building that appeared on the La Tourrette map.

63. *MCR*, February 2, 1822, and December 12, 1822. Receipts in the records of Mobile County include the following items: January 20, 1824, payment to Goodwin, surveyor for two lots for the jail; February 17, 1824, to H. Chamberlain, laying the foundation, $1,000; August 20, 1824, to Peter Brown, window irons, $6.48; to John Ward, installing the irons in three cells, $92; to H. Chamberlain construction (January 1825), $1,426; and on January 1, 1826, final payment to Chamberlain for $2,166. Also see *MCR*, November 12, 1828.

64. Police Records of the Night Patrol, 1822–1827, November 1, 1821. City Archives, number 33-3-2-1, and night of November 24.

65. MAM, January 13, 1825. The La Tourrette map shows the Powder Magazine behind the City Hospital. There are various references to the Powder Magazine in MAM, pp. 64, 67, 68; MAM, February 5, 1825, pp. 72–73, and April 28, 1825, p. 97.

66. Duke of Saxe-Weimar, *Travels through North America*, p. 39.

67. Misc. Bk. A, p. 49, August 4, 1821 (contract between Ezekias Souther and Ada Forrest and the owners, J. Wilkins and P. Paul); Goodacre, "Report on Mobile"; Misc. Bk. A, March 31, 1824, pp. 136–37 (contract between builders John Ward and Turner Stark and the owner, William Hale); Misc. Bk. B, April 19, 1827, p. 76 (contract between the builder Thomas Negus and the owner, Henry Ellis). According to one theory, the central hall evolved from the dogtrot of the pioneering cabin. This type of dwelling occurred much farther north than the Gulf Coast and did not penetrate below the thirty-first parallel until the middle or late nineteenth century. In Mobile, the hall arrived with the emigrants who were familiar with it from the Georgian and Federal homes of the Atlantic states. Also see Misc. Bk. A, May 23, 1825, pp. 229–30 (contract between the builder George Hilliard and the trustees of the Catholic Diocese).

68. Misc. Bk. B, July 1, 1829, pp. 375–76 (contract between William Moore and the owner, Charles Batre); Misc. Bk. A, March 31, 1824, pp. 136–37 (see note 67); Misc. Bk. B, July 1, 1829, pp. 375–76. The contract for the Batre House specified a

69. Misc. Bk. B, January 10, 1828, p. 124. A two-story house built by Amasa Turner for Chester Root.

70. Misc. Bk. A, March 31, 1824, pp. 136–37 (the Hale House); Misc. Bk. A, May 23, 1825, pp. 229–30 (cottage for the Catholic Diocese).

71. Misc. Bk. A, May 23, 1825, pp. 229–30; *MCR*, December 30, 1821. Henry Gunnison advertised the paint colors red lead, white (dry and in oil), ochre yellow, Spanish brown, and lamp black. In the March 1824 issue, the colors listed were cream yellow, dutch pink, gold leaf, silver leaf, ivory black, king's yellow, patent yellow, prussian blue, red chalk, white chalk, rose pink, vermillion, terre de sienna, and white lead.

72. Misc. Bk. B, January 10, 1828, pp. 124–26 (contract between builder Amasa Turner and owner Chester Root for a two-story frame building).

73. S. R. Garrow was taxed for a frame house at this location in 1829, and his deed (DB D, p. 305) stipulates a good frame dwelling. But the Tax Records also indicate that his residence was in the country near his brickworks. Like other individuals at the time, he probably had a summer home away from the city and another residence for the winter season. Mr. Garrow was married to Mary Brown, whose family was in Virginia, and the couple came to Mobile from that state.

74. In addition to the contract, the Tax Records of 1829 list two brick homes: one for T. R. Ryder on the southeast corner of Conti and St. Emanuel, valued at $6,000, the other for Nicholas Weeks, on the northeast corner of Royal and Monroe, worth $4,000. Also see Misc. Bk. A, September 9, 1824, pp. 188–89 (contract between the carpenters and builders, Mount and Company, and the owner, Thomas Dailey); Misc. Bk. B, April 11, 1829, pp. 366–67 (contract between the builder William Moore and the owner, Winslow Foster).

75. *MCR*, June 3, 1822.

76. *MCR*, February 7, 1822.

77. Mr. Vincent definitely occupied the building by 1830, as stated in DB I and J, pp. 350–51. But at least a portion of the house was there by 1827, for the newspaper of May 24, 1828, carries a list of delinquent taxes which includes a home for Mr. Vincent located on the north side of Spring Hill, with house and lot valued at $1,000. The 1829 tax value had increased to $7,000, suggesting that the house had been enlarged.

78. *MCR*, March 29, 1836, carried an advertisement for the sale of the Vincent House stating that it contained in the basement a dining room, a bedroom, a wine cellar, and a pantry and, in the upper story, three bedrooms and parlor, with additional outbuildings.

79. The Vincent House is included in the City Planning Commission's *Nineteenth Century Mobile Architecture: An Inventory of Existing Buildings* (Mobile: City of Mobile, 1974), no. 130. The date given in this publication is 1830, but with the discovery of the delinquent tax records, an earlier date can be ascribed.

80. The number of acres in an arpent varies: 1 arpent ordonnance equals 1.28 acres; 1 arpent common equals 1.04 acres; 1 arpent de Paris (used in Canada) equals 0.84 acres. *ASP* 5:130 (November 7, 1733). Deeds trace the change of ownership, with J. Chastang and B. Laurendine owning 12,145+ acres in

	1807. David Juzan and his wife, Louise Laurendine, acquired 1,930 acres of the original tract, which in turn became the property of Theophilus Toulmin and his wife, Amante Juzan, in 1828. Family tradition records that the first three children were born in a log house.
81.	The university commissioned a monograph on the house at the time it was moved. The book traces the history of the house and reproduces thirty-one matching photographs taken before and after restoration, showing the frame floor and the rebuilding of the brick foundation. A copy of the monograph is kept in the house.
82.	*MCR*, August 29, 1822, and June 29, 1824; *ASP* 4:335–36 (January 23, 1826). This was the second letter to make the request. The first, dated November 29, 1825, appears in *ASP* 4:336.
83.	The deed of July 6, 1832, made when John Elliott sold a strip from lot 42 to Jack Ross, mentions a "homestead" (DB P, p. 67). While the Tax Records do not refer to a dwelling, they do show a great increase in value between May 8, 1828 ($75; DB I and J, p. 429), and February 2, 1831, when Elliott bought from Center ($450; DB I and J, p. 450).

3. The Coming of the Greek Revival, 1830–1840

1.	A prostyle plan places the columns across the front of the building. A distyle-in-antis design has two columns between the extended side walls that are terminated in pilasters. See Stuart and Revett, *Antiquities of Athens* (London: J. Haberkorn, 1762–1816), supp. vol. (London: J. Haberkorn, 1830).
2.	Hamilton, *Colonial Mobile*, p. 253. The English purchased the hospital on September 10, 1769, for 186 pounds, 13 shillings. Information on the Mount and Tatum hospital appears in MAM, 1824–25, pp. 40, 60, 72.
3.	MAM, 1833–34, April 17, 1833, p. 88; May 8, 1833, p. 94; August 28, 1833, p. 117; September 6, 1833, p. 118; and see reports all through 1834–35.
4.	Treasurer's Day Book, August 29, 1833, bk. 1, p. 12, to September 18, 1835, p. 85, and February 1836, p. 98.
5.	The original main entrance has been replaced by an aluminum door. A torus-scotia molding is one formed by a sequence of convex and concave profiles.
6.	The exact date when the bays were added has not been documented. Further description of the building and its history can be found in MPL(SC) in "Mobile Old City Hospital," a term paper prepared by Gabriel Riesco in May 1973, while he was a student at the University of South Alabama. The 1974–75 exterior restoration and interior renovation were done by the firm of Grider and Laraway.
7.	The Town and Davis partnership, which began in 1829, had a profound effect on the development of Greek Revival and Gothic Revival architecture. The two men also established the style of state capitols still standing in many of the states east of the Mississippi. Minard Lafever was a skilled draftsman as well as an architect and did much to spread the knowledge of the nineteenth-century revivals by writing books for carpenters and builders. Regarding Charles Dakin, see Arthur Scully, Jr., *James Dakin, Architect: His Career in New York and the South* (Baton Rouge: Louisiana State University Press, 1973), p. 51.
8.	James Gallier, *Autobiography* (Paris: E. Briere, 1864), p. 21.

Gallier's Barton and the St. Charles Hotel in New Orleans both follow the same design.

9. *CD* 1839, p. xii, gives the following population counts: Mobile City, 13,621; whites, 8,594, slaves 4,470, free people of color, 557; county population including the city, 18,336; whites, 11,142; slaves, 6,474; free people of color, 720. Regarding the 1830 purchase, see Thomas N. Lane to the Board of School Commissioners, cost of purchase, $2,750. The quoted statement appears in Minutes of the Board of Education, vol. 1 (1836–45), p. 1. Also see ibid., p. 24.

10. The name Henry Hitchcock appears throughout the first third of the decade. Hitchcock was the grandson of Ethan Allen and came from Vermont to Mobile during its early formative years. He became a prominent figure in both the political and the commercial development of the area, serving as secretary of the Alabama Territory and then as the first attorney general of the state. He was a highly successful businessman and became one of the first millionaires in the area, using his great wealth generously in the interests of the city of Mobile. During the 1837 panic, he lost everything. He died during the 1839 epidemic before he could recoup his fortune. Also see Gallier, *Autobiography*, p. 21. By 1836, Charles B. Dakin and James, his brother, had established their Mobile office. Dakin is mentioned repeatedly in the Minutes of the Board of Education, vol. 1; for payments to him as architect, see pp. 6, 23, 28, 32, 35, etc. Apart from pay for "Mr. Dakin, architect," payment was made to Thomas James and John Burden for work done on the building. Throughout the days of construction, payments to James and Burden are noted. The last payment to the Dakin brothers was made January 6, 1838 (p. 35).

11. Minutes of the Board of Education, vol. 1, p. 4. On August 23, 1836, Commissioner Richard Redwood moved that authorization be granted to solicit bids for the erection of the cupola (July 20, 1837, p. 27); the authorization was given for covering the dome with lead, copper, or zinc.

12. Ibid., November 9, 1836, p. 10; the old wood schoolhouse on the lot was sold for $630.18. I quote from ibid., introduction, vol. 1, p. 1.

13. Ibid., May 3, 1837. Redwood signed a contract for a fence, to cost $4,000 (p. 25). On October 18, 1837 (p. 34), Thomas Magraw was paid $1,915 in cash and $3,320 in notes for an "iron fence."

14. Ibid., vol. 1, p. 39; vol. 2, p. 82; ibid., vol. 1, October 31, 1838, p. 41 (each organization was to pay a monthly fee of $25); ibid., vol. 1, November 4, 1840, p. 69; ibid., vol. 2, June 17, 1845, p. 3; the school was leased on a yearly basis. On July 15, 1848 (p. 24), the building was rented to Mr. Merrill for $700. A lodging on the third story was allowed but no cooking (p. 32). See ibid., vol. 2, November 5, 1851, p. 74; ibid., vol. 2, September 21, 1852, p. 100. The fees were nominal: $0.50 a week for primary students, $1.50 for grammar students, and $2.50 for high school students. It was stipulated that, as soon as finances permitted, all fees would be eliminated. Also see Bama Watson, "History of Barton Academy" (master's thesis, University of Alabama, 1949); and Minutes of the Board of Education, February 9, 1909 (volume for November 9, 1904–August 31, 1909), pp. 178–79. Information on the restoration of Barton may be obtained from Nicholas Holmes, fellow of the American Institute of Architects.

15. The Ionic order is characterized by a capital with volutes located on the sides of the carved echinus. Enriched moldings

embellish the cornice. Unlike columns of the Doric order, Ionic columns stand upon a base. Ionic columns are also taller and more slender in proportions. Also see Asher Benjamin, *The Builder's Guide* (Boston: Perkins and Marvin, 1850), plate 59.

16. Arthur Scully, *James Dakin*, p. 71. There has been a tendency in Mobile to describe as Egyptian style all doors that have crossettes at the sides of the architrave and slightly battered jambs, without considering the fact that the Greek door had these characteristics. Apart from the crossettes, the architraves are also often slightly pedimented, and none has the typical Egyptian cavetto cornice; see *New Orleans Architecture*, vol. 2: *The American Sector, Essays by Samuel Wilson, Jr., and Bernard Lemann*, ed. Mary Louise Christovich, Roulhac Toledano, Betsy Swanson, and Pat Holden (Gretna, La.: Pelican, 1972), p. 95. In the inventory the authors discussed the Greek Revival door with the crossettes and named it a Greek key door, a term that I have adopted.

17. Misc. Bk. B, March 18, 1829, p. 369. The contract was signed by J. B. Warren and Moses Wickmire. James R. Burgett's *Presbyterianism in Mobile* (Mobile: Henry Farrow, 1881) states, "The frame building was erected on a brick basement and was dedicated in May, 1829" (pp. 7–12). Also see Scully, *James Dakin*, p. 71.

18. Misc. Bk. C, August 6, 1838, pp. 166–73 (contract between the Christ Episcopal Church, the architect Cary Butt, and builder James Barnes, with specifications). On Scully's argument for Dakin as designer, see *James Dakin*, pp. 80–81; no known records verify this attribution, but information in Dakin's account book indicates that the two men had a professional relationship. Just as Dakin had learned from Town and Davis, Butt had undoubtedly learned from Dakin. Should we credit the teacher or the pupil? The contract lists Cary Butt as architect, but in the minutes of the Church, April 20, 1840, payment to Cary Butt, architect, and to Frederick Bunnell for plans is recorded. Bunnell seems to have been the actual designer. H. B. Witherell, *The Structural History of Christ Church* (Mobile: Christ Church, 1937). The drawings were done by H. B. Witherell for HABS.

19. The minutes of the board repeatedly record repairs to the steeple. Witherell, *Structural History*, p. 4. The stuccoing was finished in June 1852, at a cost of $1,444. Misc. Bk. C, pp. 166–73; the new bank mentioned in the Christ Church contract was the Planters and Merchants Bank designed by Charles Dakin.

20. A contemporary description of the 1839 fire can be found in the *Mercantile Advertiser*, October 9, 1839. See appendix 3. Also see Scully, *James Dakin*, p. 74; Misc. Bk. C, July 14, 1837, p. 103 (quoted). According to the contract, Mr. Barnes was paid $34,649 for his work.

21. Scully, *James Dakin*, p. 74; James Silk Buckingham, *The Slave States of America*, vol. 1, 2d ed. (London: Fisher, 1842), pp. 251–90; MAM, November 26, 1839, p. 127, and October 12, 1839, p. 105; Scully, *James Dakin*, p. 82 (*New Orleans Daily Picayune*, August 16, 1839).

22. Tyrone Power, Esq., *Impressions of America*, vol. 2 (Philadelphia: Carey, Lea, and Blanchard, 1836), p. 123.

23. Scully, *James Dakin*, p. 79.

24. In spite of the disasters at the end of the decade, the population increased from 3,134 in 1830 to 18,336 in 1839. *CD*

25. Misc. Bk. B, June 22, 1831, pp. 475–76 (contract with plan and specifications). John K. Collins built Charles Barney a three-story brick structure for $14,869.

26. Thomas Ellison was the architect of the Second American Theatre in Mobile. He was also awarded the contract for a city hall in August of 1835 when the Gallier-Dakin plan did not materialize. Misc. Bk. B, July 11, 1832, pp. 531–33. The contract was between the owners, John Hogan and Philip McLoskey, and the builders Thomas Ellison and William Littell.

27. This type of window is commonly known as a slide-by.

28. Misc. Bk. B, June 29, 1831, pp. 471–73 (store for Bartolomé Lopez built by Joseph Brooks).

29. Misc. Bk. C, August 15, 1838, pp. 176–77 (contract regarding store for Isaac Spear, built by James Barnes).

30. CD 1859, p. 47, lists the fire companies as they developed.

31. MAM, May 14, 1839, p. 26. The city paid Richard Redwood $1,980 for building an engine house. Also see ibid., April 9, 1831, p. 248, and ibid., October 12, 1839, p. 105.

32. Ibid., in 1833 over a period of time, pp. 133, 160–64, 170–71, 177. Also see the La Tourrette map; check blocks 48b, 92a, and 130b and engine houses on 92b and 130d.

33. Misc. Bk. C, May 18, 1839, pp. 325–26 (contract for a mill for the owner, Adam Hollinger, built by Ellis Drake and William Woodward). Other mills recorded in the archives include the Union Steam Press, valued at $150,000, and the large Hitchcock Press in block 86 of the La Tourrette map.

34. Two separate financial arrangements were made in order to obtain funds. In May 1834, MAM record that the city borrowed $50,000 from the Phoenix Bank of New York, issuing fifty bonds worth $1,000 each. In July 1836 it borrowed an additional $190,000, with 190 bonds valued at $1,000 each for the purpose of buying the square of land. The lots were subsequently purchased over the years from 1834 to 1849 and are recorded in DB N, pp. 84–85; DB N, pp. 329–30; DB P, pp. 100–1; DB Q, pp. 352–53; DB Q, p. 603; DB S, pp. 24–25; DB S, pp. 34–35; DB S, pp. 35–36; DB 4 o.s., pp. 223–24; DB 5 o.s., pp. 97–98; DB 1 n.s., pp. 93–95, and DB 1 n.s., pp. 91–93; Mobile Treasurer's Day Book, March 13, 1835, p. 59. "Longheus" may have been "Longhers"; the writing is difficult to decipher. Gallier, *Autobiography*, p. 21.

35. MCR, August 28, 1835; The Troost map, vol. 4, ward 4, p. 4. In the archives of the Mobile Engineers' Office at City Hall is an index of properties owned by the city. P. 148 has a brief description in block 92 of the old Price tract, on the east side of St. Emanuel and south of Conti, where the Police Station, the city Court House, the City Jail, the Police Patrol Station, and the Board of Health were located.

36. MAM, May 17, 1829, p. 32, June 17, 1829, p. 35, and September 25, 1833, p. 123. On the same day the committee was ordered to sign a contract with J. Turner for the erection of the cupola and clock not to exceed $1,050. Some years earlier, a clock tower had been planned for the top of the Customs House but had been deemed too expensive (MAM, April 23, 1831, p. 257). Also see ibid., April 1, 1839, p. 1, and ibid., June 15, 1839, p. 157. The minutes state that Mr. Bloodgood was paid $4,148 for the work, with a balance due of $2,231.03. Iron

doors for the Guard House were ordered from I. D. Spear and Company.

37. The Delage map, DB T, p. 302. The location of the Prison is further documented by the Troost map, 1840–46, vol. 7, p. 41, and by the Robertson map of 1853. *CD* for 1844 locates the Prison on the corner of Jefferson and Congress streets. The 1891 "Bird's Eye View of Mobile" shows the Jail as having two wings in addition to the central block. DB T, November 18, 1837, p. 302, records the purchase of the land from Joshua Kennedy for $11,185.50. The property consisted of 215 feet 4 inches on Jefferson, west along the Hospital lot for 221 feet 8 inches, to Broad and thence north for 215 feet 4 inches to Congress, and thence east along Congress for 221 feet 8 inches. Misc. Bk. C, August 28, 1839, pp. 379–87; specifications are detailed. The granite used for the building has been preserved in a house in the western part of the city. It is made of black hornblend, quartz, and white feldspar. The granite contained no pink particles, so the color appeared to be a soft gray. Its source was not mentioned in the contract (see figure 239 in appendix 5).

38. Misc. Bk. C, pp. 142–43 (contract for brick fence to be built by John Williams and James Murphy for Mobile County).

39. All the maps (see n. 36) locate the Jail correctly. The Diard map is incorrect in showing the Jail on the former site of the Powder Magazine. MAM, November 23, 1833, p. 135.

40. Misc. Bk. C, August 23, 1837, pp. 5–6 (specs; cost, $2,100).

41. I have selected six contracts from Misc. Bk. C for the purpose of summarizing the characteristics of the cottages. They appear on pp. 86–87, 159–62, 165–66, 182–83, 184–85. Misc. Bk. C, June 16, 1838, pp. 165–66 (specs; cost, $2,100) (see appendix 5).

42. Ibid., April 6, 1838, pp. 86–87 (specs; $650).

43. The HABS drawings and photographs were made in 1935. The house had been adapted to accommodate a small private school run by Mrs. Katherine Ayers Robert, and the building was long known as Madame Robert's School.

44. The Pascal Larrouil cottage was photographed in 1963.

45. Research on Carpenter locks was done by Mr. Carter Smith of Mobile, who corresponded with Josiah Parkes and Company, Ltd., in England. The original letters are in the private collection of Mrs. Carter Smith, Mobile. Information appeared in the *Ironmonger* and is included in the correspondence in the Carter Smith research.

46. In 1840, Bishop Portier wrote a letter to the Vatican, saying it was time that he "fixed" his stay in Mobile. In Archbishop Lipscomb's "The Administration of Michael Portier," p. 161, Portier is quoted: "The Episcopal house which is composed of ten rooms cost me—$7000.00." Before 1834, Bishop Portier had lived in a two-room cottage adjacent to the Cathedral.

47. Contract for the Hamilton House, Misc. Bk. C, February 11, 1839, pp. 279–83. Three builders' names appeared on the original contract—Charles Shaw, Joseph Vaughan, and Benjamin White—but Shaw and White withdrew with a memorandum signed between Hamilton and Vaughan. The contract has specs; cost was $6,760.00. Also see the contract for Benjamin Dorman, Misc. Bk. C, June 9, 1838, pp. 132–33. Builders were Nodine and Walker. The contract has the builders' plan; cost was $6,500.

48. The structural elements are specified in the contract. The forty supporting piers of brick were five feet high and stood on

cypress planks. All framing members were cypress, as were the weatherboarding and the roof shingles. The measurements for all structural members were itemized.

49. Charles Torrey of Fairhope, Alabama, is a descendant of Judge Torrey, who had a winter and summer home. Charles has several letters describing the journeys made between the two residences during the 1850s. The founding of Widows' Row is described in a history of the Episcopal Church of St. John written for the church in 1960 by Lucy Nelson (copy in church archives).

50. Misc. Bk. C, March 26, 1840, pp. 471–73. Cost was $4,000.

51. Misc. Bk. C, April 16, 1839, p. 359 (Thomas James for L. Brown), and Misc. Bk. C, January 3, 1838, p. 48 (Thomas James for Walker and Nodine).

52. There is still a question about the Ottenstein ownership. The Troost map, 1840–48, shows the corner as Ottenstein property, but the city directories do not list an Ottenstein until the late 1860s, and a Nathan Ottenstein appears in 1870. In 1863 the chain of title lists an Ottenstein for the first time.

53. The Sanborn map of 1880 shows the house as having two stories. The 1885 Sanborn map has two and one-half stories. The 1880 map could be in error, or the dormers may have been added between the two dates.

54. Frances Beverly was employed by the Federal Works Project in 1938 to do some research on Mobile history. She wrote an account of Widows' Row with oral recollections as well as written accounts. Her article is in MPL(SC); unfortunately she did not record her sources.

55. The following are some of the street improvements: MAM, March 31, 1830: "extension of Conception Street from Monroe to Choctaw Point" (pp. 79–80); MAM, March 12, 1831: "to the platting and streets of Orange Grove Tract" (p. 221); MAM. July 3, 1833: "recommended that Dauphin Street be extended westwardly to the City limits agreeable to the diagram of James Dowell, commencing at Bayou" (p. 107). Old Shell, then known as Isabel Street, did not extend beyond Stickney's Hollow, at about Monterey Place. Also see Misc. Bk. C, January 1, 1838, pp. 56–57 (plan and some specs). The two-story frame house was built on Spring Hill Road and includes a front and rear "piazza" at a cost of $2,500.

56. Misc. Bk. C, March 20, 1840, pp. 470–72 (with specs). Though this cottage was built in the first year of the next decade, in style it belongs to the 1830s. It was two-story frame structure on Spring Hill Road, three and one-half miles west of the city limits. The front gallery was two stories, the rear, one story with end rooms. The cost was $3,000. Also see ibid., September 21, 1831, p. 8 (a country home three and one-half miles from the city: a one-story frame structure with hall plan); ibid., June 7, 1839, pp. 311–13; house out Dauphin Road. The book includes specs and plan; the cost was $3,350.

57. DB Z, June 14, 1839, p. 209 (map of the Collins property, in which ten parcels of ten acres each were platted). On lot 3 the Collins-Marston-Robinson cottage was built. The original land grant was made in 1833. Charlotte Robinson, the present owner, has the enlargement contract in her possession.

58. Mrs. Vernon White, a descendant of the John O'Donnell family, has an early painting of the house.

59. A history of Oakleigh has been written by Lucy Nelson and can be obtained from the office of HMPS. I also obtained information during an interview with Herbert Cole, who was

born in the house and whose family owned the property until 1927; with Mrs. Dan McCall, who was a frequent visitor to the house during the Cole ownership; and with Mrs. Alfred Dennison Staples. The Dennison family owned the property from 1827 to 1945 (personal communication, April 1979).

60. The Post Road to New Orleans was advertised in *MCR*, December 23, 1831, to encourage emigration to the Spring Hill area. It also facilitated the journey to Spring Hill College. The history of Spring Hill College has been carefully traced in several publications. See Lipscomb's "Administration of Michael Portier"; Father Michael Kenny, S.J., *The Torch on the Hill* (New York: American Press, 1931); *Spring Hill College, 1830–1905* (Mobile: Commercial Printing, 1906); and Frances Sheffield, "The Development of Education in Mobile prior to 1860" (master's thesis, University of Alabama, 1935).

4. Architecture in Transition, 1840–1850

1. MCC, August 9, 1848, p. 369, and August 18, 1848, p. 371. For information about the 1840s I used three minute books: MAM, 1839–42, MAM, 1843–47, and MCC, 1844–49. Some of the meetings recorded in the Minutes of the Common Council included meetings with the mayor and Board of Aldermen. MAM, October 19, 1841, p. 180; contract signed November 23, 1841, p. 184 (quoted); January 18, 1842, p. 192 reported the building nearly finished; MCC, March 22, 1848, p. 323.

2. MAM, September 28, 1841, p. 173.

3. MAM, March 17, 1840 (unpaginated), and June 15, 1841, p. 157; also May 4, 1842, p. 221; May 23, 1843, p. 545, and June 20, 1843.

4. Ibid., April 25, 1845, p. 186. The Troost map was authorized by the Board of Aldermen. On January 26, 1846 (see p. 268), Troost asked for a review of his work and a monthly stipend so that he could finish the task. On April 15, 1848 (MCC, p. 330), he again asked for a review. On May 4, 1848, p. 339, the volumes of maps were declared completed, and he was paid an additional $200. *MCR*, April 4, 1839, no. 209; U.S. Treasury Department, *History of Public Buildings under Control of the Treasury Department*, comp. W. H. Hills and J. A. Sutherland (Washington, D.C., 1901); Marine Hospitals, Outgoing Letters, Set M, no. 1, April 8, 1833, to May 30, 1848; Marine Hospitals, Incoming Letters, Set M, 1837 to 1839 and 1839 to 1840; *MCR*, April 4, 1839, no. 209.

5. Charles A. Harrington, 1972 Summer Project Report, Report ALA/781, HABS, p. 2 (August 8, 1972).

6. MCC, April 5, 1848, p. 328. The gutters were made of flat stones or bricks. The ditch was sixteen inches wide at the bottom, and the outer edges were rounded out so that they were about three feet apart. At the street intersection the gutters were covered with planks placed over iron bars. MAM, June 22, 1841, p. 160; MCC, March 9, 1847, p. 210; MCC, May 3, 1848, p. 339; MAM, June 21, 1842, p. 240; MCC, February 16, 1848, pp. 306–7; Misc. Bk. D, November 12, 1840, pp. 192–95 (contract for the Stein Water Works).

7. MAM, December 13, 1843. The office of superintendent of chimney sweeps had been established in 1827.

8. MCC, November 17, 1848, pp. 392–93.

9. Misc. Bk. D, January 24, 1844, pp. 481–82; James Deas, mason, for R. D. James, executor for the Erwin estate. Plan and specs are shown; the cost was $1,000.

10. Ibid., March 3, 1841, pp. 173–74; J. F. Hutchisson, builder, for

A. Dumée, two stores and a dwelling with a passageway. Specs are included. The cost was $6,000. Ibid., February 20, 1841, pp. 153–54; J. F. Hutchisson for Burns and Riley. Specs are included. The cost was $5,000. Misc. Bk. D. July 8, 1842, pp. 352–55; Robert Walker, builder, for Bartolomeo Lopez. Specs are included. The cost was $4,300.

11. Ibid., April 18, 1840, pp. 12–14; William Smith, builder, following the plans of Neville and Silver, for John Lyons. The contract includes specs. The cost was $2,300.

12. Ibid., April 30, 1840, pp. 18–20; John Collins, builder, for George Davis. Specs are included. The cost was $2,300. Ibid., April 18, 1840, pp. 12–14; see n. 11.

13. A common bond has one row of headers between five to seven rows of stretchers.

14. See n. 12.

15. Misc. Bk. D, May 25, 1840, pp. 58–61; F. Bunnell, architect, and J. Collins, builder, for A. Payan. Specs are included. The cost was $8,108. Ibid., July 8, 1842, pp. 352–55; Robert Walker, builder, for B. Lopez. Specs are included. The cost was $4,300.

16. Ibid., May 25, 1840; see n. 15.

17. Contracts for wharves show little change in construction methods from the previous decade. The main difference was that in the 1840s wharves were larger. Misc. Bk. D, November 27, 1845, pp. 577–78, has a contract calling for a wharf 350 feet long and 100 feet wide, with specs, at a cost of $1,500. I have copies of the contracts for warehouses. Misc. Bk. D, February 29, 1842, pp. 304–6; James Deas, builder, for William Sayre, agent for William Pritchard; the contract has specs, and the cost was $10,093. Ibid., July 19, 1840, pp. 85–86; J. F. Hutchisson, builder, for M. Eslava and A. Dumée. The contract has specs; the cost was $16,250. Misc. Bk. E, July 13, 1847, pp. 190–91; Robert Ellis and Jonathan Kirkbride, builders, for Davis Chandler; the contract covers a warehouse and press, with specs, at a cost of $6,000.

18. *Nineteenth Century Mobile Architecture*, p. 46, illustration 108.

19. Misc. Bk. E, March 27, 1849, pp. 451–52; B. W. Van Epps, builder, for the I. W. Irwin estate; the contract covers a two-story livery stable with specs, at a cost of $2,000.

20. MAM, p. 268.

21. Lipscomb, "Administration of Michael Portier," pp. 159ff.

22. Misc. Bk. D, August 7, 1843, pp. 636–37 (contract between the Cathedral building committee, Bishop Portier, and Claude Beroujon).

23. Lipscomb, "Administration of Michael Portier," pp. 173–74.

24. Ibid., p. 182; the Cathedral committee presented a silver pitcher with an engraving to James F. Hutchisson for his work on the roof and cornice. The pitcher is in the possession of a descendant.

25. Lipscomb, "Administration of Michael Portier," pp. 184–85.

26. *Mobile Daily Herald and Tribune*, August 22, 1849, quoted in Lipscomb, "Administration of Michael Portier," pp. 184–85.

27. Misc. Bk. D, April 13, 1828, recorded February 9, 1843, pp. 321–22. Contract between Bishop Michael Portier and the Benevolent Society, giving them land and the use of buildings for an orphanage. The complex consisted of an old chapel and a three-story frame house "lately finished." Two of the rooms were reserved as vestry rooms.

28. Misc. Bk. D, October 24, 1844, pp. 568–71. I. P. Pond, B. H. Scattergood, and E. W. Irvin, builders for the Second Presbyterian Church. The contract includes specs; the cost was $7,850.

29. The cottage was restored by Nicholas H. Holmes, Jr., fellow of the American Institute of Architects, and is being managed by the Museum Board of the city of Mobile. The house is open to the public.

30. William Charles Macready, *His Reminiscences, Diaries, and Letters*, 2d ed., ed. William Toynbee, vol. 2 (London: Chapman and Hall, 1912), p. 552.

31. In reading the chain of title and the deeds, the sequence of names of the streets can be traced. Summerville was located out Spring Hill Road, in the vicinity of the Convent of Visitation.

32. Misc. Bk. D, July 1, 1843, p. 446 (F. Bunnell, architect, Joseph Silver, builder, for William Scott, at a cost of $4,120).

33. The original configuration can be seen in the Sanborn map of 1880, plate 3. *CD* for 1840 still has no advertisements for decorative cast iron, only for sheet iron. During the decade, decorative iron was imported.

34. Mary Harrison Waring to Stephen Croom, copy on file in the City Planning Commission in the research files for *Nineteenth Century Mobile Architecture*.

35. MCC, April 19, 1848, p. 333; January 27, 1849, pp. 415 and 418.

36. Ibid., July 19, 1848, p. 362, and January 22, 1849, p. 414.

5. The Golden Age, 1850–1860

1. Charles Olliffe, *Scènes Américaines* (Paris: Amyot, 1853), trans. Ernest Falbo and Lawrence Wilson (Painesville, Ohio: Lake Erie College, 1964), 3:29–35.

2. Fredrika Bremer, *The Homes of the New World*, trans. Mary Howitt (New York: Harper, 1854), 2:217.

3. Misc. Bk. F, pp. 71–72; pp. 99–105; April 15, 1853: contract between the county Board of Revenue and James Barnes, by which Barnes was commissioned to construct the new County Court House upon the plans of William S. Alderson at a cost of $70,259 (see appendix 6).

4. Triglyphs are found in the Greek Doric entablature in which a projecting rectangular block of the frieze has vertical grooves. The frieze consists of triglyphs alternating with metopes.

5. MAM, June 11, 1852.

6. DB, 7 n.s., pp. 392–400; DB 202 n.s., p. 352.

7. MAM, February 1, 1855, and December 27, 1855.

8. Ibid., June 1, 1855.

9. Ibid., December 27, 1855; there is recorded a contract signed by James Barnes to finish the building.

10. New York Wire Railing Company, *New Phase of Iron Manufacture* (New York, 1857), chap. 28 (catalogue).

11. Mobile Writers' Workshop, *Historic Churches of Mobile* (Mobile, 1971), pp. 71–77.

12. John Harris and Jill Lever, *Illustrated Glossary of Architecture*, 850–1830 (New York: Potter, 1966), plate 36 (east window of All Saints in Sharrington, Norfolk, England).

13. Architectural drawing in the collection of C. L. Hutchisson, Jr., Mobile, Alabama.

14. There was a small Presbyterian church in Spring Hill about which the Misses Mary and Flora Gaillard, who used to attend it, provided me with information. There are no surviving photographs, and the building was dismantled. The material was reused in a chapel in the Davis Avenue community.

15. The history of Providence Infirmary was described in an undated letter signed by Sister Mary Ellen Sherloch [MPL(SC)].

16. The summary of architectural characteristics was compiled from contracts in the following: Misc. Bk. F, p. 41, December 30, 1852 (northwest corner of Church and Lawrence; Mather Anderson, owner; James F. Hutchisson, builder; cost, $1,500). Misc. Bk. F, pp. 57–58, April 14, 1853 (two-story brick; north side of Dauphin, between Conception and Joachim; P. F. Pepper, owner; A. H. Swasey, builder; cost, $3,100). Misc. Bk. F, pp. 68–69, April 19, 1853 (four-story brick; Royal Street; Mechanics Saving Company, owners; James Barnes, builder; cost: $13,423). Misc. Bk. F, p. 70, April 18, 1853 (three-story brick; southwest corner of Water and Smith Alley; Robert Smith, owner; James Barnes, builder; cost $10,414); Misc. Bk. F, pp. 285–86, May 17, 1855 (three-story brick; northwest corner Dauphin and Water streets; Th. McCoy, owner; James Barnes, builder; cost, $6,235).

17. Misc. Bk. E, pp. 454–55, May 10, 1850 (three-story brick, next to the Mansion House; Charles Cullum, owner; James F. Hutchisson and A. M. Quigley, builders; cost, $2,050).

18. Misc. Bk. G, pp. 97–98, February 7, 1859 (three-story brick store and residence; southwest corner of Dauphin and Claiborne). The structure was built on land rented from Bishop Portier on condition that McGanahan erect a "suitable building" measuring fifty-nine feet by ninety feet, to cost between $7,000 and $10,000. There are other contracts of this rental nature in which the builder had to pay both rent and the costs of construction.

19. Misc. Bk. E, pp. 388–89, June 26, 1849 (a forty-room, two-story addition to the Mansion House; Charles Cullum, owner; James F. Hutchisson, builder; cost, $7,100).

20. Misc. Bk. E, pp. 453–54, May 7, 1850 (second addition to the Mansion House; three-story brick; Charles Cullum, owner; James F. Hutchisson and A. M. Quigley, builders; cost, $5,500).

21. James F. Sulzby, Jr., *Historic Alabama Hotels and Resorts* (University: University of Alabama Press, 1960), pp. 41–48. Also see the *Mobile Press Register*, December 13, 1852.

22. *Mobile Press Register*, September 28, 1852.

23. Joel Lambert, "The Old Battle House" (senior thesis, University of South Alabama, 1970), p. 4. Copy in MPL(SC).

24. Henry F. Withey, *Biographical Dictionary of American Architects, Deceased* (Los Angeles: New Age, 1956), p. 521.

25. Misc. Bk. E, p. 474, May 29, 1850; contract for two frame cottages on Franklin Street; John Carter, owner; J. F. Hutchisson, builder; cost, $1,600.

26. Charlotte Page and Mary Cummings, *Under Sail and in Port in the Glorious 1850s, May 1 to October 3, 1852* (Boston: Peabody Museum, 1950), p. 12.

27. An example of the side-hall plan in a large frame dwelling that once stood on the north side of Government, recorded in Misc. Bk. E, pp. 557–59, October 1, 1851; Francis Palmer, owner; A. Tabor, builder; cost $2,300.

28. Misc. Bk. F, p. 11, 1852 (no month), contract for three two-story kitchen houses on Square 72, Orange Grove; house fifteen feet by thirty feet, with two-story galleries; J. Bloodgood, owner; James F. Hutchisson, builder; cost, $1,800.

29. Misc. Bk. E, p. 577, January 8, 1852; contract for small house; rear of northeast corner of Cedar and St. Michael; Mary Andrews, owner; William Dutton, builder; cost, $900.

30. I do not discuss the origin of the shotgun house in this book, since there is still much disagreement as to its source. It did not become an important element in Mobile architecture until after the Civil War.

6. War and the Changing Order, 1860–1870

1. CCM, bk. 3, pp. 40–41; April 10, 1860 (contract with Charles T. Liernur, civil engineer, for the addition of the east wing of the County Jail).

2. *Illustrations of Iron Architecture Made by the Architectural Iron Works of the City of New York* (New York: Baker and Godwin, 1865), reprinted in *The Origins of Cast Iron Architecture in America: A Catalogue of the Architectural Iron Works of D. D. Badger and Company* (New York: Da Capo Press, 1970).

3. Ira W. Parker is listed in *CD* for 1859 as bookkeeper for the architect Thomas James. By 1861 he owned a building materials and hardware store at 19 South Royal.

4. For other examples, see the City Planning Commission publication, *Nineteenth Century Mobile Architecture*.

5. *MCR*, January 31, 1864; CCM, bk. 3, p. 253, February 2, 1864; *MCR*, February 2, 1842, advertisement for rent of the newly finished Hagan building; CCM, bk. 3, pp. 281–378, June 7, 1864, to April 3, 1866: reports on the repairs on the Hagan building for use as a county court. Bk. 4, pp. 146–76, March to August 16, 1869: reports on the enlargement of the site at the southwest corner of Government and Royal by the purchase of the rear lot, with Cahill employed to clear the land at the site of the burned building and to make improvements on the rented building. (See appendix 6.)

6. William Howard Russell, *My Diary, North and South*. (Boston: T. O. H. P. Burnham, 1863), pp. 89–91.

7. Interview with John Stark, Professor of Chemical Engineering, University of South Alabama, who worked with Dr. Mohr for several years, December 6, 1982.

8. Harris and Lever, *Illustrated Glossary of Architecture*, plate 159; Marcus Whiffen, *American Architecture since 1780* (Cambridge, Mass.: MIT Press, 1969), p. 71; Wayne Andrews, *Architecture, Ambition, and Americans* (London: Free Press of Glencoe, Collier-Macmillan, 1964), p. 142.

9. Misc. Bk. H, pp. 56–57, February 13, 1869 (contract for a wharf built by John King for Edward Townsend, a New York investor; cost, $4,100); *MCR*, May 10, 1866, p. 3.

10. MAM, December 18, 1866.

11. Misc. Bk. H, p. 67, June 23, 1869 (charter for the Magnolia Sugar Refinery); Misc. Bk. H, p. 88, August 11, 1869 (charter for the Mobile Fertilizer Company); Misc. Bk. G, pp. 549–50, September 10, 1866 (contract for the sale of the Skates Iron Foundry to the Mobile Foundry, with a list of all equipment and materials); *CD* 1866.

12. Frank Daugherty, *Azalea City News*, July 30, 1981; *Souvenir History of the Mobile Fire and Police Departments, 1819–1902*

(Mobile: Commercial Printing, 1902). Thomas Price, chief of the Fire Department; C. W. Soost, chief of the Police Department. The other three buildings constructed by the volunteer fire companies are located at 6 St. Joseph, 208 St. Francis, and 7 North Lawrence. The Phoenix Fire Station of 1859 was moved from its original location at 154 South Franklin to 203 South Claiborne, where it has been reconstructed as part of the City Museum complex. Theresa Beyer and Rebecca Zurier, *The American Firehouses: An Architectural and Social History* (New York: Abbeville Press, 1969).

13. Diane S. Woodward, "The Medical College of Alabama" (senior thesis, University of South Alabama, 1976). DB 13, p. 351, May 23, 1859 (contract for the land purchase at $600).

14. Misc. Bk. H, pp. 17–18 (February 5, 1869); *MCR*, March 28, 1890 (spire constructed, $1,000); *MCR*, January 1, 1908 (building stuccoed, facade modified, and a new tower constructed; C. L. Hutchisson, Sr., architect; cost $12,000).

15. Otis D. Crawford, *Mobile Chronicle*, February 4, 1882; "Emerson Institute: Editor's Chronicle," report on the fire and the history of Emerson College, known as the "Blue College" for blacks (courtesy of Mrs. Carter Smith). *Harper's Weekly*, October 3, 1868; drawing of Emerson College building reproduced in the *Mobile Chronicle*, February 4, 1882.

16. *MCR*, trade edition, September 1, 1885, $13,000; Kenny, *The Torch on the Hill*.

17. *MCR*, trade edition, September 1, 1885 (reports the enlargement of the Visitation Convent building and the addition of the three-story veranda; James H. Hutchisson, architect).

7. The End of an Era, 1870–1880

1. Melton McLaurin and Michael Thomason, *Mobile: The Life and Times of a Great Southern City* (Woodland, Calif.: Windsor Books, 1981), pp. 72, 79.

2. Edward King, "Mobile, the Chief City of Alabama," in *The Great South*, ed. W. Macgruder Drake and Robert R. Jones (Baton Rouge: Louisiana State University Press, 1972), pp. 319–28. The material was first published in 1875 under the title *The Southern States of North America*, after a series of articles in *Scribner's Monthly* during 1874. King was the Massachusetts journalist for *Scribner's* and the *New York Times*.

3. CCM, bk. 4, p. 321, September 28, 1872; CCM, bk. 4, pp. 327–45, October 1, 1872 (contract between W. O. Pond, architect, and the County Court House Committee; includes contract with the builder); CCM, bk. 4, pp. 322–27 (contract with the builder, Charles Fricke, and the County Court House Committee). Fricke agreed to finish the construction by October 1, 1873, at a cost of $101,000.

4. Misc. Bk. H, p. 501 (subcontract between Fricke and McDonald, March, and Company to furnish the stone and sculptural work for the County Court House at a cost of $16,850). (See appendix 6).

5. *MCR*, March 25, 1976; CCM, bk. 7, p. 353, January 27, 1888 (report to the council concerning the fire of January 20, 1888).

6. *MCR*, November 29, 1871: an announcement that "the hotel will open at 8 o'clock this evening." In 1840, C. L. Hutchisson, Sr., and C. L. Hutchisson, Jr., were the architects

7.   for the addition of twelve rooms on the western end of the La Clede Hotel and the continuation of the gallery. The drawings for this addition are in the private collection of C. L. Hutchisson, Jr. *MCR*, December 5, 1871: a report on the grand opening of the La Clede Hotel.

7. Misc. Bk. I/J, December 12, 1875, pp. 223–44: the listing of the sale of contents of the La Clede by the owner, Caleb Price, securing his mortgage debt to H. Monroe and Phillipe. Misc. Bk. I/J, January 16, 1877, pp. 365ff. The listing of the sale of the contents of the St. James Hotel by the owners, Van Buren Gunnison and Simon Grey. The St. James was located on the east side of Royal, two doors south of Dauphin, the site of the present Goldstein Jewelers. Misc. Bk. I/J, December 23, 1879, pp. 255–59. John Forsythe, editor of the *Mobile Daily Register*, was forced to secure a loan by putting up as collateral all the equipment in his newspaper business. The list of equipment is instructive regarding the publishing methods of the times. Misc. Bk. I/J, June 17, 1874, p. 14. Henry Nobring gave Frascati a right-of-way through his property to the Bay Shore Rail Road. Misc. Bk. I/J, February 3, 1876, pp. 253–54 (incorporation of the Order of Myths).

8. *MCR*, September 9, 1877. From the 1870s onward, the newspapers occasionally ran a column on new construction. Beginning in the mid-1880s a special edition, the *Trade Journal*, was devoted to city improvement. It was issued on or about September 1.

9. Ibid.; Rudolph Benz is the subject of a master's thesis now being prepared by Rowena Van Hoof for Newcomb-Tulane University. Benz was born in Tubingen, Germany, lived in Stuttgart, and spent some years in Heidelberg. He was a lieutenant in the German army, traveled in Europe, South America, and Asia, and came to the United States in 1870. He worked first in Chicago as a draftsman in an engineering firm, which sent him to Mobile on a geodetic survey in about 1875. He then moved to Mobile, bought out the architectural practice of Mr. Brown, and advertised in the newspaper of 1875. Benz introduced the high Victorian style into Mobile, designing commercial, civic, and residential buildings.

10. *MCR*, September 9, 1877, p. 1.

11. *MCR*, May 26, 1877: an unsigned editorial titled "Impressions of Mobile" described a two-hour walk through the city.

12. Ibid.

13. Frederick J. Vogel, a great grandson, found a contract between Charles Fricke and Henry Bernstein among the family papers. A copy of the contract is in MHDC files. The contract was signed January 16, 1872.

8. *The High Victorian Period, 1880–1900*

1. *MCR*, September 9, 1886; file on hurricanes, MPL(SC); Hodding Carter and Anthony Raguzin, *Gulf Coast Country* (New York: Duell, Sloan and Pearce, 1951), p. 199.

2. McLaurin and Thomason, *Mobile*, p. 93.

3. *MCR*, April 9, 1892, p. 5; *Mobile Weekly Register*, March 25, 1893 (clipping file in the collection of Mrs. Carter Smith).

4. In 1907 a rear addition to the County Court House was added, extending to Church Street on the south, with Benz and Sons as architects. See *MCR*, September 1, 1907. Reports on the fire, with details regarding insurance, temporary location, and new construction plans, appear in CCM, bk. 7, pp. 353–58, 371–74, 382–84, 400, 414, 482, and bk. 9, pp. 63–64, 77, 128,

176–77, 221, 224–25, 255–57. Also see *MCR*, January 21, 1888, p. 4.

5. CCM, bk. 7, pp. 382–84 (contract with Benz); CCM, bk. 7, p. 414 (contract with Monin for construction).

6. *MCR*, September 1, 1889, with photos.

7. CCM, bk. 9, p. 128; January 25, 1889.

8. *MCR*, April 3, 1889.

9. *MCR*, September 1, 1895.

10. DB, 77 n.s., pp. 532–33; December 5, 1895.

11. *MCR*, September 1, 1896, drawing on p. 11, also a description.

12. The German Relief organization first occupied an earlier building that can be seen to the left of the entrance to the Guard House in figure 77c. It has a two-story gallery with a decorative scrolled parapet above. *MCR*, August 31, 1890, describes the remodeling of the original building by Benz before the new building was undertaken.

13. YMCA, drawings and description in *MCR*, January 14, 1897, p. 5 [also pamphlets and the YMCA publication *HY-SHY-NY* in MPL(SC) files.]

14. *MCR*, March 17, 1907, clipping in local history files, MPL(SC); dedication of the new auditorium.

15. *MCR*, September 1, 1891, p. 5 gives a description of the Gothic Revival Church on the southwest corner of Government and Broad. It was replaced some sixteen years later by the Spanish Revival Church of George Rogers. St. Francis Street Methodist Church was designed by Watkins and Johnson, as noted in the article in *MCR*, September 1, 1896, with photos and description. In the *MCR*, September 1, 1895, the building was incorrectly ascribed to Rudolph Benz. The State Street A.M.E. Zion Church belongs to two building periods. In *MCR*, August 31, 1884, p. 10, James H. Hutchisson redesigned the facade, adding the central tower. In *MCR*, September 1, 1896, there is a description of the enlargement of the sanctuary and the renovation by Watkins and Johnson. Benz was again incorrectly credited in *MCR*, September 1, 1895. *MCR*, March 28, 1890 (St. Michael A.M.E. Church), and *MCR*, September 1, 1891; *MCR*, September 1, 1895 (Methodist Church on Broad and Elmira by Benz); *MCR*, September 1, 1896 (the Bethel A.M.E. Church); *MCR*, March 28, 1890 (the Union Baptist Church); ibid. (report of the St. Louis Street Baptist Church spire); *MCR*, September 1, 1899 (the Baptist Church on Dearborn and Palmetto).

16. *MCR*, August 31, 1890, and September 1, 1895. Account of the completion of the Cathedral facade and towers. There is still a question as to which architect actually designed the facade, but James H. Hutchisson held the contract for construction in 1873, and the structure was finished by his son after his father's death in 1887. In Oscar Lipscomb, "The Administration of John Quinlan, Second Bishop of Mobile, 1859–1883," *Records of the American Catholic Historical Society of Philadelphia*, vol. 78, nos. 1–4 (March–December 1967), p. 147, appears the statement that James Freret of New Orleans had been acting as architect but by 1873 had been relieved of his appointment; the contract was then given to Hutchisson. Edwin L. Jewell, ed., *Jewell's Crescent City* (New Orleans, 1873), p. 127, contains the statement that James Freret designed the facade. The local newspaper account seems to indicate that the final design was that of Hutchisson. *MCR*, September 1, 1887: the vestry of Christ Church cost $9,000.

17. *MCR*, September 1, 1894: reproduction of an architectural drawing of the building as it appeared in 1894. *MCR*, August 31, 1884, and *MCR*, September 1, 1896. The first building program of 1884 was undertaken by James H. Hutchisson, the second in 1895–96 by Watkins and Johnson, who constructed the sanctuary. The Hutchisson building replaced an earlier structure that had been built in 1853–54 by Richard Redwood and Albert Quigley, according to the research of Louise Erskine.

18. *MCR*, September 1, 1896: St. Francis Street Methodist Church, drawing with a description at the time of dedication. The Church was designed by the architects Watkins and Johnson but through some error was attributed to Rudolph Benz in the newspaper.

19. E. B. Gould, "An Architectural Survey," *Catholic Week*, January 28, 1983, p. 5.

20. *MCR*, August 31, 1884: Spring Hill addition by Freret. The three-story addition called for an auditorium on the second level and a chapel on the third. *MCR*, September 1, 1885: Spring Hill refectory and brick kitchen built by James H. Hutchisson.

21. *MCR*, September 1, 1896: the McGill Institute, with photograph of the building and a description of both the exterior and the room arrangements of the interior.

22. *MCR*, September 1, 1899. The brewery had been built in 1892, but the drawing and complete description appear in the 1899 paper. The article explains the process and the machinery involved. *MCR*, September 1, 1896: the grain elevator with drawing and description. The construction was contracted to the Heidenreich Construction Company of Chicago.

23. *MCR*, September 1, 1885: carriage factory on the site of the present Rousseau's Restaurant in Church Street East.

24. *MCR*, August 31, 1884: the Kling Foundry; Hutchisson, architect; *MCR*, September 1, 1886: the skating rink; $10,000; *MCR*, September 1, 1895: remodeling of the skating rink to create the Princess Theatre; *MCR*, September 1, 1899: description of the new Pollock commercial and theater building with a sketch of the interior of the theater.

25. *MCR*, September 1, 1897: drawing for an advertisement for the Dreaper and Burns Building; *MCR*, September 1, 1893: description and illustration.

26. *MCR*, September 1, 1885: the McCaw Building, 210 Dauphin Street; *MCR*, September 1, 1891: the Spira Building; *MCR*, September 1, 1893: the Scheuerman Building, with description.

27. *MCR*, September 1, 1897: the J. H. Masson Building; *MCR*, September 1, 1899: the Spira and Pincus Building, drawing and description.

28. *MCR*, September 1, 1886: the English Block, drawing and description; *MCR*, September 1, 1886: the Cotton Exchange, with drawing and description; *MCR*, August 31, 1890: the Pincus Building (under restoration in 1983); *MCR*, September 1, 1896: the Spira and Pincus Building (burned 1899).

29. *MCR*, September 11, 1882: list of permits granted for the year.

30. *MCR*, September 1, 1889: Scott House on Jefferson, moved to Cedar in 1980; *MCR*, September 1, 1891: the Kilduff House on George Street.

31. *MCR*, September 1, 1891: the McCoy House, with description; *MCR*, September 1, 1893: the Festorazzi House, with

	description; *MCR*, September 1, 1889: the Hopkins House with alterations.
32.	1552 Monterey Place: the Shepherd House (MHDC files).
33.	*MCR*, September 1, 1899: the Quill House; *MCR*, September 1, 1899, sec. 2: "Mobile's Expansion Year."

9. The Early Twentieth Century, 1900–1918

1.	*MCR*, September 1, 1908, sec. 4: George B. Rogers house for Ralph Richards on Michigan Avenue; ibid., Hutchisson and Garvin for Mrs. Dickens; *MCR*, September 1, 1909, sec. 2: Hutchisson and Garvin for B. H. Davis, Ashland Place.
2.	From 1906 through 1909, *MCR* trade journals recorded new suburban developments: September 1, 1906, sec. 3, for Spring Hill; September 1, 1908, sec. 4, for Flo-Claire; September 1, 1909, sec. 2: several suburbs and photographs.
3.	*MCR*, September 1, 1910: report on street paving and sidewalk installation, including Washington Square in Oakleigh.
4.	Ibid.: city report on the addition to City Hall and other improvements.
5.	*MCR*, September 2, 1907, sec. 3: report on the addition to the county court building, with photographs, also sec. 2, and, on the Leinkauf School, September 1, 1908, sec. 4, with photographs.
6.	John T. Faris, *Seeing the Sunny South* (Philadelphia: Lippincott, 1921), pp. 175–76.
7.	*MCR*, September 1, 1910, sec. 7: Hutchisson and Garvin plan for the Mobile Infirmary, with photograph; *MCR*, September 1, 1902, and September 1, 1903: drawing by R. L. Mulligan, architect.
8.	*MCR*, September 1, 1907, sec. 5: photographs of the Jewish Temple and a description at the time of dedication.
9.	*MCR*, September 1, 1909, sec. 2: Government Street First Baptist Church, with photographs and description.
10.	*MCR*, September 1, 1900: the Fidelia Club with photographs and description.
11.	*MCR*, September 2, 1901: architect's drawing of the Masonic Temple.
12.	MHDC files, Scottish Rites nomination to the National Register; *MCR*, September 1, 1921: photographs and description.
13.	*MCR*, September 1, 1906, sec. 2: full-page architect's drawing. *MCR*, September 2, 1907, sec. 2: photographs and description.
14.	*MCR*, September 1, 1903, sec. 3: the Lowenstein Bank with drawing; *MCR*, September 1, 1904, sec. 2: drawing of the Bank and Trust Building.
15.	*MCR*, September 1, 1906, sec. 3: drawing of the First National Bank.
16.	*MCR*, September 1, 1893: buildings at Monroe Park; *MCR*, September 1, 1906, sec. 2: description of the fire and hurricane destruction at Monroe Park and the rebuilding of the casino, with photos.
17.	*MCR*, September 1, 1900: full-page drawing of the Bienville Hotel, with description; *MCR*, September 1, 1906, sec. 4: full-page drawing of the Cawthon Hotel, with description.
18.	*MCR*, September 1, 1906: burning of Battle House with drawings of proposed new building; *MCR*, September 1, 1908,

19. sec. 2: description at time of dedication. The architect, Frank M. Andrews, also designed the state capitol at Frankfort, Kentucky, and hotels at Indianapolis and Louisville.

19. *MCR*, September 2, 1901: facade of Hammel's Store; *MCR*, September 1, 1902: description and drawing.

20. *MCR*, September 1, 1906, sec. 2: proposed Van Antwerp Building; *MCR*, September 2, 1907, sec. 4: drawings and description; *MCR*, September 1, 1908, sec. 3: building completed.

21. Clem Labine and Patricia Poore, "The Comfortable House: Post-Victorian Architecture," *Old House Journal* (January 1982), p. 7 (with photographs of the typical four-square house); *MCR*, September 1, 1905: advertisement for the sale of houses of the same type, with photographs.

22. *MCR*, September 1, 1904: description of the house, with a photograph.

23. DB 132, p. 425, states that the party releases all his rights for the "cement residence." *MCR*, September 2, 1907, sec. 4: photograph of the house. Recent repair work on the house also verifies the size of the concrete blocks, which were cast solid.

Bibliography

Selected Books

Acker, Marion F. *Etchings of Old Mobile*. Mobile: Gill Printing and Stationery, 1938.

———. *Glimpses of Old Mobile*. Mobile: Gill Printing and Stationery, 1955.

Agee, Rucker. *Maps of Alabama*. Birmingham: Public Library Collection, 1955.

Alvarez, Eugene. *Travels on Southern Antebellum Railroads*. University: University of Alabama Press, 1974.

American Heritage. *Pictorial Atlas of United States History*. Edited by Hilde Heum Kagan et al. New York: American Heritage, 1966.

Andrews, Wayne. *American Gothic*. New York: Random House, 1975.

———. *Architecture, Ambition, and Americans*. 1947. Reprint. London: Free Press of Glencoe, Collier-Macmillan, 1964.

Baldwin, Joseph G. *Flush Times in Alabama and Mississippi*. 1853. Reprint. New York: Sagamore Press, 1957.

Bartram, William. *Travels through North and South Carolina, Georgia, East and West Florida, the Cherokee Country, the Extensive Territories of the Muscogulges, or Creek Confederacy, and the Country of the Choctaws, Containing an Account of the Soil and Natural Productions of those Regions Together with Observations on the Manners of the Indians*. 1791. Edited by Mark Van Doren. New York: Dover, 1928.

Baumgart, Fritz. *A History of Architectural Styles*. New York: Frederick A. Praeger, 1970.

Beck, Mary. *Ghosts of Old Mobile*. Mobile: Haunted Book Shop, 1946.

Beers, Henry Putney. *The French in North America: A Bibliographical Guide to French Archives, Reproductions, and Research Missions*. Baton Rouge: Louisiana State University Press, 1907.

Bell, Robert E. *Bibliography of Mobile*. University: University of Alabama Press, 1956.

Benjamin, Asher. *The American Builder's Companion*. 1827. Reprint of 6th ed. New York: Dover, 1969.

_____. *The Builder's Guide*. Boston: Perkins and Marvin, 1850.

_____. *Rudiments of Architecture*. 1814. 2d ed. Boston: R. P. and C. Williams, 1820.

Berney, Stafford. *Handbook of Alabama*. 2d ed. Birmingham: Roberts and Son, 1892.

Bernhard, Duke of Saxe-Weimar Eisenach. *Travels through North America, 1825–1826*. Vol. 1. Philadelphia: Carey, Lea and Carey, 1828.

Berquin-Duvallon. *Travels in Louisiana and the Floridas in the Year 1802*. Translated from the French by John Davis. New York: I. Riley, 1806.

Beyer, Theresa, and Rebecca Zurier. *The American Firehouses: An Architectural and Social History*. New York: Abbeville Press, 1969.

Bossu, Jean-Bernard. *Travels in the Interior of North America, 1751–1762*. Translated and edited by Seymour Feiler. Norman, Okla.: University of Oklahoma Press, 1962.

Brannon, Peter. *Southern Indian Trade*. Montgomery: Paragon Press, 1935.

Bremer, Fredrika. *The Homes of the New World*. Vol. 2. Translated by Mary Howitt. New York: Harper, 1854.

Buckingham, James Silk. *The Slave States of America*. Vol. 1. 2d ed. London: Fisher, 1842.

Burchard, John, and Albert Bush-Brown. *The Architecture of America: A Social and Cultural History*. Boston: Little, Brown, 1966.

Burgett, James R. *Presbyterianism in Mobile*. Mobile: Henry Farrow, 1881.

Carter, Hodding, and Anthony Raguzin. *Gulf Coast Country*. New York: Duell, Sloan and Pearce, 1951.

Caughey, John W. *Bernardo de Gálvez in Louisiana, 1776–1783*. Gretna: Pelican, 1972.

Chafetz, Henry. *Play the Devil: A History of Gambling in the United States from 1492 to 1950*. New York: Potter, 1960.

Chapman, Herman Hollis. *The Iron and Steel Industry in the South*. University: University of Alabama Press, 1953.

Chipley, William D. *Pensacola, The Naples of America*. 1877. Reprint. Pensacola: T. T. Wentworth, Jr., 1962.

Christian, Marcus. *Negro Iron Workers of Louisiana, 1718–1900*. Gretna: Pelican, 1972.

City Planning Commission, City of Mobile. *Nineteenth-Century Mobile Architecture: An Inventory of Existing Buildings*. Mobile: City of Mobile, 1974.

Clark, Thomas D. *Travels in the Old South: A Bibliography*. 3 vols. Vol. 1: 1527–1783. Vol. 2: 1750–1825: Vol. 3: 1825–1860. Norman: University of Oklahoma Press, 1956, 1959.

Condit, Carl W. *American Building Art: The Nineteenth Century*. 5th ed. Chicago: University of Chicago Press, 1975.

Coulter, Ellis Merton. *Travels in the Confederate States: A Bibliography*. Norman: University of Oklahoma Press, 1948.

Cumming, Kate. *Gleanings from Southland*. Birmingham: Roberts, 1895.

Cumming, William Patterson. *The Southeast in Early Maps during the Colonial Period*. Chapel Hill: University of North Carolina Press, 1962.

Cutter's Commercial Guide to Mobile, Alabama, Queen of the Gulf. Mobile: Cutter's Guide, 1899.

Davey, Norman. *A History of Building Materials.* London: Phoenix House, 1961.

Delaney, Caldwell. *The Story of Mobile.* Mobile: Gill Printing and Stationery, 1962.

Dodd, Donald. *Historical Atlas of Alabama.* University: University of Alabama Press, 1974.

Dodd, Donald, and Wynelle Dodd. *Historical Statistics of the South, 1790–1970.* University: University of Alabama Press, 1973.

Downing, Andrew Jackson. *The Architecture of Country Houses, Including Designs for Cottages, Farm Houses, and Villas, with Interiors, Furniture, and the Best Modes of Warming and Ventilating.* New York: D. Appleton, 1850.

———. *Cottage Residences; or, A Series of Designs for Rural Cottages and Cottage Villas, and Their Gardens and Grounds Adapted to North America.* 2d ed. New York and London: Wiley and Putnam, 1844.

———. *Rural Essays.* Edited by George William Curtis. New York: Leavin and Allen, 1857.

———. *A Treatise on the Theory and Practice of Landscape Gardening . . . , with Remarks on Rural Architecture.* New York: Putnam, 1853.

Eberlein, Harold Donaldson, and Charles Van Dyke Hubbard. *Colonial Interiors: Federal and Greek Revival.* New York: William Helburn, 1938.

Ellicott, Andrew. *Journal of Andrew Ellicott, 1754–1820.* 1814. Reprint. Chicago: Quadrangle Books, 1962.

Ellison, R. C. *History and Bibliography of Alabama Newspapers in the Nineteenth Century.* University: University of Alabama Press, 1954.

Ellsworth, Lucius F., ed. *The Americanization of the Gulf Coast, 1803–1850.* Pensacola: Historic Pensacola Preservation Board, 1972.

Engelhard, Zelma. *Beyond the Bayous: Acadians in Louisiana.* Baton Rouge: Claitor, 1962.

Faris, John T. *Seeing the Sunny South.* Philadelphia: Lippincott, 1921.

Ferris, Robert G., ed. *Explorers and Settlers: Historic Places Commemorating the Early Exploration and Settlement of the United States.* Vol. 5. Washington, D.C.: National Survey of Historic Sites and Buildings, U.S. Department of the Interior, National Park Service, 1968.

First National Bank of Mobile. *Highlights of 100 Years in Mobile.* Mobile: Mobile Press Register, 1965.

———. *Through Mobile Gates.* Mobile, n.d. [Compiled from newspaper advertisements]

Fitch, J. *American Building: The Environmental Forces That Shaped It.* Boston: Houghton Mifflin, 1966.

Forbes, James G. *Sketches Historical, Topographical of the Floridas,* 1821. Introduction by James W. Covington. Reprint. Gainesville: University of Florida Press, 1964.

Forman, Henry C. *The Architecture of the Old South: The Medieval Style, 1585–1850.* Cambridge, Mass.: Harvard University Press, 1948.

Franzwa, Gregory M. *The Story of Ste. Genevieve*. St. Louis: Patrice Press, 1967.

Gallier, James. *Autobiography*. Paris: E. Briere Publishers, 1864.

Gardiner, F. B. *How to Paint Your Victorian House*. [Facsimile of *Everyman His Own Painter*.] 1872. Reprint. Library of Victorian Culture. New York: Watkins Glen, American Life Foundation and Study Institute, 1978.

Glennon, J. *Where Time Bears Witness to Sound Building*. Mobile: First National Bank, 1934.

Hall, Captain Basil. *Travels in North America in the Years 1827–1828*. 3 vols. Edinburgh, 1829.

Hall, Mrs. Basil. *The Aristocratic Journey: Letters Written by Mrs Basil Hall during a Fourteen Month Sojourn in America, 1827–1828*. Edited by Una Pope Hennessy. New York: Putnam, 1931.

Hamilton, Peter J. *Art Work in Mobile and Vicinity*. Chicago: W. H. Parish, 1894.

―――. *Colonial Mobile*. 3d ed. 1897. Reprint. Mobile: First National Bank, 1952.

―――. *The Colonization of the South*. Vol. 3 in *History of North America*. Philadelphia: Barrie, 1905.

―――. *The Founding of Mobile, 1702–1718*. Mobile: Commercial Printing, 1911.

―――. *The Reconstruction Period*. Vol. 16 in *History of North America*. Philadelphia: Barrie, 1905.

―――. *Under Five Flags*. Mobile: Gill Printing and Stationery, 1913.

Hamlin, Talbot Faulkner. *Greek Revival Architecture in America*. New York: Dover, 1964.

Hammond, Ralph Charles. *Antebellum Mansions of Alabama*. New York: Architectural Book, 1951.

Harris, John, and Jill Lever. *Illustrated Glossary of Architecture, 850–1830*. New York: Potter, 1966.

Harrison, Mary Douglas Waring. *Miss Waring's Journal, Being the Diary of Miss Waring of Mobile during the Final Days of the War between the States*. Edited by T. Holt, Jr. Chicago: Wyvern Press, 1964.

Higginbotham, P. Jay. *Mobile, City by the Bay*. Mobile: Azalea City, 1968.

―――. *Old Mobile: Fort Louis de la Louisiane, 1702–1711*. Mobile: Museum of the City of Mobile, 1977.

―――. *Pascagoula, Singing River City*. Mobile: Gill Printing and Stationery, 1967.

Historic Records Survey. *American Imprints Inventory 8. Check List of Alabama Imprints, 1807–1840*. 1939. Reprint. New York: Kraus, 1964.

Holly, Henry. *Country Seats*. New York: Appleton, 1863.

Howard, Ann S. *Enchantment in Iron*. Mobile: Rapier House, 1950.

Howard, Clinton. *The British Development of West Florida, 1763–1769*. University of California Publications in History, 34. Berkeley: University of California Press, 1947.

Hutchins, Thomas. *An Historical Narrative and Topographical Description of Louisiana and West Florida*. 1784. Floridiana Facsimile and Reprint Series. Gainesville: University of Florida Press, 1968.

Illustrations of Iron Architecture Made by the Architectural Iron Works of the City of New York. In *The Origins of Cast Iron*

Architecture in America: A Catalogue of the D. D. Badger and Company. 1865. Reprint. New York: Da Capo Press, 1970.

Issac, I. J. *Mobile Up to Date.* Mobile: Mobile Stationery, 1895.

Jordy, William H. *American Buildings and Their Architects. Progressive and Academic Ideals at the Turn of the Twentieth Century.* Garden City, N.Y.: Doubleday, 1972.

Kenny, Father Michael, S.J. *The Torch on the Hill.* New York: American Press, 1931.

King, Edward. "Mobile, the Chief City of Alabama." In *The Great South*, edited by W. Macgruder Drake and Robert R. Jones. Baton Rouge: Louisiana State University Press, 1972.

Lafever, Minard. *The Beauties of Modern Architecture.* 1835. Reprint. New York: Da Capo, 1968.

Land, John E. *Mobile: Her Trade, Commerce, and Industries.* Mobile: By the author, 1884.

Levasseur, Auguste. *Lafayette in America: Journal of the Travels in the United States.* Vol. 2. New York: White, Gallalee and White, 1829.

Lewis, Arnold, and Keith Morgan. *American Victorian Architecture.* New York: Dover, 1975.

Loveman, Louis Vandiver. *Historical Atlas of Alabama, 1519–1900.* Special ed. Gadsden, Ala.: n.p., 1976.

Lowery, Woodbury. *The Lowery Collection: A Descriptive List of Maps of the Spanish Possessions within the Present Limits of the United States, 1502–1820.* Edited by Philip Lee Phillips. 1905. Reprint. Washington, D.C.: Government Printing Office, 1912.

McAlester, Virginia, and Lee McAlester. *A Field Guide to American Houses.* New York: Alfred A. Knopf, 1984.

McDermott, John, ed. *The French in the Mississippi Valley.* Urbana: University of Illinois Press, 1965.

McKee, Harley. *Introduction to Early American Masonry: Stone, Brick, Mortar, and Plaster.* Washington, D.C.: Preservation Press, 1973.

McLaurin, Melton, and Michael Thomason. *Mobile: The Life and Times of a Great Southern City.* Woodland Hills, Calif.: Windsor Books, 1981.

McMullin, Phillip W., ed. *Grass Roots of America: A Computerized Index to the American State Papers.* Serial set numbers 28–36. Washington, D.C.: Universal Printing, 1972.

McNeely, S. Blake. *Bits of Charm in Old Mobile.* Mobile: Gulf States Engraving, 1946.

Macready, William Charles. *His Reminiscences, Diaries, and Letters.* Edited by Sir F. Pollock. 2d ed. Edited by William Toynbee. Vol. 2. London: Chapman and Hall, 1912.

Manucy, Albert. *The Houses of St. Augustine, 1565–1821.* St. Augustine: St. Augustine Historical Society, 1962.

Marchand, Sidney. *Acadian Exiles in the Golden Coast of Louisiana.* Donaldsonville, La.: Ascension and St. James Parishes, 1943.

Meek, Alexander B. *Romantic Passages in Southwestern History.* 1857. Reprint. Spartanburg: Reprint, 1975.

———. *The Southwest: Its History, Character, and Prospects: A Discourse for the Eighth Anniversary of the Erosophic Society of the University of Alabama, December 7, 1839.* Tuscaloosa: C. B. Baldwind, 1840.

Mémoire Justificatif du Chevalier Montault Monberaut, 1763–1765. Translated by Milo B. Howard, Jr., and Robert R. Rea. University: University of Alabama Press, 1965.

Mereness, Newton Dennison, ed. *Travels in the North American Colonies and the West Indies, 1764–1765.* 1916. Reprint. New York: Antiquarian Society, 1961. [Includes: Lord Adam Gordon, "The Journal of an Officer, 1764–1765"; Captain Harry Gordon, "The Journal of Captain Harry Gordon from Pittsburg down the Mississippi to New Orleans, Mobile and Pensacola, 1966"]

Michigan Pioneer and Historical Society Collection. *The Haldiman Papers.* Vol. 9 (1816). Vol. 10 (1886). Vol. 11 (1887). Vol. 19 (1891). Vol. 20 (1892). Reprint. Lansing, Mich., 1908–12.

Milfort, General Louis. *Mémoire; ou, Coup-d'Oeil Rapide Sur Mes Différents Voyages et Mon Séjour Dans La Nation Creek.* 1802. Translated and edited by Ben C. McCary. Kennesaw, Ga.: Continental Book, 1959.

Millar, John Fitzhugh. *The Architecture of the American Colonies.* Barre, Mass.: Barre Publishing, 1968.

Mitchell, Donald G. *Rural Studies.* 1867. Reprinted as *Out of Town Places.* New York: Scribner, 1884.

Mitchell, Louis Dumas, and Others. *Burial Records, Mobile County, 1820–1856.* Mobile: Mobile Genealogical Society, 1963.

Mobile Alabama in Photogravure from Recent Negatives. Mobile: Zadex Jewelry, 1892.

Mobile Writers' Workshop. *Historic Churches of Mobile.* Mobile, 1971.

Moogk, Peter N. *Building a House in New France.* Toronto: McClelland and Stewart, 1977.

Morrison, Andrew, ed. *Mobile: The New South.* New Orleans: Metropolitan Star Publishing, 1877–88.

Morrison, Hugh. *Early American Architecture from the First Colonial Settlements to the National Period.* New York: Oxford University Press, 1952.

Myers, Denys P. *Gas Lighting in America: A Guide for Preservation.* Washington, D.C.: Department of the Interior, 1978.

Nelson, Col., and Mrs. Soren Nelson. *A History of the Church Street Graveyard.* Mobile: Historic Mobile Preservation Society, 1963.

New Orleans Architecture. Vol. 1, *The Lower Garden District* (1971). Vol. 2, *The American Sector* (1972). Vol. 4, *Creole Faubourgs* (1974). Vol. 5, *The Esplanade Ridge* (1977). Gretna, La.: Pelican, 1971–77.

New York Wire Railing Company. *New Phase of Iron Manufacture.* New York, 1857.

Olliffe, Charles. *Scènes Américaines.* 1853. Translated by Ernest Falbo and Lawrence Wilson. Vol. 3. Painesville, Ohio: Lake Erie College, 1964.

Olmsted, Frederick Law. *A Journey in the Seaboard States, 1853–54.* 1856. Reprint. New York: Putnam and Sons, 1904.

Page, Charlotte A., and Mary Cummings. *Under Sail and in Port in the Glorious 1850s: May 1 to October 3, 1852.* Boston: Peabody Museum, 1950.

Panek, R. T. *American Architectural Styles, 1600–1940.* Dover, Me.: Architectural Styles, 1976.

Parker, James C. *The Development of the Port of Mobile, 1819–1836.* Auburn: Auburn University Press, 1968.

Peterson, Charles, ed. *Building Early America: Contributions toward a Great Industry.* Radnor, Pa.: Chilton, 1976.

———. "The Houses of French St. Louis." In *The French in the Mississippi Valley*, edited by J. F. McDermett. Urbana: University of Illinois Press, 1965.

Pickett, Albert J., and Thomas McAdory Owen. "History of Alabama, and Incidentally of Georgia and Mississippi from the earliest period," and "Annals of Alabama, 1819–1900." 2 vols. in 1. 1900. Reprint. Spartanburg: Reprint, 1975.

Pierson, William H., Jr. *American Buildings and Their Architects.* Vol. 1: *The Colonial and Neoclassical Styles.* Garden City, N.Y.: Doubleday, 1970.

Post, Lauren C. *Cajun Sketches: Acadians in Louisiana.* Baton Rouge: Louisiana State University Press, 1962.

Power, Tyrone, Esq. *Impressions of America.* Vol. 2. Philadelphia: Carey, Lea and Blanchard, 1836.

Ramsey, Carolyn. *Cajuns on the Bayous.* New York: Hastings House, 1957.

Rifkind, Carole. *A Field Guide to American Architecture.* New York: New American Library, 1980.

Ritchie, Anna Cora. *An Autobiography of an Actress* [Anna Cora Mowatt]. 1854. Reprint. University of South Alabama Library. Microfilm.

Robin, Claude C. *Voyage to Louisiana, 1803–1805.* 3 vols. 1807. Abridged translation by Stuart O. Landry. Gretna: Pelican, 1966.

Romans, Bernard. *A Concise Natural History of East and West Florida.* 1775. Reprint. Gainesville: University of Florida Press, 1962.

Rowland, Dunbar, ed. *History of Mississippi, the Heart of the South.* Chicago: S. J. Clarke, 1925.

Rowland, Dunbar, and A. G. Sanders. *French Dominion, 1729–1740.* Jackson, Miss.: Press of the Mississippi Department of Archives and History, 1927.

Royall, Anne N. *Letters from Alabama, 1811–1822.* University: University of Alabama Press, 1969.

Russell, William H. *My Diary, North and South.* Boston: T. O. H. P. Burnham, 1863.

Scully, Arthur, Jr. *James Dakin, Architect: His Career in New York and the South.* Baton Rouge: Louisiana State University Press, 1973.

Severens, Kenneth. *Southern Architecture.* New York: Elsevier, Dutton, 1981.

Shippee, Lester B., ed. *Bishop Whipple's Southern Diary, 1843–44.* Minneapolis: University of Minnesota Press, 1937.

Sloan, Samuel. *City and Suburban Architecture.* Philadelphia: Lippincott, 1859.

Sloane, Eric. *A Museum of Early American Tools.* 2d ed. New York: Ballantine Books, 1974.

Smith, J. Frazier. *White Pillars: Early Life and Architecture of the Lower Mississippi Valley Country.* New York: William Helburn, 1941.

Smith, Richard. *A Guide to the Deep South: Alabama: A Bibliography.* W.P.A. Writer's Program. New York: Richard R. Smith, 1941.
Smith, Sidney, and C. C. Carter Smith, eds. *Mobile, 1861–65: Notes and a Bibliography.* Chicago: Wyvern Press, n.d.
Southworth, Susan, and Michael Southworth. *Ornamental Iron.* Boston: David R. Godine, 1978.
Souvenir History of the Mobile Fire and Police Departments, 1819–1902. Mobile: Commercial Printing, 1902.
Stuart-Wortley, Lady Emmeline [Charlotte Elizabeth *née* Manners]. *Travels in the United States, 1849–1850.* New York: Harper, 1851.
Sulzby, James F., Jr. *Historic Alabama Hotels and Resorts.* University: University of Alabama Press, 1960.
Summersell, Charles Grayson. *Mobile: History of a Seaport Town.* University: University of Alabama Press, 1949.
Thomason, Michael, and Melton McLaurin. *Mobile: American River City.* Mobile: Easter Publishing, 1975.
Thompson, Alan Smith. *Mobile, Alabama, 1850–1861.* Ann Arbor: University Microfilms International, 1982.
Thompson, Helen. *Magnolia Cemetery Records, 1828–1871.* New Orleans: Polyanthus Press, 1974.
Ullman, Edward L. *Mobile: Industry, Seaport, and Trade Center.* Chicago: University of Chicago Press, 1943.
Vaux, Calvert. *Villas and Cottages.* 1864. Reprint. New York: Dover, 1970.
Waite, Diana S., ed. *Architectural Elements: The Technological Revolution, 1854–1879.* American Historical Catalogue Collection. Princeton: Pyne Press, n.d.
Waugh, Edward, and Elizabeth Waugh. *The South Builds.* Chapel Hill: University of North Carolina Press, 1960.
Whiffen, Marcus. *American Architecture since 1780.* Cambridge, Mass.: MIT Press, 1969.
Wilson, Eugene N. *Alabama Folk Houses.* Montgomery: Alabama Historical Commission, 1975.
Wilson, Samuel Jr. "Colonial Fortifications and Military Architecture in the Mississippi Valley." In *The French in the Mississippi Valley,* edited by J. F. McDermott. Urbana: University of Illinois Press, 1965.
Witherell, H. B. *The Structural History of Christ Church, Mobile, Alabama.* Mobile: Christ Church, 1937.
Withey, Henry F. *Biographical Dictionary of American Architects Deceased.* Los Angeles: New Age Publishing, 1956.

Articles and Pamphlets

Abernethy, Thomas. *Florida and the Spanish Frontier, 1811–1819.* Pensacola: Historic Pensacola Preservation Board, 1972.
American Gazette. London, 1798.
Ballou's Pictorial Drawing Room Companion. June 1857.
Beer, William. "The Surrender of Fort Charlotte, Mobile." *American Historical Review* 1 (1896), pp. 696–99.
Bromberg, Frederick G. "Reconstruction Period in Alabama." *Papers of the Iberville Historical Society,* nos. 3–4 (1911–14), pp. 1–18.
Brown, J. A. "The Panton, Leslie and Company." *FHQ* 37, nos. 3–4 (January–April 1959), pp. 328–37.

Burns, Francis P. "Lafayette's Visit to New Orleans." *LHQ* 29, no. 2 (April 1946), pp. 296–340.
Cunningham, Charles H. "Residencia in the Spanish Colonies." *Southwestern Historical Quarterly* 21, no. 3 (January 1918), pp. 253–78.
Dana, David. "The Mobile Fire Department." In *The Firemen*. Boston: James French, 1858.
DeBow, Thomas D. B. "Mobile: Its Past and Present." *Review* (Charleston) 28 (March 1960), pp. 305–13.
Deupree, Mrs. N. D. "Some Historic Homes of Mississippi." *Mississippi Historical Society* 6 (1902), pp. 245–64.
Doherty, Herbert J. "Ante Bellum Pensacola, 1821–1863." *FHQ* 37, nos. 3–4 (January–April 1959), pp. 337–57.
Fondé, C. H. "The Great Explosion." *Mobile Bound Pamphlets* 2 (May 25, 1865), p. 13.
Gaines, George. "Notes on the Early Days of South Alabama." *Alabama Historical Quarterly* 26, nos. 3–4 (Fall and Winter 1964), pp. 133–229.
Gallilee, Jack D. "Andrew Ellicott and the Ellicott Stone." *Alabama Review* 18, no. 2 (April 1965), pp. 92–105.
Goodacre, Robert. "Report on Mobile." *Mobile Commercial Register*, February 19, 1828. [Reprinted from the *Nashville Whig and Banner*]
Gould, Elizabeth B. "Transition and Adaptation in Mobile Architecture." *Antiques* 112, no. 3 (September 1977), pp. 466–76.
Grosse, Sir Edmund William. "Travel Book." Compiled by George Fremault. *MCR*, May 1839.
Hamilton, Peter J. "British West Florida." *Mississippi Historical Society* 7 (1903), pp. 399–426.
———. "Some Southern Yankees." *American Historical Magazine* 3, no. 4 (October 1898), pp. 303–12.
Holberg, Ralph, Jr. "Mobile." *Confederate Echoes* 1, no. 11 (April 1963), pp. 3–10.
Holmes, Jack D. L. *Alabama Colonial Settlers: Spanish Period, 1780–1813*. Louisiana Collection Series 2. New Orleans: Holmes, 1970. Microfilm of Spanish Documents, University of South Alabama.
———. "French and Spanish Maps and Charts of Colonial Alabama in French and Spanish Archives." *Alabama Historical Quarterly* 27, nos. 1–2 (Spring–Summer 1965), pp. 7–21.
———. "Genealogical and Historical Sources for Spanish Alabama, 1780–1813." *Deep South Genealogical Quarterly* 5, no. 3 (February 1969), pp. 130–38.
———. *A Guide to Spanish Louisiana, 1762–1806*. Louisiana Collection Series of Books and Documents of Colonial Louisiana. New Orleans: Jack D. L. Holmes, 1970.
———. "Notes on the Spanish Fort San Esteban de Tombecbé." *Alabama Historical Review* 18, no. 4 (October 1965), pp. 281–90.
Howard, C. N. "The Interval of Military Government in West Florida." *LHQ* 22 (April 1939), pp. 18–30.
"Inventory of the Property of Joseph Bock, Mobile, April 4, 1762." *LHQ* 23, no. 3 (July 1940), pp. 917–19. [Reprinted from the *Records of the Superior Council of Louisiana*, no. 8131, p. 9]
Jenkins, C. "West Florida Revisited." *Journal of Mississippi History* 28, no. 2 (May 1966), pp. 121–32.

Jenkins, William H. "Alabama Forts, 1700–1838." *Alabama Review* 12, no. 3 (July 1959), pp. 163–79.

Johnson, Cecil. "Missouri French Houses: Some Relict Features of Early Settlements." *Journal of the Pioneer American Society* 6, no. 2 (July 1974), pp. 1–12.

Kirby, Ephraim. "Letters to the President, May 1, 1804." *MTP* 5:322–26.

Kniffen, F. B. "Folk Housing: Key to Diffusion." *Annals of the Association of American Geographers* 55, no. 4 (December 1965), pp. 549–77.

Labine, Clem, and Patricia Poore. "The Comfortable House: Post-Victorian Architecture." *Old House Journal* (January 1982), pp. 1–8.

Lancaster, Clay. "Greek Revival Architecture in Alabama." *Alabama Architect* 4, no. 1 (January–February 1968), pp. 6–18.

"Letters from Major Farmer to Lord Egremont." *Mississippi Provincial Archives* 1 (January 1764), pp. 137–38.

Lipscomb, Oscar H. "The Administration of John Quinlan, Second Bishop of Mobile, 1859–1883," *Records of the American Catholic Historical Society of Philadelphia* 78, nos. 1–4 (March–December 1967).

McAlister, Lyle N. "Pensacola during the Second Spanish Period." *FHQ* 37, nos. 3–4 (January–April, 1959), pp. 281–327.

Manucy, Albert. "The Founding of Pensacola: Reason and Reality." *FHQ* 37, nos. 3–4 (January–April 1959), pp. 223–41.

Mulcrone, Thomas F. "Antoine de Laval, S.J., at Dauphin Island, 1720." *Alabama Review* 20, no. 1 (January 1967), pp. 69–76.

Myers, Denys Peter. "The Recently Discovered Diaries of Isaiah Rogers." *Columbia Library Columns* 16, no. 1 (November 1966), pp. 25–32.

Parkhurst, Helen. "Don Pedro Favrot: A Creole Pepys." *LHQ* 28, no. 3 (July 1945), pp. 679–735.

Peterson, Charles E. "Early Ste. Genevieve and Its Architecture." *Missouri Historical Review* 35, no. 2 (January 1941), pp. 207–32.

Ravesies, Paul, Sr. "Scenes and Settlers of Alabama." In *Sub Rosa*. Mobile: Mobile Public Library, n.d.

Robinson, Willard. "Military Architecture at Mobile Bay." *Journal of the Society of Architectural Historians* 30, no. 2 (May 1971), pp. 119–39.

Rowland, Dunbar, ed. "Letters and Enclosures to the Secretary of State from Major Robert Farmer and Governor George Johnstone of West Florida." *MPA* 1, "English Dominion, 1763–1766" (October 1911).

Schuyler, Montgomery. "The Old Greek Revival." Pt. 4. *American Architect* 99, no. 815 (May 3, 1911).

"Skates and Company: Mobile Foundry." *Mobile Bound Pamphlets* 2 (n.d.), p. 53.

Smith, Herndon. "Spain and Mobile." *Deep South Genealogical Quarterly* 5, no. 3 (February 1968), pp. 117–27.

"A Verbal Process of the Cession of the Port of Mobile to Mons. Robert Farmer, named Commander by His Britannick Majesty of Mobile." *MPA* 1, "English Dominion, 1763–1766" (October 1911), pp. 77–79.

Wilson, Samuel, Jr. "Religious Architecture in French Colonial Louisiana." *Winterthur Portfolio* 8 (1973), pp. 63–106.

U.S. Government Documents

American State Papers: Legislative and Executive (ASP). 38 volumes. Washington, D.C., 1832–61. Vol. 1 (1789–1809); vol. 2 (1809–15); vol. 3 (1815–24); vol. 4 (1824–28); vol. 5 (1828–34).

Historic American Building Survey (HABS). Washington, D.C.: National Park Service, Department of Interior, 1972. (Surveys of Mobile, including photographs and measured drawings, housed in the Library of Congress).

Territorial Papers of the United States (USTP). Edited by Clarence E. Carter.

    Vol. 5: *Territory of Mississippi, 1798–1817 (MTP)*. Washington, D.C., 1937.

    Vol. 18: *Territory of Alabama, 1817–1819*. Washington, D.C., 1952.

    U.S. Treasury Department. *History of Public Buildings under Control of the Treasury Department*. Compiled by W. H. Hills and J. A. Sutherland. Washington, D.C., 1901.

Works Progress Administration. Writers Program. *Alabama: A Guide to the Deep South*. New York: Hastings House, 1941.

Alabama State Documents

Department of Education. "History of Education in Alabama." Bicentennial Intern Project. *Educational Bulletin* 7 (1975).

Digest of the Laws of Alabama. Compiled by Judge Harry Toulmin. Ed. John G. Aiken. Cahawba, N.Y.: Ginn and Curtis, 1823.

"Minutes of the First Session of West Florida Assembly, 1766–1767." *LHQ* 22 (April 1939).

"Spanish and French Record." Vol. 1: 1715–1812. Translated by Joseph Caro, 1840. Mobile Probate Court.

Mobile City Records

Annual Report of the General Council. March 15, 1895. City Vault.

Burial Records. Vol. 1: 1820–56; vol. 2: 1857–79. MPL(SC).

City Directories (CD). 1839, 1842, 1844, 1852, 1855, 1856, 1858, 1859, 1861, 1865, 1866, 1867, 1870, 1871, 1872, 1873–1918. MPL(SC).

City Planning Commission. Research files for *Nineteenth Century Mobile Architecture: An Inventory of Existing Buildings*.

Maps. Pillans maps. 1868. City Engineer's Office. Sanborn maps. 1880, 1885, 1891, 1904, 1924. MHDC. Troost maps. 5 vols. City Engineer's Office.

Minutes of the Mayor and Board of Aldermen (MAM). Vols. for 1824–29, 1829–32, 1833–34, 1839–43, 1843–47, 1850–55, 1851–59 (vol. 2), 1857–61, 1859–66 (vol. 2), 1861–66, 1866–69, 1875–79, 1887–96. City Vault.

Minutes of the City Common Council (MCC). Vols. for 1839–40, 1844–50, 1857–61, 1871–74, 1887–89, 1899–1900. City Vault.

Mobile Historic Development Commission (MHDC). Research files on the Mobile historic districts, historic buildings, and buildings on the National Register.

Police Records of the Night Patrol, 1822–27. Mobile City Archives. #33-3-2-1.

Tax Records, 1836–1912. City Archives.

Treasurer's Day Book. Book 1. City Vault.

Mobile County Records

County Board of Education. Minutes. Vol. 1: 1836–45; vol. 2: 1845–52. Barton Academy.

Minutes of the County Council, the Road Commissioners, and the Revenue Board (CCM). Vol. 1: 1844; vol. 3: 1860–69; vol. 4: 1872–73; vol. 7: 1884–88. County Archives.

Miscellaneous Books (Misc. Bks.). Vol. A: 1821–25; vol. B: 1826–32; vol. C: 1833–40; vol. D: 1840–45; vol. E: 1846–52; vol. F: 1852–58; vol. G: 1858–66; vol. H: 1867–73; vol. I/J: 1874–79. County Archives.

Probate Court. Deed Books (DB).

Tax Records. Microfilm, 1881–. Tax Assessor's Office.

Newspapers

Newspapers are on microfilm in the Mobile Public Library, Local History Division. One newspaper changed names so frequently from 1820 to 1868 that for the purposes of this manuscript it is indicated as *Mobile Commercial Register (MCR)* unless there is a special reason for specifying the name at a particular time. In general, names took the following forms: *Mobile Gazette*, 1813, *and Commercial Advertiser*, 1819; *Mobile Daily Commercial Register and Patriot*, 1821–41; *Mobile Daily Register and Journal*, 1842–49; *Mobile Daily Register*, 1850–60; *Mobile Daily Advertiser and Register*, 1861–67; *Mobile Daily Register*, 1868–. Also see the following other newspapers: *Azalea City News*, 1981; *Mobile Evening News Supplement*, 1856; *Mobile Chronicle*, 1882.

Unpublished Material

Bailey, Francis. "History of the Stage in Mobile, 1824–1850." Master's thesis. University of Iowa, 1934.

Barker, Ronald. "USER Handbook: Fort Condé." Vol. 1: 1720–60; vol. 2: 1810–38. Mobile: City of Mobile, Fort Condé, 1981. [Copy in the MPL(SC)]

Brown, Edward Devereaux. "History and Theatrical Activities at the Mobile Theatre, 1860–1875." Master's thesis. Michigan State College, 1952.

Gould, Elizabeth B. "The Marx House of the 1870s." Mobile: University of South Alabama, 1968. [Monograph and documentation with thirty-seven photographs taken before and after reconstruction]

———. "The Toulmin House, 1828." Mobile: University of South Alabama, 1976. [Contains thirty-one photographs taken before and after restoration]

Leland, Levi Lengel. "Keeper of the Peace in the West Florida Controversy: Harry Toulmin, 1805–1813." Master's thesis. Duke University, 1962.

Lipscomb, Oscar H. "The Administration of Michael Portier, Vicar Apostolic of Alabama and the Floridas, 1825–1829, First Bishop of Mobile, 1829–1859." Ph.D. diss. Washington, D.C.: American University, 1965.

Sheffield, Frances. "The Development of Education in Mobile Prior to 1860." Master's thesis. University of Alabama, 1935.

Watson, Bama W. "History of Barton Academy." Master's thesis. University of Alabama, 1949.

Woodward, Diane S. "The Medical College of Alabama." Senior thesis. University of South Alabama, 1976.

Index

Abba Temple, Rudolph Benz, architect, 224–25
Alderson, William S., architect, 132
American four-square, 247, 250, *251*, *252*
Andrews, Frank, architect, 228, 240–41, *242*, *243*–44
Andry, Paul, architect, 206, *207*, 227, 238
Antomanchi store, 174, *175*
Arcade, 33, 43, 112, 135, 163, 181, 202, 238
Arch:
  blind, 76
  cusped, trefoil, 141, 205, 240
  jack, 155
  lancet, 44, 140, 141
  reverse, 76, 77, 115, 138
  relieving, 208, 211
  segmental, 34, 77, 93, 169, 212, 237
Architects in Mobile: Alderson, William S.; Andrews, Frank; Andry, Paul; Benz, Rudolph; Beroujon, Claude; Brunns, Hermann; Bunnell, Frederick; Butt, Cary; Cumming, David, Jr.; Dakin, Charles B.; Dakin, James; Denham, W. L.; Dougherty, Philip; Downey, Andrew; Freret, James; Gallier, James, Sr.; Garvin, Joseph; George, Captain William; Giles, J. H.; Giraud, T. E.; Hammond, W. R.; Harrod, B. M.; Holmes, Nicholas, Jr.; Holmes and March; Hunt, Reubin Harrison; Hutchisson and Chester; Hutchisson, Clarence L., Sr.; Hutchisson and Denham; Hutchisson and Hutchisson; Hutchisson, James F., 2nd; Hutchisson, James H.; James, Thomas; Karwinski, Thomas F.; Knodel and Thomas; Liddel, Charles T.; Lockwood and Seymour; Maritzen, August; Marye, Philip Thornton; McCrary and Slater; Moffat, Henry; Mulligan, R. L.; Noraman, C. L.; Pearson and Ashe; Pond, W. O.; Rogers, George; Rogers, Isaiah; Smith, T. J.; Stevens and Nelson; Stone Brothers; Sully, Thomas; Taylor, James Knox; Van Antwerp, Cooper; Watkins, George; Watkins and Hutchisson; Watkins, Hutchisson and Garvin; Watkins and Johnson; Willis and Dudley; Young, Ammi B. *See also* Builders; individual listing of architects
Architectural sculpture, 184, 197, 216, 232, 237, 248
Architecture: English, French, and Spanish. *See* English Colonial Period; French Period; Spanish Colonial Period
Architrave, 62, 69, 86, 114, 121, 125, 181, 233
  crossetted, eared, 99, 121, 150, 153, 159, 281 (n. 16). *See also* Crossettes; Greek key door framing
  pedimented, 153, 159, 181
Armory, 105, 133
Arpent, 52, 278–79 (n. 80)
Ashland Place, 228
Attic. *See* Garret
Ayers cottage, 82, *83*

Badger, Daniel, 163, *164*
Balconies, 23, 41, 67, 80, 102, 108, 109, 125, 200, 220, 222, 250
  interior, 67, 142, 243
  iron balconies, 80, 92, 125, 139, 144, 148, 159, 185, 200
  stone, 136
Baluster, wood:
  flat patterned, 192
  square, 81, 85, 117
  swallowtail, 56, 82, 99, 117, 120
  turned, 82, 222, 248
  See also Balustrade; Railing
Balustrade, 33, 34, 48, 50, 56, 71, 82, 89, 92, 117, 118, 202, 248. *See also* Baluster; Railing
Bank of Mobile (1820), 29, *30*, 34
Bank of Mobile (1904), George B. Rogers, architect, 238
Banks, 29, *30*, 31, 34–35, 74, 224, 227, 238, *239*

Barbaud de Boisdore, Joseph, 11
Barge board, 172, 173
Barnes, R. James, builder, 68, *69*, 70, 72, 77, 132
Barnes, W. R., architect, 107
Barney store, 75–76
Baroque influence, 122, 233, 234, *239*, 247, 248
Barton Academy, Gallier and Dakin, architects, 62, 63, *64*, 65, 66, 280 (n. 14)
Bartram, William, 21
Baseboard, 110, 118, 171
Basement, 45, 90, 109, 115, 197, 202
Batter, 67, 99, 121, 125, 153, 159, 236
Battle House (1852), Isaiah Rogers, architect, 148, *149*
Battle House (1906), Frank M. Andrews, architect, 240, *242*, *243*, 244
Bay, 60, 61, 63, 73, 117, 159, 163, 222, 248
Bayshore Rail Road, 187
Bay window. *See* Windows
Beal-Gaillard House, 96, *97*, 98
Beal-Hunter cottage, *88*
Bendernagle (Andry and Bendernagle), architects, 238
Benjamin, Asher, 44, 57, 66, *67*
Benz, Rudolph, architect, 192, 200, *201*, 210, 212, 213, 214, 215, 216, 217, 218, 219, 222, 223, 227, 229, 241, 291 (n. 9)
Bernstein House, James H. Hutchisson, architect, 191, *192*
Beroujon, Claude, architect, 88, 102, 113, *114*
Berryman, contractor, 230
Bethel A.M.E. Church, 203
Bienville, Jean Baptiste Le Moyne de, 15, 52
Bienville Hotel, C. L. Noraman, architect, 228, 240
Bienville Square, 58, 80, 108
Big Zion A.M.E.Z. Church, 203
Big Zion A.M.E.Z. Rectory, George B. Rogers, architect, 233
Bishop Portier cottage, attributed to Claude Beroujon, 86–88

Black education, 178
Blakeley, Josiah, 23, 24
Blakely House, James McGill, builder, 190, 191
Bloodgood, Charles, builder, 80, 104, 106
Bloodgood, John, 155
Bloodgood Row, 94, 95
Board-and-batten. *See* Door; Walls: siding, exterior
Bock, Joseph, cottage, 9–11
de Boispinel and Sieur de Pauger map, 7, 8
Bolduc House, Sainte Genevieve, Missouri, 11–12, 13
Boston, Tremont House, 72, 149
Boundaries. *See* City boundaries
Bousillée. *See* Construction methods
Brace frame. *See* Construction methods
Bracketed style, 191, 192
Brackets, 118, 122, 135, 136, 146, 150, 156, 159, 163, 170, 171, 178, 188, 189, 191, 200, 202, 219, 222, 224, 233, 234, 238, 239, 248
Bragg-Mitchell House, ii, 150
Brick buildings. *See* Civic architecture; Commercial, industrial buildings; Governmental buildings; Religious architecture; Residential architecture
Brick construction, 33, 36, 76, 91, 105, 174
Brick-making machine, 144
Bricks: gray, 228, 234, 238, 240; molded, 109, 176; pressed, 231
Brick sources: Baltimore, 76, 109, 113, 144; Mobile, 144; Nashville, 206; Philadelphia, 144; Roman, 202; St. Louis, 200; Zanesville, 215
Brick veneer. *See* Walls: siding, exterior
Broad Street A.M.E. Church, 203
Brown, Charles, store, 38
Brunns, Hermann, architect, 206
Builders in Mobile: Barnes, R. James; Bloodgood, Charles; Butt, C. W.; Clements and Kellog; Collier and Weeks; Collins, John K.; Cook and Laurie; Cox, George; Davenport, B.; Dargan, E. S.; Deas, James; Durden, John; Ellison, Thomas; Emrich, J. P.; Farley, Charles; Foster, W. S.; Franklin, Lawyer and White; Fricke, Charles; Garrow, S.; Garrow and Center; General Supply Construction Company; Gregory, George; Griffin, C. C.; Heuston and Richards; Hill, James; Hilliard, J.; Hilliard, George; Hobart, Peter; Hutchisson, James F.; Interstate Construction Company; James, Thomas; Jennings, Legrande; Jett Brothers; Kearns, Henry; Kellog, Thomas; Knapp, Samuel; Knoxville Building Company; Lamb, Edward; Lewman, M. T., and Company; Little, William L.; McAdory, J.; McBride, James; McDonald, March, and Company; McGill, James; MaGraw, Thomas; McGuire and Lyndall; Miller, Thomas; Monin, Louis; Monin and Farley; Negrus, Thomas; Neville, William; Newberry, John, and James Prescott; Nicol and Legee; Overton, V.; Pauly Jail Company; Pond, I. P., E. W. Irvin and B. H. Scattergood; Quigley, A. M.; Quigley, William; Railey, Thomas; Redwood, Richard; Sadler, William; Scattergood, Benjamin; Sellitt, Oliver; Shaw, C.; Shaw and White; Shoemaker, E. B.; Silver, Joseph; Silver and Neville; Smith, William; Sossaman, B.; Southern and Forrest; Springsteel, John; Stark, Turner; Tompkins, Thomas; Turner, Amaso; Vaughan, Joseph; Walker and Nadine; Waltan, Alfred Wm.; Ward, E. S.; Ward, John; Warren, Knight and Davis; White, B. H.; Wickwire, Moses; Williams, John; Williams, Robert; Williamson, Robert; Zachary and Zachary. *See also* individual listing of builders
Building codes and ordinances, 43, 77, 108, 144, 174, 276 (nn. 40, 54)
Bungalow style, 246, 247
Bunnell, Frederick, architect, 69, 80, 107, 110, 163
Burgess House, George B. Rogers, architect, 248, 250
Burke Building, 189
Burns and Riley store, 109
Bush-Sands Memorial House, 169, 170, 171
Butt, Cary, architect, 69, 281 (n. 18)
Butt, C. W., builder, 166
Butt House, 164, 166
Buttress, 141, 236
Byzantine influence, 207, 209

Cabinet windows. *See* Windows
Campo Santo, 22, 44
Canada, Charlesbourg, The Paradise House, 11, 12
Caribbean influence, 11, 12
Carlen cottage, 118
Car line, 139
Carolina Hall, 121–23
Carpenter Gothic, 169, 171
Carpenter locks. *See* Hardware
Carriage houses. *See* Dependencies
Carriage way, 42, 109, 135, 159, 211
Cartouche, 170, 181
Casement windows. *See* Windows
Cathedral of the Immaculate Conception, Claude Beroujon, architect; portico, James H. Hutchisson, architect; towers, James F. Hutchisson, 2nd, architect, 44, 102, 114, 115–16, 205, 292 (n. 16)
Catholic Chapel (1827), 44, 148 (nn. 59, 60)
Catholic Orphanage, 116
Caulfield House, 159
Cavallero House, 92–93, 95
Cawthon Hotel, Watkins, Hutchisson, and Garvin, architects, 240, 241
Ceilings, 43, 48, 49, 50, 71, 74, 81, 89, 110, 122, 132, 196, 201
Cellar. *See* Basement
Cement. *See* Concrete
Census, 15, 17, 21, 22, 30, 63, 131, 280 (n. 9), 281 (n. 24)
Center-Gaillard House, 54, 55, 56
Chair rail, 110

Chamberlain-Rapier Double House, 158, 159
Chandler House, 126
Chapel of the Sacred Heart, Harrod and Andry, architects, 205, 206, 207, 208
Charleston, South Carolina, Miles Brewton House, 121
Chase Brothers, iron, 145
Chevillot, Sieur Guillaume-Philbert, 4–5, 6, 253–54 (Appendix 1)
Chicago Commercial School influence, 234, 235, 240, 241, 244, 245
Chickasaw Bogue, 31
Chighizola Building, 145, 146
Chimney: exterior, 37, 49, 76, 91, 113, 118, 125, 144, 155; interior, 118
Christ Church Vestry, James H. Hutchisson, architect, 205
Christ Episcopal Church, Cary Butt, architect, Frederick Bunnell, plan, 69–71
Christ Episcopal Church Rectory, 233
Church buildings. *See* Religious architecture
Church plans. *See* Plans: church
Church Street East Historic District, 140, 174, 191
City Bank and Trust, Andry, Bendernagle, and Rogers, architects, 238
City boundaries, 21, 27, 31, 94, 140, 198, 228, 273 (n. 2)
City growth, 27, 29, 57, 129, 139–40, 183, 195
City halls, 78, 79, 80, 133, 134, 135, 229, 282 (n. 14)
City incorporated, 30
City Jail and Police Station, Rudolph Benz, architect, 198, 199, 200
City jails, 23, 28, 29, 46, 80, 104, 105–06, 199. *See also* City Jail and Police Station; Guard House; Old Spanish Guard House
City plans, 5, 12, 20, 22, 23, 27, 31, 108, 129, 140, 198, 228
Civic architecture, 184–85, 196–200, 201, 202, 203, 229–30, 234, 235, 236, 292 (n. 12). *See also* Fire Station Number Five
Cladding. *See* Walls: siding, exterior
Clarke, G. C., House, 248, 249–50, 251
Clements and Kellog, builders, 29
Clemmons cottage, 119
Closets, 90
Collier and Weeks, contractors, 210
Collins, John K., master builder, 60, 72, 75, 76, 80, 107
Collins property map, James Dowell, 97
Collins-Robinson cottage, 95–96, 97
Colonial periods. *See* English Colonial Period; French Period; Spanish Colonial Period
Colors. *See* Painting
Columbage. *See* Construction methods
Columns, 9, 10, 37, 43, 45, 48, 50, 53, 57, 60, 64, 66, 67, 69, 71, 74, 81, 82, 88, 89, 96, 98, 99, 105, 109, 112, 114, 116, 120, 132, 163, 248, 250
capitals:
Corinthian, 67
Doric, 45, 69–70, 88, 150, 178, 232
Ionic, 64, 66, 69, 184, 197, 239, 248, 250
Square, 45, 53, 96, 99, 117, 132, 191

Tuscan, 115, 150, 159, 208
uncut posts, 11
shafts:
arris, 70, 233
entasis, 60, 71, 82
fillet, 70
shaft, 60, 71
types:
cast iron, 108, 113, 116, 142, 201. *See also* Galleries
cottage, 47, 82
chamfered, 57, 98, 120
fluted, 70, 74, 88, 90, 115, 122, 184, 233
plastered, 45, 60, 71, 116
square, 20, 45, 48, 82, 96, 99, 109, 117, 132, 150, 191
turned, 81
twin, 248
twisted, 232
unfluted, 60
Style. *See* Bungalow style; Greek Revival style; Italianate style; Neoclassical influence; Queen Anne style; Victorian style
Commercial, industrial buildings, 19, 22, 27, 28, *30*, 31, *32*–42, *43*, 71–72, *73*, 74–78, 108–10, *111*, 112–13, 129, 132–33, 140, 144–48, *149*, 156, 163, 174–78, 186, *187*, 188–90, 209, *210*, 211–19, 227–28, 237, *238*, 239–40, *241*, *242*, 243–46, 282 (n. 33), 286 (n. 17), 288 (n. 16)
Common bond, 109, 286 (n. 13)
Community Development Program, 94, 219
Concrete, 181, 201, 228
reinforced, 234, 238, 239, 244, 245. *See also* Flooring
Concrete block, 248, 250. *See also* Houses: concrete block
Construction methods:
assembly line, 247
brick. *See* Brick construction
concrete. *See* Concrete block; Concrete: reinforced
earthen, 7, 11, 14
steel. *See* Steel skeleton
wood:
brace frame, 28, 47, 96, 118
half-timber, 7, 11, 12, 47; bousillée, 7; colombage, 12, 269–70 (n. 9); nogging, 28; poteaux sur sole, 7, 12, 269–70 (n. 9)
Contracts, 28, 29, 33, 35–37, 38, 43, 45, 48, 49, 50, 67, 68, 69, 72, 75, 76, 77, 80, 81, 82, 89, 91, 94, 96, 108, 110, 112, 113, 116, 117, 125, 132, 133, 144, 147, 155, 178, 184, 197, 275 (n. 32)
Convent of Visitation, 101, *181*, 182
Cook and Laurie, contractors, *244*
Coping, 35, 109
Corbels, 141, 146, 159, 181, 189
Corbel table, 142, 229
Cornice, 41, 49, 73, 75, 76, 109, 114, 117, 122, 125, 142, 144, 182, 184, 229, 230, 237
bracketed Italianate, 122, 136, 146, 150, 156, 159, 163, 164, 165, 170, 171, 176, 188, 208, 234, 240
cavetto, 236
terra cotta, 238, 245
Victorian, 222

Cottages:
French Creole style, 7, 10–*11*, 29, 47, *83*, *84*
Gulf Coast development, 47–49, 57, 81–82, *83*–88, 94–95, *96*, *97*, 98–99, 117, 191
late Gulf Coast, 117, *118*, *119*, 120, 121, 150, *151*, 192
worker's cottages, *190*, 191
Victorian. *See* Victorian cottages
Cotton Exchange and Chamber of Commerce Building, Rudolph Benz, architect, *215*, 216
Cotton presses, 28, 33–34
County Court Houses, 29, 45–46, 131–32, 167–68, 184, *185*, 196, *197*, 229, 265–67 (Appendix 6)
County Prison, Frederick Bunnell, architect, 80–81, 163, 283 (n. 37)
Cox, George, master mason, *169*, 170, *171*
Crawford store, *237*
Crenelation, 44, 161
Creole Fire Station Number One, James H. Hutchisson, architect, 176, *177*
Cresting, 140, 209, 222; wood, 140; iron, 200, 209
Crocket, 140
Cross bracing, 7
Crossettes (eared). *See* Architrave: crossetted; Greek key door framing
Crown moldings. *See* Moldings
Crozar, Antoine, 14–15
Cullum, Charles, 144
Cumming, David, Jr., architect, *140*, 141, *157*
Cupola, 23, 64, 71, 80, 180

Dade cottage, *83*, 103
Daily house, 50
Dakin, Charles B., architect, 62, 63, *64*, 66, *67*, 69, 71, *72*, *73*, 74, *79*, 102
Dakin, James, architect, 62
Daniels and Elgin store, Badger Iron Works, 163, *164*, 211
Dargan, E. S., contractor, 133, *134*
Davenport, B., builder, 88
Davis, B. H., house, Hutchisson and Garvin, architects, 228
Davis Avenue development, 198, 228
Dawson, John, builder, 142
Deas, James, master builder, *111*
De Batz Map, 7, *10*
Decorative designs:
beeding, 37
cavetto cornice, 171
Greek Revival
acanthus, 71, 122, 159, 170, 212
anthemion, 67, 159
arcadian, 76, 129
bead and reel, 122
egg and dart, 122, 174, *181*
fret, 67
leaf and dart, *169*, 181
palmette, 122, 212
rosette, 71, 233
Italianate
arabesque, 129
organic, 122, 129, 156, 160, 166
rinceau, 129
shell, 171
scroll, 150, 159, 188
swag, 129, 239, 240

wreath, 234
Linear-geometric, 215, 231, 233, 237, 238
Victorian, 124
Delage, Charles, map, *80*
Demouy store, *188*
Denham, W. L., architect, 227, 228
Dentils, 49, 67, 75, 88, 91, 93, 109, 122, 145, 153, 156, 184, 188, 197, 239
Dependencies:
bath houses, 89
carriage houses, 94, 109
kitchens, 10, 11, 56, 89, 90, 94, 109, 146, 181
privies, necessaries, 77, 89, 94, 109, 178
sheds, 36, 37, 108
stables, 42, 89, 94, 109, 200
Descriptions of the City of Mobile, 35, 37–38, 38–39, 42, 129, 131, 168–84, 191, 195, 196
Develle, Peter Hanibal, 15
Deverges, Bernard, 9
Devin, Sieur, 5, 7, 8
Dickens House, Hutchisson and Garvin, architects, 228
Digest for the Laws for the State of Alabama, 53, 261 (Appendix 4)
Distyle-in-antis, 57, 66, 69, 70, 116, 279 (n. 1). *See also* Greek Revival; Plans
Doctor LeVert's Office, 146, *147*
Dome, 63, 71, 74, 180, 238, 242
Door:
exterior, 34, 35, 37, 38, 41, 45, 46, 49, 50, 54, 56, 61, 76, 81, 82, 86, 90, 94, 99, 105, 108, 109, 112, 117, 119, 125, 188, 211, 219, 248
types
arched heading, 35, 77, 142, *185*, 231
batten, 66, 108
iron, 80, 105, 109, 165
jib, 76, 95, 99, 109
louvred, 153
paneled, 90, 117
segmental heading, 34
Venetian, 50
interior
board-and-batten, 82, 94
folding, 89, 94, 110, 112, 166
paneled, 45, 50, 82, 94, 117, 185
sliding, 110, 201
styles
Federal, 41, 86
Greek Revival, 150, 153, 159, 233. *See also* Greek key door framing
Italianate, 137, 160, 170
Victorian, 200
Dorman house, Walker and Nadine, builders, 89
Dormer windows, 76, 85, 88, 92, 93, 109, 113, 118, 199, 125, 216, 223
Dougherty, Philip, architect, 156, *157*
Downey, Andrew, architect, 227, 228
Downey and Denham, architects, 228, 233
Downing, Andrew Jackson, architect, 44, 171, 227
Drainage, 32, 108, 274 (n. 19), 274 (n. 6)
Dreaper and Burns store, George Watkins, architect, *211*, 212
Drought, 103
Dunlap house, *221*

Durden, John, builder, 63, *64*
Durnford, Elias, 20

Early statehood, 30–56
  architectural elements, 33–34, 41, 43, 45, 54, 56
  buildings
    cotton presses, 30, 33–34
    banks, 30, 34–35
    government buildings, 43, 45–46
    hotels, 30, 39, 41–42
    religious buildings, 44–45
    residential, 42, *47, 48, 49, 50, 51,* 52–53, *55*–56
    sawmills, 32
    stores, 30, 35–39
    theater, 30, 39–41
    warehouses, 36, 39
    wharfs, 36, 39
  census, 30–31
  city plan, 31
  description of city, 35, 37, 38, 39, 42
  emigration, 30, 34
  Federal style, 33, 34, 41
  fires, 34, 38, 42, *58*
  Georgian influence, 33
  maps, *26,* 30, *55*
  streets and roads, 31
  water supply, 32
Early twentieth century, 209, 215
Economic recession, 103, 105, 182, 183
Educational buildings, 62–63, *64,* 65, 66, *101, 102,* 131, 178, *179,* 180, 181, *208,* 209, *229,* 230
Egyptian style influence, 67, *68,* 236, 281 (n. 16)
Electric cars, 195
Electric companies, 195
Electric lights, 206
Elkus House, *156,* 159
Ellicott boundary stone, 5, 21, 272 (n. 43)
Elliott, John, House, 94
Ellison, Thomas, brick mason-architect, 76, 78, 282 (n. 26)
Emerson College, 178
Emigration, 15, 21, 27, 30, 34, 270 (n. 17)
Emrich, J. P., contractor, *203*
English Block, Rudolph Benz, architect, *215,* 216
English Colonial Period, 16–21
  agriculture, 17
  architecture, military, 18–19
  architecture, nonmilitary, 20
    churches, religious, 20
    columns, 20
    court house, 20
    description of the town, 17, 18
    elements, 18, 20
    Fort Charlotte, 16, 18–19, 30
    Georgian influence, 20
    hospital, 19, 20
    house, Pensacola, 16
    land grants, 17, 20
    maps, *14,* 20
    materials, 18
    Pensacola. *See* Pensacola
    plantation house, 18
    porches, 20
    windows, 20
  trade law, 18
  Treaty of Paris, 16

English Perpendicular style, *233*
Entablature, 56, 60, 61, 64, 66, 69, 86, 88, 99, 114, 117, 163, 208, 233
Entasis, 60, 71, 82
Eslava, Don Miguel, 41, 153
Eslava and Dumée store, James F. Hutchisson, builder, 109
Eslava-McMahon cottage, 82, *84*

Fan lights, 45
Farley, Charles, builder, *215*
Farmer, Major Robert, 14, 15, 16, 17, 18
Fascia, 156, 166
Fearn Company, 228, 250
Federal influence, 30, 33, 34, 41, 45, 86, *87,* 155, *156, 157,* 159
Female Benevolent Society, 93
Fencing, 42, 49, 65, 88, *89,* 90, 109, 110
  wall fencing, 80, 92, 105–06, 110
Fenestration, 35, 63, 73, 75, 144, *145,* 174, 188, 212, 215, 237, 240, 250. *See also* Windows
Ferard home, Neville, Silver, Miller, and Sadler, builders, 91
Festorazzi House, Rudolph Benz, architect, *223,* 293 (n. 31)
Fezende, René-Jean-Gabriel, 15
Fidelia Club, Pearson, and Ashe, architects, 234, *235*
Fines levied on builders, 33, 47
Finial, 140, 141, 216
Fire companies, 77, 138, *139,* 176, *177,* 196, 289–90 (n. 12)
Fireplaces, 37, 89, 93, 185, 248. *See also* Mantlepieces
Fires, 34, 38, 42, 45, 57, *58,* 71, 75, 77, 103, 148, 168, 195, 275 (n. 27)
Fire Station Number Five, 138, *139*
Firewall, 35, 75, 76, 77, 109, 132, 144, 174
First Baptist Church, Rubin Harrison Hunt, architect, *232,* 233
First County Court House, Peter Hobart, architect, 45–46
First Government Street Presbyterian Church, Moses Wickwire, builder, 67–68
First National Bank, Watkins, Hutchisson, and Garvin, architects, 238, *239*
First Protestant Church, 30, 44
Flo-Claire, 228, 247, 250
Flooring, 19, 36, 37, 42, 50, 68, 74, 77, 82, 98, 110, 132, 185
  brick, 42, 77, 110
  concrete, 239, 240
  flagging, 110, 132
  marble, 74, 198
  parquetry, 221, 234
  plank, 36, 82, 98
  rough, 82
  tile, 148, 198, 248
  tongue-and-groove, 36–37, 50, 77, 98, 110
Forbes, John, 22, 27
Forbes and Company, 27, 272 (n. 45)
Forcheimer, M., House, *222*
Forcheimer, second house, *224*
Forsythe, John, 186
Fort, Red Bluffs, 19
Fort Condé:
  elements, 7, 12, 15–16, 18–19
  demolition, 30, 274 (n. 17)
  description, 15–16

  inventory, 15, 16
  maps, *6, 8, 9, 10, 13, 14*
  See also English Colonial Period; French Period; and Spanish Colonial Period
Fort Condé-Charlotte. *See* English Colonial Period
Fort Louis de la Louisiane, 6
Fort San Esteban de Tombeché, 21
Foster, W. S., contractor, *203*
Foundations, 7, 14, 28, 36, 48, 57, 60, 71, 75, 77, 81, 102, 112, 115, 118, 137–38, 209, 234
Framing elements:
  iron. *See* Iron structural elements
  steel. *See* Steel skeleton
  wood:
    braces, 7, 28, 47
    girders, 37, 174
    joists, 28, 36, 37, 77, 174
    lath, 29, 49, 76, 95, 118
    plate, 37
    posts, 7, 11, 28
    rafters, 28, 33, 141
    sleepers, 16, 28, 36
    studs, 29, 47, 76
    summer beam, 52
    truss: cusped, 205; king post, 110; scissors, 141
  sills,
    door:
      stone, 71, 76, 109, 114;
      wood, 28, 36;
    window:
      brick, stuccoed, 125;
      iron, 169;
      stone, 46, 71, 76, 114, 125, 185;
      wood, 170
Franklin, Lawyer, and Whitehouse, masons, 38
Franklin Society Building, Rudolph Benz, architect, 189
Frascati Recreational Park, 187
French Period, 4–16
  agriculture, 15
  census, 15
  churches, 7, 14
  city plan, 4–5, 13
  cottages, 7, 9–10, *11, 12, 13*
  fort. *See* Fort Condé
  hospital, 12, 14, 58
  hurricane, 12
  map. *See* Maps
  plantations, 15
  trade, 14–15
  streets, 5, 13
French Second Empire style, *197,* 198
Freret, James, architect, *180,* 181, 184–85, 208
Fricke, Charles, contractor, *180,* 184, *185,* 191, *192*
Frieze, 69, 86, 114, 189, 233
Frolichstein-Goldsmith houses, *165,* 166–67

Galeries, 7, 9, 10, 11, 23, 37, 48, 52, 53, 54, 61, 71, 81, 94, 96, 98, 99, 109, 116, 118, 120, 125, 180
  iron galleries, 33, 61, 75, 76, 91, 125, 126, 143, 145, 155, 160, 165, 182, 211
  See also Porches

Gallery:
  exterior. *See* Galeries
  interior, 41, 71. *See also* Balcony: interior
Gallier, James, Sr., architect, 62, 63, *64, 67, 78, 79,* 102
Gálvez, Bernardo de, 21
Garçonnière, 126
Garden, 42, 130, 150, 191
Garret, 28, 41, 56, 125
Garrow, Samuel H., 49
Garrow House, *49, 50,* 278 (n. 73)
Garvin, Joseph, architect, 227. *See also* Watkins, Hutchisson, and Garvin
Gates Houses, *120*
Gazzam House, *90, 94*
Geary, Dan, map, 272 (n. 46)
General Supply and Construction Company, 216, *242*
George, Captain William, 60
Georgia cottage, *120*
Georgian influence, 20, *30,* 33, 34, *49, 121, 122,* 248
Georgian plan. *See* Plans: style
German Relief Hall, Rudolph Benz, architect, 200, *201,* 292 (n. 12)
Giles, J. H., Badger and Company, 163, *164*
Giraud, T. E., architect, *114,* 115
Glass:
  art glass, 198, 200, 211, 223
  beveled, leaded, 171
  Bohemian, 122, 159, *160*
  diamond shaped, 142
  etched, 122
  French, 132, 212
  plate, 212
  sizes, 37, 50, 76, 82, 109, 112, 219
  stained glass, 70, 141, 206, 207, 221, 224, 243
Globe Hotel, *30,* 41–42
Goodwin and Haire Map, *30, 31, 33, 34–35, 39–41, 43–44*
Gordon, Lord Adam, 18, 19, 20
Gothic Revival influence, *30,* 35, 44, 122, *123,* 140, 142, *143,* 161, *162,* 169, 172, *173,* 203, *205,* 220, 233
Gothic Revival plan. *See* Plans: style
Governmental buildings, 28, 29, 46–47, 78–81, *104, 105, 106,* 107–08, 129–33, *134*–39, 140, 163, 184, *185,* 196, *197, 199,* 229, 230, *262* (Appendix 4), 282 (n. 34), 283 (n. 37)
Government Street, 31, 131
Government Street Baptist Church, Reuben Harrison Hunt, architect, *232,* 233
Government Street Hotel, Charles B. Dakin, architect, *71, 72,* 73
Government Street Methodist Church, B. D. Price, architect, 203
Government Street Methodist Church, George B. Rogers, architect, 232
Government Street Presbyterian Church, Gallier and Dakin, architects, *59,* 62, 66, *67*–68
Government Street Presbyterian Church, Moses Wiskwire, builder, 67, 68
Grain elevator, A. Maritzen, architect, 209
Graining, 82, 94, 110, 116, 185. *See also* Painting
Greek key door framing, 67, 99, 121, 150, 153, 159. *See also* Architrave: crossetted
Greek Revival moldings, 67, 71, 121, 122, 137, 169, 181–82. *See also* Decorative designs
Greek Revival orders. *See* Columns: capitals
Greek Revival style, 34, 56, 58–63, *64–65,* 66, *67–70,* 71, *72–74,* 78, *79,* 82–84, *85,* 88, 90, 91, *92–93, 99–100,* 107, 116, 122, 137–38, *139,* 150, *154–55,* 159, *171,* 178, *208,* 232, *251*
Greek Temple of Vergina, Greece, 150, 154
Gregory, George, contractor, 133, *134–35*
Griffin, C. C., builder, *213*
Groined vaults, 132
Grondel, Mme, 14, 58
Grotz Building, 188, 212, *213*
Guard House, Quigley and Henderson, builders, 80, 153 (n. 36)
Guatamalan house, Livingston, 11, *12*
Guesnard House, David Cumming, Jr., architect, 141, *156, 157*
Gulf, Mobile, and Ohio Railroad Station, Philip Thornton Marye, architect, 228, *238*
Gunnison, Henry, 28, 29
Guttae, 69

Haldimand, Brigadier General Frederick, 19
Half-timber, 7, 11, 12, 47
Hall, Edward, developer, 228
Hallett, William, 113
Hall-Ford House, *85*
Hall plan. *See* Plans: residential, cottages and houses
Hall warehouse, 110
Hamilton, Reverend William T., 68
Hamilton home, Vaughan, Shaw, White, builders, 89–90, 283–84 (n. 48)
Hammel's Department Store, Stone Brothers, architects, *244*
Hammond, W. H., architect, 227
Hardware, 37, 71, 85, 90, 95; carpenter locks, 85, 90, 95, 98
Harrison, D. G., contractor, *217*
Harrod and Andry, architects, 206, *207*
Health, 18, 19, 50–51, 103, 116, 184, 195
Hellen-Croom House, 191, *192*
Henderson, builder, 80
Henshaw and James Map, 58, *62*
Heuston and Richards, masons, 211
Hexastyle, 232
Hill, James, builder-mason, *157*
Hilliard, George, carpenter, *48*
Historic Mobile Preservation Society, 99
Hitchcock, Judge Henry, 63, 68, 71, 75, 93, 103, 280 (n. 10)
Hitchcock Row, 137, *145*
Hobart, Peter, architect-builder, 24, 45, 131
Hogan-McLoskey Building, Ellison and Littell, builders, 76
Holmes, Nicholas, Jr., architect, 66, 118
Holmes and March, architects, 66
Hood moldings, 161, 171, 172, *173,* 176, 178, 188, 189, 229
Hopkins House, 223
Horst House, George Cox, master mason, *169,* 170

Hospitals, 12, 14, 27, 31, 46, 58–62, 107–08, 143, 230
Hot air furnace, 132
Hotels, *30,* 39, 41–42, 71, 72, 73, *112,* 113, *146,* 147–49, 186, 227, 240, *241, 242*–44, 290 (n. 6), 291 (n. 7)
Houses:
  brick, 47, 50, *91–93, 94, 95,* 124–27, 145, 155, *156*–62, 164, *165–67,* 169–71, 191, 248
  brick veneer. *See* Walls: siding, exterior
  concrete block, *247, 248, 249, 250, 251*
  country, 15, *51, 52–53,* 54, *55–56,* 94–96, *97,* 99–100, *101,* 119, *120*–25, 150, *151–54*
  shingle, 228
  shingle and stucco, 228
  stone, *225*
  wood, one story, 11, 81, 82, *83*–88, 96, 97, 98–101, *118, 119,* 150, 151, *152–53, 172, 173,* 190, 191, *218–20,* 246, 247. *See also* Cottages; Bungalows; Shotgun cottages
  wood, two story, ii, 48, 49, 52, *85,* 88, 89, 90, 94–96, 121–22, 150, 155, 191, 192, *220–25,* 248, *251, 252,* 278 (n. 73), 293 (n. 31)
Housing, colonial. *See* English Colonial Period, French Period, Spanish Colonial Period
Hull, D. B., and U. S., builders, *199,* 200
Hunt, Reubin Harrison, architect, 228, *232*
Hunter Cottage, 82, *232*
Hurricane, 12, 68, 70, 132, 141, 180, 195, 198, 206, 240
Hutchisson, Clarence L., Sr., 68, *178,* 227, 228, 246, 248. *See also* Watkins, Hutchisson, and Garvin
Hutchisson, James F., builder, 109, *114,* 115, 144, 147, 155
Hutchisson, James F., 2nd, architect, 113, *114,* 192, 197, 203, 205, 207, 212, *218,* 219, 220, 227
Hutchisson, James H., architect, *83,* 113, 174, 176, *177,* 181, *182,* 191, 192, 204, 205, 207, 211
Hutchisson and Chester, architects, 51
Hutchisson and Garvin, architects, 228, 230, *233,* 248
Hutchisson, Holmes, and Hutchisson, architects, 52
Hutchisson and Hutchisson, architects, *146*

Imbrication. *See* Walls: siding, exterior
Indian Assembly House, "haugard, sovager," 14, 19, 20
Indian trade: English, 18; French, 14–15; Spanish, 22, 23
Interstate Construction Company, *239, 245*
Investment mass housing, 248
Iron foundry. *See* Kling Foundry; Lang Brass Foundry; Mobile Foundry; Park and Lyon Foundry; Skate Foundry; Spear Iron Foundry; Water Street Phoenix Foundry
Iron structural elements, 80, 105, 108, 109, 110, 115, 116, 132, 135, 142, 146, 163–64, 169, 185, 189, 201, 233. *See*

Galeries; Balconies; Verandas; Moldings; Doors; Shutters
Isabella Street, 120, 284 (n. 55)
Italianate plan. *See* Plan: styles
Italianate style, *ii*, *121*, 129, *136*, 138, 146, *147*, 150, 155, 156, *157*, *159*, *160*, *164*, *165*, *169–70*, *171*, *172*, *173*, 178, *187*, 188, *191*, *192*, *208*, 209, 210, 212

Jack arch, 155
Jail. *See* City jails
James, Thomas, builder-architect, 63, 68, 92, 133, *134*, 145, 166
Jennings, Legrand, builder, 46
Jett Brothers, builders-contractors, 66, *232*, *233*, *235*, *241*
Jib doors, 76, 95, 99, 109, 155. *See also* Doors: arched heading
Jig saw. *See* Saws
Johnstone, Governor George, 17, 19
Joinery, 53, 56, 96, 118, 136
Jones cottage, *118*
Judson, Lewis, 22, 24, 29, 45

Karwinski, Thomas F., architect, *84*, 95, *187*, 211, 212
Kearns, Henry, mason, *213*
Kellog, Thomas, builder, 28, 29
Kennedy, Joshua, 24, 107
Kennedy, William, 24
Kennedy House, *162*
Ketchum, Dr. George, House, *171*, *172*
Ketchum, William, House, *164*, *165*, 166
Keystone, 114, *189*, *239*, *240*
Kilduff House, James F. Hutchisson, 2nd, architect, *220*, 221
Kimball House, *172*, *173*
King, Edward, traveler, 184
King, John, wharf, 174
Kling Foundry, 166, 211
Knodel and Thomas, architects, *233*, *234*
Knoxville Building Company, *202*, 214
Krebs, Hugo, 12
Kreb's "Bird's Eye View" map of Mobile. *See* Maps

Label. *See* Hood moldings
La Clede Hotel, *146*, 291 (n. 7)
Lafayette Hotel, 112, *113*, 186
Lamb, Edward, builder, *157*
Lancet arch. *See* Arch
Land grants and claims, 17, 20, 21
Lang Brass Foundry, 176
Larrouil Cottage, 57, 82, *85*
Lath, 29, 49, 76, 95, 118
La Tourrette Map, 57, *59*, 66, *72*, *73*
Lauber Carriage Factory, James H. Hutchisson, architect, *209–10*
Leinkauf School, Watkins and Hutchisson, architects, *229*, *230*
Leprete, John, and Thomas Townsley Cotton Press, 30, *33–34*
LeVert office, *146*, *147*
Lewman, M. T., and Company, contractors, *206*, *207*
Liddel, Charles T., architect, 221
Lintels, 35, 76, 125, 155, 200, 240
  cast iron, 115, 169, 233
  rusticated stone, 200
  stone, 109, 115, 125, 136, 155
  stucco, 35, 76, 125, 155

terra cotta, 238, 239
Victorian, 212
Lisloy, plantation house, 15, *18*
Littell, William, mason, 76
Little, William L., mason, 35, 76, 275 (n. 32)
Livery stable, 112
Lockwood and Seymour, architects, 68
Loggia, *171*, *234*, *248*
Lopez store, 77
Lorimer, Dr. John, 19
Lots, city, 20, 29, 91, 146, 273 (n. 50), 273 (n. 8), 228 (n. 18)
Lott House, Hutchisson and Garvin, architects, *248*
Louis XIV, 7, 14, 15
Louis XV style, *248*, *249*
Lowenstein Bank, Stone Brothers, architects, *227*, *238*
Lower Dauphin Street Commercial Historic District, 174, 212
Lyon House, *160*, *161*
Lyons, John, store, William Smith, builder, 109

McAdory, J., contractor, *201*, *214*
McBride, James, *223*
McCaw Building, *212*
McCoy House, *222*, 293 (n. 31)
McCrary and Slater, architects, *227*, *228*
McDonald, March, and Company, *184*, *211*, *213*, *214*, *217*
McGanahan Store, *146*, *147*
McGill, James, builder, *191*
McGill Institute, *208*, 209
McGill Building, *174*, *175*
McGillvrey, Lachlan, 20, 22, 271 (n. 36)
McGowin, Joseph, House, T. J. Smith, architect, *247*, *248*, *249*
McGuire and Lyndall, builders, 212
McGuire Building, *145*, 146
MacKenzie, Roderick D., 11, *47*, 48
McMillan, Reverend Leighton, 153
Macy House, *172*, *173*
Magnolia Sugar Factory, 176
MaGraw, Thomas, iron fencing, *65*
Malaga Inn. *See* Frolichstein-Goldsmith houses
Mandeville Tract development, 198, 240
Mansard roof. *See* Roof
Mansion House, 144
Mantlepieces, 94, 110, 224, 248. *See also* Fireplaces
Maps:
  Boispinel-Pauger, 7, *8*
  Chevillot-Pailloux, 4, *5*, *6*
  Collins property, 95, *97*
  De Batz, 7, *10*
  Delage, *80*
  Geary, 272 (n. 46)
  Goodwin and Haire, 30, *31–44*
  Henshaw and James, *62*
  Kreb's "Bird's Eye View" of Mobile, *116*, *183*
  La Tourrette, 57, *59*, 66, *72*, *73*
  Matzenger (1888), *198*, *199*
  Mobile Fires, *58*
  North America, 1689–1748, 1, *2*
  North America, 1763–1774, 1, *2*
  Pauger and Devin, 5, 7, *8*
  Phelypeaux, 12, *13*, 22
  Pittman, *14*, 20

Robertson (1828), 54, *55*, 96
Robertson (1856), 129, *130–31*, 140
Sanborn (1885), 93, 125, 220
Schematic Map of Mobile, 26, *27*
Spanish, 22
Spanish plan for Mobile, 23–24, *25*
Troost, 75, 78, 107, 285 (n. 4)
United States Map of Claims and Cessions, 1, *5*
United States map, 1812–1822, 1, *4*
Marble. *See* Stone material
Maritzen, August, architect, *209*
Market. *See* Public markets
Marshall, Benjamin, 153
Marshall-Hixon House, 150, *151–53*
Marye, Philip Thornton, architect, 228, 238
Masonic Temple, Stone Brothers, architects, *234*, *235*
Masson Building, *214*, *215*
Mayer, Franz, stained glass, 70
Medallion, 54, 71, 90, *121*, *122*, 170, 232, 238
Medical College Building, 178, *179*
Metope, 69, 86, 208
Military architecture. *See* English Colonial Period; French Period; Spanish Colonial Period
Miller Farmhouse, 98, *99*
Miller, Thomas, mason, 91
Millfort, General Louis, 23
Mobile and Ohio Rail Road, 127
Mobile boundaries. *See* City boundaries
Mobile Brewery, August Maritzen, architect, *209*
Mobile Daily Register, 186
Mobile Fertilizer Manufacturing Company, 176
Mobile Foundry, 176, 211
Mobile Historic Development Commission, 219
Mobile Hotel, 30, 41
Mobile Infirmary, Hutchisson and Garvin, architects, *230*
Mobile Lighting Company, 195
Mobile Omnibus Company, 139
Modillion, *163*, 166, *188*
Moffat, Henry, architect, 116, *117*
Mohr, Dr. Charles, 171
Moldings, 54, 56, 61, 88, 90, 114, 117, 121–22, 136, 159, 174, 182, 248
  crown, 122, 153, 166, 171, 206, 212, 233. *See also* Greek Revival moldings
Monin, Louis, builder, 197, *215*
Monin and Farley, contractors, *215*
Monin Building, *174*, *175*
Monroe Park Pavilion, *240*, *241*
Montault de Monberaut, Chevalier, 15, 18, 271 (n. 26)
Monterey development, 228
Montuse Tavern, 27
Moogk, Peter, 11, 269–70 (n. 9)
Moorish influence, 223, *240*, *241*
Mortar joints, 36, 109, 110, 125, 136, 146, 155, 206, 215–16
Mottus, Catalina, 45
Moog grocery warehouse, 174
Mount and Company, carpenters, 58
Mount and Tatum Hospital, 58–59
Mulligan, R. L., architect, 230
Murphy, James, mason, 80
Mutuals, 69
Mystic Society, 187

Neoclassical influence, 45, 120, 150, *158*, 178, *179*, 184, *185*, 191, 196, 202, 225, 241, 251
Neville, William, mason, 91
New Lyric Theatre, Stone Brothers, architects, 227
New York Wire Railing Company, 133
Nicol and Legee, contractors, 231
Nogging. *See* Construction methods: wood
Noraman, C. L., architect, 228, 240
Notman, John, architect, 136, *139*, 171

Oakleigh, *99–100*
Oakleigh Garden Historic District, 191, 228
O'Conner country home, 94
Old Chandler House. *See* McGill Institute
Old City Hospital, William George, architect, 59, 60, 61, *61*, 62, 229
Old Government Street (Airport Boulevard), 250, *251*
Old Shell Road, 119, 140, 198, 284 (n. 55)
Old Spanish Fort, Pascagoula, Mississippi, 12, *13*
Old Spanish Guard House and Jail, Bloodgood, builder, *104*, *105*, *106*
Orange Grove development, 94, 155, 289 (n. 28)
Ordinances. *See* Building codes and ordinances
Osborne House, 169
Ottenstein House, Thomas James, builder, *92*, *93*
Overton, V., contractor, *218*

Page Store, James H. Hutchisson, architect, 174
Pailloux, Barbazant de, 4, 5, 6
Painting, 28–29, 42, 47, 49, 71, 82, 89, 110, 118, 198, 206, 223, 230, 239, 243, 248, 278 (n. 71). *See also* Graining
Palladian window. *See* Windows
Paneling. *See* Walls: siding, interior
Panton and Leslie, 20, 22
Parapet, 41, 42, 44, 64, 73, 76, 91, 113, 125, 132, 155, 161, 170, 174, 176, 189, 208, 238, 250
Park and Lyon Foundry, 176
Parks, 187, 240, *241*
Parmly Houses, *124*, 125
Partition walls, 60, 76, 89, 174, 201
Party walls, 35, 75, 159, 174, 189
Pattern books, 57, 66
Pauger, Adrien, Sieur de, 5, 7, 8, 14
Pauly Jail Company, *199*, 200
Pavilion, 63, 102, 181, 206
Pavillon roof, 7
Pearson and Ashe, architects, 227, 234, *235*
Pediment, 50, 66, 88, 181, 184, 197, 209, 216, 233, 239, 250
Pensacola, Florida:
    English period, 17, 19, 23
    Spanish period, 23
    Old Spanish Jail, 23, *24*
Pest house, E. B. Shoemaker, builder, 105
Peters, Joseph, store, *146*, 186
Phelypeaux Map. *See* Maps
Philadelphia, Pennsylvania, Athenaeum, John Notman, architect, 136, *139*
Piazzas, 43, 45, 47, 89. *See also* Galeries; Porches
Piers, 33, 43, 48, 53, 54, 77, 112, 202, 234, 242, 245
Pilasters, 53, 61, 62, 63, 66, 68, 70, 85, 86, 90, 93, 110, 114–15, 116, 122, 125, 132, 159, 163, 171, 178, 181, 184, 202, 206, 216, 231, 234, 243, 245, 248
Pincus Building, Rudolph Benz, architect, *216*, 217
Pinnacle, 44, 70, 141
Plans:
    church
        basilica, 141
        Greek cross, 207
        rectangular, temple, treasury: apse, 206; chancel, 70, 141; nave, 115, 142; side aisle, 115, 141, 205. *See* Greek Revival style
    residential
        bungaloid, 247
        cottages, 7, 4, 47, 49, 81, 82, 94, 117, 120, 150; two rooms, 10, 11, 29
        cottages and houses: central hall, 47, 48, 50, 53, 81, 96, 98, 118, 150, 277 (n. 67); cross hall, 172; side hall, 56, 89, 91, 121, 125, 154, 155, 166; T, 99; temple, 66; wing, double, recessed, 90, 150; wing, single, 91; wing, offset, 155, 165, 166, 208, 219
    store, 35, 36–37, 75, 76, 108–09
    styles:
        Greek Revival, 57, 66, 70, 116, 184, 197, 232. *See also* Distyle-in-antis; Hexastyle; Prostyle
        Georgian, 49
        Italianate, 156, 159, 165, 170
        Gothic Revival, 172
        Shotgun, 155, 172, 191, 289 (n. 30)
        Victorian, 222
Planters and Merchant Bank, Charles and James Dakin, architects, 74, 94
Plaster on lath. *See* Walls: siding, interior
Plaster relief ornamentation, 122, 129. *See also* Decorative designs
Podium, 45, 116, 185, 197
Pollock and Bernheimer, 211
Pollock and Bernheimer Building, Rudolph Benz, architect, 209, *210*
Pollock and Bernheimer Store (1903), *210*
Pollock and Bernheimer warehouse, *187*, 188, 209
Pollock Building, Thomas Sully, architect, 211
Pond, I. P., E. W. Irvin, and B. H. Scattergood, builders, 116
Pond, W. O., architect, 184, *185*, 192, 196
Porches, 20, 47, 48, 50, 73, 85, 92, 95, 107, 121, 142, 154, 162, 165, 172, 191, 219, 222, 247, 248, 252. *See also* Galeries; Piazzas
Portico, 45, 47, 60, 61, 63, 64, 71, 78, 102, 107, 113, 116, 122, 178, 184, 197, 250. *See also* Greek Revival style
Portier, Bishop Michael, 44, 86, 101, 146, 180
Post of La Balise, 7, 9
Poteaux sur sole. *See* Construction methods

Powder House, 46, 81, 105
Prefabricated cast iron units, 163
Price, Larimar, store, *146*, 186
Privies. *See* Dependencies
Progress Light and Motor Company, 195
Prostyle, 57, 88, 197, 279 (n. 1). *See also* Greek Revival style
Protestant Children's Home, Henry Moffat, architect, 116, *117*
Providence Infirmary (1854), 143, *144*
Providence Infirmary (1903), R. L. Mulligan, architect, 230
Public markets, 28, 39, 43, 132–35, 276 (n. 54). *See also* City halls
Purvis, Robert, House, 94

Queen Anne style, 212, *213*, *218*, 222–25, *246*, 247
Quigley, A. M., mason, 144, *157*
Quigley, William, mason, 46
Quigley and Henderson, builders, 80
Quill House, 225
Quoin, 135, 136, 164, 165, 181, 234, 250

Railing, 37, 42, 48, 50, 56, 81, 82, 99, 117, 132, 185. *See also* Balustrade; Baluster
Railroads, 127, 187
Ranch style, 250
Rapelje House, George Cox, master mason, 170, *171*
Rapier-Boone House, Clarence L. Hutchisson, Sr., architect, 248
Redwood, Richard, mason-contractor, 65, 72, 94, 96, 133, *134*, 156
Religious architecture, 7, 14, 20, 30, 31, 44–45, 59, 66, 67–70, 71, 94, 101–02, 113, *114*, 115, *116*, 117, 131, 140–43, 179, 180, *181*–82, 203–05, 206, 207, 208–09, 231–33, 234, 292 (nn. 15, 16)
Renaissance influence, *128*, 129, *134–35*, 136, 162, 163, 164, 180–82, 202, 230, 234, 235, 238, 239, 244, 248
Residential architecture, 7, 9–10, 11, 14, 23, 29, 42, 47–56, 57, 81–101, 117–25, 150–62, 164–67, 169–73, 191–93, 219–25, 228, 247–52, 283 (n. 41), 283–84 (n. 48). *See also* Bungalow style; Cottages; Houses; Shotgun cottages; Victorian cottages
Reverse arches. *See* Arch
Richards, Ralph, home, George B. Rogers, architect, 228
Richards House, 156, 159, *160*
Richardsonian and Romanesque influence, 200, 205, 206, 207, 208, 225, 229, 231
Riley, Thomas, contractor, 133, *134*
Riley House, *158*, 159
Roberts-Abbott House, 154, *155*
Robertson Map of Mobile (1856), 129, *130–31*, 140
Robertson Map of Spring Hill (1828), 54, *55*
Robertson and Barnwall store, 35
Rochon, Pierre, 18–19
Rogers, George B., architect, 121, 203, 227, 228, 231–32, 233, 236, 238, 244, 245, 250, 275–76 (n. 41)
Rogers, Isaiah, architect, 40, 148, *149*, 276 (n. 41)
Romans, Bernard, 17

Roof, 33
    cottage, 82. *See also* Roof: double-pitch
    deck, 23, 54, 248
    double-pitch, flared, 7, 9, 11, 52, 54, 82, 270 (n. 10)
    gable, 7, 36, 42, 43, 48, 64, 75, 82, 106, 117, 122, 125, 172, 191, 197, 200, 202, 206, 220, 222
    hip, 7, 48, 77, 121, 156, 200
    Mansard, 7, 198, 209, 216
    Norman "Pavillon," 7
Roofing material:
    bark, 9, 11
    copper, 108
    tile, 250
    shingle, 9, 13, 14, 28, 43, 95
    slate, 37, 38, 60, 77, 105, 108, 110
    tin, 71, 108
Roper House, *99–100. See also* Oakleigh Garden Historic District
Rosettes. *See* Decorative designs
Rowan country cottage, Richard Redwood, builder, 94
Row buildings, 35, 39, 73, 75, 91, 93, 108, 125, 129, 144, 183
Royal East Indies Steamship Line. *See* Steamboats
Rue de Tournée, 13, 22
Rustication. *See* Stone treatment

Sadler, William, mason, 91
St. Francis Street Baptist Church, 141–42, *143*
St. Francis Street Methodist Church, Watkins and Johnson, architects, 203, 206
St. Genevieve, Missouri, Bolduc House, 12, 13
St. James Hotel, 186
St. John Episcopal Church, David Cumming, Jr., architect, 94, *140–41*
St. John House, 156, *157*
St. John Orphanage, 94
St. John, Richard, House and Shop, John Springsteel, builder, 81
St. Joseph Chapel, Downey and Denham, architects, *233*
St. Louis Street Baptist Church, 178, *179*, 203
St. Martinville, Louisiana, La Couteau, 5, 6
St. Michael Street Emanuel A.M.E. Church, facade, James F. Hutchisson, architect, 203, *205*
St. Michael Street Hotel, Charles B. Dakin, architect, 73
St. Paul Chapel, John Dawson, Albert Stein, builders, 142, *143*
Sanborn Map. *See* Maps
Sash windows. *See* Windows
Sawmills, 31, 32, 78, 144, 282 (n. 33)
Saws:
    crosscut and vertical, 144
    jig saw, 172, 191, 219
    woodpecker, 144
Saxe-Weimar Eisenach, duke of, 33, 41, 47
Scattergood, Benjamin, builder, 116, 133, *134*
Scattergood-Grey House, *167*
Scheffelin Multiple Dwelling, *158*, 159

Schematic Map of Mobile. *See* Maps
Scheuerman Store, Rudolph Benz, architect, 212, *213*
Scott House, James F. Hutchisson, 2nd, architect, *220*
Scottish Rite Bodies, George B. Rogers, architect, *236*
Screening, 171
Scully, Arthur, 66, 72
Second Presbyterian Church, I. P. Pond, B. H. Scattergood, E. M. Irvin, builders, 116
Segmental arch. *See* Arch
Sellitt, Oliver, and Company, contractors, *238*
Sha'arai Shomayim Temple, Watkins and Hutchisson, architects, *231*
Shaw, C., carpenter-builder, 89
Shepherd House, *223*, 224
Shoemaker, E. B., builder, 105
Shotgun cottages, 155, 172, 191, 289 (n. 30)
Shutters:
    exterior, 11, 37, 38, 47, 50, 81, 105, 108, 112, 142
    interior, 185, 198
    iron, 105, 110, 132, 185, 198
Sidelights, 41, 45, 56, 88, 108, 112, 117, 150, 159
Sidewalks, 38, 75, 108, 228
Silver, Joseph, mason, 91
Silver House, *125*
Skate Iron Foundry, 109, 119, 176
Skating rink, 211
Slide-by windows. *See* Windows
Smith, Murray F., House, 161, *162*
Smith, T. J., architect, *247*, 248, *249*
Smith, William, carpenter, 109
Smith store, *145*, 146
Sodality Chapel, 180
Soffits, 156, 166
Sossaman Brothers, contractors, *213*, 220
Southern Hardware Company, Stone Brothers, architects, 227
Spanish Colonial Period, 21–25
    architecture, 23
    boundary, 21
    census, 21
    church, 22, 44
    description, 23
    hospital, 58, 74
    land grants, 21
    map. *See* Maps
    Old Spanish Jail, 23, *24*
Spanish influence: Churrigueresque, Plateresque, and Mission, *232*, 238, *247*, 250, *251*
Spear Iron Foundry, 109, 129
Spear store, 77
Spindles, *223*, 224
Spira and Pincus Building (1886), Rudolph Benz, architect, 216, *217*
Spira and Pincus Building (1899), *214*, 215
Spira Building, Rudolph Benz, architect, 212, *213*
Spire, 140, 205, 206, 216
Sprague House, 224
Spring Hill, 50, 54, 94, 142
Spring Hill College, First Administration Building, Claude Beroujon, architect-builder, 101, *102*
Spring Hill College, Refectory and

Kitchen, James H. Hutchisson, architect, 181
Spring Hill College, Second Administration Building, James Freret, architect, *180*, 181
Springsteel, John, builder, 81
Stables. *See* Dependencies
Stairways:
    exterior, 45, 52, 81, 90, 99, 116, 132, 153, 185, 197
    interior, 37, 45, 50, 52, 56, 90, 118, 122, 135, 138, 148, 160, 172, 185, 198, 206, 221, 224, 234, 237, 248
Stark, Turner, master builder, 43
Statehood, 30
State Street A.M.E. Zion Church, Watkins and Johnson, architects, facade, James H. Hutchisson, architect, 203, *204*, 205–06, 293 (n. 17)
State Street store, *75*
Staylor House, *91*, 92
Steamboats, 28, 38, 127
Steel skeleton, 201, 228, 234, 239, 240, 245
Steeple, 68, 71, 115, 140
Stein, Albert, 142
Stein Waterworks Company, 78, 108
Stevens and Nelson, architects, 66
Stewartfield, 150, *154*
Stone Brothers, architects, 227, 234, *235*, *238*, 244
Stone material:
    Durand, 109
    limestone, 206, 231, 234
    granite, 76, 89, 109, 114, 115, 116, 132, 136, 206, 231, 239, 240
    marble, 46, 71, 74, 132, 155, 200, 224, 230, 234, 239
    marble graining, 94. *See also* Painting
Stone sills. *See* Framing elements: sills
Stone treatment, texture:
    ashlar, 136
    beveled, 136
    rusticated, 200, 202, 206, 212
Stone veneer. *See* Walls: siding, exterior
Store plans. *See* Plans
Stores, 28, 30, 35, 36–39, 43, 74, 75–76, 77, 108, 109, 110–13, 130–31, 144, 145–47, 148–49, 163, *164*, 174, *175*, 187, *188–89*, 209, 210–17, 237, 238–39, 244–45
Street numbers established, 84
Streets and roads, 5, 13, 22, 31, 54, 94, 102, 108, 119, 140, 198, 228, 284 (n. 55)
String course, 34, 63, 75, 165, 202, 234; stone, 200, 206
Stucco. *See* Walls: siding, exterior
Studs. *See* Framing elements: studs
Styles and influences. *See* Baroque influence; Bungalow style; Cottages; Early twentieth century; English Colonial Period; Egyptian style influence; Federal influence; French Period; French Second Empire style; Georgian influence; Greek Revival style; Italianate style; Neoclassical influence; Queen Anne style; Renaissance influence; Shotgun cottages; Spanish Colonial Period; Victorian cottages
Suburbia, 50, 51, 94, 101–02, 119, 142, 198, 228, 250

Sully, Thomas, architect, 211
Summerhouse, 98
Summerville, 51, 102, 119
Swags. *See* Decorative designs
Swanson and McGillivray, 20

Tacon-Tissington House, *224-25*
Tardy cottage, 150, *151*
Tarleton House, *124*, *125*
Taylor, James Knox, architect, *230*
Terra cotta, 234, 238, 239, 245
Territorial years, 27-30
 architectural elements, 28-29
 boundaries, 27
 buildings, 28-29
Texture, 35, 136, 202, 212, 216, 222, 234, 237
Theater, 30, 31, 39-41, 74, 227
Theatre (1823), Isaiah Rogers, architect, 30, 31, 40-41
Three Mile Creek, 27, 31
Toises, 5, 269 (n. 2)
Tongue and groove. *See* Flooring; Walls: siding, exterior
Toulmin, Judge Harry, 23, 24, 32, 52-53
Toulmin House, *52-53*
Tower, 44, 106, 113, 141, 142, 171, 198, 200, 206, 209, 216, 222, 231, 233
Town, Davis, and Dakin, 62, 66, 279 (n. 7)
Tracery, 140, 141, 142
Transom, 41, 46, 56, 61, 82, 88, 90, 117, 125, 150, 153, 159, 171, 185, 200, 206, 219
Treaty of San Lorenzo, 21
Trefoil. *See* Arch
Triglyph, 69, 86, 132, 208, 287 (n. 4)
Trinity Episcopal Church, Robinson Memorial Parish House, Hutchisson and Denham, architects, 233
Trinity Episcopal Church, Willis and Dudley, architects, 141, *142*
Troost Map. *See* Maps
Trudeau, Carlos, 12
Turner Building, Rudolph Benz, architect, 189
Tuscan Order. *See* Columns: capitals

Union Baptist Church, 203
United States Custom House, Ammi B. Young, architect, *136-38*
United States Hotel (1818), *30*, 41
United States Hotel (1836), Charles B. Dakin, architect, 72 (same as the Government Street Hotel)
United States Map of Claims and Cessions. *See* Maps
United States Marine Hospital, Frederick Bunnell, architect, *107*, 108

United States Post Office, James Knox Taylor, architect, *230*

Van Antwerp, Cooper, architect, 198
Van Antwerp Building, George B. Rogers, architect, 244, *245*
Vaughan, Joseph, carpenter-builder, 89
Vault, 243, 244
Veneer. *See* Walls: siding, exterior and interior
Verandas, 33, 42, 66, 108, 148, 150. *See also* Porches
Verge boards. *See* Barge board
Vickers House, *251*
Vickery House, Philip Dougherty, architect, 155-56, *157*
Victorian cottages, *218*, *219*
Victorian plan. *See* Plans: styles
Victorian style, 118, *126*, 189, 196, *197*, 198, *199*, 200, *201*, 202, *203*, 206, 209-10, 211-12, *213*, 214, *215-20*, 221-23
Vincent House, 51, *52*
Visitation Monastery. *See* Convent of Visitation
Voussoirs, 200, 239, 240

Wainscoting. *See* Walls: siding, interior
Walker and Nadine, carpenters-builders, 89
Walls:
 construction. *See* Construction methods
 siding,
  exterior: board-and-batten, 56, 122, 141, 142, 171, 172, 173; brick veneer, 228, 238, 240; concrete block veneer, 248; imbrication, 220, 223; marble veneer, 230; painted (*see* Painting); plank, 12, 14, 56; shingle, 228; stone, 206, 225; stone veneer, 230, 234, 240; stucco, 7, 12, 22, 23, 34, 35, 61, 70, 106, 132, 135, 161, 181, 228, 233, 250; terra cotta, 234, 238; tongue-and-groove, 81, 95; weatherboarding, 28, 29, 47, 48, 54, 81, 95, 223
  interior: beeded, 37; painted (*see* Painting); paneling, 74, 90, 198, 224, 243, 248; plank, 28; plaster, 29, 37, 49, 76, 89, 110, 118, 122, 273 (n. 7); tapestry, 240; wainscoting, 71, 198, 224, 234, 239, 248
Ward, E. S., contractor, 250
Ward, John, master mason, 33, 36-37, *43*
Warehouses, 22, 28, 36, 39, 110, *111*, 174, 186-87, 209, *210*
Waring Texas, 126, *127*
Warren, Knight, and Davis, contractors, 107

Warren, Reverend John, 67
War years, 167-69
Washboard. *See* Baseboard
Washington Fire Engine Company Number Eight. *See* Fire Station Number Five
Water Street Phoenix Foundry, 144
Water supply, 18, 32, 77-78, 108. *See also* Stein Waterworks Company
Watkins, George, architect, 211, 212, 227
Watkins, Hutchisson, and Garvin, 238, *239*, 240, *241*
Watkins and Hutchisson, 229, 230, *231*
Watkins and Johnson, 202-03, 205, 206
Weatherboarding. *See* Walls: siding, exterior
Wharfs, 14, 20, 22, 28, 36, 39, 110, 129, 174, 286 (n. 17)
White, B. H., builder, 89
Wickwire, Moses, carpenter, 67-68
Widows' Row, 93-94, *95*
Williams, John, mason, 80
Williamsburg, Virginia:
 Wythe House, 5, *6*
 Charlton House, 49, *50*
Williamson, Robert, mason, 107
Willis and Dudley, architects, 141, *142*
Windows, 33, 35, 37, 38, 50, 70, 75, 81, 108, 112, 117, 126, 161, 170, 174, 176, 189, 205, 216, 219, 222, 223, 234, 237, 244, 245
 arcaded, 202
 bay, 240
 cabinet, 211
 casement, 11, 88
 diamond shaped, 172
 lancet, 44, 141, 142
 oriel, 116
 Palladian, 248
 pedimented, 153, 181, 248
 pointed, 172
 sash, 49, 82, 93, 109, 117, 132, 155
 segmental, 93, 119, 169, 229
 semi-circular, 20, 114-15, 142, 162, 171, 178, 181, 185, 189, 198, 200, 202, 206, 212
 showcase, 100, 212, 237
 slide-by, 76, 109, 155, 219
 stairway, 33, 221, 224
Window framing. *See* Architrave; Lintels; Pediment
Workman's cottage. *See* Cottages

YMCA, Watkins and Johnson, architects, 200, *202*
Young, Ammi B., architect, 126, *136*

Zachary and Zachary, contractors, *235*